BAD MUSIC

D0143697

WITHDRAWN

BAD MUSIC

The Music We Love to Hate

Edited by

CHRISTOPHER WASHBURNE
and **MAIKEN DERNO**

Routledge

New York & London

Published in 2004 by
Routledge
270 Madison Avenue
New York, NY 10016

Published in Great Britain by
Routledge
2 Park Square
Milton Park, Abingdon
Oxon, OX14 4RN, U.K.

Library of Congress Cataloging-in-Publication Data

Bad music : the music we love to hate / edited by Chris Washburne and Maiken Derno.
    p. cm.
  Includes bibliographical references (p.) and index.
    ISBN 0-415-94365-5 (hardcover : alk. paper) — ISBN 0-415-94366-3 (pbk. : alk. paper)
    1. Music—Philosophy and aesthetics. 2. Music—History and criticism.
  I. Washburne, Christopher. II. Derno, Maiken, 1972–
  ML3800.B13 2004
  781.1'7—dc22   2004016591

For August

Contents

Preface

The seed for this book emerged during a discussion between Tim Taylor and Christopher Washburne concerning the discrepancy between the music addressed in the scholarly literature and what most people in this world actually listen to. With only few exceptions, scholars tend to focus on music that has special value in terms of influence, competence, and historical genealogy all the while avoiding the mundane music of the everyday. Inspired by the work of Simon Frith, among others, we decided to address this disjuncture by organizing a panel on the topic of "Bad Music" for the October 2001 meeting of the Society for Ethnomusicology in Detroit, Michigan. Participants on that panel were Jason Lee Oakes, Elizabeth L. Wollman, Tim Taylor, and Christopher Washburne (their original papers have been expanded and included in this volume). We are indebted to the provocative work of those panelists and the engaging discussion that followed, encouraging us to pursue the topic further.

The enthusiasm of Richard Carlin and Routledge Press to publish a collection of essays prompted us to post an open call for papers on the topic, as well as approach some of the most respected thinkers in music to contribute. We were overwhelmed by the sheer number of responses and the truly original nature of that work. Quite obviously, there is a sense within the scholarly community of real lacunae associated with the subject, as well as an eager desire to fill that void. Everywhere we turned for feedback and editorial advice, especially from our colleagues at Columbia University and University of Copenhagen, respectively, we encountered generous support and encouragement. In particular we would like to thank Tim Taylor, Steven Feld, Aaron Fox, Walter Frisch, Torben Sangild, and Martin Zerlang for generously giving their time and constructive feedback. It is so valuable to be working in an environment with such esteemed and inspiring colleagues.

We would also like to acknowledge Mark Burford, Ana Maria Ochoa, Robert Christgau, Dieter Christensen, Kai Fikentscher, Toby

King, Ingrid Monson, Kate McQuiston, and Heather Willoughby who generously offered their assistance in the editorial process and whose efforts greatly enhanced this project.

We are grateful to Bärenreiter Verlag and Gustav Bosse Verlag, the publishers of Carl Dahlhaus' work on *Trivialmusik*, for granting permission to translate and publish his work, excerpts of which have been translated into English for the first time and appear at the end of this volume. Many thanks go to Uli Sailer for agreeing to take on the formidable task of translating such a dense and sophisticated text and to Nikolaus Bacht for expeditiously reading and critiquing this translation.

Lastly, we wish to express our sincere gratitude to all of the contributors: Eliot Bates, Giorgio Biancorosso, Richard Carlin, Aaron A. Fox, Walter Frisch, Simon Frith, James Koehne, Jason Lee Oakes, Angela Rodel, Uli Sailer, Torben Sangild, Matthew Wheelock Stahl, Timothy D. Taylor, Elizabeth Tolbert, Deena Weinstein, and Elizabeth L. Wollman, whose invaluable and dedicated efforts have made work on this volume such a pleasure.

CHRISTOPHER WASHBURNE
AND MAIKEN DERNO

Introduction

CHRISTOPHER WASHBURNE AND
MAIKEN DERNO

B ad music is everywhere! Just hit the scan button on your radio while driving down any highway in any state and listen to the constant regurgitating drone of the same formulaic pop song. Arrive at your destination, whether it be a mall, dentist's office, or grocery store and listen. Call any company and try to maneuver through the menu options in search of "the next available representative." While on hold, listen. Turn on the television, tune into any commercial station. Close your eyes, and listen. Bad music is everywhere.

Artist Fernand Léger once commented that in the United States "Bad taste is . . . one of the valuable raw materials."[1] Needless to say, this dictum now holds true for most parts of the "old" and "other" worlds, too. Far from being limited to the odd, individual experience of some disgruntled driver, the repetitive encounter with a notoriously "bad artifact" is something which is shared (and endured) by millions of people on a daily basis. This rather bleak state of affairs has been poignantly diagnosed by Jacques Attali, whose usual, sly irony encapsulates the nihilism of our times: "Today, it [i.e., music] is unavoidable, as if, in a world now devoid of meaning, a background noise were increasingly necessary to get people a sense of security."[2] A mass-produced commodity par excellence, music (and especially the vast array of popular, standardized sounds emanating from so many boom-boxes, stereo speakers, cell phones, and iPods in public and private spaces alike), stands in constant danger of dissolving into mere noise—the undifferentiated soundtrack of human deprivation and cultural decay.

Bad music, however, should not necessarily be equated with pop music, nor does it refer to inherent qualities in any other musical style or genre per se. Rather, in one meaning of the term, it can be loosely understood along contextualist lines to be music that is somehow unwanted, played in the wrong contexts for the wrong reasons; music that is forced upon us in all kinds of possible and impossible situations

1

as we attempt to navigate through the saturated soundscapes of our complex postmodern lives. Yet, even such a tentative definition would seem to ignore the complicated logic of desire and agency at stake in the discursive uses of the term. As the subtitle of this book betrays, there is a virtual love–hate relationship behind most of our trade in musical value judgments, and one that renders any Attaliean pronounce-ments of cultural pessimism somewhat paradoxical. For just as musics that are deemed "good" and "valuable," bad music is first and fore-most a social construct. Not only are we the passive victims of some intrusive bad music onslaught, we are very much its deliberate creators, consumers, and perpetuators.

Nevertheless, popular music has often served as the contested site for extensive debates on negative value. Cultural critics from Walter Benjamin to Susan Sontag have reminded us that the traditional divide between low and high culture was based primarily on the difference between unique and mass–produced objects, and that anything with mass appeal has typically been regarded as culturally suspect.[3] Fur-thermore, the historical nature of the link between the popular and the vulgar, between "low" and "bad," and in particular the groundedness of this connection in the cultural climate of the late 1800s, has been pointed out by Lawrence Levine, among others: "The exaggerated antithesis between art and life, between the aesthetic and the Philis-tine, the worthy and the unworthy, the pure and the tainted, embodied at the turn of the twentieth century, has unquestionably colored our view of culture ever since."[4] Levine's observations amount to the im-portant insight that these categories are far from stable ones, but rather betray infinite, historically inflected transformations.

Since the heyday of the old divide, of course, the legitimization of popular culture as an object of serious academic study is gradually eroding the grounds for such suspicions of everything popular. As Alfred Appel comments on the present blurring of these hierarchichal deline-ations, now ". . . rappers and rock'n'rollers are all called 'artists' just as readily as the journalists who cover them are billed as 'critics'. 'What isn't art?' is now a challenging, defining question for a culture that, for better or worse, has all but eliminated the distinctions between 'high' and 'low' art."[5]

Several types of dichotomies, albeit blurred at times, lie couched in the common assumptions about musical taste conjured up by the label "bad music." Some of these include: high vs. low, popular vs. avant-garde, commercial vs. art, desired vs. unwanted, formulaic vs.

original, and so forth. And underlying all these prejudices is an even more basic delineation between *real* experiences of auditive discomfort vs. the passing of aesthetic judgments as strategic acts of positioning oneself within a given *discursive* landscape. But whereas the former may seem to depend on idiosyncratic, psychological factors such as past experiences and personal associations (i.e., highly individualized factors that are hard to theorize), the latter category is predominantly made up of collective and communicational choices, which certainly invites further systematic scrutiny.

Despite the obvious historical inflection of value judgements, then, and even though the predominantly discursive nature of taste is now widely recognized, "musical badness" still remains somewhat of a fetishized cultural commodity; something that is very much "out there," submerged in the reality of mundane experience; but also something which is being circulated, broadcast, repeated, and traded exactly because it holds functional, aesthetic, and social value in a variety of different contexts previously undiscovered by the guardians of "good taste."

Anytime anyone makes a discursive judgment of "good" or "bad" this is first and foremost a positioning gesture, which serves to construct or reimagine specific modes of subjectivity or to restructure social relationships by asserting deliberate musical agency. What on the surface may appear to be miniscule gestures of random alliances (somebody switching radio stations, fast-forewarding CD tracks, or expressing distaste for a particular song, for instance) turn out to have a vitally important impact on our own sense of identity as well as on how we chose to present ourselves to the world. The very act of passing an aesthetic judgment assumes and bestows authority upon the judge. By explicitly disaffiliating ourselves with certain forms of musical expression, we make a claim for being "in the know" about things, we demonstrate an educated perspective and activate a wide range of underlying assumptions about what is "good."

Bad music is everywhere, available at all times and to each one of us. It is mostly undesired, of course, yet surprisingly often it is a fully intentional accompaniment to our paradoxical and multi-layered auditive lives. One thing is clear: the circumstances surrounding each localized act of musical judgement defy easy, categorical definition.

***

Traditionally, music scholars have sought out uncharted or unspoiled territory of inquiry, searching a domain (geographically, historically, or intellectually bounded) to eke out a claim of academic ownership. For instance, in the early twentieth century, ethnomusicologists sought alterity in the musics of isolated and tribal communities. Later on, they turned to more familiar urban environments, this time under the guise of seeking out unique subcultural enclaves. Similarly, musicologists sought historically significant trends or figures, archeologically unearthing musical gems whose significance presumably had been buried under the sediments of time, thereby (re-)constructing and (re-)interpreting historical narratives at the core of Western civilization. More recently, and within the same methodological parameters, some musicologists and ethnomusicologists have turned toward popular music studies and questions of value formation, thereby broadening the traditional scope of both disciplines and spawning some innovative contributions in the process. However, traditional tropes of inquiry, invested in the "great divide" between high brow and low brow categorization, frequently inform this more recent trend which is still permeated by the politics of canon-building that seek to identify masterpieces, master musicians/performers, cultural gems, influential musical moments, tradition-changing events, innovative trends, as well as exceptional cases within their prospective domains.

There is great value in this type of endeavor, especially if the study in question is the first of its kind for a particular genre or style. However, due to the exclusionary nature of canon construction a vast residue of music and musicians that are considered mediocre, non-influential, un-exceptional, and generally lacklustre are being omitted from the scopes of analytical scrutiny. Those gems, then, float like miniscule planets in a vast universe of presumably indistinct and mundane music, which perpetually gets overlooked. Why? Because the gatekeepers of academic inquiry do not value this segment of music. They feel it is "bad," "valueless," and "unworthy," regardless that it is loved, despised, ignored, and consumed by multitudes serving as the soundtrack of our daily lives. As scholars, we tend to write about the music we value, simultaneously serving as critics and advocates, while avoiding that which we disdain or take for granted. Besides, even if, say a Beethoven scholar, an individual whose musically educated perspective has yielded a successful academic career, actually indulges in, consumes, and enjoys top 40 radio, Madonna, or ABBA, she will often be reticent to publically admit her guilty pleasures, let alone incorporate them in her professional work. Academic inquiry, then, has

rarely addressed this vast body of "bad" music (simultaneously unwanted and desired) which permeates modern society.

With the present collection of work, we have set out to explore
this neglected, yet omnipresent domain; the bad, the spoiled, and the
vapid musics of our everyday lives, and in particular, the strategic discourse which we constantly generate concerning our alliances with
certain musical tastes. The 17 contributors have sought out the unrec-
ognized value of various musical genres or styles, as these may function as parameters for complex patterns of political, ideological, and
identificatory affiliations. For it turns out, of course, that musical badness—even as it borders on noise or kitsch—proves a much more fruit-
ful site for the decoding of social inscriptions than Attali's dismal
soundtrack to oblivion seemed to imply.

The present effort, then, is not just a matter of recuperating yet
another "undiscovered" country, of retrieving the marginalized, or of
paying lip service to the musically bad in a similar fashion to what
scholars of music have been doing for "good music" over the centuries.
With the advent of popular culture studies in the humanities, the very
raison d'être of the analytical venture has changed. Instead of seeking
out inherent value in a string of exceptional artistic moments, our culture as a whole is now perceived as a dynamic and ever-changing field
of forces, just as local events within one discipline are seen to be capable of setting adrift virtual continental plates within others. Our reasons
for studying a particular musical phenomenon are less to capture a
certain Zeitgeist or extract inherent value from its anatomical make-
up, than to demonstrate how even the seemingly idiosyncratic phenomena possess the ability to characterize or redefine entire strata of
our cultural self-understanding and identity construction.

"Bad" is obviously a subjective category, but it is also marked by
particular cultural and historical contestations over what is thought to
be good and bad within a variety of differing contexts. It is these broader
cultural and historical dimensions of valuation that concern the present
volume. Its purpose is not to define an inherent badness (which is most
likely impossible and, at best, undesirable), nor is it to focus on what
is obviously bad or lacking in terms of competence in relation to individual performances. Rather, we explore musics that, for whatever reasons, invite disdain and disapprobation, even though some of these
musical styles may have a multitude of fans and a wide circulation
within the popular sphere. By addressing this large segment of music
which has a real impact in the daily lives of millions, but which is

systematically ignored by the scholarly literature, we hope to lay bare
the complex dynamics and dialogical interaction which underpin and
perpetually redefine the relationship between the "good" and the "bad."[6]
George Lipsitz's comment on the potential benefits of looking at the
popular music domain could just as well be taken to apply specifically
to that of bad music: "It calls for an understanding of how people make
meaning for themselves, how they have already begun to engage in
grass-root theorizing about complicated realities . . . Anxieties aired
through popular music illumine important aspects of the cultural and
political conflicts that lie ahead for us all."[7]

The main goal of this volume, then, is to discover how aesthetic
concerns previously thought to be intrinsic to the work/performance
itself, might be routinely set aside in favor of a set of alternative evaluative criteria based on, variously: the communality of the listening
experience; the dynamics of participation; the politicized message of
the lyrics; the positionality of the musician and/or listener as a
racialized/ethnicized/gendered/classed subject; business and marketing
factors; the impact of globalization; as well as the cultural affiliation
listeners feel for a particular musical style or genre with all of the
identity-constructing, community-making, and boundary-policing processes that accompany such affiliation. In choosing to contextualize
questions of individual and public tastes, our investigation, involving
the stakes of canon-building and generic transformation, takes place
at the crossroads of aesthetics, cultural analysis, musicology, reception
theory, and related disciplines, where discourses on and of the "bad"
are intrinsically tied to musics that are highly valued.

This volume not only provides an overview of the traditions of
classical twentieth century debates on value formation, but brings the
discussion into the twenty-first century by developing a valid and useful
methodology to address the role played by bad music in society as well
as in individual lives, thereby filling a perceived gap in the conceptual
framework surrounding this precarious topic.

***

Charles Ives, in a note on the Second Movement of his *4th Symphony*, wrote; "Nature builds the mountains and the meadows and man
puts in the fences and labels."[8] In much the same vein, one might be
tempted to ask: to what an extent is "bad music" to be considered a
discursive (as opposed to a real) phenomenon? In his extensive opening
chapter, Simon Frith poses a string of basic questions appertaining to
various possible meanings of "badness," and while discussing the com-

plex mechanisms underlying acts of value-formation he grapples with the fundamental question "What Is Bad Music?" The most simple answer, he concedes, is that ". . . 'bad music' is a matter of taste, and involves a judgment that depends on the social and psychological circumstances of the person making it." But for Frith, this is not merely a matter of taste, however, but also a matter of argument; "An argument that matters," because these judgments of value are a necessary part of popular music pleasure serving as identity-constructing formulations that establish our place in various musical worlds. He argues that there is a strong need a for concept of 'bad music' "even if we know full well that we won't be able to agree on how the label should be applied." Frith's relentlessly comprehensive and systematic approach amounts to a book introduction in its own right, and his chapter deserves to be read as such. By resorting to a basic communications model to pin down a concept which otherwise stands in danger of remaining slippery and elusive, he astutely demonstrates how discourses of value can and must be theorized if we hope to disentangle the ideological premises of their making.

In the following section, Value & Identity Politics, four writers set out to explore the intimate relationship between music and value as these categories become inflected (both discursively and literally) with complex identity-defining signifiers such as race, class, gender, geography, and even with the very essence of becoming coded as a human being. It is widely recognized that the affiliation of certain demographic groups with particular "bad" musical genres—often in the sense of rebellious, marginalized, counter-hegemonic or even conspicuously mass-produced—may come to serve as important markers of self-expression and identity formation within the cultural landscape at large. Only seldom, however, have localized instances of such idiosyncratic affiliations with musical badness been scrutinized in the thorough, scholarly manner they deserve.

But what exactly, one may be tempted to ask, does the redistribution of apparently valueless and defunct objects at an auction fundraiser in a redneck bar on the cusp of the Texan desert have to do with the discourses on value in popular music theory? Quite a good deal, if we are to believe Aaron A. Fox's thick ethnographic tale of community-sustaining philanthropy and romantic mythology as mediated through what is perhaps the epitome of "white," American, working-class musical identity. His chapter treats "badness" as interestingly as its ostensible topic: country music. First, he eloquently orchestrates the

demonstration of a notoriously "bad" issue, namely the intricate dynamics of desire and racism lurking beneath the surface of the country
scene's aesthetic, thereby effectively problematizing the relationship
between the forbidden, the unattainable, and the real. Next, the expli-
cation of the self-hating alchemy of "white trash" is deftly executed in
a manner that revives the opening auction image in a telling way. The
private guilty pleasures characteristic of smokers' culture in today's
prohibitive and regulatory climate serve as an apt metaphor for the
dynamics at work in a depressed rural community of country-loving
'common folk'.

Indulging in one's own secret guilty pleasures, however, can also
be a highly public and musically affirmative affair. Thus, a night at
New York City's "Loser's Lounge" is less a matter of suicidal self-
deprecation, than of a sophisticated traffic in musical parody, cheese,
camp, irony, experimentation, and celebratory masquerade. Jason Lee
Oakes' discursive tour de force into this institution of canonized musical
bad taste touches upon many crucial social and linguistic matrices of
value formation as these intersect with, say, the racial politics of performing tribute-paying acts within the framework of a conspicuously
"white" genre. The demographic signifiers of mainstream Western pop
music are treated with a humorous edge as part of a larger ideological
construct, which followed in the wake of the lounge music revival in
the early 90s. Here, as elsewhere throughout this volume, the racial
stratification of "bad" musical affiliation is featured prominently as an
entry ticket into the world of "good" society.

Far from being a solely personal business, music as index of identity is also a matter of big business and calculated marketing strategies.
In his discussion of world music and its crucial rapport with the urban
experience, Timothy D. Taylor explores the exclusionist mechanisms
employed by the music industry in its efforts to govern the nuts and
bolts of market shares. Why, he asks, is it that some of this music
doesn't qualify as world music even though it is made "by people of
colour from European and American Elsewheres?" The key word here
is authenticity, that is: political authenticity or "authenticity as
positionality," as convincingly demonstrated in the analysis of the very
different fates of Robby Bee's two records. Joining in a favored practice
of the poststructuralist school—the deconstructing of binaries—Taylor
points to the paradox of the anti-essentialist stance of this school
combined with its adaptation by post-colonialism and its cult of
authenticity.

Fine-tuned distinctions between rural, urban, and colonial discourses aside, the basic role of music as an evolutionary force in human development has long presented a virtual enigma to evolutionary biologists and music theorists alike. What functional value may we ascribe to the apparently inherent ability in members of the human species to make structured sounds and take pleasure in listening to them, too? And what is the relation between such functionality and the semiotics-inspired concept of "the musically abject?" From a Kristevean perspective, Elizabeth Tolbert explores the nature of our guilty pleasures at the unexpected intersection of evolutionary discourses and linguistic theory, by addressing questions of "badness" in terms of narratives of identity-constructing adaptations. In three diverging case stories about the process of human becoming, she convincingly makes the point that far-reaching claims about music's unmediated sonic power lie couched in our complex web of Western music/language ideologies.

For decades, tensions between commercialism and artistic integrity have been points of contention within the music world. Quite often, these debates have centered on performers who straddle stylistic lines drawn up between different genres and market shares, as well as on the incorporation of "mundane" experiences into artistic spheres. The second section of this volume, Canonizing the Popular, Discovering the Mundane, consists of chapters addressing dual issues of canonization in the writing of historical narratives within the realm of popular music, as well as the urgency of economic factors when traditional high art institutions are pressured to take upon themselves the uncomfortable role of catering to the tastes of mass audiences. The key word, here, is the exploration of "the everyday" and the search for its serendipitous value when introduced into new and unlikely contexts.

Jazz is one musical genre which has experienced a real transformation from "low" popular to "high" art; a transformation that, in turn, has triggered a general retreat of this music to the concert hall, public radio, and the ivory tower of academic reflection. This shift of realms has been due, in part, to economic factors as well as to the changing landscape of mass tastes. However, one type of jazz remains firmly rooted in the popular, namely "smooth jazz." In his chapter on the disputed genealogy of this label, Christopher Washburne focuses on Kenny G, the archetypal smooth jazz musician, as a case study to address a litany of questions concerning the policing of generic boundaries and the attribution of stylistic labels. Is Kenny G's music jazz, and if so, is it "bad jazz?" Who determines what jazz is? As scholars, musicians, and critics, the self-appointed custodians of the jazz tradition, why do we listen to his music with such disdain? Why is he omitted from the jazz canon and historical narratives? What shared relationship, if any, does artistic and commercial value have in jazz today?

The difficult task of making pragmatic choices vis-à-vis a persisting culture of disdainful elitism is also the topic of chapter 7, and one which attempts to negotiate the precarious balance challenged by the introduction of audience-pleasing works by contemporary composers into the near-petrified repertoire of the classical symphonic world. In his capacity as Artistic Director for the Adelaide Symphony Orchestra, James Koehne provides a refreshing "practitioner's" perspective from Down Under, focusing on the very real dilemmas faced by music institutions whose job it is to attract new audiences in the face of dwindling attendance, while at the same time protecting and cultivating a cultural heritage in danger of slow extinction. Accusations such as "too sentimental" or "too Hollywood," which have fallen upon composers such as Christopher Rouse and John Adams, are countered by Koehne who launches a scathing critique of the stubborn conservativism still characteristic of the classical music establishment at large. In particular, his discussion of Theodor Adorno takes issue with out-dated notions of music as a noble edifying power, and advocates a need to radically rethink our automatic aversion to contemporary music's blurring of new sounds with more familiar citations from the realm of popular entertainment.

Whereas Koehne is mainly concerned with "bad" motivation for renewal on an institutional level, Richard Carlin is interested in how our individual perception of "poor proficiency" is intimately linked to historical context and other circumstantial factors. The history of "folk" as a key idea in romanticism, nationalism, and other ideological formations of modernity, provides the backdrop for a discussion of the parameters against which folk revivalists have discovered and recorded their artists. It soon becomes apparent that false dichotomies of "good" and "bad" musicians have too long dominated concepts of what "folk" is.

Another genre which is haunted by a virtual lacuna in our understanding of how mechanisms of "good" and "bad," "significant" and "insignificant," "central" and marginal" function is film music. Not too long ago, the sounds that accompany the mainstream Hollywood motion picture were viewed as mere secondary creations, exercises in sentimentality devoid of any inherent artistic merit, and certainly as undeserving of any serious scholarly attention in their own right. Even less attention has been paid to those fragmentary pieces of music which appear as background ambience inside the fictional world of film narratives themselves (i.e., the odd juke-box playing in the corner of a bar), often referred to by film critics as "diegetic music." By redirecting our focus to the surfacing of the musically banal, Giorgio Biancorosso challenges this traditionalist neglect, making a strong case for such hardly noticeable soundtracks as productive objects of study. Through careful analysis of a number of examples in which everyday sounds enter a film scenario, he uncovers the social roots of aesthetic judgments and calls for "redemption of the mundane." What upon first hearing tends to escape the moviegoer's attention, turns out to play a significant functional role in the narrative-constructing mechanisms of cinematic representation.

Humiliation rather than redemption plays an important role within the world of another visual media, namely that of television and its recent obsession with the more-than-mundane musical talents of mundane people. Thus, the overwhelming success of recent mass media broadcast reality shows, especially those that feature teen, wannabe musicians in audience-decided song contests, calls for further analysis. And yet, the obvious "badness" of many such amateur performances is far from the only point in question here. In his detailed discussion of the television program *American Idol*, Matthew Stahl sets out to investigate ideas about American meritocracy in what he describes as "musically-themed discourses of opportunity and upward social mobility." The shows' ostensible traffic in reality, Stahl argues, serves the strategic purpose of staging telegraphic narratives of sincerity and pretense, advancement contra failure, musical craftsmanship vis-à-vis obviously untalented acts, and as such may be used to decipher both commercial and utopian mappings of character and opportunity structures in our present-day society.

The third section in this volume, Noise, Malfunction, and Discourses of (In)Authenticity, is concerned with an array of more recent phenomena which deals self-consciously in perceptions of musical badness; from an aesthetics of badness that blurs the boundary between noise and music, to a technological badness that becomes reshuffled into the basic building blocks of a new emergent genre, and to the central role of a discourse of authenticity in the assessment of value.

The bland background "noise" of most mainstream mass media productions is seriously challenged by a quite different kind of very literal noise, as Angela Rodel astutely argues in her chapter on a punk affiliated genre which goes by the name of "extreme hard core." Jacques Attali's seminal book on noise serves as a stepping-stone towards a larger discussion about the role played by radical modes of musical expression and their subversive potential for a critique of the mechanisms of appropriation by hegemonic discourses. She argues that by using a "bad aesthetics" to set itself apart from mainstream music production, extreme hardcore introduces new dimensions to the idea of "badness" as a means of challenging the musical status quo. Within various frameworks of artistic and social resistance Rodel, then, explores the ways in which punk's "short, fast and loud" incarnation of badness may be theorized.

The creative and critical potential inherent in new electronic music genres provides the topic of two chapters, both of which explore the historical origins and technology-driven aesthetics of "glitch," a relatively recent genre appellative which demarcates a style where sounds of mechanical malfunction and damage serve as the primary colors for its sonic palette. In his chapter, Torben Sangild works to open our ears to the beauty of malfunction, mapping out the newly discovered terrain of glitch artists, such as Yasunae Toné, German Oval, and Ryoji Ikeda. These artists transform traditionally bad and unwanted sounds (part and parcel to recording and sound reproduction processes) into good and desirable musical gestures. Eliot Bates adds to this discussion by exploring glitch in the context of high fidelity and the inevitable deterioration of reproduced sound. He asks what may be the implications concerning such definitions of a musical work when machine-additions, degeneration, and playback malfunction are taken into consideration? He answers, among other things, that recording and playback idiosyncrasies and their obnoxious defects have always had a profound effect on musicians and listeners, and that unsolicited glitch and its artistic alter ego simultaneously worsen the work of art and make listening to recordings a unique experience. It is from this historical perspective that he traces the emergence of glitch music as a separate genre.

In order to understand the need of most rock critics to define their tastes against a negation, Deena Weinstein uses their almost universal disdain for metal as a case study for the exploration of the underlying cause-and-effect of these debates. In her chapter she takes rock critics to task for their communal bashing rituals of "bad music"; a need, which turns out to be rooted in their personal status anxiety and resentments of youth culture on a broader scale. Further reasons for this reliance, she demonstrates, include age and class difference, the demise of the 1960s counter culture, economic structures, and the need to cater to mass tastes. However, she also sees the discourse of "authenticity" as the central issue at stake. In opposition to commercially successful music, this discourse preserves the critic's position "as uncorrupted and as a member of a select, hip group, still linked to the counter-cultural past." In Weinstein's discussion, bad music (disguised as metal) functions as the backdrop for defining and affirming the critic's authoritative position, while constructs of authenticity serves as their tool for assessing such value.

The question of authenticity is further explored by Elizabeth L. Wollman. Focusing on the unfortunate fate of many rock musicals, she sets out to discuss the troubled hybridization of the apparently incompatible genres of rock and musical theater. Through ethnographic examination she evaluates the circumstances surrounding three rock musicals in-the-making, addressing the dynamics involved in their particular versions of hybridization and supplies some answers to why the end results were almost inevitably rejected both commercially and critically as "bad rock" and/or "bad musical theater." Such failures, Wollman maintains, are not solely the result of clashes between genre-specific performance practices and conventions, but rather can be traced back to fundamental ideological differences and fan profiles. With rock intrinsically tied to notions of authenticity and with musical theater, by contrast, reveling in artifice and explicit commercialism, the generic gulf often proves too wide to navigate, a fact which further illustrates the inherent conceptual nature of value judgments.

With the addition of the final section of this volume, Historical Afterthought, we hope to historicize and theoretically broaden our discussion of more contemporary musical phenomena. Originally published in 1967, Carl Dahlhaus' monumental tome *Trivialmusik,* along with the inspirations from which he drew, shares an uncanny resemblance to our motivations for embarking on the current volume. Prompted by the notion that throughout the nineteenth century popular genres occupied a large portion of Europe's musical reality, Dahlhaus believed that music historians working on this period needed to address the complex web of distinctions between high and low musics. He subsequently compiled and edited a collection of essays focusing on a sphere of "bad" music from the nineteenth century, known as "trivial music." In the Preface and first chapter of his 1967 publication, both of which are included in the last chapter of this book, he discusses this banal, worn, and functional music, stressing the importance of developing an analytical approach that is genre-specific and different from that used for autonomous art music. For Dahlhaus, function and contextual factors must always be considered in order to make appropriate "aesthetic judgments" and value assessments of trivial music. Newly translated from the German into English by Uli Sailer and with introductory comments by Walter Frisch, this is the first complete English translation of Dahlhaus' work.

We sincerely hope that this compilation will serve as fodder for future explorations into the value discourse of music and that it will spawn studies which examine the seemingly endless plethora of "bad" musics that permeate our everyday lives.

NOTES

1. Léger's interview with James Johnson Sweeney was published in the *Museum of Modern Art Bulletin* in 1946.
2. Jacques Attali, *Noise: The Political Economy of Music*. (Minneapolis: University of Minnesota Press, 1985), 3.
3. Benjamin (1968), Sontag (1966).
4. Lawrence Levine, *Highbrow/Lowbrow: The Emergence of Cultural Hierarchy in America.* (Cambridge: Harvard University Press, 1988), 232.
5. Alfred Appel, *Jazz Modernism from Ellington and Armstrong to Matisse and Joyce.* (New York: Alfred A. Knopf, 2002), 39.
6. Some of the ideas and wording of this paragraph derive from Tim Taylor's original panel abstract. We are greatly indebted to his efforts and ideas.
7. George Lipsitz, *Dangerous Crossroads: Popular Music, Postmodernism, and the Poetics of Place.* London: Verso, 1994), 3.
8. Levine, *Highbrow/Lowbrow: The Emergence of Cultural Hierarchy in America,* 141.

REFERENCES

Appel, A. 2002. *Jazz modernism from Ellington and Armstrong to Matisse and Joyce.* New York: Alfred A. Knopf.

Attali, J. 1985. *Noise: The political economy of music.* Minneapolis: University of Minnesota Press.

Benjamin, W. 1968. The work of art in the age of mechanical reproduction. In *Illumination* (re-published 1968). New York: Schocken Books, pp. 217–51.

Levine, L. 1988. *Highbrow/lowbrow: The emergence of cultural hierarchy in America.* Cambridge: Harvard University Press.

Lipsitz, G. 1994. *Dangerous crossroads: Popular music, postmodernism, and the poetics of place.* London: Verso.

Sontag, S. 1966. *Against interpretation and other essays* (re-published 1990). New York: Anchor Books.

1
What is Bad Music?

SIMON FRITH

From my scrapbook.

> First there is the *innocently stupid*, the insipid song; then the
> *intentionally stupid*, the song ornamented with all the stupidities
> that the singer takes into his head to make . . . Next comes the
> *vicious song* which corrupts the public and lures it into bad
> musical paths by the attraction of certain capricious methods of
> performance, brilliant but with false expression, which is
> revolting to both good sense and good taste. Finally we have the
> *criminal song*, the wicked song, that unites with its wickedness a
> bottomless pit of stupidity, which proceeds only by great howls
> and enjoys adding noisy melees to the long drum rolls, to the
> sombre dramas, to the murders, poisonings, curses, anathemas,
> to all the dramatic horrors that provide the occasion to show off
> the voice. It is this last which, I am told, reigns supreme in
> Italy . . .
>
> HECTOR BERLIOZ C1840

> Sloppy versification, sophomoric diction, clichés, maudlin
> sentiments and hackneyed verbiage.
>
> LORENZ HART ON 1920S POP

> If Sibelius' music is good music, then all the categories by which
> musical standards can be measured . . . must be completely
> abolished.
>
> T. W. ADORNO C1940

> The Stones are fake-simple, without gift. The design of their
> 'Devil' lacks arch, the sonic element is without sensibility, much
> less invention, and the primary harmonies are not simple but
> simplistic. Neither does the melody flow anywhere, nor does its
> stasis invite hypnotism rather than boredom . . . Misfired

simplicity, then, makes this music bad. The words, too, pretend . . . What makes Jagger's lyrics bad is their commercial up-
to-date before-the-fact intent . . . The vocal performance is
doubly false . . . Jagger's inability to revamp plagiarism into
personal style because of superficial (even dishonest: he's a
white Englishman) instinct for choice (of vocal models—
'parents') makes his performance bad . . .

NED ROREM 1969

It's a contributory factor to epilepsy. It's the biggest destructor in
the history of education. It's a jungle cult. It's what the Watusis
do to whip up a war. What I see in the discos with people
jogging away is just what I've seen in the bush.

HARVEY WOOD, DIRECTOR GENERAL OF THE RHODESIAN
BROADCASTING CORPORATION, ON DISCO, 1979

No single song has done more for the pro-choice movement than
this sexist piece of wretchedness.

CITATION FOR PAUL ANKA'S "(YOU'RE) HAVING MY BABY,"
NUMBER 1 IN *THE BOTTOM FIFTY. SONGS THAT MADE
THE WHOLE WORLD CRINGE*, GANNETT NEWS SERVICE, 1991

There are six main reasons why unrestrained pop music is a
grave social evil. First, with very few exceptions it is artistically
worthless. The intolerable amplification which is essential to
projecting it, and which is one of the chief reasons for its appeal,
makes musical creativity impossible. It destroys the aural
perception of the children who grow up accustomed to it, makes
it difficult for them to cast off its spell, and thus denies them the
love of true music . . .

PAUL JOHNSON 1995

Kissin has been appearing in Britain for 14 years, since he was
17. His platform appearance now is just as mechanical as it has
ever been—one suspects the back of his tailcoat hides the hole
for a giant wind-up key—and his fingers are as stunningly
accurate as ever, but all traces of spontaneity have been progressively obliterated . . . On Thursday he rampaged through
his programme in a totally repellent and scarcely credible
manner . . . the paeans of the final Great Gate of Kiev carried no
weight or majesty because all the sound and fury that preceded
them had generated no tension or excitement, except of the most
primitive kind . . . [Kissin] started out on his career as a musical

talent of apparently limitless potential, and has turned into the biggest pianistic circus act since David Helfgott; there's nothing there but technique.

ANDREW CLEMENTS 2002

L ike Nicolas Slonimsky, editor of the *Lexicon of Musical Invective,* I have long been a collector of musical abuse, but I should make it clear at the beginning of this chapter that I am not going to answer my question—what is bad music?—directly.[1] I did think about this: rather than prepare a chapter, I could compile a list of bad records, a guide to dreadful songs. I decided not to for two reasons. First, what intrigues me is not music I don't like (and other people might) but music I do like (and other people don't).[2] Day-to-day bad music is music that my family and friends beg me to take off or turn down, to stop playing because it is so ugly or dull or incompetent.[3] Second, there is no point in labelling something as bad music except in a context in which someone else thinks it's good, for whatever reason. The label "bad music," that is to say, is only interesting as part of an argument. There is no purpose (and it would be no fun) to discuss music which everyone agrees is bad (a tape of me singing in the shower, for example). And this is not an argument we can have blind. I can't, in other words, persuade someone that the music they like is bad (and this is the most common setting for the use of the concept) unless I know their tastes, the way they make sense of their listening pleasures (which is not to say that the arguments here are *just* a matter of taste).

In short, I'm more interested in examining ways of arguing about music (good *versus* bad) than in setting up a taxonomy, this is bad music of one sort, this is bad music of another sort. I'll come back to this momentarily; first, an aside on taxonomies.

There are, by now, various albums (and radio and TV shows) featuring "bad music." The first I can remember is a 1970s K-Tel anthology of the *Worst Records Ever Made,* selected and introduced by the British disk jockey, Kenny Everett. There are three sorts of tracks featured in such collections and shows:

- Tracks which are clearly incompetent musically; made by singers who can't sing, players who can't play, producers who can't produce. Such acts (Tiny Tim springs to mind) used to be the stuff of certain sorts of television variety shows.

• Tracks organized around misplaced sentiments or emotions invested heavily in a banal or ridiculous object or tune. Jess Conrad's "My Pullover" is much anthologized in Britain, for instance.

• Tracks involving a genre confusion. The most common examples are actors or TV stars recording in the latest style: Telly Savalas sings Bob Dylan, Steven Seagal ("extending his creativity") writes and performs his own songs.[4] I'd add almost any opera singer performing almost any rock song. And, come to that, the Kiri Te Kanawa/José Carreras recording of *West Side Story*.

Bad music here means essentially *ridiculous* music, and the sense of the ridiculous lies in the gap between what performers/producers think they are doing and what they actually achieve. Such recordings reflect a complete musical misunderstanding: this is bad music as naïve or foolish music (rather than immoral or corrupting music). Anthologies of bad music thus offer listeners tracks at which to laugh, to regard with affection, and above all about which to feel *knowing*: we, as listeners, understand this music—and what's wrong with it—in a way in which its producers do not.

Rock critical lists of the worst records ever made, which nowadays feature routinely in the press and in books of rock ephemera, rest on a rather different approach to musical taxonomy. The tracks cited here are usually well known and commercially successful (rather than being oddities or commercial flops); the object of such lists is a critique of public taste, and the judgment involves the explicit assertion that these records are simply *heard too often*, as staples on classic pop or oldies radio stations, at weddings and in shopping malls.

There seem to be two sorts of tracks on these lists:

• Tracks that feature sound gimmicks that have outlived their charm or novelty (from "Disco Duck" to "The Ketchup Song" via "Bohemian Rhapsody"; Christmas and summer holiday hits generally).

• Tracks that depend on false sentiment (like Paul Anka's "(You're) Having My Baby"), that feature an excess of feeling molded into a radio-friendly pop song (songs about birth and death generally, in fact; most 9/11 songs, for example).

There's still a knowingness here, but the critical contempt seems less for the recordings than for the people who like them, who take them seriously, who still find them funny or sad. And while one could imagine buying a bad record collection and playing it to friends as a camp gesture (re-framing kitsch as art), these critical lists of bad records are intentionally identifying tracks that are irredeemable. These are, it seems, records that no one could want to play who has any sense of good music at all![5]

I'll come back to this argument. What I want to do immediately, moving back from taxonomy to analysis, is to make clear the premises of what follows. First, then, I am going to assume that there is no such *thing* as bad music. Music only becomes bad music in an evaluative context, as part of an argument. An evaluative context is one in which an evaluative statement about a song or a record or performer is uttered communicatively, to persuade someone else of its truth, to have an effect on their actions and beliefs (the quotes that introduce this chapter are all arguments in this sense).

There are more or less appropriate circumstances for musical evaluation, but probably the most significant (significant in that evaluations here have the most effect materially) involve music making rather than music listening: the judgments made at the piano or the keyboard, in rehearsal rooms and recording studios, at run throughs and sound checks.[6] Musicians, interestingly, are more likely to use the term "wrong" than the term "bad": "that's the wrong chord, the wrong tempo, the wrong sound, the wrong mix." One question that arise here is what is the relation, if any, between *wrongness* and *badness?*[7]

Second, I am going to assume that even if bad music doesn't exist, "bad music" is a necessary concept for musical pleasure, for musical aesthetics. To put this another way, even if as a popular music scholar I can't point authoritatively to bad music (my authority will undoubtedly be rejected), as a popular music fan I do so all the time. This is a necessary part of fandom. A self-proclaimed rock or rap or opera fan who never dismissed anything as bad would be considered as not really a *fan* at all. And what interests me here is what we are doing when we make such judgments and why it is that we need to make them. My question, in short, is not what is bad music but what is "bad music"?

The first analytic problem is to clarify the discursive basis of this concept. Conceptually, that is to say, most *judgments* of bad music are simultaneously *explanations* of bad music: the judgment is the explanation, the explanation is the judgment (and people's musical judgments often, in fact, combine or confuse explanations, or move imperceptibly from one sort of explanation to another). In very broad terms (making an artificial separation for analytic purposes), the most common discourses in popular music judgment refer either to how the music was produced or to its effects, and we can therefore note immediately that although it is music that is here being judged "bad," the explanation is not musical but sociological. What's going on, in other words, is a displaced judgment: "bad music" describes a bad system of production (capitalism) or bad behavior (sex and violence). The apparent judgment of the music is a judgment of something else altogether, the social institutions or social behavior for which the music simply acts as a sign.

I can clarify this by going through the most common arguments in a little more detail. First, in *arguments about production* there are two familiar positions.

Music is judged bad in the context of or by reference to a critique of mass production. Bad music (in the argument made most influentially by T. W. Adorno) is "standardized" or "formulaic" music. The implicit contrast is with "original" or "autonomous' or "unique" music, and the explanation built into the judgment depends on the familiar Marxist/Romantic distinction between serial production, production to commercial order, to meet a market, and artistic creativity, production determined only by individual intention, by formal and technical rules and possibilities.

Among other things, this means that "formula" or "standard" production that is not commercial is not, in this discursive context, usually judged bad: the fact that all disco numbers in the late 1970s "sounded the same" is a mark of unhealthy (commercial) formulaic production; the fact that all folk songs collected in Norfolk or Virginia in the late 1870s sounded the same is a sign of their healthy (noncommercial) roots in a collective history. More generally, one could say that such formula criticism tends to be genre-dependent: minor variations in boy band music are taken to be insignificant; minor variations in rural blues guitar tunings or madrigal polyphonics are of great aesthetic importance.

A second sort of criticism, which refers to production but without a Marxist edge, equates bad music with *imitative* music. Again, the implicit contrast is with "original" or, perhaps, "individual" sounds, and I am sure that every music listener has sometime dismissed a record or artist for sounding just like someone else (or, indeed, for sounding just like themselves), for "cashing in" on a successful musical formula.

There are many variations on this sort of argument. Take, for example, shifting attitudes to the "cover version," British imitations of U.S. hits. When I first started arguing about pop, in the mid-1960s, rock fan orthodoxy was that the cover version was necessarily inferior to the original. This was obviously true of white pop versions of black r&b songs (Pat Boone's "Tutti Frutti" is probably the nearest thing to a consensual bad record in popular music history), but was soon applied in playground argument to the Beatles' versions of Chuck Berry songs (which we actually heard afterward), and I can admit now that the logic of the argument didn't always reflect my listening habits. Nearly all the records I first bought in the late 1950s and early 1960s were cover versions. And soon white British r&b versions of black American r&b songs were raising different questions again—a guitarist like Eric Clapton acquired his reputation by sounding *more* like the blues originals than anyone else.

By the end of the 1960s rock critics were making a quite different sort of argument, drawn from both folk and jazz, in which creative musicians (whether Billie Holiday or Charlie Parker, Ray Charles or Bob Dylan) were heard to make something original out of standards. A "version" of an old song could be just as original as a new song. From an academic point of view, then, particularly in this age of hiphop and sampling, there is no clear position on originals and copies; judgments can only be made on a case to case basis.[8] In lay terms, though, the old assumptions about race and authenticity, commerce and inauthenticity, still have considerable purchase. On August 15, 2002, to mark the twenty-fifth anniversary of Elvis Presley's death, the *Guardian* published an article by Helen Kolaoke dismissing his music on the grounds that "for black people Elvis more than any other performer epitomises the theft of their music and dance." This led to a flurry of correspondence in which fifty years of critical argument about race and rock'n'roll were replayed in miniature: when does "borrowing" become "appropriation," when does "cultural exchange" become "theft"?

At the core of this dispute, though, was a simple but unstated point: people who liked Presley's music were defending him from the charge of racial exploitation; people who didn't sought to develop the charge. The confusion of musical judgment and social explanation was obvious, but there is also an implicit argument here about value and intention. The fact that Pat Boone's "personal stamp" was put on "Tutti Frutti" is clearly a bad thing; the fact that John Coltrane's personal stamp was put on "These Foolish Things" is clearly a good thing. There's an assumption here about motives as well as race—Boone making a marketing decision, Coltrane an artistic judgment (years later Puff Daddy's use of Sting's "I'll Be Watching You" would equally be dismissed as cynical, commercial, bad). And so while I can't think of a rock critic who wouldn't agree that the Peter Frampton version of *Sgt. Pepper* is one of the worst albums ever made, there would be disagreement about Paul Young's version of Joy Division's "Love Will Tear Us Apart." Rip off or tribute? The judgment rests not on what Paul Young says about the record but on how it sounds.

The law, of course, has always had its own (non-aesthetic) interest in authorship and plagiarism and this is the source of another kind of argument about bad music and production. Following the 1988 Copyright Act, British law (unlike U.S. law) was brought into line with the law in other European Union countries and now acknowledges authors' moral rights in their work. Under this clause, the "integrity" of a composer's work is protected; "bad music" by this definition, illegal music, is that which in arrangement or interpretation brings a composition or its composer into "disrepute," fails to "respect" the work and its author's intentions. Few cases have been heard under this clause (though injunctions against the use of samples have referred to it) but it seems clear to me that in practice the intention of the "interpreter" will be less significant in judging the moral value of their work than its effect on listeners, on the original composer and, indeed, on the judge.

Even here, though, on the evidence of straight plagiarism cases, the musical judgment will refer to production processes and depend on particular sorts of knowledge. To condemn a record as derivative or disreputable we must know (or know about) the "original" (the kind of knowledge displayed so ostentatiously by both classical and popular music critics faced with new work, by musicological "experts' in court). To describe a song as "standardized" means that we have heard (or heard of) other songs of a similar type. Such knowledge may be more or less extensive, more or less valid; judgments here often rest on hypothetical knowledge, on unexamined assumptions about record company, studio and marketing decisions. (This was obvious in the *Guardian*'s Presley correspondence.) Listeners read from a record how they think it must have been produced, and then condemn it (or not) accordingly. Hence the familiar enough experience (to which people are often loath to admit) that we need to know who a record is by before we can evaluate it.

Production arguments do tend, then, to be deployed by fans; they depend on certain sorts of musical knowledge and engagement. At the same time, though, even the most well informed fan is still, in the end, referring "bad music" to the something "in the music itself" that led him or her down this discursive path in the first place (again the Presley point). And the recurring negative musical judgment in all these discussions of the original and the derivative, the individual and the standardized, seems to be in terms of excessive *familiarity*: a piece of music is bad because it uses musical clichés; because its development is easily predictable; because nothing unexpected happens. And the critical problem here is not just that there can be pleasure in the predictable, but that not everyone has the same expectations. Few people who bought Atomic Kitten's 2002 U.K. hit, "The Tide is High," knew the Blondie record it faithfully copied (itself a cover version).

Arguments, about musical *effects* are rather different. Bad music is, it seems, responsible for bad things, for hysteria and sexual arousal, for violence and crime. In their entertaining history of "the opposition to rock'n'roll," Linda Martin and Kerry Seagrove quote a typical 1950s editorial about this new form of bad music, this one from the worthy *Music Journal*. Teenagers listening to rock'n'roll were, the journal argued,

> Definitely influenced in their lawlessness by this throwback to jungle rhythms. Either it actually stirs them to orgies of sex and violence (as its model did for the savages themselves), or they use it as an excuse for the removal of all inhibitions and the complete disregard of conventions of decency . . . [rock'n'roll] has proved itself definitely a menace to youthful morals and an incitement to juvenile delinquency. There is no point in soft-pedalling these facts any longer. The daily papers provide sufficient proof of their existence . . . It is entirely correct to say that every proved delinquent has been definitely influenced by rock'n'roll.[9]

Such dire warnings about its effects have accompanied every popular music trend since—the twist, rock, disco, punk, rave, rap. Even as I was writing the final draft of this chapter, in January 2003, a British culture minister, Kim Howells, was denouncing rap in general and the

U.K. garage act So Solid Crew in particular, in the aftermath of a gun battle in Birmingham which left two teenage girls dead: "Idiots like the So Solid Crew are glorifying gun culture and violence." Howells was echoing comments made earlier by a senior policeman, Tarique Ghaffur, "who blamed a 'backdrop of music' for alienating young men and encouraging them to use weapons as fashion statements."[10]

The subsequent public debate about music and violence in Britain has almost exactly replayed the U.S. debate about music and violence in the early 1990s, following the success of gangsta rap. There were hearings in 1994 in both the Senate and House of Representatives to consider the problem of "violence and demeaning imagery in popular music," and, as Doug Simmons then wrote, the underlying question was this: "does reality shape rap or does rap shape reality?"[11] What is remarkable is how many politicians have so strong a belief in the power of music to shape society when music analysts themselves are ever more wary of such a description. At its most ludicrous, this political belief becomes the certainty that the most evil music (usually heavy metal) gets its effects subliminally, by including backward messages. Judas Priest had to go to court in 1990 to defend themselves from the charge of inducing two teenage boys to attempt suicide as a result of such a devilish musical ploy.[12]

The suggestion that music is evil comes from all parts of the political spectrum. In Europe, for instance, white nationalist skinhead groups like Skrewdriver have long been accused of fomenting fascism, violence and political mindlessness, while the rap and ragga acts denounced by policemen and politicians for glamorizing violence are equally condemned from the left for promoting misogyny and homophobia.[13]

Such arguments about rock's dreadful effects are familiar and I must resist the temptation to document even more outlandish examples, but some general points are worth noting here. First, musical judgments in terms of musical effects are usually made by people from outside the musical worlds concerned, and involve no informed pop or rock knowledge at all (which is why such arguments seem plain silly to the fans and musicians themselves, even if they have to take them seriously to protect their music from censorship or regulation).

Second, despite (or maybe because of) this, effect arguments, unlike production arguments, are surprisingly influential institutionally, in terms of record labelling, banning and censorship. These accounts of bad music do affect what we can hear on the radio, see on stage, buy in shops. Indeed, the moral logic of such music criticism is that *something should be done*! Ban Eminem/So Solid Crew/Buju Banton![14]

Third, there is, nonetheless, very little evidence that bad music has the effects it is purported to have, whether on crowd behavior, individual attitudes, social beliefs, or whatever. It follows, paradoxically, that the focus here is much more closely on the music itself than in production criticism. The "effects" of the music, that is to say, are deduced from the music itself because there is no independent evidence that they actually exist. (Compare the way in which Soviet officials could only determine what music was decadent, what music was not, by formal analysis.)

Opponents of rock usually reduce "the music itself" to a small number of effective elements: *rhythm; lyrics; performance.* I discuss the long association of rhythm, race, sexuality, and the "primitive" in *Performing Rites.* Here I will focus on lyrics and performance.

Nearly all indictments of "bad music" leading to censorship or airplay bans concern lyrics, as exemplified by the "parental guidance" labelling of albums following the Parents' Music Resource Centre's successful U.S. lobbying campaign in the 1980s.[15] In his account of the Mosely-Brown Senate Committee hearings on demeaning imagery in popular music, Doug Simmons describes "the sheets of graphic lyrics stacked on the press tables." The demeaning imagery was, it seems, verbal rather than musical.[16]

Are there circumstances in which a pop melody or arrangement or instrumental texture is censored? Totalitarian regimes have certainly banned whole musical genres because of their supposed political or oppositional or "foreign" implications. Religious authorities have on occasion decided that instrumental music is incompatible with godliness (I'm not just thinking here of the Taliban's denunciation of all music, but also of the way the Church of England banned all musicians except choirs and organists from its services in the late nineteenth century). The arguments here are not so much about bad music as that music— all music—is bad per se.

Music performance raises different questions. The most widely discussed examples of offensive performance over recent decades have been the pop videos condemned by right and left alike as sexist, racist, homophobic. A more interesting case of "bad music" being explained by reference to its offensive performing conventions, though, is minstrelsy, white people aping blacks, and, in particular, *The Black and*

White Minstrel Show, which ran on British television from 1957–1973, and which is still occasionally revived as a live attraction.[17] Even as a child I found the minstrels' show unsettling: the falseness and excess of the make-up made the musical emotions of the standard Tin Pan Alley songs seem false and excessive too (I had much the same reaction to the Rolling Stones' stage spectaculars in the late 1970s).

In retrospect, though, at least *The Black and White Minstrel Show* had the virtue of drawing attention to its performing conventions, to the problems of staging musical authenticity and inauthenticity, to what it means to *be an act*. In her illuminating account of the 1990 Florida court case in which 2 Live Crew were charged and acquitted of staging an obscene performance, Lisa Jones makes the point that 2 Live Crew are just such an act. Decidedly offensive and unpleasant, but still an act. The turning point in the trial came when the police witnesses had to "translate" to the court the meaning of what they'd seen. "After lunch there's a breakthrough. The jury has sent a note to Judge Johnson asking if they're allowed to laugh. It's a deciding moment in the case."[18]

Ten years later and we have to make the same argument about Eminem. I know of no credible rock critic who thinks Eminem makes bad music. On the contrary, his records provide some of the best popular music of the turn of the century. But then I know of no credible rock critic who's not made uneasy by their pleasure in these words, this sensibility. "He's an act," we comfort ourselves, "a brilliant act, Eminem (like James Dean or Johnny Rotten before him) is *playing* a disturbed and disaffected young white man." In denying that the rise in gun violence in the U.K. had anything to do with music, a spokeswoman for So Solid Crew suggested that their own music reflected society "just as Robert de Niro reflected American gangster society in his film roles."[19] And what's at issue in drama criticism is how well a role is played; to articulate a sensibility musically is not to endorse it.

I'm not entirely convinced that this argument describes musical (as against dramatic) performance but before dealing with that I want to take stock of my argument so far. I've been describing uses of the term "bad music" that refer more or less explicitly either to how it was produced or to its presumed effects. What is going on here, to repeat my starting point, is the entanglement of a musical judgment—the music is bad—with an explanation of why it is, and I think most day-to-day arguments about music are conducted in this way: aesthetic judgments are necessarily tangled up with ethical judgments. I suggest that what's involved here are not accounts of bad music as such but justifications for using the label, "bad music."

To clarify this point I need to discuss briefly a third kind of critical discourse, derived from the arguments used in music making. For musicians, bad music seems to fall into two broad categories. First, *incompetent* music, music that is badly played, that reflects inadequate skill, technique and so forth. But even here technical, "objective," judgments (this player is lagging behind the beat, has erratic pitch, played the wrong note) are often confused with an ideological, subjective, ones. Musicians' incompetence can be explained in two ways. Either they are *untutored* (they can't do certain things because they haven't been taught how) or they are *unprofessional* (they are unwilling to learn proper techniques). The former argument implies that bad musicians want to play differently but can't, the latter implies that there are pop genres in which "bad musicianship"—erratic pitch, wrong notes— is actually welcomed. Even in classical criticism reviewers tend to favor a "passionate" performance, wrong notes and all, over something that is technically flawless but "cold."

This argument spills over into a second sort of conception of bad music, that it is *self-indulgent*. At least three different points are conflated here. Musicians may be criticized for selfishness or egocentricity; bad musicians are musicians who forget or deny that good music is a collective practice; they use a performance to show off their own virtuosity or character, to dominate the microphone or sound mix, to play too long or loudly. Such musicians don't listen to their performing colleagues and the resulting music is bad because it is "unbalanced." Musicians may also be criticized for emptiness; bad musicians indulge in form at the expense of content, make music that "has nothing to say" but says it elaborately anyway. Their music is not made for any reason except as a display of technical skill. Cecilia Bartoli, writes Tim Ashley,

> could be accused of unearthing second-rate music for the express purpose of showing off, for what she now presents us with is a vocal olympiad, at which we are primarily invited to marvel at her technique . . . Bartoli is always impressive but rarely moving. It is artifice rather than art."[20]

Musicians may also be criticized for their incomprehensibility; bad musicians play in a completely introverted way, for self-satisfaction or for therapeutic reasons, as a matter of private obsession. Their music is not communicative; it does not acknowledge or address an audience. This is the standard workaday musician critique of "arty" music, for example.

All the arguments here are, indeed, about communication. Bad music is music that doesn't communicate—between musician and audience, between musician and musician, between performer and composer. The implication is that musical decisions are communication decisions, and certainly one kind of judgment of bad music is that the composers'/performers' choices—to write/play this note rather than that—have been made randomly, with no communicative point at all. And this leads me to my final set of questions. What do people want from music? What it is that they're *not* getting when they describe a song or performance or work as bad music? I would suggest three rather grand answers: truth, taste and intelligence.

The most common account of bad music (of bad rock music certainly) is that it is *inauthentic*. This certainly refers to its production, but not in any coherent way. "Inauthentic," that is to say, is a term which may be applied evaluatively within genres which are straightforwardly, cynically, commercial. Fans distinguish between authentic and inauthentic Eurodisco or TV pop idols, and what is being described is not how something was actually produced, but a more inchoate feature of the music itself, a perceived quality of sincerity and commitment. It's as if people expect music to mean what it says, however cynical that meaning, and music can be heard as being false to its own premises (which is one reason why I have difficulty in treating Eminem—or Madonna—as "just an act"). How do people hear music in such ethical ways? What is it about a record that makes us say "I just don't believe it," not necessarily agreeing with anyone else on this at all. This is, I think, related to the ways in which we judge people's sincerity generally. It is a human as well as a musical judgment.

Bad music may also be described as music in *bad taste*, and this involves a different kind of judgment, in terms of its appropriateness or inappropriateness to a particular function or occasion. Post-9/11, the U.K. TV news service, ITN, was thus censured by the Independent Television Commission for broadcasting a "sick and tasteless" sequence of news in which "the collapse of the World Trade Center in New York was set to music." The music (from Charles Gounod's *Judex*) may have been, as ITN claimed, suitable, with "a sombre, funereal tone," but the very attempt to show these images in time to music "was inappropriate and breached the programme code." There are both specific and general questions here: is this piece of music suitable for this event (Elton John's "Candle in the Wind" at Princess Diana's funeral service)? Is any sort of popular commercial music suitable to deal with disease or pain in general, to deal with them *entertainingly*?

Third, bad music may be considered *stupid*. This is a common term in popular discourse even if it is not often articulated by professional critics. And it is an interesting term because it is not only applied to words or lyrics; people can and do find tunes and arrangements and sounds stupid too. What is meant here? Clearly the analogy is with the way we call a statement (or the person making a statement) stupid, a suggestion not just that their account of the world is wrong, but that it is also somehow demeaning, that it demeans us through our involvement, however unwilling, in the collusive act of listening to someone making, say, a racist or sexist remark, to *The Black and White Minstrel Show,* to Eminem. Stupid music in this (non-academic) context is offensive because it seems to deny what we're capable of, humanly, rationally, ethically, aesthetically. Which is why we can loath a tune that we can't get out of our heads.

And that brings me to my final set of arguments. I'm happy to concede that "bad music" is a matter of taste, involves a judgment that depends on the social and psychological circumstances of the person making it. I doubt if the readers of this book could come up with an agreed list of bad records and I agree that it would be foolish to try. On the other hand, whatever the individual bases of our judgments, once made we do seek to justify and explain them, and my concern here has been to survey the language that seems available to us, and to point out some of its problems.

From this perspective it is clear that we need a concept of "bad music" even if we know full well that we won't be able to agree on how the label should be applied. The marking off of some tracks and genres and artists as "bad" is a necessary part of popular music pleasure; it is a way we establish our place in various music worlds. And "bad" is a key word because it suggests that aesthetic and ethical judgments are tied together here: not to like a record is not *just* a matter of taste; it is also a matter of argument, an argument that matters. My students have always been agreed on this: other people's musical tastes have a decisive effect on friendships, courtship, love.

Throughout this chapter I've been treating the evaluative process as a matter of discourse: what is happening when we talk about music?

As a music lover, though, I know that what's equally at issue is feeling: what is happening when we listen to music? "Bad music" describes to begin with an emotional not an ideological response. I don't like a record; I then try to account for that dislike, to justify it. When we label something as "bad music" it is because it is music that, if nothing else, upsets or offends us, that we don't want to listen to. *Please* play something else! Do I *have* to listen to this? It grates, hurts, bores; it's ugly, it's painful, it's driving me *mad*. Is there anything I can say as a sociologist about such responses?

Well, to begin with, I don't believe that music in itself just *is* ugly or painful or boring. What's at issue here is not the sound but the emotional response to the sound. And looking back at my schematic account of evaluative language and evaluative circumstances, at my discussion of when and why music is labelled "bad," two themes become apparent. First, musical arguments (whether referring to production or effects) call into question musical *intent*. They are judgments of musicians' motivations; they call to account the reasons *why* the music sounds as it does. They are thus judgments of performers' attitudes to their listeners; they are arguments about communication. Bad music is heard to be music made in bad faith. But this is to suggest a second theme, musical *expectation*. People don't just read off musicians' intentions from their music, they interpret what they hear in the light of what they believe music could or should be. (And certainly one difference between music critics and committed fans, on the one hand, and "ordinary" or casual listeners, on the other, is that the former have higher expectations of music in general and specific performers in particular, and are therefore more often disappointed.)

The question, then, is how to relate the emotional response to music to these understandings and expectations of the musical experience. Or, to put this the other way round, when does not *liking* a piece of music mean judging it *"bad"*? When does a piece of music make someone so angry that they have to speak their objections?[21] There can be no doubt that this happens, famously, for example, at the first performance of Stravinsky's *Rite of Spring*. One source of listeners' displeasure seems to have been a sense of sacrilege. The problem was not just that the music was difficult, that it lacked the melodic and sonic qualities the audience expected, but that it somehow ridiculed such qualities, bringing "primitive" elements to a highly serious occasion. A reading of contemporary music criticism suggests that anger at a performance is still imbued with this sense that it, the performance, is somehow making a mockery of what the critic believes music is supposed to be. I would classify such critical anger under three headings:

- Anger that other people are enjoying something that is *not worthy of enjoyment*. (This is what one might call the David Helfgott problem—critics are particularly incensed when someone they regard as musically sloppy if not meretricious is rapturously applauded for "sentimental" reasons.)[22]
- Anger that performers or composers are *betraying their talent*. (This is often seen to be in the pursuit of crowd-pleasing, whether emotionally or commercially. The most familiar version of this argument is the rock cultural concept of "selling out," but classical critics are often similarly upset—the more talented or "promising" the musician the greater the critic's anger.)
- Anger that a performer or composer or record company is dishonouring music by *corrupting its original integrity*. (This is the language, as we've seen, of moral rights, the source of legal injunctions against dance music producers "adapting" the work of Carl Orff, of ethnomusicologists' despair at the way in which local ritual and spiritual music is sampled for Western entertainment.)[23]

In all these cases the performance is heard to be insulting, and the performers to lack respect, whether for their music, its composers, or their listeners. It's the same sense of insult that makes people angry about the *inappropriate* use of music—as muzak, on advertisements, in television shows. People are most annoyed, that is to say (going by anecdotal evidence), when music they particularly *like*, whether it be Verdi or the Rolling Stones, is used to soothe nerves or sell cars, used in a way which will make it difficult for them ever to listen to this music *in their own way* again.

In all these cases a performance of music is making people angry because of what it is not. People don't just have unmet musical expectations, thwarted ideals of musical performance, occasion and experience, but feel that these ideals are being sullied. I want to note two aspects of this immediately. First, such a sense of sacrilege depends on a particular kind of musical understanding. Second, music here is making people angry because of its ethical rather than technical shortcomings (which is why we can be made angry by music in which in other circumstances we delight).

I will turn now to a related but I think different kind of anger, rooted in issues of identity. The most famous example of an angry audience in rock history (the iconic equivalent of the first *Rite of Spring*) was captured on tape at Bob Dylan's concert at the Free Trade Hall in Manchester in 1966.[24] Listen to it now and the sense of betrayal is still palpable—in the audience response to Bob Dylan playing electric rock, in Dylan's own response to his audience's disapproval. This is an example of the sheer emotional charge of the accusation of "sell out!" And for rock and pop fans the problem here seems to be less the dishonouring of an ideal or original musical concept than the betrayal of an identity, of a belief in what an artist *stood for*, and how that, in turn, reflected (and reflected back on) the identity of the listener. For Bob Dylan's folk-club followers musical taste was a key to the way they differentiated themselves from the mainstream of commercial pop consumers. Dylan going pop thus had for his folk fans something of the same emotional impact as betrayal by a lover. Their musical trust had been abused; the new Bob Dylan called their very sense of themselves into question. The source of anger here, in short, was not so much the music itself as who was playing it.

Audiences can be angered by another kind of betrayal of trust, when they feel that a musician is cheating or exploiting them. In the days when I was reviewing a lot of concerts I did occasionally see audiences get very angry indeed. This was either because they thought they had been short-changed—numbers performed perfunctorily, with mistakes and sloppiness, musicians displaying a kind of contempt. Or because they detected the use of backing tracks or drum machines or other kinds of pre-recorded assistance (in fact used by most rock bands, but usually well concealed). Here too, if without the sense of self involved in the more intense kinds of fandom, music can be seen as a relationship in which both sides have certain obligations. (My own rages at concerts were with audience members who failed to meet their obligations as listeners—talking all through the quiet bits.)

I want to turn finally to a third and rather different (if more familiar) kind of anger. I will summarize this as the problem of *noise* because, in general, it is anger expressed at music being played *too loud*! In fact, though, I think the problem is not volume as such (measured by decibels) but the feeling that someone else's music is invading our space, that we can't listen to it as music, a pleasurable organization of sound, but only as noise, an undifferentiated din.[25] This is an increasing problem in everyday life and these days musical disputes are probably more often arguments about noise than taste. "Turn it down!" is the eternal parental cry (even when the music isn't actually being played that loudly), and so, over the last few months, I've found myself being most irritated at home by one child's habit of playing Bob Dylan's *Greatest Hits* in the kitchen—too loud!—whenever he gets the chance to do so, tracks that I'll happily put on myself when I'm home alone.

"Noise" in such domestic disputes refers to people's sense of spatial integrity, and the question becomes how music works to include and exclude people from this kind of aural space, and when and why other people's music is felt to invade it. It's clear to begin with that the music itself is not really the issue, just that it is not, at that moment, *our* music. And certainly in domestic life some records come to carry traces of battles past, to symbolize particularly charged arguments not so much about good and bad music as about the personal right to make such judgments (and enforce them)!

My grand opening question—what is bad music?—has ended up with musical judgment as the banal currency of domestic squabble. But there is a grand point I want to make about this, as I draw to a conclusion. Our feelings about a piece of music are, of course, drawn forth by the music: we listen, we respond. But we listen on the basis of who we are and what we musically know and expect, and we respond according to how and where and why we're listening. I've been arguing throughout this chapter that musical judgments are also ethical judgments, concern the perceived purposes as well as sounds of music, and that judgment is, by its nature, an attempt to persuade other listeners of the rightness of one's own responses. What I want to conclude is that the aesthetics of music, therefore, involve a particular mix of individualism and sociability.

I don't think there can be any doubt that for both technological and cultural reasons the twentieth century experience of music became highly individualized. Music listening became tied up with personal identity and the sense of self; music became something through which one laid claim to and identified one's own physical and geographical space. This in turn led to a new kind of demand being placed on music: it was expected to meet its listeners' individual (and shifting) emotional needs, to confirm their sense of individuality. At the same time, music became something to which one could be, individually, more or less committed; it was no longer just a shared part of communal life.

In different but related ways music critics and music fans developed evaluative positions in which greater knowledge and better taste (derived from the individual devotion to music of much time and attention) meant a superior way of *listening*. The self became invested in musical judgment as never before.

The paradox is that this egocentric aesthetic ("I" is the most common word in all forms of music criticism) is driven by a passionate desire to make other people listen differently. In both published criticism and everyday argument, "good" and "bad" music are terms used to persuade people to change their listening expectations. Even as the musical experience has been individualized, it has remained necessarily and undeniably sociable. I haven't dealt here at all with music and dance, with collective music making, with musical pleasures that are social pleasures (and therefore not subject to the same sort of aesthetic judgment). But, more pertinently, the peculiar thing about music is that even in these days of the personal sound systems, it is not, and cannot be, just an individual experience. These days, when music accompanies every conceivable public and private activity, we can't help hearing what other people are listening to and, if we think of ourselves as any sort of music lover, wanting to do something about it.

NOTES

1. The first version of this chapter was prepared for a seminar in the Musicology Department, University of Stockholm, in 1994, and published by the Department as part of its report on that event, *We're Only In It For The Money*. I wrote it as a companion paper to "What is Good Music," *Canadian University Music Review* 10(2), 1990. Arguments from both papers fed into my *Performing Rites. On the Value of Popular Music* (Cambridge, MA: Harvard University Press, 1996).

2. This is the everlasting appeal of Slonimsky's *Lexicon*, first published in 1953 (and kept in print by the University of Washington Press). What makes this collection of "critical assaults on composers' such compulsive reading is its examples of critics getting things wrong. It is less about bad music than about bad music criticism.

3. The original spoken version of this paper was illustrated by the following records: Dub Syndicate's *One Way System* ("boring" and "repetitious"); Midi, Maxi and Efti's "Bad Bad Boys" (unoriginal, standardized disco pop complete with tacky rap); Tommy Tune and Twiggy's "Room in Bloomsbury" from *The Boyfriend* (parody of the Tin Pan Alley heterosexual love song at its most lyrically and melodically banal); Joseph Spence's "Santa Claus is Coming to Town" ("incompetent" performance and production); an unknown country singer's "Ice Cream Cones and Soda Pops' ("bad taste" death of a child song); Meat

Loaf's "Rock and Roll Dreams Come Through" (sexist, offensive, over-produced, commercial formula white rock). I'm fond of all of these but can only play them at home when I'm alone.

4. Savalas did sing Bob Dylan, just as Robert Mitchum sang calypso before him. Seagal's songs so far only exist as promises on his Web site. It seems somehow safe to assume that they will be dreadful—see John Sutherland's column in the *Guardian*, January 13, 2003 (G2, 5)

5. For the last ten years I've chaired the judges of the Mercury Music Prize, which is awarded to the best British record of the year, of any genre. We sometimes consider producing a list of the worst records of the year too. There are two kinds of bad music on which we are all agreed: albums by 70s rock stars success-ful enough to indulge themselves in some religious or philosophical fad and attempts to give classical music pop appeal (Bond, Opera Babes, Planets, and the like). The former are ridiculous and therefore have kitsch potential; the latter are irredeemable.

6. In the art music world the value judgments made by grant and commission giving bodies might be equally important materially (in determining which musicians can make a living from their music and which can't; which works are heard by audiences and which not). Such funding bodies rarely articulate publicly the reasons why somebody was *unworthy* of support.

7. I address this question in *Performing Rites*.

8. For two excellent recent discussions of the issues here see Dai Griffiths: "Cover versions and the sound of identity in motion," in D. Hesmondhalgh and K. Negus eds., *Popular Music Studies* (London: Arnold, 2002), 51–64; Michael Coyle: "Hijacked hits and antic authenticity: cover songs, race and postwar marketing," in R. Beebe, D. Fulbrook and B. Saunders eds., *Rock Over the Edge* (Durham and London: Duke University Press, 2002), 133–157.

9. Quoted in Linda Martin and Kerry Seagrove, *Anti-Rock. The Opposition to Rock'n'Roll* (Hamden, Connecticut: Anchor Books, 1988), 53.

10. Fiachra Gibbons, "Minister labelled racist for attack on rap 'idiots.'" *Guardian*. January 6, 2003, 3.

11. Doug Simmons: "Gangsta Was the Case," *Village Voice,* March 8, 1994, 63.

12. See Ivan Solotaroff, "Subliminal Criminals," *Village Voice,* September 4, 1990, 24–34.

13. A campaign in Glasgow in 2001 to prevent Marilyn Manson and Eminem head-lining the annual Festival on the Green thus involved an unusual alliance of fundamentalist Christians and gay activists.

14. For a useful recent survey of global music censorship and regulation see Mar-tin Cloonan and Reebee Garofalo eds., *Policing Pop* (Philadelphia: Temple University Press, 2003).

15. For a good contemporary discussion of the PMRC campaign and its historical context see James R. McDonald, "Censoring Rock Lyrics," *Youth & Society*, 19, no. 3 (1988): 294–313.

16. Simmons op. cit., 63.

17. For a sophisticated discussion of minstrelsy as British entertainment see Michael Pickering, "John Bull in blackface," *Popular Music* 16, no. 2 (1997): 181–201.

18. Lisa Jones: "The Signifying Monkees," *Village Voice,* November 6, 1990, 171.

19. Gibbons op. cit.
20. Tim Ashley: "Cecilia Bartoli," *Guardian,* November 7, 2002, 27.
21. Some of the arguments that follow were first presented in "Why does music make people so cross?", a paper given to the 4th Nordic Music Therapy Conference in Bergen in May 2003. Thanks to the participants for their comments.
22. David Helfgott was the Australian pianist whose story of mental breakdown and recovery was told in the emotionally and commercially effective film, *Shine*. His subsequent concert hall appearances were rapturously received by audiences but almost universally panned by critics.
23. See, for example, Steven Feld, "The Poetics and Politics of Pygmy Pop" in G. Born and D. Hesmondhalgh, eds., *Western Music and Its Others* (Berkeley: University of California Press, 2000)
24. The tape was issued as a bootleg record, misleadingly titled *Dylan Live at the Albert Hall*. For the true story of this event, see C. P. Lee, *Like the Night. Bob Dylan and the Road to the Manchester Free Trade Hall* (London: Helter Skelter, 1998).
25. For further discussion of some of the issues here see Simon Frith, "Music and Everyday Life" in M. Clayton, T. Herbert and R. Middleton, eds., *The Cultural Study of Popular Music* (New York and London: Routledge, 2003).

PART I

Values and Identity Politics

2

White Trash Alchemies of the Abject Sublime
Country as "Bad" Music

AARON A. FOX

> *[T]he products of labor become commodities, social things whose qualities are at the same time perceptible and imperceptible by the senses. In the same way the light from an object is perceived by us not as the subjective excitation of our optic nerve, but as the objective form of something outside the eye itself.*
>
> KARL MARX, *CAPITAL*, VOL. 1

Turning Trash Into Gold

Hoppy's band had just finished an energetic rendition of "Release Me," done in the Ray Price style and capping a set of Marty Robbins, Merle Haggard, George Jones, and Waylon Jennings songs.[1] The musicians were heading for the bar and the bathroom, and the dancers back to their tables and conversations. Miss Ann, the owner of this redneck bar ("Ann's Other Place") by the side of the state highway north of Lockhart, Texas, walked to the floor in front of the stage. Holding the microphone in one hand, she gazed authoritatively across the smoky dance hall, quieting the raucous crowd of local families as she introduced the afternoon's main event. She stressed the seriousness of the situation that had inspired this "benefit" party for Jerry Meese, a respected regular patron facing a new and expensive diagnosis of advanced lung cancer:[2]

> **ANN:** Ladies and gentlemen
> We gonna have an auction!
> I've never seen such diVERSE stuff
> in an AUCtion before
> in my life
> we have some STRAAANGE stuff here!
> We have a GOLF-BALL picker-upper!

39

[laughter]
We have a clay PIgeon thrower!
We have Candy Sue's last BRA!
[children laugh]
We have some WEEEEEEIRD stuff!
We may have to take up a collection
to get Candy Sue another BRA!
[laughter]
We have a GOLD HARD hat . . .
We have a twenty-two [caliber] rifle
and a twenty-two [caliber] PIStol . . .
So we really run the gamut around here
We gonna auction off some posters
of . . . Clint Black
Surely there's gals in here that wants THAT
But anyway we have a lot o STUFF
But I wanna tell y'all about S . . .
I mean about Shirley and . . . and Jerry
When ANYtime anybody asks for help
They're the FIRST ones to jump in
an help . . .
When I found
a family that didn't have anything to eat
had eight children
the FIRST PEople
to bring me FOOD for them was
Shirley . . . and Jerry
And gave me money to go buy MEAT for 'em
So when they jump,
they jump in FIRST
to HELP
and I think it's TIME to PAY 'em back!

As the crowd applauded in fond acknowledgment, Hoppy, a re-
vered local singer whose band had been providing good country music
all day long, took the microphone from Ann and introduced Tony
Collins, who had agreed to serve as the first auctioneer of the afternoon. Tall, gaunt, bearded, and merry, Tony (who worked at a local
chicken processing plant) took quick command of the crowd:

TONY: Alright ladies an gentlemen
Miss ANN forgot to say one thing

She was advertisin' all these WEIRD things
we're gonna have to auction off?
She just forgot to mention that you got a CHICKen-plucker for a
auctioneer!

For the next hour, Tony proceeded to cajole, beg, demand, and manipulate nearly every person in the audience who could spare a few dollars—and the few who could spare more—to part with surprisingly large sums of money in exchange for goods that, in any objective sense, were worth little or nothing. The few items—especially the guns—that did have real value sold for extraordinarily high prices, to men whose careers had taken them into the higher strata of working-class earning power. Such men were not among the more regular patrons of the bar, but were bound by networks of obligation, kinship, patronage, and solidarity to appear at such events as this auction. To this end, the organizers had obliged by holding the benefit on a warm September day when a group of such men had planned a trail ride, the local term for a boozy re-creation of a nineteenth century cattle drive, complete with horse-drawn wagons and elaborate cowboy costumes. This event always drew a sizable contingent from the "Wild Bunch," a loose association of local men with a passion for such rituals and the drunken, carnivalesque sociability they entailed. The dance hall was full of men in curled-brim hats and high leather boots, lubricated, relaxed, and ready to subsidize the back-breaking health care costs Jerry and Shirley suddenly faced.

Of course, the room was also full of the bar's many regulars—truck-drivers and mechanics, nursing home workers and school bus drivers, roofers and electricians, teenage moms and retirees like Jerry. Many patrons had brought their children, as was customary for week-end afternoon events in the local bars. Toddlers wandered around the tavern, cajoling their parents or other adults to bid on baubles they desired. Invariably, such bids were accepted and the newly purchased trinket (say, a plastic watch) was immediately given to the supplicant child. Conversations at various tables zeroed in on the objects being offered, as bids were shouted into the noisy storm of talk. Then these conversations returned to the traditional themes—country music, someone's crazy antics, someone's infidelity, and the generally screwed-up state of the world. Bellowing bidding wars ensued, sometimes in response to bids shouted out by Crazy Jane, one of the bar's most performative "fools," who seemed to delight in making bids everyone knew she could not afford on items she couldn't possibly want, secure in the knowledge that none of the men in the "Wild Bunch" would allow themselves to be out-bid by a woman.

The hard hat sold for fifteen dollars. A wooden salad bowl sold for ten. A cassette recording of Hoppy's band went for a cool twenty. And the ethnographer in the room was also expected to chip in, right after Tony reminded everyone in the room again why it all mattered:

> **TONY:** Most . . .
> of you folks know what we're out here for
> We're out here to help
> a couple people here in
> Lockhart, Texas
> Good friends
> About everybody in Lockhart knows 'em
> Need some HELP
> That's what this is ALL about
> This is tryin to help
> Jerry
> Shirley and the kids
> to make it through this thing . . .
>
> This is gonna be ONE special item only
> for the NIGHT
> you'll never have another chance to bid on
> this next item
> but this is ec-specially for YANkees
> Do we have any Yankees in the HOUSE?
> [yells and whoops]
> HEY LEMME SEE THEM HANDS
> WILL YOU PLEASE KEEP EM HOLDIN UP!
> [. . .]
> What we're gonna do is go around right here
> and we're gonna auction OFF
> ONE
> Gen-U-WINE
> ARMA-DILLA EGG!
> And here it is!
> This is one of these TEXAS SIZE
> Arma-dilla eggs!
> Can I get a bid on this ARMA-dilla egg
> from a YAN-kee?

[bidding ensues]
I wanna tell you ONE thing man!
When you take this cross the Red River with YA . . .
Now this is a GREEN one!
You gonna have to take it back with ya!
And put it under your old SETTIN hen
to get this thing to turn BROWN
That's the only way it WORKS!
Somebody take this thing back up NORTH
You probly get a HUNDred dollar BILL for it
Cause they never SEEN one like it before!
[bidding, banter]
You take em back to Illinois
Chicago
Anything north the Red River
You got something to SHOW!
[bid by AF]
I got a SIX dollar bid!
That man knows the value of these things
They keep goin' UP!
This thing is like DIAMONDS in Yankee land!
They last forEVER!
I'll guarantee ya
it'll last FOREVER!

On Lasting Forever: Country as (White) Trash

As the proud owner of a six dollar plastic "Armadillo Egg," I am compelled to use this brief episode in the life of a peri-urban working-class community in Texas to think through some aspects of the complex notion of *value* in relation to fields of popular musical practice, and specifically in relation to country music's strong but complicated claim to the title of "bad" music. Country music occupies a privileged place in the pantheon of American musical badness, a place reserved for (white) trash.

Country isn't bad the way background music is bad—stripped of symbols of cultural difference and devoid of the Romantic aura of music as a site of sacred experience in opposition to the textures of commercial life. Country asserts cultural identity—and increasingly, cultural difference (Ching 2001), and though it appears to be relentlessly and crassly commercial, country embraces a key Romantic mythology of the sacredness of the folkloric ordinary. Nor is country "bad" the way a school orchestra's performance of a Brandenburg concerto might be bad, marking amateur fealty to elite hierarchies of cultural value. Country may seem, like a school orchestra performance, to index, dimly, a deeply valued tradition (in this case, of "folk" vernacular expression), but the hierarchies of value country embraces are anything but elitist. In that sense, its badness is not only an index, but an icon of the abject status of its fans and creators. And while country is sometimes "bad" the way some jazz (Kenny G, perhaps) and blues (the Rolling Stones, perhaps) are bad—skimming the textural surface of a deeply complex musical style or producing a clowning minstrelsy of poverty—the standard of authenticity to which country is consequently held is not the racialized cultural essence of "real" jazz or "real" blues, but the historicized essence of "real" country music—an originary badness, always receding into the nostalgic mists of a preceding generation of stars and consumers.

On the other hand, country music is widely disparaged in racialized terms, and assertions of its essential "badness" are frequently framed in specifically racial terms. For that reason, I will focus my discussion in this chapter first on the question of whether country is racist, and if so, whether that explains its particular and exaggerated reputation for "badness," before moving into a more general discussion of the framework of social value that accusations of "racism" perhaps merely exemplify.

For many cosmopolitan Americans, especially, country is "bad" music precisely because it is widely understood to signify an explicit claim to *whiteness,* not as an unmarked, neutral condition of lacking (or trying to shed) race, but as a marked, foregrounded claim of cultural identity—a bad whiteness. As "white" music, unredeemed by ethnicity, folkloric authenticity, progressive politics, or the *noblesse oblige* of elite musical culture, country frequently stands for the cultural badness of its adherents. Country is, in this sense, "contaminated" culture (Stewart 1991), mere proximity to which entails ideological danger. (One example: while I have never seen a personal advertisement in a newspaper that lists a preference for any other musical genre among the disqualifications for potential romantic partners, the stipulation "no country music fans" is quite common in such ads.)

The taint of whiteness in country aligns with the taint of rural idiocy and working-class psychopathology. William Ivey, an academic folklorist who at one time was the director of the Country Music Foundation, was chosen by President Clinton to head the embattled National Endowment for the Arts in 1996. In an interview with the *New York Times* correspondent Peter Applebome, Mr. Ivey assured sophisticated readers (who might be concerned about the direction in which he might take the Endowment) that he actually preferred Charlie Parker to Garth Brooks (and, the article asks by implication, just *who* wouldn't?). Applebome himself pointed out that Ivey drove a BMW and piloted a small plane. True, he expressed some fondness for country music that had "real connections to the music's roots, like Allison Krauss and Alan Jackson." But it might be argued that Garth Brooks' genre-bending showmanship might be equally true to the roots of commercial country music, that Allison Krauss' modernized bluegrass is the descendant of an urbane invented tradition, or that the "roots" of Alan Jackson's style are in the hard country idiom that emerged in the 1940s to serve the needs of post-war working class–migrants from the country to the industrial cities of the South, West, and Midwest.

For Applebome, Ivey's *bona fides* as "not really country" (and thus, likely to be a decent steward of all the good cultural idioms supported by the NEA) are most clearly evident in his history of supporting revisionist historical efforts by the Country Music Foundation to de-whiten country music, through such efforts as the lavish boxed CD set *From Where I Stand: The Black Experience in Country Music* (1998), and his unsuccessful attempt to include rural blues musicians in the CMF museum (which Applebome equates with embracing "the best parts of the country tradition"). The message is clear: Ivey has had his hands dirtied by extended contact with bad (white) music, but his sins are absolved by black music. Even more pointedly, Ivey's embrace of white, working-class art is redeemed, for Applebome, by the possiblity that the Ivey's entire relationship to popular culture is cynical: ". . . those who know [Ivey] say that he is eminently qualified to run the agency and that if his populist cultural credentials help politically, so much the better" (Applebome 1998).

As Ivey took pains to indicate, country music isn't *all* bad. It too can be redeemed, after all, both by the discriminating judgment of the professional folklorist (much is made of Ivey's PhD in ethnomusicology), and as a source of "populist cultural credentials," in a vaguely nostalgic, mythologizing key. Elite uses of country music for credentialing purposes have a long history. Ivey's arm's-length embrace resonates strongly, for example, with Ralph Peer's ambivalent relationship to what he once called the "pluperfect awful" sound of a music then known as "hillbilly," a music he did so much to conjure into a potent commercial product (Peterson 1997, 33–48). It evokes, too, Henry Ford's sponsorship of barn dances for workers to promote the health of white culture, which he viewed as under assault by Jewish bankers and ethnic minorities (Peterson 1997, 59–66). Literary scholar Cecelia Tichi finds redemption in the unacknowledged (she claims) artfulness and complexity of country music, which she discovers in a curiously narrow and nonrepresentative sample of artists and songs with a distinctively bourgeois appeal, and which she forcefully and forcedly equates with the paintings of Edward Hopper and the poetry of Walt Whitman (1994; see Whisnant 1995).

When President George H. W. Bush declared October, 1990 to be "Country Music Month," he began by limning the genre in question as lying between "the spirited sound of bluegrass" and "the soulful melodies of traditional ballads"—leaving out the songs about getting drunk, killing people, and having sex. The proclamation continues: "Encompassing a wide range of musical genres, from folk songs and religious hymns to rhythm and blues, country music reflects our Nation's cultural diversity as well as the aspirations and ideals that unite us. It springs from the heart of America and speaks eloquently of our history, our faith in God, our devotion to family, and our appreciation for the value of freedom and hard work. With its simple melodies and timeless, universal themes, country music appeals to listeners of all ages and from all walks of life" (Bush 1990). Whiteness, racism, poverty, and alienated labor are, it seems, quite as irrelevant as country music's obvious failure to appeal to listeners from at least *some* walks of life.

But then, "bad" can be *good*—or at least good to think with. In one of the more amusing denigrations of country music I have seen, the Web site of the "Schiller Institute" (a nonprofit cultural organization founded by the wife of Lyndon LaRouche), country music receives special mention as "the 'musical culture' of the pessimistic American populist, wallowing in nostalgia for the Good Old Days and the glorious Lost Cause of the Confederacy . . . Where did Country and Western come from? You guessed it, again: not from the hills and hollers of rural America, but from testtubes [sic] of such cultural warfare centers as Theodore Adorno's Princeton Radio Research Project" (Schiller Institute, n.d.). Leaving aside the impossibly rich image of

Adorno inventing country music in the 1930s, we can see in this flat dismissal exactly the judgment of value that William Ivey, Cecelia Tichi, and George Bush invoke (through a pointed absence) as a foil for their own enlightened appreciations.

Debates about the boundaries of authenticity in country music are so common in the academic and journalistic literature on country as to virtually define the intellectual terrain across which country can be critically approached (Ching 1993, 2001; Dawidoff 1997; Fox 1992; Jensen 1998; Malone 2002; Peterson 1997). The general consensus of recent scholarship—that the discourse of authenticity is an elaborate and cynical construction of value—has become a hackneyed point. And yet the logics of this construction, devolving around key oppositions between old and new songs, hard and soft textures and attitudes, rural and urbane sensibilities and biographies, masculine and feminine affects, subcultural and mass markets, and acoustic and electric performance technologies, continue to compel the same scholars who would reject them. Even more, they compel virtually all serious criticism of country music, and much of the discourse of country fans and marketers. In general, old, hard, rural, masculine, subcultural, and acoustic qualities appease the discriminating sensibility. But the rapidity and ease with which such judgments become marketable signs of affected authenticity, available for a price to people whose judgment cannot be assumed to be adequately discriminating, puts anything "country" under immediate suspicion of falseness. The vanishing real remains always out of reach, and that's bad.

Badness is also available as the engine of a powerful ironic nostalgia characteristic of so many postmodern appropriations of country as a symbol of ambivalence about the "end of history" (Fukuyama 1993; see Stewart 1988). Such ambivalence can shade toward gleeful deconstruction of "roots" mythologies (as in the music of Southern Culture on the Skids), or toward the reverent nostalgic cultivation of these same mythologies within a cosmopolitan sensibility (as in most "alternative country" music). Quite often, as in the case of the *O Brother Where Art Thou?* phenomenon (and indeed, all forms of American minstrelsy [Lott 1997]), these tendencies are combined and interlaced in ways that cannot be adjudicated, intentionally taking maximum advantage of the power of irony to mean whatever one wants it to mean (and to render any potentially damaging implication deniable on its face).

Such effects—historical revisionism, selective essentialism, etc.—
are increasingly important even for curatorial and nominally respect-
ful projects, such as the PBS series "American Roots Music" (2001),
in which country music features prominently as both an unproblematic
"folk" tradition and as the place where folk music went to die. The
documentary series also stumbles on the issue of race. In *American
Roots Music,* the figure of DeFord Bailey, the long-time African American harmonica-playing star of the *Grand Ole Opry,* stands rather impossibly for a subtle revisionism in which the only point his career
makes is that—*in spite of the stereotype*—African Americans really
have contributed significantly to country music. The series fails to
mention that Bailey embodied an important stereotype of African
Americans for *Opry* fans, that he was treated with racist contempt by
Opry management throughout his career, or that he died in poverty
and obscurity. The film also fails to present "the Black experience in
country music" in the more interesting terms of a long history of (white)
country's presence in African American communities, especially in
the rural South, and with the even longer history of white appropriations of black expressive idioms as the source of almost every significant
stylistic development in the history of country as a commercial genre.

Such facts—DeFord Bailey's mistreatment, and embarrassment
at the legion of African American country fans—are inconvenient re-
minders that country *is* bad music, whatever else it may be. They sub-
vert the judgment of taste exercised as a privilege and a condition of
cultural distinction (Bourdieu 1981) by the likes of Bush, Ivey, and
Tichi. And they lend some credibility to the naïve judgement of taste
that is the hallmark of middlebrow rejections of country music—at
least, in other words, such judgments are intellectually honest. By any
conventional standard of value in American pop, country is bad stuff.

And there's a whole hidden history of badness to discuss, a history
that is virtually unrecoverable from official accounts, scholarly or commercial, documentary or promotional, even as it is widely imagined
by people who casually hate country music. The point is that this imagined badness is closer to the truth than all the imagined goodness George
Bush can summon. It's this badness that potentially taints William Ivey's
resumé.

But to look at country's "badness" directly is to discover a more
complicated badness than all these imaginings taken together suggest.
Those who suspect country music is racist, for example, might find

their opinion strengthened by the underground race-baiting, hate-filled music of country singer/songwriter "Johnny Rebel" (Clifford "Pee Wee" Trahan) whose records have circulated widely since his commercial heyday in the 1960s. Among his most popular songs: "Nigger Hatin' Me."[3]

Rebel is mentioned, occasionally, in the academic and critical literatures, usually as a fringe phenomenon, more curious than threatening (though his records are now widely hawked on white-power Web sites). Virtually invisible in these literatures, however, are two far more complex and problematic cases. As far as I know, the two most prominent uses of the word "nigger" in modern country music have never been mentioned in the academic literature.[4] David Allan Coe's 1977 "If That Ain't Country," although not a radio hit, is a widely known song that can be found on thousands of jukeboxes across the American South. In the midst of an edgy evocation of "poor white trash" poverty, Coe's narrator frankly recalls "working like a nigger for my room and board."

The usage is more complex than anything Rebel ever recorded, hurled not as an insult but as a term of shocking comparison, a recognition that whiteness is hardly a singular identity, yet still evocative of a racist mindset Coe never disowns. (Coe, a controversial figure in country music history, also recorded two albums of racist and pornographic songs, some of which also use the word "nigger" in more immediately offensive ways. Those records—*Nothing Sacred* [1980] and *Underground* [1982]—are well known among country fans. Released originally as mail-order-only products, these records now circulate widely on copied tapes and on the Internet.)

But then, there's "Blackbird." Written by Chip Taylor, and recorded in 1975 by Stoney Edwards for Capitol, the song reached number forty-one on the *Billboard* country music singles charts, marking a late hit for one of the most successful African American country singers of the modern period. The song was controversial even in its day for its repeated use of the phrase "just a couple of country niggers." The phrase is remembered by the song's narrator (the "Blackbird" of the song's title) first as the reported speech of his father, a local fiddler who taught him his musical craft. Blackbird's father urges the young man to "hold your head high," even though he was "born poor, Black, and hungry"— even though they are just "country niggers"—because he has been "taught to understand the good in every man," and to "sing about it when you can." The phrase then recurs, in a manner that is utterly canonical in country music, spoken by the narrator's mother, imploring her son to recall his father's wisdom as they witness the interment of the old man. Thus, in both cases, the phrase is uttered by an elderly African American character, and the usage is pointedly ironic, bluntly contrasted with an ethical mandate to see all people as equally good.

Here we see the space of country's ultimate badness—its racist badness—both more starkly and with more complexity than in all the critiques, commentaries, enconiums, and documentaries that avoid or minimize the issue of country's racial politics. Excluding this history of racialized discourse in country music is the essence of the judgment of taste exercised by President Bush and Cecilia Tichi. In the space of this exclusion, the question of country's racial politics is trivialized. The monolithic association of country with a singular and unmarked whiteness is allowed to stand as, apparently, uninteresting, good or bad. Racial boundaries remain intact: either country is fundamentally a racist expressive form, or its whiteness is a historical accident, or the African American contribution to country is underacknowledged, or (most commonly in my experience) country's whiteness simply speaks for itself as evidence of a foundational racism. Johnny Rebel represents the extreme, and still widely held, stereotype of the kind of racist sensibility that embraces country music as a sign of identity. David Allan Coe's overtly racist work, with its wide popularity up to the present day, confirms the truth of that stereotype, despite the efforts of the country music industry to shed its whiteness. Stoney Edwards has been (deservedly) rediscovered as evidence of a Black contribution to country music.[5] But "If That Ain't Country" and "Blackbird," taken seriously as discourse *about* race, class, poverty, and "country" identity, tell a story at once more disturbing and far more complicated than any elitist judgment or any common sense stereotype of country's racial politics allows. For in both songs, "nigger" signifies ironically, and counter-hegemonically, marking the ambivalent and blurred character of whiteness from the point of view of working-class poverty.

One could tell a similar story about other kinds of country music badness. Stereotypes of incestuous rural kinship, for example, are figured humorously, tragically, and ironically in country music (Homer and Jethro's "I'm My Own Grandpa" might be juxtaposed with Frenchie Burke's "Mama's Picture," or Billy C. Wurtz's "Inbred in the U.S.A.," for example) and in anti-rustic polemics casually tossed off as jokes by cosmopolitan urbanites and as explanations in horror movies. The evident inbreeding of America's aristocracy, of course, visible in the phenomenon of political dynasties, has no musical or cinematic equivalent. The right-wing political sentiments expressed by artists such as Merle Haggard ("Okie From Muskogee") and Hank Williams, Jr. ("A Country Boy Can Survive") are by no means obviously sincere or unironic.

Haggard has, for example, himself frequently disclaimed the political views assigned to him on the basis of "Okie," which he asserts is more of an abjectly humorous portrait of small-town parochialism from the perspective of a touring musician. Yet, he has also expressed sympathy with that "parochial" way of life, leaving the listener to choose or to live with the contradiction. In a recent interview, he said of "Okie" that "[the song is a] documentation of the uneducated that lived in America at the time, and I mirror that. I always have. Staying in touch with the working class . . . but it's pretty easy to lie to me. You could lie to me" (Phipps 2001). In the same interview, he expressed anger at the outcome of the 2000 presidential election, yet his ultrapatriotic "The Fighting Side of Me" was frequently heard on country radio in the days after September 11, 2001.

Such songs—and the artists who create them—dwell within the fundamental opposition between law-and-order authoritarianism and the image of "outlaw" authenticity, an opposition that has structured country's discourse of masculinity since the days of Jimmie Rodgers. They dwell, as well, within a fundamental opposition between heroic and antiheroic understandings of working-class identity. Racism is only the most obvious, and simultaneously the most inchoate, of the many kinds of "badness" associated with the genre by its detractors, a "badness" bound up with the other regressive, despised qualities of working-class culture in general, with a goodness only recoverable through the erasure—and the e-race-er—of the exercise of good taste, sound historical judgment, and a patronizing gaze past the conditions of blue-collar existence—what Sennett and Cobb (1972) once famously called "the hidden injuries of class" and Lillian Rubin (1976) referred to as "worlds of pain"—at the misty, patriotic, sepia-toned images of dignified labor stripped of a history of violence, conflict, disease, disaster, and scapegoating.

But how then can we make "sense" of such contradictions? What is the alternative to the opposition between rural idiocy and cosmopolitan snobbery? Must "badness" or "goodness" be absolute qualities, assigned to genres or music or particular performers, or is there another possibility? The discussion of country's race politics, *above*, suggests that country music invites numerous possible readings. Here, I would suggest that perhaps the most compelling alternative to the discriminating, elitist judgment of taste *or* the ignorant embrace of regressive political and cultural values is country music's own poetic self-regard as a commodity, at once disposable and profoundly obsessed with the loss such disposability signifies. And to the extent that so much music—good, bad, and indifferent—now circulates in a commodified form—I would further argue that country offers an object lesson (quite literally) in how to think about the question of value in relation to modern musical culture. Indeed, from the perspective of a Texas country music bar, country makes a strong case for its own badness, but precisely as a precondition for a striking conversion of bad into good. Country music's working-class fans *embrace* what is "bad" about the music's—and their own—cultural identity and meaning, as a way of discovering and asserting what is valuable and good about their lives and their communities. This is what I mean by the apparently contradictory phrase "the abject sublime." Country is not only bad music—it is bad for you. Pathetic or foolish, it is meant to be hated, and it is loved for that, as a symbol of working-class experience. It's not just country's detractors, in other words, or those who would selectively subject the music to the discriminating gaze of the educated arbiter of authenticity, who hate country music. Nobody hates country more than a country music fan, as many great country songs acknowledge.

I Hate These Songs: Badness as a Condition of Abjection

> *Yeah, but I mean, a lot of people don't want to get tore UP,*
> *y'know? And that's the—that's a lot of the BITCH about country*
> *music. God do you want to cry in your beer? No!*
> —JIM HODGSON, TEXAS COUNTRY MUSIC FAN

There's bad, and there's *bad*. All popular music is, to some extent, "bad" music in the sense that disposability is essential to the commercial cycle that organizes music industries. The dialectic of canon formation and its essential ephemerality structure almost all critical discourse about popular music in the modern era, academic and vernacular. Country may be especially "bad" for the reasons discussed above—especially its deep association with the supposedly unique level of racism characteristic of its working-class and Southern constituency, requiring the particularly vigorous effort to scrub it clean evident in the views of Bush, Tichi, Ivey, and so many other apologists and revisionists. Country makes a convenient scapegoat for the badness of popular music in particular, but with all modern music distributed as a commercial product (including normatively "good" musics like classical and jazz), it shares a more banal, but no less fundamental sort of "badness."

I have a box in my office containing (or rather, that once contained) approximately 500 CD singles found in the trash bin at a commercial country music radio station. These are records that were sent out to radio stations by major label record companies to promote new artists and new songs by both well-known and obscure artists. Well over ninety percent of these records never achieved commercial success, and many that did receive extensive airplay are now utterly forgotten by country music fans, historians, and marketers. The vast majority of these recordings are musically competent performances of acutely generic songs. Indeed, within certain subcategories many of these records are nearly indistinguishable except on a very superficial level. For fun, and to make a point, I occasionally grab a handful of these discs and bring them into the college classrooms in which I teach academic courses on popular music. Usually, I drop these CDs on the floor, roughly, and stomp on them until the jewel boxes break. Sometimes, I systematically remove individual CDs and shatter them with a bending and twisting motion that took several attempts to perfect. The effect is predictable on students used to viewing the musical compact disk as a fifteen dollar product (though the drama diminishes year by year as my students themselves have come to the same realization on which I will now elaborate, thanks to the rise of file-sharing and CD burning technologies.)

You can find the same musical trash in the dumpsters of radio stations playing hip-hop, R & B, hard rock, Latin music, or bubblegum pop (and perhaps even the few stations that play jazz and classical music as well). The singers on the covers may wear different clothes, have a different skin pigmentation, and perform in different musical idioms, but under the surface and the generic variations in sound, trash is trash, and bad is bad. Music CDs consist of a dollar's worth of plastic and paper, holding the often calculated work of teams of marketing specialists and a few relatively disempowered artists. The point I make by destroying these bad CDs (admittedly, I have not been able to destroy my Merle Haggard collection!) is that recordings aren't music, and the great error of popular music scholarship (rooted in the ambivalences of highbrow criticism, quite as much as in the naiveté of ordinary fandom) is to confuse the economic value of the commodity with the cultural value of organized sound, thus reproducing the ideological effect of authenticity popular music scholars so often claim to deconstruct.

I learned this critical point from years of engagement with country music, which frequently regards itself, in many of its classic songs and in the everyday musical discourse of many of its working-class fans, precisely as a debased commodity in search of an alchemical transformation, a bending and twisting of the commodified object into a speaking, feeling subject. This transformation is fundamentally figured in the tropes of country's genre poetics (Fox 1992; Stewart 1993; Ching 2001). In song after song, across decades of stylistic change, country music's *real* star performer is the speaking object—the talking jukebox, the house full of furniture but emptied of love, the bitter goodbye heard on an answering machine or read on a Post-It Note stuck on the bathroom mirror, the bottle or glass that ruthlessly seduces the drunken fool, the picture of a lost love on the wall that continues to accuse across the years.

Abjection and alienation are not the sole topic of country's poetic discourse, nor are they exclusive to country music, of course. But abjection—musical and social—is the dominant ethos of many country music songs, especially in the "hard country" subgenre, and the dominant interpretive stance of working-class country fans for whom "hard country" is, as they often say, "*real* country." Country often affects the stance that it is trashy music for trashy people, with a knowing wink or a line like Texas singer Dale Watson's self-loathing 1997 composition "I Hate These Songs:"

> *Note by note, Line by line*
> *It cuts to the bone*
> *Man, I hate these songs*[6]

Despite these sentiments, the song's narrator, of course, lovingly demonstrates a deep familiarity with and passion for the songs he professes to despise, as he wallows in his own drunken misery. The verses of the song consist almost entirely of the titles of classic hard country hits strung together to tell a story of loss and self-destruction. Such narratively embedded intertextuality is a canonical trope in hard country music.

An analogy to another "hated" (but also globally beloved) product may make the irony of country's abjection—or its abject aspect—more obvious. Country music is like a cigarette between the lips of a sweaty, grease-drenched mechanic at happy hour. Richard Klein has said of cigarettes that "[they] are bad. That's why they are good" (1993, 2). But it is in this apparent contradiction, this alchemical transformation of the hated, killing object into the object of intense desire, that the sublime also resides, as Julia Kristeva also famously proposed (in a more psychoanalytic than social scientific sense) in her classic essay on abjection, *Powers of Horror* (1982). Indeed, Klein adds: "if cigarettes were good for you, they would not be sublime" (1993, 2). Or, as a sign behind the bar at the Liar's Inn, a rather brutal dive near Lockhart, Texas, put this point: "This is a smoking area. If you insist on not smoking, you will be asked to leave." The sign was meant, in part, to scare away bourgeois patrons—or to attract them to the abject *mise en scène* should they ever enter such place in search of rustic authenticity (if so, the sign was a failure); it was also meant, in its pointed parody of the kind of sign patrons of the Liar's Inn might encounter in the morning as they entered their workplaces, to signify the transformation effected by the hard country music always playing on the jukebox, and to claim a place where their objectified laboring bodies became, temporarily, their own property again, the site of their subjective agency. At the Liar's Inn, everyone (including this bourgeois patron) smoked.

Like a cigarette, a country song (bad or good, canonical or disposable) arrives in the form of a consumable commodity—with a price. It is consumed in a fit of self-assertion mixed with self-loathing, with a passion for pain as a feeling one can at least inflict sometimes on oneself, at a moment and under conditions of one's own choosing (conditioned, of course, by the physiology of addiction). It hurts going down, and you wake up regretting the indulgence—before you have the first of the morning at least; but in the moment the pain is pleasurable, whether it is pain artfully evoked in a brilliant turn of phrase or a gorgeous crying inflection placed on precisely the right verb in a song text, or the more prosaic pain of listening to yet another forgettable musical exercise from yet another handsome man in a cowboy hat that's never seen a drop of rain. After all, a cigarette is a nicotine delivery device, whether it's a Dunhill or a no-name generic brand. Given a choice, most smokers would take the smooth flavor of the Dunhill, but in a pinch any cancer stick will do.

The analogy goes further. As any smoker—including this one—will tell you, there's a big difference between smoking alone and smoking in a group of fellow smokers. The former is pleasurable, but the pleasure is guilty and shameful. The badness of smoking becomes, when smoking alone, an object of reflexive consideration: *I shouldn't do this.* Smoking in a group of fellow smokers is profoundly sociable. The sociability of smokers is mediated by elaborate rituals of offering cigarettes to others (or, conversely, "bumming" a smoke), of handling cigarettes performatively, of lighting both one's own cigarette and those of others, and of organizing the rhythm of conversation around the rhythms of smoking.

Just so country music. The ultimate transformation of the leaden commodity into the gold of (white, working-class, Southern) identity occurs in collective rituals of musically mediated sociability. In the working-class bars of Texas, these rituals occur nightly, as country music becomes a prime topic of talk, a saturating soundtrack, and a powerful metaphor for the covert prestige of badness. In the process, country music becomes *our music,* experienced not as a pleasurable diversion or a solipsistic exercise in the judgment of aesthetic worth, but as a brilliant way of re-valuing trash, of making the "bad" song, bad feelings, and the bad modern ("redneck") subject not only good, but sublimely good.

On Redemption: From Bad to Good

Which brings me back to the auction for Jerry Meese. For although I have described the logic of the "abject sublime" as a specifically musical phenomenon, a way of understanding what's bad about country music, I want to conclude by moving beyond the obvious implication that badness is a function of context and perspective, not an inherent property of objects or expressions or genres or performances. My point is that formations of *musical* "badness" emerge within discourses of *social* judgment—which is to say, within social power relations in all their historical and psychodynamic and cultural complexity. The logics of value that appear to structure hierarchies of musical styles and performances and talents are in fact the same logics, in a symbolically condensed and projected form, that structure hierarchies of people in social groups: logics of race, class, gender, otherness, similarity, and ultimately, of the value of individual human beings and their communities.

The benefit auction, as a genre of ritual practice within working-class communities like Lockhart, is, frankly, essentially a socialist institution. In a community beset by poverty and its consequences, almost every member can anticipate a financial crisis triggered by a medical disaster at some point in his or her life. In a place where a majority of families lack adequate health insurance, institutions like the benefit auction function much like an insurance system. Each community member contributes what s/he can, according to ability, on every occasion when help is needed; those who participate in this way can expect to be similarly supported when their crisis occurs. This point is made explicitly by Miss Ann, when she describes how Jerry and his wife Shirley had quietly given her food and money to distribute to needy members of the community (as a bar owner, Ann was in a privileged position to receive intimate knowledge of such situations). There are two implications made here. First, Ann's comment emphasizes the secrecy with which Jerry and Shirley practiced their generosity toward others in need. Among working-class Southerners, white and non-white, and certainly within the community around Ann's Other Place, dependence on charity (including government assistance) is sharply disdained. Among the most deeply cherished qualities of "country" identity is a mythologized autonomy. The discourse of self-reliance is pervasive and elaborate, although of course many members of the community must seek "charity" (from both government and private sources). Out of respect for the recipient, however, charity must be given and received in secrecy, or else disguised as something else. The alternative is shame, a despised and feared condition.

The auction disguises community charity, on a scale that could never be kept secret, as a grand sociable ritual of the economic exchange of goods for money (or other goods), a highly honorable source of wealth, locally referred to as "trading." A number of factors shape the event as a simulacrum of a ritual of ordinary commercial exchange. High-value items (guns and alcohol) are interspersed among the detritus that is generally offered (most of which is donated by local people from the large collections of junk many keep just for such purposes). Participants engage in sometimes vigorously competitive bidding wars, as if it mattered deeply to them whether they secured the used videotape of *On Golden Pond*. Organizers and members of the crowd (like "Crazy Jane") maneuver the total situation so that people with more to give (such as the members of "The Wild Bunch" at Ann's) actually have an appropriate opportunity to do so. The rhetorical skills of the auctioneer are typically virtuosic, offering up compelling arguments for the unconsidered value of absurd objects ("Armadillo Eggs" may be worthless in Texas, but valuable North of the Red River).

Slowly, but surely, significant amounts of money (in this case, nearly $3,000) are transferred from those who have to those who need. Slowly, but surely, "bad" commodities, slouching toward the status of abject trash, become charged—even sublime—embodiments of the profound use value they have suddenly acquired through the mimesis of alienated exchange (for a specifically musical example of this process, see Fox 1997). This is still commodity fetishism—trash is still trash—but with a counter-hegemonic thrust under-theorized in Marxist social thought. Here, the commodity no longer appears alienated from the hierarchical class relations it mediates. Rather, egalitarian social relations reclaim the commodity for a critical purpose. What was disposable, used up, worthless, trashy, ephemeral, and low quality becomes performatively filled with goodness. Such objects then enter new collections of trash, on someone else's mantle or shelf, where they are frequently touchstones for reflection, recollection, and narration, until they are recirculated yet again, for someone else's benefit. What was bad becomes, temporarily, something good. And if it acquires the elevated status of a "mem'ry," as such objects often do, the sublime quality perseveres well after the exchange is completed.

Tony Collins (the auctioneer) himself makes this linkage between "stuff" and people explicit in his clever and self-deprecating opening remarks. Miss Ann, he notes, had already mentioned some of the "weird things" that were to be sold at the auction. But "She just forgot to mention that you got a CHICKen-plucker for a auctioneer!" Chicken-plucking is a "bad" job, a job many Americans could not imagine doing. Although it is mechanized, it is difficult and dirty work (although it's worse for the chicken). An aura of symbolic pollution attends to the handling of dead animals on an industrial scale, separating the trash (the feathers) from the valuable commodity (the meat). To say of your-self that you are a "chicken plucker" is to embrace a trashed identity, to declare yourself *bad*. To do so as the skillful officiant of a sociable ritual of fundamental generosity, is of course, to deploy the trope of irony, but it is also to announce a symbolic transformation of the chicken-plucking self quite as much as the pending transformation of trash into gold.

So what does this have to do with understanding country as *bad music?* Just this: badness is a cultural logic, determined by social rela-tions structured in hegemonic dominance and resistance, ease and abjection. It is, from this perspective, a futile task to theorize badness as a condition of style, as a quality of performance, as a property of texts, as an effect of mass production, or as an entailment of mass consumption. You can argue all day long about whether Shania Twain makes bad country music or Alan Jackson makes good country music, and many people do argue all day long about such questions, just as people almost certainly argued, in the late 1920s, about whether Jimmie Rodgers' music was really country (or rather hillbilly) or whether his music embraced its commodity status (as pop) too abjectly—the same argument stimulated in later decades by Hank Williams, Patsy Cline, and (yes) Garth Brooks and Shania Twain. At least for country, as working-class music, discriminating judgments of *musical* badness and goodness miss the rhetorical point of the music itself, and the cultural essence of its practice. It's all good *because* it's all bad.

NOTES

1. Ethnographic descriptions and transcripts in this chapter are based on five years of musical and linguistic field research in small towns and working-class bars in South and Central Texas and in Central Illinois. This fieldwork is reported in more detail in Fox (1995; 1997; 2004). Quoted dialogue is transcribed from tape-recordings made with full knowledge and permission of the participants. Some names are pseudonyms.
2. I use the following transcription conventions (cf. Fox 1995):

Notation	Interpretation
Line breaks	prosodic junctures (marked by a pause)
CAPS	syllables marked by strong prosodic stress
Italics	voice quality marked by heightened intonation
...	lengthy pauses
[Brackets]	contextual glosses, and paralinguistic descriptions
(Parentheses)	inaudible or questionable on tape.
[...]	elided material

3. I will use the word "nigger" several times in this section of the chapter, and am aware that it may offend some readers. I apologize for any offense, which is of course not intended. The term is analyzed here *as discourse,* better confronted than ignored (Kennedy 2002).
4. Barbara Ching has discussed Coe's "If That Ain't Country" brilliantly (2001: 24). But she chooses not to discuss the use of "nigger."
5. Three of Edwards' hit songs (though *not* "Blackbird") are featured on the *From Where I Stand* compilation. Edwards is likewise discussed in the article "Color Me Country," in a special issue of the *Journal of Country Music* devoted to "Black artists in country music" (Woods 1992), although again, "Blackbird" is not mentioned. (The article does, however, report that Lefty Frizzell did call Edwards "nigger" to his face in 1973). In the same issue David Morton and Charles Wolfe downplay racial discrimination as a factor in the destruction of DeFord Bailey's career, describing a complicated set of economic motivations as the reason for Bailey's firing from the *Grand Ole Opry* (Morton and Wolfe 1992).
6. "I Hate These Songs." Copyright 1997 by Dale Watson. Published by Bug Music, Songs of Windswept Pacific, and Watson Texas Music (BMI). Originally released on the Hightone Records album *I Hate These Songs* (1997). All Rights Reserved.

REFERENCES

Applebome, P. 1998. Endowment nominee's broad view of the arts; Moving beyond country music to a political stage. *New York Times,* March 23.

Bush, G. H.W. 1990. Country Music Month. Presidential Executive Order 6205. (Oct. 12).

Ching, B. 1993. Acting naturally: Cultural distinction and critiques of pure country. *Arizona Quarterly* 49(3): 107–125.

———. 2001. *Wrong's what I do best: Hard country music and contemporary culture.* New York: Oxford University Press.

Dawidoff, N. 1997. *In the country of country: People and places in American music.* New York: Pantheon Books.

Fox, A. A. 1992. The jukebox of history: Narratives of loss and desire in the discourse of country music. *Popular Music* 11(1): 53–72.

———. 1995. *"Out the country:" Speech, song, and feeling in American rural, working-class culture.* PhD Dissertation in Anthropology, The University of Texas at Austin.

———. 1997. 'Funny how time slips away': Talk, trash, and technology in 'redneck' culture. In *Knowing your place: Rusticity and identity,* eds. G. Creed and B. Ching, 105–130. New York: Routledge.

———. 2004. *Real country: Music and language in working-class culture.* Durham: Duke University Press.

Fukuyama, F. 1993. *The end of history and the last man.* New York: Avon Books.

Jensen, J. 1998. *The Nashville sound: Authenticity, commericalization, and country music.* Nashville: Country Music Foundation and Vanderbilt University Press.

Kennedy, R. 2002. *Nigger: The strange career of a troublesome word.* New York: Pantheon Books.

Klein, R. 1998. *Cigarettes are sublime.* Durham: Duke University Press.

Kristeva, J. 1982. *Powers of horror: An essay on abjection.* New York: Columbia University Press.

Malone, B. C. 2002. *Don't get above your raisin': Country music and the southern working class.* Urbana: University of Illinois Press.

Morton, D. C., and C. K. Wolfe. 1992. DeFord Bailey: They turned me loose to root hog or die." *Journal of Country Music* 14(2): 13–17.

Peterson, R. 1997. *Creating country music: Fabricating authenticity.* Chicago: University of Chicago Press.

Phipps, K. 2001. "Merle Haggard" (interview) In *The Onion AV Club* 37, Issue 9 (March 2001) Online at: http://www.theonionavclub.com/avclub3709/vfeature_3709.html

Rubin, L. B. 1976. *Worlds of pain: Life in the working-class family.* New York: Basic Books.

Schiller Institute. n.d. "Schiller Institute exposes fraud of country and western music!" http://www.schillerinstitute.org/conf-iclc/1990s/mgm_9-1-96.html

Sennett, Richard, and Jonathan Cobb. 1982. *The hidden injuries of class.* New York: Vintage Books.

Stewart, K. 1988. Nostalgia: A polemic. *Cultural Anthropology* 3: 227–241.

———. 1991. On the politics of cultural theory: A case for 'contaminated' critique. *Social Research* 58(2): 395–412.

———. 1992. Engendering narratives of lament in country music. In *All that glitters: Country music in America,* ed. G. Lewis, 221–225. Bowling Green: Bowling Green State University Popular Press.

Tichi, C. 1994. *High lonesome: The American culture of country music.* Chapel Hill: The University of North Carolina Press.

Whisnant, D. E. 1995. Gone country: 'High lonesome' and the politics of writing about country music. *Journal of Country Music* 17(2): 62–66.

Woods, J. 1993. Color me country: Tales from the frontlines. *Journal of Country Music* 14(2): 9-12.

3

Pop Music, Racial Imagination, and the Sounds of Cheese
Notes on Loser's Lounge

JASON LEE OAKES

Music critics and aestheticians are, on the surface, advocates and guardians of good music. But what exactly is "good music?" Most would argue that it's impossible to say objectively what good music is, that it cannot be quantified or contained in a single, simple definition. This means that "good music," in truth, is defined by a lack, by absence; in other words, it is good because it isn't bad. The boundaries around "good music" are drawn not by what they include, but by what they exclude, what they actively keep out, and how they mark off terrains of Otherness. This is most likely why critics and everyday observers—while claiming to be interested in good music—seem to spend so much time discussing bad music and what makes it that way. Besides, it's often easier and more fun to describe the myriad ways in which music can be bad than it is to try to explain when and why it's good. As a result, there is a semantic richness when it comes to describing "bad music" which is largely absent for "good music." Bad music can be cheesy, lame, corny, gay, or it can just plain suck, but what do each of these facets of badness connote? It is a crucial question as vocabularies of badness do more than simply describe bad music; at the same time they actually create it. The category of "bad music" is produced, then, in the interplay between discourse and musical sound. Thus, it is important to look at the language, the words, that are used to describe "bad music." For any outsider to a given musical tradition, bad music could never be identified solely in reference to the sounds themselves. Arguments about "good" and "bad" music, even those that go against conventional wisdom, can only be meaningfully expressed when one is reasonably fluent in the prevailing narratives and histories that situate good/bad distinctions in a given setting. Since it cannot be understood outside the social and linguistic matrices in which it operates, any examination of "bad music" must consider the questions of *who* supposedly makes and listens to bad music, *how* people talk about and perform bad music, and *why* and by whom the music is labeled "bad."

The Losers

In New York City, a discourse on bad music is enacted at an event called Loser's Lounge (herein abbreviated LL). LL is not a place, but refers to a regular series of performances that pay homage to various "pop music" songwriters. Taking a songbook approach, the repertoire of a particular songwriter or songwriting team is interpreted at each individual show. Past shows have been dedicated to Burt Bacharach, Jimmy Webb, Henry Mancini, Carole King, Lee Hazlewood, Neil Diamond, post-Beatles Paul McCartney, Serge Gainsbourg, Paul Williams, Elvis Costello, Brian Wilson, the Monkees, the Bee Gees, Queen, Devo, Roxy Music, ABBA, ELO, XTC, and the Zombies among others (see www.loserslounge.com for a complete list). A number of immediate questions are raised by this event, such as: Why pay elaborate tribute to music that is considered by many to be "bad" (e.g., Neil Diamond, ABBA, Paul McCartney's solo material)? What is the basis of the eclectic musical canon formed at LL, especially since some shows are dedicated to critical-darling exemplars of "good music" like Elvis Costello and Brian Wilson? Why are these particular songwriters grouped together as producers of music that appeals to "losers," however ironically the label might be applied?

To address these questions, I must first situate LL in terms of its history, locale, and personnel. LL is the creation of pianist/keyboardist Joe McGinty, who for ten years has been the event's producer and MC. Standing well over six-feet tall, McGinty's gangly nonchalance, dry wit, and expert's knowledge of pop music history (assisted by his mammoth LP and CD collections) have shaped LL. McGinty grew up near Atlantic City, and his musical career has encompassed everything from a high-school prog-rock cover band, a hotel-lounge group playing 80s pop, a stint as keyboardist for the British post-punk band Psychedelic Furs, session work and touring support for various acts from the Ramones to Ronnie Spector, and the leading of his own chamber-pop band, Baby Steps. In 1992, while living in New York, McGinty went to a club to see a performance by a man dressed in a cheap sports jacket, overemotively singing a Peter Frampton song while standing on a milk crate. Performing as his alter-ego, Nick Danger (by day a city schoolteacher) comes across as an unnervingly earnest lounge lizard, with a voice that veers aggressively out-of-tune and a body besieged by a series of twitches and tics—something like Neil Diamond with Tourette's.[1] McGinty subsequently teamed up with Danger and established the Loser's Lounge at the Pink Pony, a Lower East Side coffee bar, where they performed twisted-yet-affectionate renditions of "the corniest 70s AM-radio songs." At the end of 1993, with its growing popularity, LL moved to a larger venue and added a full backing band. Joe McGinty describes how the show came together:

> The idea was just supposed to be a loungy vibe and I was thinking, 'We'll do some Jimmy Webb, some Burt Bacharach, and some Scott Walker.' But then I noticed that everybody I mentioned the idea to really seemed to be focusing on Burt Bacharach [so] that I actually thought it would make sense to do it with a particular artist …And I was surprised because this was when Nirvana was still really popular, and Pearl Jam, and the East Village was still viewed as a noise-art rock kind of scene. It was letting everybody in on this secret. I guess that's what people like about the Loser's Lounge. It's things that you might have been ashamed to admit liking, but you're in this room where everybody else likes it too. It's like, 'Wow, even with ABBA!' You know it's kind of like, 'Wow, I love this! It's okay to like this.'[2]

For most of its run, LL has been held at Fez, a nightclub and lounge in Manhattan's East Village. The performance space resembles a small cabaret setting: candlelit tables, burgundy decor, and gold lamé curtains. It's further thematized for LL shows with kitschy decorations fashioned after the popular iconography of the tributee (one commentator describes the space as "done up in chintzy cardboard decorations to replicate the feel of kids partying in a rec room while the parents are away for the weekend"). At a given LL, twenty-five to thirty songs composed by the tributee are performed. The regular LL house band, the Kustard Kings, is a versatile instrumental combo that includes two or more guitarists (including David Terhune, the group's founder), a bassist, a keyboardist, trap-set drummer, percussionist, several backup singers, with a small string and/or brass section added at some shows. Since the group has no lead singer, vocal duties are rotated between each individual song, meaning that twenty-five to thirty singers are featured at an average show. The singers are drawn from a variety of bands and local music scenes, with their vocal renditions informed by their own singing styles and musical influences. Reflecting this variety, the original musical arrangements composed by McGinty and the Kustard Kings are highly varied—sometimes remaining loyal to the source material, but often filled out to suit the expansiveness of the band or stripped down to the barest essentials (for example, piano and voice).

The end result is like hearing the tributee's music refracted through a musical prism: straight renditions are followed by radical interpretations. Popular hits are played alongside the rarest obscurities. Songs that were once self-serious are played for laughs, while more lightweight material is played with unswerving ardor. From one song to the next the perspective is shifted, treating the music as high art, low trash, or somewhere in between. On the one hand, the high art sensibility is further conveyed through the distribution of written programs (albeit including inside jokes and illustrated caricatures of the tributee), the musicians' use of written notation on some songs, and the very act of canonization that a tribute show suggests. On the other hand, a kitsch sensibility comes across in the garishness of the visual setting and costumes, the satiric approach to some of the material, and the sheer "let's put on a show" performativity of the event.

As might be expected, audience members view LL through a variety of interpretive lenses. Based on a written survey,[3] I found that the audience is highly eclectic in their musical tastes, and highly diverse in terms of age ranging from twenties to fifties (the median is thirty-something). However, they are more homogenous when it comes to race and class, being mostly (but not exclusively) white, middle class, and well educated. When I asked audience members to give adjectives that would describe a typical LL performance, their responses were often contradictory, using words like entertaining, educational, professional, playful, spontaneous, theatrical, fun, serious, campy, and cheesy. Asked why they think the event is called "Loser's Lounge," responses included "the tribute performers haven't hit it big;" "it's a hangout for people who don't fit in;" "because they play goofy tunes by goofy artists;" "it's the intentional cheesiness of the karaoke-like setting;" "because the songs they play are not necessarily the hits by an artist;" and "the artists they select to cover are typically cheesy (culturally disenfranchised)." The losers in question, accordingly, are either seen to be the performers, the audience, the tributed artists, the individual songs, the venue, or some combination thereof. At the same time, though, positive associations are made with the label "loser": including attributes such as uniqueness, altereity, a sense of community, and a sense of humor.

Situated somewhere between tribute, satire, nostalgia, fantasy, music-nerd appreciation, and emotionally-resonant identification, it is precisely this ambiguity, this polysemeity, that makes LL such a rich case study for examining the shifting terrain of "bad music." LL functions effectively as both a musical performance in the traditional sense, and as a form of musical discourse where explicit commentary on the original music is made through performative and verbal choices (clothing, decorations, comments by performers or printed in the program) and musical signifiers (e.g., arrangements that draw links to specific musical genres and their attendant associations). The commentary enacted at LL straddles usually exclusive approaches to musical value, borrowing both from rock discourses of authenticity and masculinity, and pop music's celebration of ambiguity and excess. By playfully dancing around the peripheries of "good" and "bad" music—continually blurring and reworking the boundary erected between these categories—the never-yielding work that goes into good/bad boundary-making (while usually hidden) is brought to light. In this upsetting of stable value distinctions, there is a concomitant upsetting of related ideological distinctions. As a category that is brought into being through social exchange, "bad music" is closely aligned with other formations which shape social exchange. At LL and elsewhere, the good/bad binary—along with related binaries of authentic/inauthentic and natural/artificial—become embedded in intersecting vectors of race, gender, sexuality, class, age, locality, and other social identifiers. While the "bad music" side of the good/bad equation is typically aligned with the Other, participants at LL, to some extent, turn this practice inside out by locating the 'loser' within. In the following section, then, I will consider some of the ways in which discourses of "good" and "bad" are—whether explicitly or implicitly—intertwined with discourses of social identification. I will focus primarily on the relationship negotiated at LL between "bad music" and constructions of race, with the caveat that this is my particular reading of the racial discourse at LL, and the recognition that race can never be separated out from related discourses of class, gender, and other markers of identity.

Central to any consideration of race at LL is the event's origins in the "lounge music revival" of the early 1990s. First, it is significant to note that what the lounge revival "revived" was a categorization that

Figure 1   Joe McGinty performs at the Roxy Music Loser's Lounge on February 10, 2001.

wasn't previously in existence; lounge music as a term was not in popular circulation at the time of the original music's creation, but is an amalgamation of past genre headings such as exotica and easy listening. Thus, like "bad music," "lounge music" is a construct that has been created retrospectively and discursively (i.e., by inventing a new genre label which is closely attached to contemporary social formations). In 1993, the San Francisco-based RE/Search Publications, known for their minutely detailed surveys of various underground cultures, put out the book *Incredibly Strange Music*.[4] Compiling interviews with the "strange" music's producers and most avid collectors, the book is a celebration of kitschy, cast-off garage sale records under subheadings of ethno-exploitation and exotica, easy listening, celebrity-vanity records, and other such novelty genres. In 1994 Bar/None records, a small label in Hoboken, New Jersey, further solidified the lounge music revival with their compilation album *Esquivel!: Space Age Bachelor Pad Music*, featuring music by the then-forgotten

Mexican bandleader Juan Esquivel. In his second career go-around, Esquivel was both lampooned for his kitschy musical excesses and lauded for his musical audacity (e.g., exotic instrumentation, over-the-top arrangements), as were other revived artists such as Martin Denny and Les Baxter.[5] In many quarters, the new fans of lounge music were accused of responding to it in a blankly parodic way. However, the reality of the lounge music revival is more nuanced than this. Led by urban hipsters who didn't subscribe to grunge and alternative-rock notions of white male naturalism (i.e., authenticity), the lounge revivalists championed cheesy 'bad music' by situating it in terms usually reserved for 'good music.' Referring to lounge music recording artists as "songwriters" and "composers," even if they were more popularly known as performers and stars in their own right, acted as a rhetorical move to portray lounge musicians as skilled individuals who were the creators of musical works. Likewise, LL is conceived as a tribute to songwriters, where the notion of songwriting highlights the effort, the deliberate work, put into crafting pop music (that is, a musical work which requires purposeful work).

Despite the central role played by Esquivel, lounge music has for the most part been reimagined as an emphatically white music culture. Lounge music, in its more ironic guises, is closely linked to strained attempts by white males to be "hip" circa 1950s–early 1960s, with associated images including tiki furniture, martinis, wide lapels, and expensive stereo systems. From the happy days of the 1950s to the Kennedy 1960s, this period has often been portrayed in the mass media as a golden age of idealized, if naive, whiteness that preceded the racial upheaval of the later-1960s and the subsequent fragmentation of whiteness as a cohesive (and categorically dominant) racial category. Current fans of lounge music make an ironic identification with this era in which they both align themselves with, and distance themselves from, an idealized white identity. In the camping up of outdated white music, there lies the potential for a dual expression of discomfort and repressed longing for an unequivocal and privileged whiteness.

Although LL is not exclusively focused on lounge music, its overall ethos reflects that of the lounge revival with its overlapping and upsetting of the boundaries between "good" and "bad" music, and its negotiation of musical and performative markers of whiteness. Burt Bacharach—the most popular personification of lounge music—was the first tributee and still serves as a central reference point in the show's development. In the 1990s, Bacharach experienced a career resurgence

Figure 2   David Terhune, Jeremy Chatzky, Joe Hurley, and Kris Woolsey (from left to right) perform "Rock 'n' Roll Suicide" at the David Bowie Loser's Lounge on November 17, 2001.

that was based on two different, if not incompatible, readings of his music and image. The "bad music" Bacharach is portrayed as the archetypical lounge lizard, a campy icon of the Swinging Sixties who wrote cheesy pop songs. This image is most clearly expressed in the Austin Powers films,[6] the first of which featured Bacharach himself in a cameo appearance. He became a popular subject for parody; however, at the same time, Bacharach was reassessed as one of the greatest auteurs in the history of pop music songcraft. Whereas his rock music contemporaries disparaged his music as lightweight and disposable pop made to order, fans of the "good music" Bacharach have enshrined his music in terms usually reserved for art music. His songs are praised for their complexity of compositional strategies including unusual chord progressions, elaborate instrumental arrangements, shifting time-signatures, and circuitous melodies.

How is Bacharach's image as a good (complex) composer reconciled with his image as a bad (campy) songwriter? While the two may seem antithetical, they are in fact closely linked. One would expect that compositional craft and visible effort would be associated with "good music," but just as often the opposite standard is applied. Irwin Chusid—host of the Incorrect Music radio show on station WFMU out of Hoboken, New Jersey—claims that lounge music "was reviled at the time by hipsters [because] it was meticulous: the artists and producers were perfectionists. This aesthetic flies in the face of rock 'n' roll, which values energy and spontaneity over technique."[7] In contemporary popular music worlds music is often valued for being natural, and by extension, authentic. Since the mid-1960s, rock music has been organized in large part around discourses of authenticity, just as hip-hop culture has come to be consumed with signifiers of "realness." Conversely, pop music has been situated as the flip side to rock and rap; used to describe music that is supposedly more concerned with craftsmanship (i.e., its status as a commodity) than with self-expression (i.e., its status as an artistic statement). In this way, pop music has been positioned as a sort of doppelgänger to rock, hip-hop, and other forms of popular music (not to mention classical music), that absorbs the brunt of anxiety felt by musicians and audiences over the highly technologized production and commodity status of their own favored music.

As a default category that's defined mostly by what it isn't, the boundaries of pop music are absurdly far-reaching, extending to include everything from Cole Porter to the Carpenters to Christina Aguilera. Whatever the musical style, though, pop music has most often been noted (whether vilified or lauded) for its *madeness*—that is, the songwriting and/or technological craft that goes into its production. A cliché statement often heard in relation to cheesy cultural artifacts is that they're "so bad they're good," where the lack of good taste is taken as a guilty pleasure. When it comes to pop music, however, one could just as easily say that it's "so good that it's bad," where an overabundance of artifice and calculated exertion overflows the boundaries of refined taste. It's no coincidence that to refine literally means to remove impurities from something through a process of pruning and polishing. The purity of refined culture, then, serves to mask the messiness and the exertion that underlies its own production. Bad taste, on the other hand, is unrefined in that it exhibits "a tendency toward excess, amplitude, and abundance" that does not shun "paradox, ambivalence, [and] mixture."[8] It is these qualities that signal the madeness of an object. Ironically, it is this madeness, this forthright display of the human effort and calculation that went into a product, that leads "bad music" to be labeled as artificial and inauthentic. Thus, the acknowledgment that "bad music" has been methodically forged (brought

Figure 3   Kris Woolsey, Julian Maile, David Voigt, Connie Petruk, Tricia Scotti, and Sean Altman (from left to right) perform "My Little Town" at the Simon and Garfunkel Loser's Lounge on December 11, 2002.

into being through an obvious expenditure of effort) is taken as proof that it has been *forged* (constructed or faked with intent to defraud).

Of course, all music is deliberately made and created; music is by definition *constructed*, created out of intentionally organized patterns of sound. Madeness, however, is a matter of perception, where certain aural and formal qualities have come to function as markers of artifice. At LL, madeness is signified variously in the music of the different tributees. For Burt Bacharach it's expressed in the elaborate instrumentation, unusual chord progressions, and shifting time signatures. For Queen it's in the intricate harmonies, virtuosic musicianship, unusual song structure, and operatic pretension. For Lee Hazlewood it's the experimental production, surreal lyrics, cinematic arrangements, and his shaping of Nancy Sinatra's image. For Devo it's the plastic hats, synthesized sounds, and deliberate nerdiness. The Monkees themselves were *made*, a fictional band assembled for a TV show, and the list of examples could go on. Despite the wide-ranging stylistic diversity heard at LL, all of the music has been framed by commentators in terms of deliberate constructedness. In the following examples, I have borrowed terms from the All Music Guide (AMG) Web site,[9] which surveys users in compiling a list of descriptive adjectives for various

Figure 4   Flaming Fire perform "Lemon Incest" at the Serge Gainsbourg Loser's Lounge on July 11, 2003.

artists. AMG describes Henry Mancini as 'refined' and 'stylish' while Neil Diamond is 'mannered' and 'theatrical,' David Bowie is 'ironic' and 'campy,' Roxy Music is 'elegant' and 'cerebral,' Carole King is 'literate' and 'reflective,' Devo is 'detached' and 'ironic,' Dusty Springfield is 'sophisticated' and a singer of 'blue-eyed soul.' The traits listed here—which could be summarized as artifice, aestheticism, intellectualism, and cultural appropriation—all converge around one feature: a deliberate madeness and associated inauthenticity of music and image alike.

Besides these musical signifiers of madeness, one of the most obvious commonalities between tributees at LL is that most of them have been racially white.[10] This in itself may not be meaningful, but I would argue that most if not all of the artists are highly representative of whiteness as a category that operates socially and is coded musically. Like bad music, whiteness has no quantifiable (or biological) basis, but rather it is a discursive construct which does have real-world social and material consequences. As the editors of *Music and the Racial Imagination* state in their introduction to the subject, "as a key signifier of difference, music in America . . . historically conjures racial meaning."[11] For instance, the music of Burt Bacharach is usually thought of as archetypally "white," while the music of Serge

Gainsbourg reinforces images of the racially white Frenchman. Brian Wilson musically personifies the white-teen California dream, while The Kinks, The Who, and the Zombies hold an appeal to the Anglophile pop music fan. Genre categories such as new-wave rock, singer-songwriter, rock musical, surf music, glam, Brill Building, Nordic pop, and corporate rock are all clearly coded as white musical categories, and what's more, some of the *whitest* of white music. Of course, such generalizations about white music run the risk of appearing as crude stereotypes (which, to a large extent, they are), but it must be recognized that whiteness, as a discursive construct that has been defined historically in contrast to equally conjectural notions of blackness, is inevitably one dimensional (especially in ignoring the many hues between black and white). The very fact that some music made by white people is considered whiter than other music by whites confirms the operation of whiteness as an imagined construct rather than an internalized essence. Like other conjectural social categories, the meaning of whiteness is in a constant state of flux and contradiction. So while the sounds and images presented at LL may revolve around whiteness, the event also makes the point that whiteness is an ideological construct that is deliberately made, and once made it is open to revision and reinflection.[12] Thus, LL provides an example of how music is used not to express or reveal race, but instead is a major factor in bringing racial identities and associations into being in the first place.

In support of this point, Ingrid Monson has observed that the linkage of blackness and hipness in receptions of jazz has served to reinforce associations of black identity with naturalism and authenticity.[13] It follows, then, that whiteness—embodied in the sounds and the discourse around white music—is linked to artifice and artificiality, and is thus defined as the antithesis of hip. Here, ironically, it is the sheer intentionality of the subject which is associated with the inauthentic. Given the aesthetics of cool, to demonstrate obvious effort is to lose authenticity. While the etymology of cool in this context is fairly apparent, why is it that music or musicians who aren't cool are commonly referred to as cheesy or corny? For one thing, I would note that these two pejorative terms both originally refer to foods associated with the midwestern United States—the perceived cradle of whiteness in the national imagination. Following from this, it is an excess of whiteness, historically and culturally constructed, that makes a musician uncool.

In recent years, cheesy has become the most common term to describe music that is excessively white. In it's current usage cheesy is a colloquial adjective referring to anything that's tacky, artificial, cheap, showy, and/or stilted. The word cheesy has been around since the mid-nineteenth century, when it's believed to have alluded to the pungent smell of overripe cheese. Accordingly, the common denominator of cheesy music is it's overripeness, it's unseemly excessiveness. It is music that is overwrought, overdetermined, overemotive, overproduced, overplayed, or generally over the top. It is music that highlights its own fabrication, its own artificiality, with sounds that are coded as unreal and thus immediately recognizable as having been *made*. This linkage of whiteness and madeness is confirmed in the following comment made by regular Loser's Lounge performer Cathy Cervenka: "I am from Central Florida so you're really destined to know a lot about malls and artificially-themed environments and Disneyworld and arena rock, because that's literally what I remember . . . [When I was growing up] it was all about white suburban rock music, I mean, I never heard any black artists or not much R&B."[14] Although the meaning of 'urban' has shifted in past decades to become a sort of code word for the black diaspora in the U.S., negotiations of white identity have recently taken on a new prominence in settings such as New York City. The popularity of television shows such as *Friends* and *Seinfeld* (and their many imitators depicting hip, white urbanites), along with the "Disneyfication" of New York's Times Square, has given whiteness an increased profile in public imaginations of the city. Going beyond these recent articulations of race, the history of whiteness in New York City can be traced, in large part, through the well-known institutions of pop music songwriting that have shaped racially-white perceptions of that city, such as Tin Pan Alley, Broadway musicals, and the Brill Building. Thus, LL finds itself at the intersection of various imaginings of race and its relation to place. While LL is firmly situated within these other discourses, the event positions itself as more critical, or at least more ambivalent, in its approach to whiteness.

The self-critical stance taken towards whiteness at LL is most clearly demonstrated by the loser status associated with a tributee's (or performer's) excessive whiteness. At the same time, the event's recuperation of cheesy, "bad" music demonstrates the conflicted stance that participants hold in relation to the music and to their own racial identity. The combined guilt and pleasure that people may find in cheesy "bad music" runs parallel to the guilt and pleasure of being a politically liberal, middle-class white person, cognizant of the privileges that are attached to one's racial and class status. In highlighting the performativity of whiteness, one might ask if LL has as its end result the deconstruction of racial stereotypes and the dismantling of racial inequalities. Or, could it have the opposite effect of naturalizing and reinforcing essentialisms related to race? The not-so-simple answer is that it can do either, or both, or, at times, neither—it depends almost entirely on individual and collective readings of the event which, as already noted, are highly variable. However, by highlighting sonic markers of whiteness, musicians at LL do approach race as something that's collectively imagined and deliberately *performed*. By exaggerating—or one could say camping—racial signifiers, the multiple facets and implications of whiteness (as a form of identity and discursive practice) are explored.

Camp vs. Cheese

With its penchant for madeness, theatricality, and parody, not to mention the occasional drag performer on vocals, camp (like cheesy) is a word that comes up repeatedly in relation to LL. Joe McGinty, however, is careful to qualify the event's campiness: "It's fun to camp it up and that adds another element to [the performance]. But we really are sincere, we love playing the songs and we're fans. It's kind of like having fun with the songs rather than making fun of them . . . It's fun to present both, to present them as great songs and then present them as songs you can have fun with."[15] McGinty's formulation is remarkably similar to an early explanation of the camp mindset—possibly the first mention of camp in print—by Christopher Isherwood: "You can't camp about something you don't take seriously. You're not making fun of it; you're making fun out of it. You're expressing what's basically serious to you in terms of fun and artifice and elegance."[16] What are the implications of this camp stance at LL?

Susan Sontag, in her landmark "Notes on Camp" (1964),[17] argued that camp is strictly an apolitical "aesthetic," a position that has subsequently been criticized (and reversed by Sontag herself). Countering this argument, feminists and queer theorists have made a case for the camp aesthetic acting as a means of breaking down essentialisms related to sexuality and to gender. Camp, with its transparency in relation to the work that goes into a performance, exposes the labor and constant vigilance that must be put into the performing of sexual and gender roles. Viewed in this way, camping can work to destabilize the boundary between manufactured and authentic identities, demonstrating that "the 'real' and the 'natural' are no less made than the 'artificial'."[18] In other words, the status of the natural and the authentic is denied. This helps to explain why bad music is sometimes referred to as gay. When used in this context, gay is not necessarily meant as an explicit homosexual slander, but rather as a synonym for cheesy or inauthentic. Of course, the implicit linking of gayness with inauthenticity serves to stabilize hetero-sexual identity as normative, and homosexuality as unnatural. Although camp may serve to denaturalize these boundaries between inauthentic–authentic, masculine–feminine, and gay–straight, for some audiences it may have exactly the opposite effect. Given the polysemeity of the camp aesthetic, its exaggerated roleplaying can actually end up reifying gender and sexual distinctions, reinforcing stereotypes that some au-diences hold. Depending on its positioning, then, camp can be received either as a criticism or confirmation of social and sexual mores.

The other major distinction traditionally discussed in relation to camp is its perspective on good taste vs. bad taste, or high vs. low culture. As with gender and sexuality, the perspective that camp ex-presses on matters of taste can be read in directly contradictory ways. Some have taken camp's deconstructive ethos to its logical conclu-sion, claiming that it's subversion of good/bad distinctions levels the field between high and low culture. Others, however, have theorized camp from the exact opposite standpoint. Susan Sontag argues, "detach-ment is the prerogative of an elite; and as the dandy is the nineteenth century's surrogate for the aristocratic in matters of culture, so Camp is the modern Dandyism. Camp is the answer to the problem: how to be a dandy in the age of mass culture." As Andrew Ross has observed, "[Sontag] suggests that what is under attack in the age of mass culture is precisely the power of taste-making intellectuals to patrol the higher canons of taste, and that the significance of the 'new sensibility' of camp in the 1960s is that it presents a means of salvaging that privi-lege.'"[19] As is the case with gender and sexuality, then, camp can be positioned as either progressive or conservative, as a way of upending existing standards of good and bad, or of reinforcing these standards along with the institutions and social classes who benefit from them.

While the relationships between camp and gender, and between camp and class, have been much debated,[20] what has scarcely been considered is the relationship of camp to race. Just as camp can highlight the performative basis of gender, could it not also be deployed to show the deliberate work that social actors put into the performing of racial and ethnic identities? As noted above, the madeness and aestheticism inherent in the camp mindset are closely linked, in the surrounding discourse, to constructions of whiteness, and canons of camp are almost exclusively white where they have been enumerated.[21] What's more, the occasional instances of black camp have held an especially uneasy relationship vis-à-vis black communities, two examples being Screamin' Jay Hawkins (who was strongly criticized by the NAACP for his campy allusions to witch doctors and cannibals) and the voguing phenomenon of the 1990s (whose practitioners were doubly marginalized for being both black and gay). It could be that, having struggled so long to achieve an effectual subject position in American culture, the majority of black people are hardly ready to turn around and deconstruct their own hard-won authenticity or to question their own agency. Furthermore, the act of camping up cultural markers of black identity veers uncomfortably close to blackface minstrelsy or other disquieting historical episodes. White musicians, especially those from a relatively comfortable socio-economic position, have more freedom to place quotation marks around their own bad taste. However, such subtleties may be missed if the performer comes from a less-advantaged social position, whose "bad music" will simply be received as *bad music*, and not as high camp.[22]

What the culturati refers to as camp, is more likely to be known as cheese when associated with lower, more popular tastes. What, then, is the difference between camp and cheese? It is not unusual for the two terms to be used interchangeably, and both have been commonly applied to LL. However, there are critical distinctions between the two. Kevin Dettmar and William Richey, in an article on "musical cheese," argue for two major differences between camp and cheese. First, cheese is "derived solely from the detritus of consumer culture . . . almost entirely a celebration of canceled TV shows, artless pop songs, and useless cultural artifacts like the lava lamp and the Chia Pet." So while Susan Sontag argued that camp was a "response" to consumer culture, cheesiness operates as part and parcel of consumer culture itself. Second, while "[camp] never really loses sight of what good taste is," with cheese "the distinction between good and bad taste threatens to break down altogether, to the point where it becomes nearly impossible to tell when something is being celebrated and when it is being parodied."[23]

Thus, cheese is even more polysemous than camp, openly accommodating a wide (and quite possibly contradictory) range of interpretations and motivations. Given both of these distinctions, LL falls squarely on the side of cheese over camp. LL is highly imbricated in consumer culture; performances and audiences (myself included) are anything but detached from pop culture and fully accustomed to equating music with commodified sound recordings. Given this aspect of musical cheese, some observers might view LL as apolitical—blankly parodic and concerned only with the surface pleasures of consumerism. However, the other important aspect of musical cheese—the subversion of good/bad distinctions—can have consequences that are undeniably political. As I have argued, the subversion of good and bad aesthetic classifications at LL is directly linked to the destabilization of other too-tidy oppositions and assumptions surrounding race, gender, class, and other means of social identification. It is this multitudinous scope of musical cheese that makes it possible for audiences at LL to describe the event as both inconsequential ("goofy," "karaoke-like") fun, and as a serious engagement with aesthetic and social categories ("educational," "culturally disenfranchised").

The Name of the Game

In this final section, I will examine how cheesiness is confronted musically at LL, using their rendition of ABBA's "The Name of the Game" as an example. The music of the 1970s Swedish group ABBA is considered by most to be unrelentingly cheesy. Despite the obvious skillfulness of their songwriting, their records have been disparaged both as musically garish and as shallow bubblegum pop. However, at LL the more embarrassingly overwrought and awkward elements of ABBA's songs are not only camped up, but they are also dressed down, treated as seriously as the music of Carole King or Henry Mancini. For example, the original 1977 studio version of "The Name of the Game" derives much of its impact from it's madeness.[24] The song opens with a repeated minor-key groove with over-compressed drums outlining a slowed-down disco beat, while the walking synth-bass and clavinet-like keyboard play syncopated polyrhythms that sound rigid and deliberate (see figure 5). After a few repetitions the female vocalists enter in unison against the instrumental backing; the music's lurching, robotic funkiness stands in contrast to the airy, affectless vocal timbres and wholesome, hopeful lyrics. The song then moves through a bridge

Figure 5

section which gradually modulates into the relative major key. Suddenly the chorus explodes in a polyphony of four-part harmonies, strumming double-tracked guitar, and synthesized horn fanfare. While the minor-key, musically plodding verse was set against lyrics describing the joys of new love, the technicolor chorus takes a darker lyrical turn with hints of doubt and anxiety. Taken together, the audible effort—the deliberateness—that went into ABBA's recording acts to highlight both the madeness and the whiteness of the song. Madeness is expressed through the blatant fakeness of the synthesized instruments, the fussiness of the production, the intricate harmonies, the clockwork rhythms, the unusual form where the verse is never repeated (ABCDCDC), the curiously juxtaposed music-text relationship, and most of all in the dogged attempt by four Swedes to be funky.

At the LL tribute to ABBA in 1999, McGinty arranged the song for piano and vocal alone, stripping away the busy arrangement and layers of studio production.[25] In this new setting, McGinty claims "you realize that even without the production it's a great song, it really almost exists in this whole other more direct emotional way."[26] This directness is attained by excavating the madeness (and by association, the whiteness) of the original version. The robotic tempo of the original is rendered more flexibly. The stately piano plays an elaboration of the vocal melody, completely eliminating the syncopated bass and keyboard lines (see figure 6). Although any attempt at funkiness is abandoned, the

Figure 6

instrumental and vocal rhythms are less rigid and more varied, sliding slightly ahead and behind of the beat and of one another. As opposed to the airy vocal timbres of the original, the LL vocalist (Martha Wainwright, daughter of singer/songwriter Loudon Wainwright III) sings with a much more throaty, dark timbre. With phrasing and timbral allusions to icons such as Carole King and Billie Holiday (e.g., behind-the-beat phrasing, ending vocal lines with a falling glissando), musical signifiers of expressivity are communicated by evoking associations with folksy and soulful singing styles. However, the authenticity associated with these styles is somewhat undercut by the preciousness of the cabaret-style arrangement. Also contributing to the soulfulness of Wainwright's rendition are subtle changes made to the lyrics (changes that might alternatively be heard as overwrought piano bar melodrama). The altering of single words—from "open-hearted" to "broken-hearted," from "does *it* mean anything to you" to "does *she* mean anything to you"—shifts the subject matter from an uncertain new romance to world-weary infidelity. Overall, then, the LL performance operates as an open dialogue with (and a commentary on) the original recording, its impact deriving from what's left out, what's added, and what's changed from ABBA's version. In this overlapping and mutating of musical signifiers, the neat oppositions between good–bad, authentic–synthetic, and black–white are destabilized. Simple racial associations made with ABBA's music are challenged, moving from the whiteness of ABBA's recording to the soulfulness of Wainwright's reading, from the disco–funk of the original arrangement to the whiteness of the cabaret-style rendition. By amplifying various signifiers that are associated with good and with bad music, the original song by ABBA is made both better *and* worse, and it is left to the audience to put the pieces back together.

So Good It's Bad, So Bad It's Good

The terms good and bad suggest something more than personal preference or immediate enjoyment. While the observation that something is *so bad it's good* is somewhat cliché, it's common usage indicates a not-so-uncommon practice of taking pleasure in *bad* things. Similarly, the warning that something is *good for you* is usually applied to an object or experience that would initially be judged as bad, like foul-tasting medicine. As much as they indicate personal taste, good and bad indicate *different modes* of perception. For instance, while good music is often discursively positioned as discourse-free (i.e., "natural"), and thus aspires towards a highly-suspicious universality and timelessness, bad music is often disparaged for its situatedness (e.g., dated, geographic specificity) and its close alignment with audiences who are marginalized on the basis of race, gender, class, age, and so forth.

In arguing that "bad music" is a social construction, however, I do not mean to remove the agency from the individual social actor in matters of aesthetic judgement. "Bad music," at the same time it's collectively negotiated, is experienced by most listeners as something intuitive and immediate; it provides a visceral response where we simply *know* that it's bad, even if we enjoy it as a guilty pleasure. What I would argue here is that this seeming paradox is not paradoxical at all, for distinctions between good and bad music *are* both self-determined/ deep-seated, *and* dependent on external social and historical forces. While the typical Western thinker might view this as contradictory, the experiential basis of musical taste demonstrates otherwise. Unique aesthetic perspectives can be formed out of shared building blocks. In discourses of good and bad, the falsity of clear-cut distinctions between individual and collective, mind and body, intuitive and intellectualized, are brought to light. "Bad music" is instructive as it exists at the point of articulation between these idealized poles, exposing the ways in which these categories are enacted and the ways they interact.

NOTES

1. Danger often performs with the HoHos, a comedic female singing duo (see www.cathyland.com).
2. Personal interview. June 28, 1999.
3. The surveys were distributed to Loser's Lounge audience members at several shows in late 2001. Of those who accepted the questionnaires, there were 40 respondents who returned completed forms. The response rate was around 30 percent.
4. V. Vale and Andrea Juno, eds., *Incredibly Strange Music*. San Francisco: RE/ Search Publications, 1993.
5. For a more complete discussion see Tim Taylor, *Strange Sounds: Music, Technology, and Culture.* New York: Routledge, 2001.
6. *Austin Powers: International Man of Mystery.* 1997. Directed by Jay Roach. Written by Mike Myers. *Austin Powers: The Spy Who Shagged Me.* 1999. Directed by Jay Roach. Written by Mike Myers and Michael McCullers. *Austin Powers in Goldmember.* 2002. Directed by Jay Roach. Written by Mike Myers

and Michael McCullers. All the films were distributed by New Line Cinema, New York and Los Angeles. In *The Spy Who Shagged Me*, LL regular Robin "Goldie" Goldwasser sings the opeing "Dr. Evil" theme.

7. Quoted in Taylor, *Strange Sounds*, 99. Chusid wrote the liner notes to the first Loser's Lounge CD (1999, Zilcho Records).

8. Barbara Kirshenblatt-Gimblett. "Disputing Taste." In *Destination Culture: Tourism, Museums, and Heritage*, 259–281. Berkeley: University of California Press, 1998.

9. For these and other adjectival descriptors, see www.allmusic.com.

10. In late May and early June 2004, a tribute to Prince was performed at LL. Since the performance had not yet taken place as of the final edits of this volume, I am unfortunately unable to comment on it here.

11. Ronald Radano and Philip V. Bohlman, eds., *Music and the Racial Imagination*. Chicago: University of Chicago Press, 2000.

12. A similar point is made in Julian Stringer. "The Smiths: Repressed (but remarkably dressed)," *Popular Music* 11(1) (January 1992): 15–26.

13. Ingrid Monson. "The Problem With White Hipness: Race, Gender, and Cultural Conceptions in Jazz Historical Discourse," *Journal of the American Musicological Society* 48(3), (1995): 396–422.

14. Personal interview. March 8, 2001.

15. Personal interview. June 28, 1999.

16. Christopher Isherwood. *The World in the Evening*. New York: Random House, 1954.

17. Susan Sontag. "Notes on 'Camp'," *Partisan Review* 31:4 (Fall 1964): 515–530.

18. Judith Butler. *Gender Trouble: Feminism and the Subversion of Identity*. New York: Routledge, 1990.

19. Andrew Ross. "Uses of Camp." In *No Respect: Intellectuals and Popular Culture*, 135–170. London and New York: Routledge, 1989.

20. For an anthology that collects and contextualizes the major writings on camp, consult Fabio Cleto, ed., *Camp: Queer Aesthetics and the Performing Subject*. Ann Arbor: University of Michigan Press, 1999.

21. See, for example, Susan Sontag, "Notes on 'Camp.'"

22. Poor rural whites (i.e., "white trash") are more often the subjects and almost never the actors of camp portrayals (e.g. Beck's "Loser").

23. Kevin J.H. Dettmar and William Richey. "Musical cheese: The Appropriation of Seventies Music in Nineties Movies." In *Reading Rock and Roll*, edited by Dettmar and Richey, 312. New York: Columbia University Press, 1999.

24. *ABBA: The Album*. 1977. Produced by Benny Andersson and Björn Ulvaeus. Distributed by Atlantic Recording Corporation, New York.

25. The performance discussed here is included on the first of two LL compilation recordings. *Simply Mad, Mad, Mad, Mad About The Loser's Lounge*. 1999. Produced by Richard Barone. Distributed by Zilcho Records, New York.

26. Personal interview. June 28, 1999.

4
Bad World Music[1]

TIMOTHY D. TAYLOR

This chapter is not about music that people think is bad. It is about music that is relegated to the margins of the "world music" category by the increasingly dominant music industry, which I take to encompass the major labels, major retailers, and major media providers. This music is marginalized because it is constructed as unsaleable—bad—by this industry, for it does not meet music industry expectations of what world music should be.

Let me make it clear from the outset that the music industry does not have much interest in world music. The most recent sales figures from the Recording Industry Association of America, the trade group that represents the music industry's interests, provides a list of the top-selling genres, and world music is not among them. Their list does include a category called "Other" with a footnote that lists "ethnic" music as one of the kinds of music included.[2]

As far as the music industry is concerned, world music scarcely exists as a profitable category. If we want to understand how the industry thinks of this music, we have to examine its perspectives based on those musics that sell the most and organize the music industry's activities. In his discussion of the contemporary musical landscape, Simon Frith describes the three discursive fields that he believes operate in contemporary culture: the art music world, the folk music world, and the commercial music world.[3] I would like to take this model and refocus it more specifically on the music industry itself. What are the discursive fields operating here? How does the music industry view music generally? I think there are three such fields that are themselves attached to specific categories of music: rock, rap, and pop. (These three discursive fields, not coincidentally, map nicely onto the larger fields described by Frith: pop is the frankly commercial wing; rock is the art music wing in which musicians are routinely called "artists," possessing an aesthetic similar to composers—anything goes in the name of their art; and rap is the folk music sector in which the authenticity of the musicians as racialized or ethnicized subjects plays a prominent role).

These three discursive fields provide the lenses through which the music industry views virtually all music, even a relatively unprofitable category such as world music. That is, the power and extensiveness of the ideologies loosely organized under these three fields influences music industry members' thinking on almost all music. Decisions made about what is good world music or what is bad are, by and large, determined by individuals in the industry whose ideas about music and profitability are shaped by these three fields.

Even though the music industry takes pains to categorize music (though the categories, and/or their contents, can always be shifted), these discursive fields can operate in overlapping ways. Criteria and ideologies from one can be employed in another. For world music, however, the dominant field in operation is that of rap music. Most world music does not sound like rap (though there is an increasing amount of rap music around the world).[4] But the ideological aspects of this field do come into play with world music, which is, drawing on the rap music field, constructed as being music by ethnicized or racialized others who are politically oppressed and reside in urban spaces, and whose music employs lyrics that are frequently political.

These criteria are only slightly modified in determining who is permitted to enter the world music category and thus the world music bins in music stores. From the music industry's perspective, world music should be:

1. by people of color from European and American Elsewheres
2. political in lyrics, employing musical signs and lyrics that signify anger, if the musician is from a known oppressed group
3. hybrid (that is, a music that does not sound traditional, but employs both traditional and western pop/rock sounds) and
4. urban

None of the items on this list are explicit, but rather comprise an underlying system of ideological maneuvers.

These maneuvers are generally organized along binary lines. In an era when much of poststructuralist theory is attempting to do away with binary oppositions as analytical tools, it is still the case that, ethnographically speaking, many people understand the world through such oppositions and organize their practices and epistemologies around them. It is therefore necessary to attempt to understand the underlying binaries that shape the music industry's perceptions of music in general, and world music in particular. The fundamental binaries at play in the music industry's construction of that category, along with the musicians who are put in it, include modern versus premodern; "normal" versus "exotic"; civilization versus (anthropological) culture. The music industry, in placing musicians in the world music category, works through a veritable taxonomy of binaries based on these fundamental ones, including the assumed race/ethnicity of the musician, the meaning of the lyrics, the cover artwork, and the sound of the music.[5]

"Good" World Music Is—

Let us examine the first three items on the above list. The first of the points I discussed in my book *Global Pop: World Music, World Markets,* and do not need to examine at any great length here, except to reiterate that world music is, perhaps first and foremost, music by people of color from Western metropoles. No matter what the music may sound like, and even if the musicians sing in English, if they are known to be Others, they will be placed in the world music category. Perhaps the most striking example is still Banig, the Filipina American singer considered in *Global Pop.*[6] Banig sings in English and is clearly attempting to be another Madonna, but was marketed by her record company as a world music musician and received as such.

World music was initially set up as a distinctly marginal category reserved for these racialized and/or geographic Others. Western pop rock musicians who make music that sounds like world music are not put in this group: their race/ethnicity permit them entry into the rock category. These style/genre categories employed by the music industry are not, in the end, style/genre categories at all, but are labels segregated by race or ethnicity that protect European and American rock musicians from racialized others. The labels also serve to protect the prestige that European and American musicians derive from being in the rock category.

On to politics. Why should politics be of concern in a supposedly postmodern era, in which politics are thought not to matter anymore? Theorists of the postmodern, when advancing this idea, tend not to make distinctions between the "dominant culture" and the various ethnic, race, and class subcultures. But the music industry's valorization of the politics of the oppressed reflects a kind of dominant cultural paternalism when a particular cultural form is made by an ethnicized or racialized person. This valorization is not the only one the music industry makes of world music musicians: they are portrayed also as spiritual, innocent, premodern, unworldly, and so on. These qualities, while rooted in the binary oppositions already noted, can nonetheless be combined and recombined in the process of representing and marketing a world music musician.[7]

Due, in large part, to the romanticization of the rebel rock musician, and, more recently, the popularity and sales of hip hop music by urban African Americans, it is increasingly the case that the cries of the oppressed can serve as a selling point. There is plenty of music by disadvantaged groups that thematizes their plight which receives notice by the music industry, whereas music just as good that does not tackle the same issues might get overlooked.

What is going on with this predilection for the political, I think, is a continuation of the music industry's, and the listening public's, interest in "authenticity." No longer, however, does the industry evince a strong interest in "authentic" *sounds*; the demand for authenticity as sound is now frequently converted to authenticity as a racialized or ethnicized person, usually signified by a CD cover photograph and/or the performer's name.

This authenticity is expected to have a musical manifestation, however, in the form of a particular affect—rage. Does the musician display anger about her racialized/ethnicized subject position and what is thought to have happened to her people? To the ears of the music industry, subaltern anger is best articulated by urban African American men in the sound of hip hop music.

The music industry's fascination with politics, for authenticity-as-oppressed positionality, may be illustrated by the example of the Native American musician Robby Bee. In 1990, Bee issued an album called *Rebel Rouzer* (see figure 1) on the then-new label SOAR (Sound of America Records), the first Native American-owned and -operated label. The cover of *Rebel Rouzer* featured a photograph of a slightly unkempt Bee, wearing jeans, a T-shirt, and a leather jacket, over the following caption: "Dedicated to James Dean, Elvis, Ritchie Valens, Buddy Holly & all the great legends of Rock N' Roll."

This album contained original rock 'n' roll and rockabilly songs by Robby and his father Tom Bee, himself a rock musician, songs that

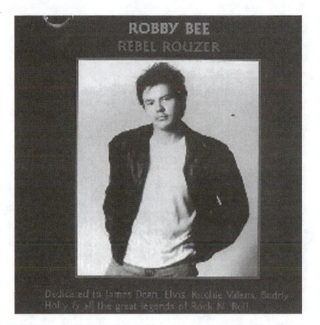

Figure 1   Robby Bee, *Rebel Rouzer*, cover.

are clearly meant to echo those of the musicians Bee named in his dedication, among others. One of Bee's songs, "Jailhouse Rocker," obviously refers to Jerry Lieber and Mike Stoller's "Jailhouse Rock," made famous by Elvis Presley; Bee's version makes references in the lyrics to early rock 'n' roll musicians such as Chuck Berry, Jerry Lee Lewis, Buddy Holly, Carl Perkins, and others. Unlike Presley's song, however, Bee's opens with a bit of verisimilitude: the sound of a key being inserted into a cell door, followed by the door slamming. In terms of reception, however, this album was never reviewed anywhere, or mentioned in print by anyone, including the Native American press, nor was it discussed online to my knowledge.

Then, three years later, Bee released a new album entitled *Reservation of Education*, (see figure 2) this time featuring Robby Bee and the Boyz from the Rez. Bee is again pictured on the cover, only this time he is wearing an earring, bolo tie, and stars and stripes bandana under a baseball cap with the bill pointed to the back.

This is a hip hop album, not rock 'n' roll or rockabilly like the first, though in terms of musical quality the two are reasonably close.

But since quality isn't the focal point of the arguments here, I want to spend some time discussing why this second album received

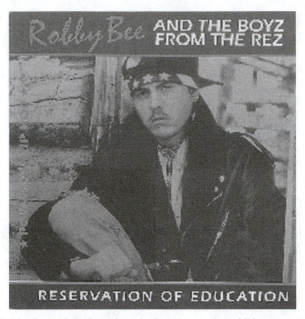

Figure 2   Robby Bee and the Boyz from the Rez, *Reservation of Education*, cover.

so much more attention than the first. If you visit the SOAR Web site,
you will find that it sells Robby Bee and the Boyz from the Rez's
music with the line: "Native American Rap!," as if the very incongruity
of these two categories marks the album exotic, and thus marketable.[8]
Indeed, one of the published reports on this album is entitled "Rappers
from the Rez?," signaling the apparent strangeness of these people
making this music.[9]

On visiting the SOAR Web site, you also discover that Bee's
second album is not in the main catalogue but in their specialty line
entitled *Warrior*. The songs continue this "warrior" attitude, for many
of the lyrics tackle political issues, ranging from the oppression of
indigenous peoples to the environment. The politics of *Reservation of
Education*, unlike the earlier album, was what seemed to attract attention to it. This album was widely written about, in the *Utne Reader*
and in George Lipsitz's insightful book *Dangerous Crossroads*; and
Bee was interviewed in a reader on music and politics, as well as an
online magazine published at an Albuquerque high school.[10] Bee's *Rebel
Rouzer* album is not mentioned in any of the published writings about
him.

I think that *Reservation of Education* received notice mainly because of its overtly political stance, and, to a lesser extent, the sheer exoticism of a Native American making hip hop music, since the music made by Native Americans that receives the most attention from the music industry is New Age, probably best represented by the flute recordings of R. Carlos Nakai.

Additionally, the invocation of the term hybridity in the marketing and critical response of Robby Bee's *Reservation of Education* represents a kind of fetish of Otherness, and thus serves as an alibi, among other things, for the lack of necessity of exercising an aesthetic judgment: Robby Bee's earlier album, which eluded all press reception as far as I can tell, does not seem to be very well regarded musically by those who have heard it. Without knowledge of Bee and the music industry-sanctioned sounds of Native Americanness, there are no criteria with which to judge it except aesthetic ones, and so it failed. Conversely, the later hip hop album received much more attention, in part, I think, because it sounds like a hybrid—it is possible to hear what might be "Native American" about it. Aesthetic judgments do not matter because this album speaks to the music industry—and the listener—expectations of what world music should be: hybrid, political, by people of color.

Also, to recall the list of criteria presented at the beginning of this chapter, there is the question of anger. Rap music is usually heard as angry music, and Bee's music is no different, employing both rap music sounds, reductionistically interpreted as signifying anger by the music industry; Bee also includes songs with political content, the titles of which convey what the songs are about: "Land of the Wanna Be Free," and "Let's Save Our Mother Earth." As far as the music industry is concerned, if a music sounds angry or embittered or militant, then there is a chance it might survive to be put in the world music bin for sale, especially if the lyrics are political. This move is, I think, predicated on some of the underlying binaries mentioned earlier. The fundamental premodern/modern binary provides an axis on which several binaries move. Authenticity in musical sound—which signifies the "premodern"—is converted to authenticity of affect in the musicians' musicalized or lyricized anger. This rage is often real, expressed by oppressed groups both in the United States and abroad, but to the music industry's ears it is more worthwhile as a signifier, perceived as a premodern affect in our postmodern era, the supposed era of the end of politics.

In short, if the musician in question is heard to possess an anger that is reasonably consistent with the modality of subaltern urban anger sanctioned by the music industry—best, but not only, exemplified by the sounds of rap music—then, regardless of the aesthetic values or quality of the music or the musical professionalism exhibited, that musician stands a chance of being noticed by the music industry. Values that we could call positional—that are concerned with the musician and her culture—prevail over the aesthetic, over musical inventiveness and professionalism.

"Retail ethnography" can provide significant insights into how the music industry, including retailers, conceptualizes and categorizes musics and musicians. It was record retailers, after all, who invented the world music category in the first place.[11] The "International Close-outs" bin at a local record store features many recordings by artists whose music can be called anything from pop to rock to schlock, but some of these artists have Asian names and faces, some have brown skins, some have white skins. Jesse Manibusan, a Californian whose parents are from Guam, provides a recent example with his album *Homeland*, the cover of which depicts Manibusan on a beach under a palm tree, guitar in hand. The album contains songs with titles such as "Forever Chamoru" (referring to the indigenous ethnic group from Guam to which he belongs), "Until I Return," and "Ode to Magellan" (with a chorus that begins, "Shame, shame, shame on you Ferdie!"), and more. All songs are sung in English, and most employ a style that is generally reminiscent of an electrified John Denver. Little has been written about this music, musician, or even the ethnic group that I can find, yet the album nonetheless is being categorized because of its placement in the "International" bin instead of rock/pop, because, it seems, of Manibusan's ethnicity and subject matter.

Like Robby Bee and the Boyz from the Rez, Jesse Manibusan's album *Homeland* (see figure 3) tackles a number of political issues, and so might qualify to be considered "good" on these grounds. It is not difficult to hear "Ode to Magellan"—in the style of a music hall waltz—as a delicious lampoon, and includes words and phrases in the Chamoru language (untranslated in the liner notes) that are clearly meant to proclaim Manibusan's indigeneity. But the sound of the music, in its joyful excess, does not signify anger, disenchantment, bitterness—which hip hop is taken by the music industry to signify, as we saw in the Boyz from the Rez case. Manibusan's music is virtually

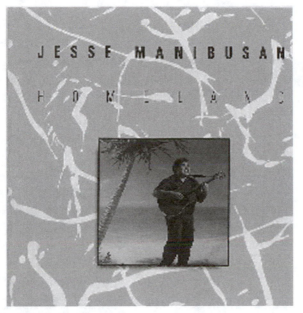

Figure 3   Jesse Manibusan, *Homeland*, cover.

unknown, consigned to the closeouts bin because the retailer thought it was "bad," or at least, unsaleable, which to them is the same thing.

Another example of a musically-enunciated politics is contained on the compilation album by the Hawai'ian duo Leahi, consisting of two young women from Kauai, Loki Sasil and Malia Kahahawai. This album, entitled *Come Ride with the Best of Leahi*, shows on the cover the two women on horseback with lush mountains in the background (see figure 4). Their version of "Pass the Dutchie," a song that was a huge hit for the British-based reggae group Musical Youth in 1983, sounds perhaps even more innocuous and sanitized than the version that the originating group made famous.[12]

And yet, if one knows anything about Hawai'ian popular music, this song has to be heard in the context of an entire movement of what was called "Jawaiian" music in the early 1990s. This music, a synthesis of Jamaican and Hawai'ian musics, was quite popular for a time. One of the reasons for this popularity was the perception by Hawai'ians that they, as an island population and oppressed people, have something in common with Jamaicans. The efforts of Bob Marley and other Jamaican musicians to unite black and brown people around the world

Figure 4   Leahi: *Come Ride with the Best of Leahi*, cover.

is well known, of course, and was heeded by musicians around the world, including in Hawai'i.[13] Leahi's music here may sound bland and ineffectual to a music industry believing that anger by ethnicized Others is best—only—expressed with the sounds of hip hop, but Leahi's music still articulates an important political stance that crosses both race and gender lines in order to find commonalities as marginalized peoples.

Having established that musicians can be political without using hip hop sounds, let's turn to the third point from the list concerning hybridity. One of the preferred modes of world music is this authenticity-as-oppressed positionality, but what about sound? The music industry's preference for authenticity-as-purity has given way to the authentic hybrid. I have written about this elsewhere,[14] and here will only note in passing how the music industry now valorizes the hybrid at least as much, if not more, than the authentic-as-pure sound or "style."[15] Musicians who were once assailed by Western critics for sounding "too Western" and thus inauthentic are now hailed as being authentic because of their very hybridity.

Simply put, ethnographic field recordings do not sell in very great quantities, and are increasingly absent from retailers' bins. The range of musical styles located in the "world music" or "international" sections of stores is becoming increasingly narrow, but the divisions between this part of the store and other parts—the divisions between "world music" and rock, in particular—are as strong as ever. Audibly hybridized musics have come to occupy the places in retailers' bins once occupied, at least in part, by ethnographic or field recordings of traditional music.

—And "Good" World Music Is Urban

It is finally time to address the last quality on the above list of what the music industry expects world music to be, and that is urban. World music is an urban phenomenon. Not all world musics are urban, emanate from urban spaces, though many, even most, do.[16] Rather, world music appeals to urbanites who tend to have a tolerance of difference, heterogeneity, and possess a cosmopolitan outlook. World music speaks a language of urbanism to city dwellers whatever its origins or intended meanings. It also speaks a language of globalization to which urban residents are susceptible, since the centers of financial power are increasingly consolidated in urban centers.

First though, understanding that this chapter appears in a volume on music and that it will probably have a varied readership, a brief overview of the writings on cities is necessary, preceded by this caveat. In discussing the aesthetic of the metropolitan I realize I am running the risk of being ahistorical, or of missing local particularities. Much of the literature on cities and the urban experience suffers from this flaw.[17] I am sensitive to this critique, and I do not wish to push here for some sort of universal city experience. At the same time, however, anyone who has visited a city recognizes that there are commonalities that scholars have attempted to theorize for quite some time. The problem with studying cities is that their qualities are transhistorical and it is easy to get lost in generalities. I am most interested in those writings that speak to the aesthetic, the consciousness, of a city dweller.

One point repeatedly made by writers on cities concerns the heterogeneity and diversity of cities; cities as sites where people from different social and ethnic groups can intermingle. For example, Chicago sociologist Louis Wirth noted in a classic article that the city is like a mosaic of juxtaposed social worlds that produces in the urbanite a toleration of difference.[18] Not just toleration, however; for Wirth, the city rewards individual differences, even encourages them.[19] Another example is provided by the construction of the Parisian boulevards in the mid-nineteenth century, which permitted people from different social groups to come into contact with one another as never before.[20]

A number of authors note the abundance of visual cues that bombard city dwellers.[21] Sights, sounds, and smells loom large in peoples' urban experiences. Walking through any city, one is struck not only by visual cues, but olfactory and auditory stimuli. The category "auditory" does not just refer to noise, though there is plenty of that (remembering that "noise" is culturally constructed, situational, and contingent anyway), but also: music pouring out of shops, taxicabs, boom boxes, leaking out of headphones, DJs and bootleggers selling tapes, street musicians playing live music above and below ground, and so forth.

The question is, of course, what does this juxtaposition of social worlds, this heterogeneity, diversity, and symbolic economy produce socially and musically? Much of my thinking about the synergy to be found in cities has been shaped by Raymond Williams's useful discussions of avant-garde formations in the era of modernism. I am not claiming here that world music is avant-garde (or modern or postmodern, for that matter).[22] But Williams's insights into cultural production in cities can be expanded to include other kinds of formations.

Williams is concerned with the various artistic avant-gardes between the 1890s and 1920s, writing that these characteristically have a metropolitan base. For Williams, "metropolitan" refers to entities that possess a degree of autonomy, especially cultural, and a degree of internationalization, which is often related to imperialism. Williams also notes that a high proportion of the contributors to these historical avant-garde movements were immigrants to metropoles, either from outlying regions or smaller national cultures, a point useful in understanding the rise and popularity of world music today.

Williams insists that certain factors of avant-garde culture have to be analyzed, not only in formal terms, but within the sociology of metropolitan encounters and associations between immigrants who share no common language but that of the metropolis. Williams also notes that the avant-garde formations he is theorizing develop specific styles within the metropolis, and that these formations both reflect and shape kinds of consciousnesses and practices that move beyond their immediate surroundings.[23] That is, modes of consciousness and practices developed by metropolitan avant-garde formations can be extremely influential and exert this influence beyond the confines of their place(s) of original formulation.

By drawing on Williams and other authors, I am attempting to move toward the point that city dwellers have different modes of being in the world, different consciousnesses, different experiences than non city-dwellers. The particular aesthetic of city-dwellers is one that is more tolerant, more sophisticated, more cosmopolitan, more eclectic than people whose experiences of cities is limited by comparison.

World music, I would further argue, finds a ready home in cities, where many of its sounds already pour out of doors, windows, and boom boxes. But the audience for this music is not just metropolitans, or the educated middle classes;[24] rather, the audience for world music is a new group that crosses class lines to some extent (on a familiar axis of educational and/or cultural capital), and which is now usually referred to as cosmopolitan. This is a group that predates, of course, theories about it, but in a sense has come into its own in the last decade and is beginning to be widely theorized.[25] An early view was formulated by Ulf Hannerz, who writes of cosmopolitanism as "a willingness to engage with the Other."[26] Cosmopolitanism, for him, entails the same kind of openness and receptivity that Louis Wirth wrote about as qualities of the city dweller. Hannerz also writes of the necessity of the cosmopolitan of possessing a certain competence in dealing with other peoples and cultures, and it is clear, for example, how world music guidebooks—most famously the Rough Guides[27]—are addressed at those desiring competence in the realm of world music consumption.[28]

Hannerz's notion of competence corresponds to what I have termed "global informational capital,"[29] a kind of Bourdieuian capital thought to be increasingly necessary in an era frequently touted as global. This term was chosen as a way around the familiar declaration of a new social group such as, simply, "cosmopolitan," a label that runs the risk of being ahistorical. The idea of global informational capital was meant to point out that familiar elite groups of the past are still elite but changing internally; and that there has long been a social group that contained people who could be termed cosmopolitans, but whose sense of what constitute the necessary kinds of competence and knowledge were changing.

In this discussion of cosmopolitans and capital I am attempting to invoke a broader phenomenon discussed by Scott Lash and John

Urry, who advance a more abstract and general notion of cosmopolitanism based on their conception of a new kind of aesthetic reflexivity evident in the contemporary moment in the "developed" countries. Their cosmopolitanism grew slowly out of the West's familiarity with "different physical and social environments," which helped foster a new kind of reflexivity that is "partly based on aesthetic judgments and stems from the proliferation of many forms or real and simulated mobility"; that this mobility has "served to authorize an increased stance of cosmopolitanism—an ability to experience, to discriminate and to risk different natures and societies, historically and geographically"; and, finally, that the social organization of travel and tourism (a major part of their argument) "has facilitated and structured such a cosmopolitanism."[30]

Because Lash and Urry view the developments of travel and tourism as central features of modernity and, by extension, postmodernity, they are less concerned with cosmopolitans as a new kind of social group than Hannerz. But taken together, they (and many other writers) have helped conceptualize and describe the relatively recent formation of a new social group with its own characteristics, including receptivity towards an eclectic array of other kinds of musics, e.g., world music. I would also insist on the urban character of this social group, a quality that Lash and Urry do not pursue. While I would not locate aesthetic reflexivity—or cosmopolitanism—as exclusive properties of city dwellers, it is nonetheless the case that the extreme diversity of sights, sounds, smells, and tastes make for different experiences of people in cities.

If world music speaks mainly, though not exclusively, to city dwellers, cosmopolitans, possessors of a metropolitan aesthetic, it is necessary to ask what it signifies to them. It is useful here to recall Roland Barthes's argument in *Mythologies* that a sign system can also be simply a sign.[31] That is, a complex cultural form such as any particular world music may be interpreted as a sign system that supports many shifting and complex interpretations; or it can simply serve as a sign. World music is seldom heard by these sophisticated metropolitans as a coherent musical language on its own, i.e., as a sign system; it is as a sign system that people in its place of origin might hear it (though, of course, with their own layers of sign value unrelated to the actual sound of the music). Instead, these city dwellers impose their own meanings on it: world music is simply a sign.

But a sign of what? One of the most salient of these meanings, constructed by the music industry and the advertising industry over the last few years,[32] is world music as the musical analog to globalization. World music is a sign of the globalizing world, a world apprehensible to urbanites, a world that metropolitan inhabitants increasingly view themselves to be a part of. Knowing a little world music is to possess some global informational capital.

And, indeed, some scholars have argued that globalization is mostly felt in cities, managed in cities. Economic capital is concentrated more in cities than ever before.[33] City dwellers, long accustomed to diversity and heterogeneity, as well as to participation in a symbolic economy, thus possess—in Weber's term—an elective affinity for world music, which is part of their larger metropolitan aesthetic.

Cities provide homes for many different peoples and cultures resulting in a particular synergy, and it is worth remembering that some of these people wield more power than others. For Zukin, what matters in the symbolic economy of the city isn't simply the presence of symbolic languages, though these certainly contribute to peoples' experiences of cities, but rather who has control over them, who has the power to "manipulate symbolic languages of exclusion and entitlement."[34] Zukin is making an argument about the physical space of cities here, but this argument can be easily inflected to include the physical space of retail stores—where certain musics are put—and the cognitive positioning of musics in hierarchies of prestige and sales potential.

Some of the music examples mentioned demonstrate the urban biases of the music industry. I have already discussed the industry's apparent preference for politicized urban sounds as organized in hip hop music. But there are other signs of this bias. Jesse Manibusan's and Leahi's album covers place these musicians in decidedly nonurban settings: Manibusan on the beach under a palm tree, Leahi on horseback with mountains behind them. Cover artwork generally seems to have a good deal to do with retailers' and marketers' reception of albums. Many unsuccessful world music albums use cover photos that are amateurish, inartistic, as in the Jesse Manibusan and Leahi examples above. Such photographs evoke neither ethnic "authenticity" nor urban grittiness. Also, such self-representations show these musicians to be unsophisticated consumers: they don't know what cool album covers look like, so they sanction these straightforward ones that are more like snapshots than aesthetic statements. This position is made fun of in Alan Parker's film *The Commitments*, when the band's manager says that he wants "urban decay" in the band's publicity photo instead of a picture postcard scene.[35]

Conclusions

What happens in judgments about world music is a complicated mixture of moves based on social and political indicators and cultural codes. That is, many judgments or understandings of musicians of color are based on the musician's life and objective conditions of race, ethnicity, geographical location, class position, gender, as represented in the album cover art and in the liner notes, regardless of sound. Knowledge about any of these qualities trumps music aesthetics, no matter what the music sounds like. A musician of color will be judged as a musician of color first, as a musician second, if she is fortunate enough to be judged as a musician at all.

Yet, aesthetic judgments do come into play. People in the music industry are adept at "reading" not just musical signs, but visual ones and literary ones, as they appear on album covers and liner notes. Sounds, images, and texts that are products of lesser amounts of cultural capital possessed by musicians of color, rural musicians, non-Western musicians, are judged by reading the wrong codes, codes of the musician's race, ethnicity, and positionality—urban versus rural, clean versus gritty, etc.—instead of aesthetic codes in sound.

Given the longtime racism and xenophobia of the music industry, I think that—as scholars—we should do what we can to deconstruct and critique music industry practices, as I have attempted here. This can be done from the outside, as is usually the case. But the need for ethnographic research on the industry is becoming increasingly urgent,[36] and would greatly further academic understanding of what goes on behind those closed doors.

An in depth study of music industry practices and assumptions would not simply add to academic understanding of how the industry operates, which would allow us to be more reflexive about our own preconceptions about world music, as well as other musics. Also, it is important that scholars be more reflexive about why we study particular musicians. How have our own tastes been shaped by the tastes of those in the music industry, our own habitus?

Last, I think that scholars could devote more time and published space to studying musicians constructed as "bad"—or good. Why does the music industry champion one musician rather than another? One kind of sound rather than another? One producer rather than another? The easy answer concerns marketability and thus profits, but there is also an aesthetic dimension that could stand some greater scholarly scrutiny.

In all of this, I am not advocating that we forget about race/ethnicity in favor of the aesthetic. Instead, I am advocating that we find a better way to talk about both.

NOTES

1. Thanks are due to Steve Feld, who offered insightful comments. And as always, I would like to thank Sherry B. Ortner.
2. Recording Industry Association of America, "2002 Consumer Profile," http://www.riaa.org/news/marketingdata/pdf/2002consumerprofile.pdf.
3. Simon Frith, *Performing Rites: on the Value of Popular Music* (Cambridge, MA: Harvard University Press, 1996).
4. See Tony Mitchell, ed., *Global Noise: Rap and Hip-hop outside the USA* (Middletown, CT: Wesleyan University Press, 2001).
5. It is worthwhile to reflect briefly on the mosaic-like nature of the entity "world music," which I have attempted to come to grips with for some time now. While I would still stand by my initial discussions of world music (Taylor, *Global Pop: World Music, World Markets*, New York: Routledge, 1997), some aspects of the world music phenomenon were omitted, though it should be said that "world music" has changed over time, and some of these qualities were not as clear, or salient, as they are now. One of these concerns the high cultural capital of listeners to world music, which I have considered in a forthcoming article "You Can Take 'Country' out of the Country but It Will Never Be 'World'," in *Songs Out of Place: Country Musics of the World*, eds. Aaron A. Fox and Christine Yano. (Durham, NC: Duke University Press, forthcoming). Another concerns the construction of world music as a set of sounds—even a "style" or "genre"—that can be used to signify the global informational world in which people in the so-called developed countries believe themselves to inhabit (discussed in Taylor, "World Music in Television Ads." *American Music* 18 (Summer, 2000): 162–92).
6. Taylor, *Global Pop: World Music, World Markets*, 17.
7. Thanks are due to Steve Feld for pushing me on this point.
8. From http://www.soundofamerica.com.
9. j poet, "Rappers from the Rez?" *Utne Reader*, (March/April, 1993): 38–39.
10. See Cielo Garcia, "Rap from the Reservation." *360°*, (spring, 1996), http://www.myhouse.com/michael/mag360/rhyt1195.html; George Lipsitz , *Dangerous Crossroads: Popular Music, Postmodernism and the Poetics of Place* (New

York: Verso, 1994); poet, "Rappers from the Rez?", Ron Sakolsky and Fred Wei-Han Ho, 1993; and Robby Bee, interview by Ron Sakolsky, eds. *Sounding Off! Music as Subversion/Resistance/Revolution* (Brooklyn, NY: Autonomedia, 1995).

11. See Philip Sweeny, *The Virgin Directory of World Music* (London: Virgin, 1991) and Taylor, *Global Pop,* 1997.

12. For more on Musical Youth, see Lipsitz, *Dangerous Crossroads,* 1994.

13. "Hawai'i," in *Sound Alliances: Indigenous Peoples, Cultural Politics and Popular Music in the Pacific*, ed. Philip Hayward, (New York: Cassell, 1998).

14. Timothy D. Taylor, "Some Versions of Difference: Discourses of Hybridity in Transnational Musics," in *Global Currents: Media and Technology Now*, eds. Patrice Petro and Tasha G. Oren, (New Brunswick, NJ: Rutgers University Press, forthcoming).

15. See also Simon Frith, "The Discourse of World Music," in *Western Music and Its Others: Difference, Representation, and Appropriation in Music*, eds. Georgina Born and David Hesmondhalgh (Berkeley: University of California Press, 2000).

16. Iain Chambers, *Migrancy, Culture, Identity*. (London: Routledge, 1994), 97.

17. See the useful critique in Ulf Hannerz, *Exploring the City: Inquiries toward an Urban Anthropology* (New York: Columbia University Press, 1980).

18. Louis Wirth, "Urbanism as a Way of Life," *American Journal of Sociology* 44 (July, 1938): 15.

19. Wirth, "Urbanism as a Way of Life," 10.

20. Marshall Berman, *All That Is Solid Melts into Air: The Experience of Modernity* (New York: Penguin, 1988), 158-9.

21. See, for instance, Wirth, *op. cit.*, Iain Chambers, *Popular Culture: The Metropolitan Experience* (New York: Routledge, 1986), and Sharon Zukin, *The Cultures of Cities* (Cambridge, MA: Blackwell, 1995).

22. I also argued against the notion of world music as postmodern in Taylor, *Global Pop,* 1997.

23. Raymond Williams, *Culture* (Glasgow: William Collins Sons, 1981), 84.

24. Taylor, "You Can Take 'Country' out of the Country but It Will Never Be 'World'," forthcoming.

25. This group has been theorized in other terms as well. See, for example, Leslie Sklair's *Sociology of the Global System*, 2nd ed., for a discussion of the "transnational capitalist classes" (Baltimore: Johns Hopkins University Press, 1995).

26. Ulf Hannerz, *Transnational Connections: Culture, People, Places,* (New York: Routledge, 1996), 103.

27. For example, Simon Broughton et al, *World Music: The Rough Guide,* Vol. 1, *Africa, Europe and the Middle East* (London: Rough Guides, 1999).

28. For more on cosmopolitanism, see also Aijaz Ahmad, "The Politics of Literary Postcoloniality," *Race & Class* 36 (January–March, 1995): 1–20; Homi K. Bhabha "Unpacking My Library . . . Again," in *The Post-Colonial Question: Common Skies, Divided Horizons,* eds. Iain Chambers and Lidia Curti (New York: Routledge, 1996); Timothy Brennan, *At Home in the World: Cosmopolitanism Now* (Cambridge, MA: Harvard University Press, 1997); Pheng Cheah

and Bruce Robbins, eds. *Cosmopolitics: Thinking and Feeling beyond the Nation* (Minneapolis: University of Minnesota Press, 1998); Jonathan Friedman, "Global Crisis, the Struggle for Cultural Identity and Intellectual Porkbarrelling: Cosmopolitans versus Locals, Ethnics and Nationals in an Era of De-Hegemonisation," in *Debating Cultural Hybridity: Multi-Cultural Identities and the Politics of Anti-Racism*, eds. Pnina Werbner and Tariq Modood (Atlantic Highlands, NJ: Zed Books, 1997); and Thomas Turino, *Nationalists, Cosmopolitans, and Popular Music in Zimbabwe* (Chicago: University of Chicago Press, 2000).

29.   Taylor, "World Music in Television Ads," 2000.
30.   Scott Lash and John Urry, *Economies of Signs and Space* (Thousand Oaks, CA: Sage, 1994), 256–57
31.   Roland Barthes, *Mythologies*, Annette Lavers, trans. (New York: Hill and Wang, [1957] 1972).
32.   See Taylor, "World Music in Television Ads," 2000.
33.   Saskia Sassen, *Cities in a World Economy* (Thousand Oaks, CA: Pine Forge Press, 1994), 119.
34.   Zukin, *The Cultures of Cities*, 7.
35.   The significance of cover art cannot be underestimated. Helfried C. Zrzavy argues that cover art in New Age music was more important than the sound of the music in establishing the identity of this music which, significantly, emerged around the same time as a music industry category. See Helfried C. Zrzavy, "Issues of Incoherence and Cohesion in New Age Music," *Journal of Popular Culture* 24 (1990): 33–53 and Taylor, *Global Pop,* 1997.
36.   Though see Keith Negus, *Music Genres and Corporate Cultures* (New York: Routledge, 1999).

REFERENCES

Discography

BEE, ROBBY
Rebel Rouzer. Sound of America Records 105, 1990.
ROBBY BEE AND THE BOYZ FROM THE REZ
Reservation of Education. Sound of America Records/Warrior 604, 1993.
LEAHI
Come Ride with the Best of Leahi. Rose Records, RC 005, n.d.
MANIBUSAN, JESSE
Homeland. two by two TD 1002-CD, 1992.
MUSICAL YOUTH
Anthology. One Way Records MCAD-22123, 1994.

Filmography

The Commitments. Alan Parker. 1991.

Webography

http://www.soundofamerica.com/

Books and Articles

Ahmad, A. 1995. The politics of literary postcoloniality. *Race & Class* 36 (January–March): 1–20.

Barthes, R. 1972. *Mythologies*, translated by Annette Lavers. New York: Hill and Wang. (Orig. pub. 1957.)

Bee, R. 1995. Interview by Ron Sakolsky. In *Sounding off! Music as subversion/resistance/revolution*, eds. R. Sakolsky and F. Wei-Han Ho. Brooklyn, NY: Autonomedia.

Berman, M. 1966. *All that is solid melts into sir: The experience of modernity*. New York: Penguin, 1988.

Bhabha, H. K. 1996. Unpacking my library . . . again. In *The post-colonial question: Common skies, divided horizons*, eds. I. Chambers and L. Curti. New York: Routledge.

Brennan, T. 1997. *At home in the world: Cosmopolitanism now*. Cambridge, MA: Harvard University Press.

Broughton, S., M. Ellingham, and R. Trillo, eds. 1999. *World music: The rough guide*. Vol. 1, *Africa, Europe and the Middle East*. London: Rough Guides.

Chambers, I. 1986. *Popular culture: The metropolitan experience*. New York: Routledge.

———. 1994. *Migrancy, culture, identity*. London: Routledge.

Cheah, Pheng, and Bruce Robbins, eds. 1998. *Cosmopolitics: Thinking and feeling beyond the nation*. Minneapolis: University of Minnesota Press.

Friedman, J. 1997. Global crisis, the struggle for cultural identity and intellectual porkbarrelling: Cosmopolitans versus locals, ethnics and nationals in an era of de-hegemonisation. In *Debating cultural hybridity: Multi-cultural identities and the politics of anti-racism*, eds, P, Werbner and T, Modood. Atlantic Highlands, NJ: Zed Books.

Frith, S. 1996. *Performing rites: On the value of popular music*. Cambridge, MA: Harvard University Press.

———. 2000. The discourse of world music. In *Western music and its others: Difference, representation, and appropriation in music*, eds. G. Born and D. Hesmondhalgh. Berkeley: University of California Press.

Garcia, C. 1996. Rap from the Reservation. *360°*, (Spring). http://www.myhouse.com/michael/mag360/rhyt1195.html

Hannerz, U. 1980. *Exploring the city: Inquiries toward an urban anthropology*. New York: Columbia University Press.

———. 1996. *Transnational connections: Culture, people, places*. New York: Routledge.

Lash, S., and J. Urry. 1994. *Economies of signs and space*. Thousand Oaks, CA: Sage.

Lipsitz, G. 1994. *Dangerous crossroads: Popular music, postmodernism and the poetics of place*. New York: Verso.

Mitchell, T., ed. 2001. *Global noise: Rap and hip-hop outside the USA*. Middletown, CT: Wesleyan University Press.

Negus, K. 1999. *Music genres and corporate cultures*. New York: Routledge.

poet, j. 1993. Rappers from the Rez? *Utne Reader* (March/April): 38–39.

Recording Industry Association of America. "2002 Consumper Profile." http://www.riaa.org/PDF/2002consumerprofile.pdf.

Sassen, S. 1994. *Cities in a world economy*. Thousand Oaks, CA: Pine Forge Press.

Simmel, G. 1971. The metropolis and mental life. In *On individuality and social forms*, ed. D, N. Levine. Chicago: University of Chicago Press.

Sklair, L. 1995. *Sociology of the global system*. 2d ed. Baltimore: Johns Hopkins University Press.

Sweeney, P. 1991. *The Virgin directory of world music*. London: Virgin.

Taylor, T. D. 1997. *Global pop: World music, world markets*. New York: Routledge.

———. 2000. World music in television ads. *American Music* 18 (Summer): 162–92.

———. forthcoming. Some versions of difference: Discourses of hybridity in transnational musics. In *Global Currents: Media and Technology Now*, eds. P. Petro and T. G. Oren. New Brunswick, NJ: Rutgers University Press.

———. forthcoming. You can take 'country' out of the country but it will never ne 'world'. In *Songs out of place: Country musics of the world,* eds. A. A. Fox and C. Yano. Durham, NC: Duke University Press.

Turino, T. 2000. *Nationalists, cosmopolitans, and popular music in Zimbabwe*. Chicago: University of Chicago Press.

Weintraub, A. N. 1998. Jawaiian music and local cultural identity in Hawai'i. In *Sound alliances: Indigenous peoples, cultural politics and popular music in the Pacific,* ed. P. Hayward. New York: Cassell.

Williams, R. 1981. *Culture*. Glasgow: William Collins Sons.

Wirth, L. 1938. Urbanism as a way of life. *American Journal of Sociology* 44 (July): 1–24.

Zrzavy, H. C. 1990. Issues of incoherence and cohesion in new age music. *Journal of Popular Culture* 24: 33–53.

Zukin, S. 1995. *The cultures of cities*. Cambridge, MA: Blackwell.

5

Theorizing the Musically Abject[1]

ELIZABETH TOLBERT

The Enigma of Music

Linguist and evolutionary psychologist Steven Pinker, in his treatise entitled *How the Mind Works,* claims that "music is an enigma."[2] Although this is undoubtedly the case, Pinker is referring specifically to the enigma of music's evolutionary provenance. Is it an adaptation in its own right, or an evolutionary accident, a byproduct of other evolved traits? In a bold move, Pinker proclaims music to be "auditory cheesecake,"[3] a wonderful but nonadaptive outgrowth of the 'real' adaptation, language, and thus ultimately "useless" for human life.[4]

Although the hegemony of language over music, not to mention music's mysterious uselessness, are hardly original ideas, Pinker's remarks suggest an elision between music's *adaptive* status and its *aesthetic* and *moral* value, which in turn points to a more widespread cultural anxiety over the inessential, yet essential, role of music in contemporary Western society. Whereas "auditory cheesecake" attests to Pinker's positive, if fluffy, attitude, "useless" is not so benign, leaving us to wonder if our deepest musical experiences are perhaps insignificant. In spite of the fact that Pinker claims that adaptive status is not correlated with aesthetic value,[5] he nevertheless asserts that "biologically frivolous" music is highly valued precisely because it *is* useless, a position mirrored in much Western philosophical discourse on 'art for art's sake.'[6] Furthermore, Pinker's music gains its *aesthetic* value from its "tickling" of the evolved predispositions for other clearly useful traits such as language, auditory scene analysis, emotional calls, habitat selection, and motor control.[7] While Pinker does not address the question directly, one might infer that "good music" does a better job of such tickling than "bad music."

Not surprisingly, those who critique Pinker to *uphold* music's adaptive status also adhere to this logic, similarly conflating functional and aesthetic value. For example, evolutionary psychologist Geoffrey Miller proposes that music evolved as a display of male reproductive fitness to impress choosy females,[8] implying that aesthetically good music would be a clear indicator of high mate quality. But even if music is granted adaptive status, its enigma remains. Is fitness-enhancing music the only good music? Does bad music lay waste to the gene pool, or is it merely neutral? Indeed, the conflation of aesthetic and functional value in Pinker's and Miller's supposedly antithetical formulations points to an even more intriguing incongruity, in that both scenarios are dependent upon a music that is inherently good.

To wit, bad music in these contexts refers not only to particular aesthetic evaluations of particular musics, but is paradoxically an assertion of music's fundamental Goodness, one that I claim is rooted in logocentric and phonocentric ideas of music as unmediated sound, music as a Derridean near-Transcendental Signifier.[9] In fact, it is almost impossible to conceptualize functionally bad music in terms of Pinker's and Miller's evolutionary scenarios. For example, in Miller's story, aesthetically bad music would supposedly signal poor mate quality, and thus would be good anyway in that it would discourage females from picking a less than optimal partner. Similarly, Pinker's bad music would be just as "useless" as his good music, even while being similarly judged in terms of its "tickling" of other functional traits. Indeed, these kinds of bad music aren't bad enough to distinguish them from their good counterparts. What is needed is a music that is actively *maladaptive,* that is not counterbalanced by other factors such as sexual selection.

How might we begin to imagine such a music? Following in Miller's footsteps, we might begin by asking if the "songs" of male animals such as songbirds or whales, also theorized to advertise male reproductive fitness, are more than metaphorically akin to human music making. Do men make music so that women can choose mates, and if so, how are to we interpret and aesthetically evaluate women's music making? Do women perform just to hone their mate selection skills? Or are they perhaps driven by musical penis envy, which if left unchecked will develop into the ultimate bad music, a gynocentric enactment of vicarious mate selection and a concomitant refusal to mate at all?

Obviously, Pinker and Miller are not interested in these kinds of questions, even if I maintain that they arise logically from their evolutionary postulates. Yet more to the point, they could not even argue about music's adaptive status if music's enigma could be solved by evolutionary fiat. Indeed, the issue is worth debating because neither music nor adaptive status can be imagined without their concomitant social values. Dissanayake, well aware of this fact, explicitly capitalizes on the valorization of adaptive status in her appeal to a "naturalistic aesthetics" based on "rhythmic-modal experiences" that "evolved to enable our human way of life in relationship with others."[10] Whether implicitly or explicitly, these kinds of proposals naturalize aesthetic value in terms of species-specific adaptations, intimating that music's enigma is deeply implicated in concepts of human uniqueness and its associated moral and epistemological claims to knowledge.[11]

In order to further explore the ramifications of music's enigma, I will introduce bad music into three seemingly unrelated narratives, narratives that nonetheless have a common rhetorical strategy in that they appeal to music, even if only implicitly, to make their larger points. All three are master narratives of human becoming, and all ground their claims in music's unmediated sonic power. When read across one other, they reveal a music/language ideology of astounding complexity, one that underlies a wide range of contemporary Western discourses about essential human truths.

Becoming Human

Whether music is considered to be adaptive or merely parasitic on other adaptations, the enigma of music is deeply embedded in another enigma, the enigma of language, the *sine qua non* of human uniqueness. The enigma of language does not concern its adaptive status per se,[12] which is assumed, but rather how a qualitatively novel form of communication could have evolved from the signal-like communication systems of our living primate ancestors. Music, in the guise of a rhythmic, song-like protolanguage, is central to this story, in that it is theorized to be the missing link between animal calls and full-fledged human language.[13]

The music-like character of protolanguage is thought to embody traces of species-specific emotion calls from which proto-song and/or protolanguage later emerged. Not surprisingly, the musicality of protolanguage is conceptualized in terms of contemporary Western understandings of music, in particular, its unmediated, nonsymbolic character. Indeed, Pinker's music could not "tickle," nor Miller's music index mate quality without just such an assumption of unmediatedness. The question then becomes, what is the importance of inserting this particular kind of music into evolution of language scenarios?

The intermediary status of song-like protolanguage, and by implication, music more generally, intersects provocatively with the theorized transition from the unmediated, nonarbitrary and involuntary emotion calls of animals, to the highly mediated, arbitrary, and intentionally modeled vocal sounds that serve as a vehicle for human speech. The move from unmediated to mediated vocality implies an attendant shift from a unification of voice and social essence in animal calls, where voice is interpreted as a direct expression of internal bodily and socio-emotional states, to their material separation in the arbitrary relationship between vocal sounds and their referents.[14] Similar to Pinker's "tickling" scenario, whereby musical sounds are interpreted as if they were reliable indicators of a physical environment, the song-like vocal sounds of protolanguage tickled the emotion call circuits and were thus interpreted as a direct index of an individual's emotional state.

So where, exactly, does music fit into this story? Knight, in a compelling proposal, notes that the arbitrary signs of language are inherently unreliable and potentially deceptive, which should have precluded the evolution of language because unreliable signals would have been ignored and eventually died out. To overcome the problem of vocal deception, Knight proposes that performative, ritual displays, such as music, co-evolved with language, serving to guarantee the truth of arbitrary signs through their illocutionary force. Drawing on contemporary ethnographic studies, and in a classic Durkheimean interpretation, Knight maintains that collective performance of ritualized music and dance demonstrate the commitment of the group to communicate honestly with one another, thereby creating a social context in which collective belief and symbolic representation can emerge.[15]

Although Knight's argument is persuasive and consistent with much anthropological thinking on ritual performance, he nevertheless draws on an inconsistent, albeit generally uncontested, music/language ideology. In particular, he conflates unmediated vocality with music in general, implying that music, whether vocal or instrumental, is similar to involuntary animal calls, and therefore indexical to the bodily and socio-emotional states of its producers. Following this logic, music takes on the qualities of an animal-like vocality, it is a direct and unmediated expression of a "true" social essence. This elision between social essence and vocality/music inadvertently places music on both sides of the animal/human divide; music's animal-like truthfulness paradoxically gives it the very human authority to ground the arbitrariness of language, and thus humanity itself.

Yet, as we all know, the musical voice is more than a primal cry, even if it is experienced in all its immediacy; rather, it is a symbolic *representation* of unmediated vocality, which I would maintain is a *social* entailment of the arbitrariness of the sign. In other words, to understand vocal sound qua sound, and hence a potential vehicle for arbitrary reference, both producer and receiver must possess social knowledge of each others' motivations and intentions. Specifically, they must know that both producer and receiver understand the voice as intentionally modeled, and therefore specifically *not* as an unmediated expression of inner essence.[16]

Thus, adherence to the doctrine of the arbitrariness of the sign creates a tension between *voice*, in the sense of a metaphor for social persona, and *vocality*, the physical vocal sonorities through which this social persona is enunciated, in that the material break between social essence and vocality is a precondition for the material break between signifier and signified.[17] For Knight's argument to work, for music to ground the truth of arbitrary signs, music would have to be *literally* unmediated. However, if we reconceptualize music as a symbolic *representation* of unmediated vocality, the argument transforms into the claim that because of music's ambiguous status as not-language, while also being the condition for its emergence, music becomes a trope for an imagined prior unity of voice/vocality in prelinguistic, not-quite humans. This prior unity of voice and vocality, or more accurately, its symbolic representation, then retroactively serves to naturalize the fully human, postlinguistic and socially constructed unity of voice/vocality identified with cultural authority and linguistic truth. Thus, Knight's rather simple formulation becomes a convoluted assertion that arbitrary reference is guaranteed by a *representation* of unmediated vocality, i.e., music, and that music as a representation of unmediated vocality defines the *conditions* from which arbitrary reference emerges.

These oblique references to a prior unity of voice and vocality in evolutionary accounts have counterparts in anthropological stories about the metaphysical potential of voice in ritual contexts, and in musicological stories about the transcendent potential of voice in Western art music genres such as opera. For example, in ritual trance contexts throughout the world, spirits and ancestors borrow human voices and bodies, making otherwise invisible beings perceptible through a putatively unmediated vocality and bodily presence.[18] Urban specifically locates this metaphysical potential in the voice's power to construct "a noumenal understanding of the phenomenal world in terms of community."[19] Tomlinson similarly suggests that the modern operatic voice is experienced as a physical vocality that carries the listener beyond presence to the limits of metaphysical reality.[20] Thus, the voice of not-yet-language might be considered metaphysical to the extent that it posits a prior unity of voice and vocality in order to create the social arena in which arbitrary reference, and thus humanness, can emerge in perceptible form.[21]

As in Pinker's and Miller's scenarios, the metaphysical voice of evolutionary accounts barely has room for bad music, in that the music in these stories is clearly good in its support of linguistic hegemony. Yet, the criteria of value has shifted ever so slightly; if good music allowed for the emergence of language and symbolic thought, then bad music is capable of revoking our essential humanity. By explicitly unmasking music as both pre- and posthuman, we can begin to imagine the full potential of bad music. However, an awareness of music's impossibly ambiguous status also leads to the suspicion that neither music nor language are capable of marking the human/animal divide. Perhaps bad music has a role to play after all, in that it is the only kind of music that could let us in on this secret.

Becoming a Speaking Subject

The anxiety about music's evolutionary provenance and its position vis-à-vis language is paralleled by similar anxieties in poststructuralist and psychoanalytic writings on voice, where musicality is characterized as the feminine, sonorous excess beyond language, and whose material presence and uncontained emotionality negate rational thought.[22] The evolutionary becoming-human-through-language story easily transmutes into a post-Lacanian story about a pre-linguistic, not-yet-subject who only becomes fully human by 'evolving' language and emerging full-fledged into the linguistically created symbolic order. The fully differentiated subject trades music for language, breaking with the materiality of sound and the primordial unity of self and other.[23]

As in the evolutionary stories, the naturalization of language as the arbiter of subjectivity seems to indicate that music is only as good as its ability to defend the symbolic order. Music that is a display of male fitness, or that tickles other evolved predispositions, or that is unabashedly emotional is non-threatening and therefore Good, clearly on the prelinguistic, prehuman side of things, and amenable to poststructuralist rhapsodizing and evolutionary theorizing alike.

Nevertheless, any particular musical moment always has the potential to become bad, to reveal its constructedness, to nullify claims to an essential humanity or subjectivity. Kristeva proposes that any such threat to the subject comes from the *abject*, those aspects of bodiliness which cannot be incorporated into the symbolic self.[24] Although Kristeva does not theorize music per se as abject, she does claim that the non-symbolic aspects of voice and indeed of music itself, are anchored in the *semiotic*, the undifferentiated world of bodily flows, drives and energies, and the place from which the subject-to-be will emerge in dialectical relationship to the linguistically created symbolic order.[25] Not surprisingly, the maternal, feminine semiotic that is the source of music and that harbors the positive forces of creativity and pleasure, is also the source of the abject.

The abject marks the border between the impossibly clean body, a bodiliness devoid of corporeality, and the ultra-corporeal, unclean, pre-oedipal body.[26] However, entry into the symbolic order does not require a complete break with the material body; on the contrary, the semiotic harbors those aspects of the body that can never be fully expunged from the subject.[27] The abject is thus a response to the prior unity of self and other, body and mind, and represents the contradictory desires to separate yet remain identical with the mother. As Grosz notes, the abject reminds us that "what is excluded can never be fully obliterated but hovers at the borders of our existence, threatening the apparently settled unity of the subject with disruption and possible dissolution[28] . . . Abjection is the result of recognizing that the body is more than, in excess of, the 'clean and proper'."[29]

Significantly for our purposes here, the abject acknowledgement of the failed rupture between body and symbolic self is elicited by intermediate bodily objects that themselves are the products of this failed rupture.[30] These intermediate bodily objects, such as urine, feces, semen, menstrual blood, and by implication, the *voice*, are experienced as detachable parts of the body, and as such have intrinsic psychological and social meanings though their potentially abject associations.

Kristeva does not consider the voice in and of itself abject, but rather places it at the interface of the semiotic and the symbolic,[31] and hence the abject and clean body. She postulates that language consists both of the *geno-text*, the musical aspects of voice such as prosody, which have a direct link to the semiotic, and the *pheno-text*, which strives to eliminate any connection to the semiotic and is concerned with the unity of the subject as created through the structure of language.[32] For the subject to survive, the fallacy of the unity of the subject as represented in the repressive, even murderous, pheno-text must be protected from the abject, from the processes of undoing the subject through the corporeal, libidinous, and song-like geno-text.

I have offered this admittedly selective and somewhat *ethnographic* reading of Kristeva because it draws attention to the broader topic of music/language ideologies as they intersect with ideologies of becoming human, of self-making. In particular, I propose that the enigma of music as it appears in Western culture is embedded in ideologies of a Humanity that is defined in terms of an emergent, agentive Becoming. Despite her explicit understanding of the myth of originary unity, Kristeva accepts the enigma of music at face value, and thus not only develops a story that describes an incomplete rupture between body and self, and hence the grounds of the speaking subject, but inadvertently allows us to see the cracks in her story. If we look at the points in her argument that need music, we note that in order to uphold the speaking subject and the leap into language, Kristeva finds it necessary to conflate voice and body while still maintaining their separateness, in a way that is similar to the tension between vocality and social essence in evolutionary accounts. The symbolic self is clearly separated from sonorous vocality, yet retains a material connection to the prior unity of body/self in the semiotic.

As Kristeva reminds us, the split between voice-as-social-persona and sonorous vocality can never be fully realized. The material voice as an intermediate bodily object is already tainted with the abject, yet it can only enunciate the socio-cultural self through a neutralized vocal sonority, one that speaks through language, and hence is a sonic virtualization of the "clean and proper" body.[33] In other words, the ambiguous relationship between voice and body, self and other, arises fundamentally from the ambiguous experience of vocality as both abject and clean. The sonorities of the clean voice initiate the processes of becoming, whereas the abject voice undoes them. It would seem that Kristeva has touched upon the same ubiquitous music/language ideology that pervades evolutionary accounts, whereby music is implicated in a becoming human that harkens back to an imagined pre-linguistic unity of voice and vocality. To maintain the integrity of the Subject, the social persona enunciated through the sonorous voice must symbolically represent an indissoluble voice/vocality, a social persona unmediated by abject vocality, identical with, yet unsullied by, voice.

Becoming an Authentic Musical Self

The rupture of voice and vocality precipitated by music not only defines the becoming human of evolutionary accounts and the emergence of the speaking subject, but also defines the local conditions necessary for the emergence of an authentic musical self. In the following ethnographic story, particular instances of bad music are narratively enacted to provide concrete examples of the theoretically bad music of the previous stories, musics which threaten, or at least pretend to threaten, the music/language ideology on which they depend.

I have recently embarked on a fieldwork project at Peabody Conservatory, talking to both students and faculty about their musical guilty pleasures. Although the project is at its beginning stages, it is already clear that a musician's musical guilty pleasures are measured against an autobiographical narrative of musical self-making. They are framed in terms of the voice/vocality rupture, and in ways that are similar both to Kristeva's psychoanalytical voice and the metaphysical voice of evolutionary accounts. The general story line begins with the mythical unity of voice/vocality prior to the emergence of the musical self, proceeds to the rupture of voice/vocality and a musical becoming human, and concludes with an awareness of the lifelong and impossible quest to become an authentic musical self through the reunification of musical persona, i.e., voice, and the music itself, i.e., vocality.

I will only be able to touch briefly on one such story. Reece is my former student, a brilliant, 23-year-old gay, ex-Catholic composer with a great sense of humor, who recently graduated from the Master's program at Peabody Conservatory. Reece's guilty pleasures can be traced back to adolescence, as can all of the narratives that I have recorded to date. Predictably, Reece's passage through adolescence is accompanied by music as an emblem of identity, specifically the pop music of his peer group; yet, as a composer, and thus a future shaman-to-be, Reece's adolescence is also accompanied by a musical fall from grace, an understanding that music begins with the unraveling of the voice/vocality unity, and that his quest as a composer will be to impossibly reunite the two. Just as the voices of our prehuman ancestors are conceptualized as unintentional emotion calls, and hence an index of truth, Reece's naive 18-year-old self, and the musical language he knew at that time, is now a shameful reminder of what from his present vantage point is a premusical self, or at least a pre-*authentically* musical self, yet ironically, one that in its ignorance of vocal unity was therefore enmeshed in an authentic musical presence. This shameful, dare I say *abject*, naiveté, his acknowledgement that he *was* that awful music, is also tied up with a painful experience of coming out as a gay man and hating music like ABBA that was supposedly part of his gay cultural inheritance. In proper Kristevian fashion, Reece's premusical and hence abject self is only provisionally expunged from his composer self; Reece cannot leave his shameful voices alone, knowing that the only way to regain admittance to Eden is to contain the abject by invoking primordial vocal unity.

Reece explicitly invokes his premusical self in a composition entitled the "Agnostic Altar Boy's Waltz," which deals with his becoming unCatholic. He specifically tries to reunite the musical honesty of his former self with the dishonesty of a popular style, an explicit acknowledgment of vocal rupture and the quest toward vocal reunification. Reece elaborates as follows:

> It's like an embarrassing song, it's not ironic enough . . . It's supposed to be from the perspective of 18-year old Reece, this really naïve person who doesn't know what to do, who is wondering about God and faith . . . I use the musical language that I knew at the time, to make it sound more naive, so it's really simple, and kinda sounds like a musical, at points it's just a little too saccharine. I was really aiming for that, because this person was trying to sing something so honestly, but the music was so dishonest sounding, what some people would call dishonest, because it's so formulaic and saccharine.

After we'd listened to the piece, Reece laughed uncomfortably, and we had the following exchange.

ME: To me that's not embarrassing at all, but it's embarrassing to you?
REECE: Kind of. Yeah.
ME: Because it's about your former self?
REECE: Yeah, and just the musical language it uses, too . . . It's just that I want to be really frank, shockingly frank, I guess . . . So I do that by writing music that coming out of a conservatory composer would be really banal, and shocking, I guess, and to kind of temper that with moments where composition gets more difficult or different.

For Reece, then, the abject is triggered by banal music, especially pop music. Consider Reece's reaction to ABBA. He supposedly hates ABBA, but of course, things are not so simple.

REECE: The students listen to pop, its not a big deal, it becomes more what kind of pop you're listening to. Is it what I like? If it is, it's ok, but if it's too trashy it's not acceptable. Like ABBA. (laugh) ABBA's terrible.
ME: And you like it because?
REECE: Um, well, it's *good*. It's really catchy, and everybody listens to it, it's become this huge cliché, not to mention that it's become this really big gay icon, which is something that I feel guilty listening to because I don't want to be associated with that at the same time, so it's really strange how that's happened. I used to listen to ABBA just because I really liked it, and because it was kind of a gay campy thing to do, and now I don't like listen to it because I'm trying to get away from that. I'm kinda denying my past, I guess, in a way.

ABBA continues to surface several times during our conversation, especially in reference to Reece's coming out period, and he is again drawn into the abject after thinking about ABBA for only a few seconds.

REECE: I mean, I just felt like when I was coming out, stuff that I liked, I didn't get along with anyone because I didn't ini-

> tially like ABBA or anything like that, the superficial, gay culture, and I had a hard time.

ME: So, do you like ABBA, or you don't like ABBA?

REECE: Well, ABBA's really catchy, you can't *not* like ABBA.

ME: Should we listen to ABBA?

REECE: It's just too painful . . . Um, it's really embarrassing for some reason, I didn't think it would be like that.

Not surprisingly, Reece's embarrassment over "banal" pop music is central to his compositional quest, as is strikingly illustrated in his "Piece for Viola and Turntables," where he juxtaposes a classical viola line with samples of house music.

REECE: So I wanted to create this tension between a classical viola line and this turntable music . . . So, I was weaving, it would move apart and then together, apart and together. So this is kind of how I feel about pop music in general. I don't want to laud it, but I'm kind of attracted to it at the same time anyway.

Reece's reference to vocal melding and unmelding, the coming together and moving apart of pop and classical, seems to be an astoundingly unambiguous invocation of the voice/vocality story as assimilated to his own musical and sexual becoming human.

So what are we left with? Three stories with the same plot: a primordial vocal unity, a rupture between voice and vocality and a consequent becoming human, followed by a full-fledged humanity defined by the quest to put voice and vocality back together again as a member of *homo sapiens sapiens,* a speaking subject, or a composer. I have also suggested that the enigma of music that upholds these stories can be "at least partially demystified when understood as an entailment of the voice/vocality opposition, a polythetic opposition where the distinctions between social personae and their material voices bleed into one another."[34]

And what of "bad music"? I suspect that music is bad to the extent that it reveals the abject conditions of its constructedness, reveals that there is no prior unity of voice/vocality to be experienced, no time before self. Bad music is music out of place, music that in its abjection "disturbs identity, systems, order."[35] I also suspect that such music can only be known in retrospect, music that lets us in on the secret that it can not do what it promises to do, it cannot guarantee social reality by masquerading as unmediated vocality.

However, this acknowledgement of the abject is not sufficient to characterize bad music, or even music-in-general. Despite Kristeva's homage to a *Revolution in Poetic Language,*[36] the musics of the semiotic and its protolanguage counterparts are hardly revolutionary. Indeed, imagining an actively abject role for bad music in these scenarios would require a music that *prevented* the evolutionary emergence of humans, that watered down the gene pool, that sparked a feminist revolt and a refusal to mate, or that forever barred entry to the symbolic order. This truly bad music is unthinkable, because it would never have allowed language, and thus humans or subjects, to emerge.

Reece, while he does not concern himself with this particular story, understands its implications with an uncanny precision. He knows both the limitations and potentials of bad music; he even writes pieces about it. For Reece, bad music not only gives him the narrative structure for his own musical becoming; more importantly, it reveals the social conditions of representation that allow for the making and unmaking of selves, and thus the potential to tell other stories about other things. By juxtaposing Reece's story with other narratives of becoming, I have used bad music to put the good music in music/language ideologies under siege, disputing its claims to uphold an essential humanity and subjectivity. Indeed, without bad music, that which hovers at the borders of a unified vocal presence, the rupture between voice and vocality would go unnoticed, and the fully human voice would never be heard.

NOTES

1. A draft of this chapter was first presented at the annual meeting of the Society for Ethnomusicology, Detroit, 2001. Special thanks to Reece Dano for his participation in the Guilty Pleasures Project at the Peabody Conservatory of the Johns Hopkins University, and for permission to quote him in this paper. Some parts of the argument presented here have appeared in more detail and with different emphases in previous publications. See Elizabeth Tolbert, "Untying the Music/Language Knot," in *Music, Sensation and Sensuality,* ed., Linda Austern (New York: Routledge, 2002), 77–95; Tolbert, "Music and Meaning: An Evolutionary Story," *Psychology of Music* 29:1 (2001): 84–94; Tolbert, "The Enigma of Music, the Voice of Reason: "Music," "Language," and Becoming Human," *New Literary History* 32: 3 (2001): 451-465; Tolbert, "Voice, Metaphysics, and Community" in *Pain and its Transformations,* eds., Sarah Coakley and Kay Shelemay (Cambridge, MA: Harvard University Press, in press).

2. Steven Pinker, *How the Mind Works* (New York: Norton, 1997), 528.

3. Ibid., 534.

4. Ibid., 528–29. Pinker asserts that music is "useless," a mere "technology." "Compared with language . . . music could vanish from our species and the rest of our lifestyle would be virtually unchanged. " For a critique of Pinker from a feminist and Derridean perspective see Tolbert, "Untying the Music/Language Knot," 82–84. See also Tolbert, "The Enigma of Music," 451.

5. Pinker, 521. "[T]he more biologically frivolous and vain the activity, the more people exalt it. Art, music, literature, wit, religion and philosophy are thought to be not just pleasurable but noble."

6. For a brief historical overview of this idea in reference to "autonomous music," see Wayne Bowman, *Philosophical Perspectives on Music* (New York: Oxford University Press, 1998), 133–97.

7. Pinker, *How the Mind Works,* 534–38.

8. Geoffrey Miller, "Evolution of Human Music through Sexual Selection." in *The Origins of Music,* eds., Nils Wallin, Bjorn Merker, and Steven Brown (Cambridge, MA: MIT Press, 2000), 329–60.

9. Although he does not posit music as a Transcendental Signifier, see Gary Tomlinson for discussion of the effects of Derridean logocentrism on music ideology in his "Ideologies of Aztec Song," *Journal of the American Musicological Society* 48.3 (1995): 343–79.

10. Ellen Dissanayake, *Art and Intimacy: How the Arts Began* (Seattle and London: University of Washington Press, 2000), 205. Her point is similar to Miller's but more socially nuanced, in that she understands reproductive fitness to encompass social reproduction and elaboration of the mother/infant bond. She proposes that the evolved predispositions that underlie the "arts" are also those that allowed for the social skills necessary for the evolutionary emergence of culture. Thus, music can be judged in terms of the evolved predispositions for mutuality, belonging to a social group, developing life competence, creating meaning, and elaborating on experience (8), and in a way that allows for the fact that some experiences are "qualitatively more meaningful, valuable, pleasurable, or desirable than others" (208, see also 205–25). For further commentary see Elizabeth Tolbert, "Review. Art and Intimacy: How the Arts Began, Ellen Dissanayake," *Musicae Scientiae* (2002): 275–79.

11. For a more detailed discussion of this idea see Tolbert, "Untying the Music/Language Knot," 77–80.

12. Disagreements about the adaptive status of language revolve around domain-specific vs. domain-general explanations. Interestingly, concerns about music's adaptive status are not framed this way. Although Pinker, for example, suggests that music is a byproduct of language-specific adaptations, it is not generally hypothesized that language is a by-product of music-specific adaptations (for an exception, see Mario Vaneechoutte and John Skoyles, "The memetic origin of language: modern humans as musical primates." *Journal of Memetics—Evolutionary Models of Information Transmission,* 2 (1998): http://jom-emit.cfpm.org/1998/vol2/vaneechoutte_m&skoyles_jr.html), although co-evolutionary scenarios have been proposed (e.g., Chris Knight, "Ritual/Speech Co-evolution: A Solution to the Problem of Deception," in *Approaches*

to the Evolution of Language: Social and Cognitive Bases, eds., James R. Hurford, Michael Studdert-Kennedy, and Chris Knight (Cambridge: Cambridge University Press, 1998), 69–91; Steven Brown, "The 'musilanguage' model of music evolution," in *The Origins of Music,* eds., Nils Wallin, Bjorn Merker, and Steven Brown (Cambridge, MA: MIT Press, 2000), 271–300). For a proposal supporting domain specificity in language evolution, see Steven Mithen, *The Prehistory of the Mind: A Search for the Origins of Art, Religion and Science* (London: Thames & Hudson, 1996). For an argument supporting the emergence of language from domain-general adaptations, see Merlin Donald, "Preconditions for the Evolution of Protolanguages," in *The Descent of Mind: Psychological Perspectives on Hominid Evolution,* eds. Michael C. Corballis and Stephen E. G. Lea (Oxford: Oxford University Press, 1999), 138–54.

13. For a variety of proposals on protolanguage and the evolutionary origins of music see *The Origins of Music,* especially Brown, "The "Musilanguage" Model of Music Evolution." See also Merlin Donald, *Origins of the Modern Mind* (Cambridge: Harvard University Press, 1991), especially 37–41, 180–86; idem, "Preconditions for the Evolution of Protolanguages."

14. To clarify, I am not suggesting that the indexical qualities of voice are immaterial to socio-linguistic meaning, but merely that they are logically distinct from their symbolic referents. I draw on Deacon, who using a Peircean framework and with a similar focus on the logic of sign/object relationships, suggests that the evolution of language represents a progression from indexical to symbolic reference (Terrence Deacon, *The Symbolic Species: The Co-Evolution of Language and the Brain* (New York: Norton, 1997), 69–101).

15. Chris Knight, "Ritual/Speech Co-evolution."

16. Tolbert, "Music and Meaning," 91.

17. Dunn and Jones were among the first to present the voice/vocality distinction in the context of music scholarship. As literary theorists, they challenge the concept of voice as a literary construct, and call for more attention to the non-linguistic, performative, and 'audible' voice (Leslie Dunn and Nancy A. Jones, "Introduction," in *Embodied Voices: Representing Female Vocality in Western Cultures,* eds., Leslie Dunn and Nancy A. Jones (Cambridge: Cambridge University Press, 1994), 1–3). My concept of the voice/vocality distinction has been heavily influenced by Steven Feld's and Aaron Fox's discussion of voice as both a *metaphor* for "social position and power," and as *vocality*, "the embodiment of spoken and sung performance" "Music and Language," *Annual Review of Anthropology* 23: (1994): 26. Feld and Fox conceptualize vocality as a "social practice that is locally understood as a conventional index of authority, evidence, and experiential truth," and therefore amenable to socio-cultural analysis (idem., "Music," *Journal of Linguistic Anthropology* 9: 1–2 (2000): 161).

18. There is an immense anthropological literature on the power of ritual performance to ground socio-cultural truths, much of which assumes music's unmediated status. For example, in a classic text, Maurice Bloch conflates illocutionary force with unmediated vocality by claiming that "you cannot argue with a song," i.e., music's illocutionary meaning trumps the propositional meaning of language ("Symbols, Song, Dance and Features of Articulation: Is Religion an

Extreme Form of Traditional Authority?" *Archive of European Sociology* 15 (1974): 55–81), 71 .

19. Greg Urban, *Metaphysical Community: The Interplay of the Senses and the Intellect* (Austin: University of Texas Press, 1996), 251.

20. Gary Tomlinson, *Metaphysical Song: An Essay on Opera* (Princeton: Princeton University Press, 1999), 83–92.

21. For a more detailed elaboration of this idea see Tolbert, "Voice, Metaphysics and Community."

22. The assertion of the feminization of music is almost axiomatic in contemporary feminist musical scholarship. For an overview of some of the issues see Susan McClary, *Feminine Endings: Music, Gender, and Sexuality* (Minneapolis: University of Minnesota Press, 1991), 3–34; Tolbert, "Reshaping a Discipline: Musicology and Feminism in the 1990's," *Feminist Studies* 19: 2 (1993), 399–423; Tolbert, "Paradigm Dissonances: Music Theory, Cultural Studies, Feminist Criticism," *Perspectives of New Music* 32: 1 (1994), 68–85; Ellen Koskoff, "An Introduction to Women, Music, and Culture," in *Women and Music in Cross-Cultural Perspective,* ed., Ellen Koskoff (New York: Greenwood Press, 1989 [1987]), 1–23; Ruth A. Solie, "Introduction: On "Difference","" in *Musicology and Difference: Gender and Sexuality in Music Scholarship,* ed., Ruth Solie (Berkeley: University of California Press, 1993), 1–20; Dunn and Jones, "Introduction," 1–13.

23. For further discussion of this idea from a Derridean perspective, see Tolbert, "Untying the Music/Language Knot," 82–83.

24. Julia Kristeva, *Powers of Horror: An Essay on Abjection* , trans. Louis S. Roudiez (New York: Columbia University Press, 1982). Reprinted in *The Portable Kristeva,* ed. Kelly Oliver (New York: Columbia University Press, 2002), 229–263.

25. Julia Kristeva, *Revolution in Poetic Language,* trans. Margaret Waller (New York: Columbia University Press, 1984). Reprinted in *The Portable Kristeva,* ed. Kelly Oliver (New York: Columbia University Press, 2002), 27–92. See especially 32–70.

26. Kristeva, *Powers of Horror,* 261–62.

27. Kristeva, *Revolution in Poetic Language,* 43–44.

28. Elizabeth Grosz, *Volatile Bodies: Toward a Corporeal Feminism* (Bloomington and Indianapolis: Indiana University Press), 71.

29. Ibid., 78.

30. Kristeva, *Powers of Horror,* 231.

31. Idem, *Revolution in Poetic Language,* 40. Kristeva terms this interface the *thetic,* and claims that "all enunciation . . . is thetic."

32. Ibid., 57–59.

33. Kristeva conceptualizes the body as " clean and proper . . . in the sense of incorporated and incorporable" (*Powers of Horror,* 235–36).

34. Tolbert, "The Enigma of Music," 463.

35. Kristeva, *Powers of Horror,* 232.

36. Kristeva, *Revolution in Poetic Language,* 27–31. According to Kristeva, the revolutionary irruption of the semiotic (i.e., music) in language results in "exploding the subject and its ideological limits" (29).

PART II

Canonizing the Popular, Discovering the Mundane

6

Does Kenny G Play Bad Jazz?
A Case Study

CHRISTOPHER WASHBURNE

"**K**enny G's playing is lame ass, jive, pseudo bluesy, out-of-tune, noodling, wimped out, and fucked up . . ."[1] These are the words of guitarist Pat Metheny concerning Kenny Gorelick's choice to overdub a saxophone solo on Louis Armstrong's "What a Wonderful World." The overdubbing was viewed by the jazz community as a virtual desecration, tasteless, and to some, the equivalent of committing jazz necrophilia. This track, released in 1999 on a record entitled *Classics in the Key of G* (see figure 1), provided an opportune occasion for many within the jazz community to voice their disdain for this controversial musician, specifically, and to comment upon, in their opinion, one troubling direction contemporary jazz has taken, generally.

For decades tensions between commercialism and artistic integrity have fueled numerous debates in the jazz world. Throughout the music's history there have been performers who have strategically straddled stylistic lines of popular music and jazz, such as Paul Whiteman, Louis Jordan, Frank Sinatra, Herb Alpert, and Quincy Jones. In the 1930s, jazz, often synonymous with popular music, reached the apex of its commercial appeal. At that time, jazz records represented close to 70 percent of the recording industry's market share.

The post World War II jazz scene, to the contrary, has experienced a continual downward economic trend, forcing each generation of jazz musicians to cope with their dwindling market share. Many opt for the solution that their predecessors have been using for years; namely that of turning to the popular music of the day and incorporating elements and repertoire from that body of music. Today's scene is no different. With the jazz market barely encompassing 3.3 precent of record sales at best,[2] and with fewer clubs and venues throughout the United States, America's current jazz scene has retreated to the concert

Figure 1   Cover art for Kenny G's *Classics in the Key of G* (Arista Records 1999).

hall, National Public Radio, overseas, and to the Ivory Tower. However, there are a few exceptions.

One group of musicians, in particular, has come to represent a commercially viable alternative to the lifestyle of the starving artist or professorship that a life in jazz most often entails. They play a style of music that first emerged in the late 1980s, which is derived from earlier jazz rock and fusion styles. It is known as "smooth jazz," "contemporary jazz," or more pejoratively, "jazz-lite," "Happy jazz," "hot tub jazz," and "fuzak." One musician, namely, Kenny Gorelick (Kenny G) (b.1956), an appellation that elicits much ire from many jazz musicians, critics, and serious listeners (really a pariah to jazz purists), at times has commanded roughly 50 percent of that 3 percent sliver of jazz record sales.[3] Gorelick has accomplished what most jazz musicians have not been able to do, that is, he has a lucrative music career playing his own music. His website's claim that he is "the best-selling instrumentalist/musician in the world, having sold over 30 million records . . ." is not far off the mark.[4] As a result of his wide exposure, Kenny G provides many listeners with their first introduction to music that includes the word "jazz" as part of its stylistic label and thereby he assumes a significant definitorial role in popular conceptions of what jazz is. Writer Stanley Crouch comments;

The problem emerged with fusion music in the 1960's, which made it difficult for people to tell the difference between jazz and instrumental pop music. Now, because of the title ["smooth jazz"], some people are led to believe that jazz is anything with a pop rhythm section and an instrumental improvisation. Smooth jazz makes it more difficult to know what jazz is for the average person, and when people finally hear real jazz, they always say, 'Why did I spend so much time listening to garbage?'[5]

The problem with Gorelick is that most in the jazz community claim that he is not playing jazz, and consequently he and his smooth jazz colleagues are seldom mentioned in the scholarly literature.

The discursive relationship of smooth jazz to the jazz community at large (meaning musicians, critics, scholars, industry people, as well as consumers), which often manifests itself in ways that are derisive and visceral, is particularly revealing. It is clear that a complete rupture has arisen between those who consider themselves "serious jazz listeners and performers" and smooth jazz. Smooth jazz music and its practitioners are distanced, with scorn, derision, and animosity, from the "jazz tradition" regardless of the fact that the word "jazz" is included as part of the style's name. For instance, pianist Fred Hersch comments, "My gut reaction is that it's like Paul Whiteman trying to make a lady out of jazz . . . he [Kenny G] is not a jazz musician. He's the only person I've ever seen who is able to smirk while playing the saxophone. I don't know what more I need to say."[6] Chicago critic Neil Tesser adds, "Scholarly articles discussing Kenny G are an obvious contradiction in terms. Now, if you want to consider a treatise on Kenny-G humor, I think you might have something. . . ."[7]. Another example of this pervasive humoristic approach appears in the cover story from the May 2001 issue of *Jazziz* magazine where one writer, Michael Roberts, explored the results of listening to Gorelick's music for 10 straight hours. The cover of that issue (see figure 2) portrays Kenny G in a crucified, General Custer-like caricature with South Park references. One can hardly imagine this type of treatment for other musicians. Depicting, for example, Charlie Parker or John Coltrane in this light would be considered sacrilege.

When jazz print publications devote more serious space to Gorelick, editors feel compelled to write apologetic disclaimers, something which is not typically done for other subjects. For instance, in 1999 editor Lee Mergner wrote in *JazzTimes*, "Before you cancel your subscription, let me explain why we featured Kenny G in this issue . . .

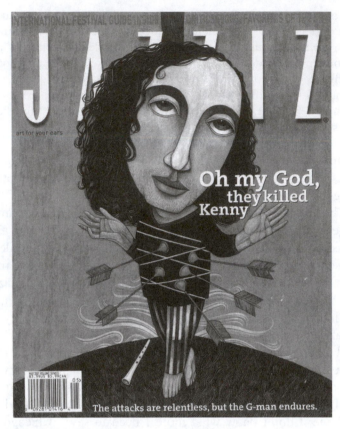

Figure 2   Cover of the May (2001) issue of *Jazziz* magazine.

we have ignored the man for many years, but it hasn't hurt any. Maybe it's time to at least hear what he has to say."[8]

It must be noted that Gorelick is not an innocent bystander simply suffering as the jazzerati's favorite whipping boy, but to some extent he fosters such ill will by publicly making naïve and irresponsible statements. One example appeared on the Barnes & Noble website in 2002 during an interview with writer Ted Pankin:

KENNY G: Charlie Parker would squeak a lot, and that's why they called him Bird, because his reed would chirp.

TED PANKIN: You think that's why they called him Bird? That's interesting.

KG: That is why they called him Bird. That was the deal. He played so fast, and his reed would chirp because it . . . I don't know, it just couldn't take the speed of his fingers.[9]

The story behind Parker's nickname is well known among jazz musicians and fans and has been widely documented and publicized.[10] That Gorelick speaks so matter-of-factly about the topic calls into question just how much he really cares about, or has made the effort to learn of the jazz greats that he claims to be so indebted to. This erroneous statement is laughable on the one hand, yet considering his popularity and prominence as a "jazz" musician in the popular imagination, such statements can prove to be destructive and viewed as an abuse of his powerful (economic/cultural/political) position.

Does Kenny G play jazz? I pose this question not in terms of what his music is in any essentialized way, but rather, I am concerned with how this genre is contested, defended, by whom, and why? Should he, along with other smooth jazz musicians, be included under the jazz tradition umbrella? Who determines what jazz is? Why is he omitted from jazz historical narratives? As scholars, musicians, critics and self-appointed custodians of jazz, why do we listen with such disdain to his music? Does he play "bad" jazz? In the analysis that follows, I shall attempt to answer these questions by taking a closer look at the historical genealogy leading up to Kenny Gorelick; at the role of economic and marketing strategies; at the racial component of his popularity; and finally, at the implications involved with the acknowledgement of his music as jazz and how that bears on canon formation within jazz scholarship. I shall venture to argue that cracking open our narrow definitions and notions of stylistic heritage will enrich our perspective of how cultural narratives come to be and are constantly renegotiated.

What Smooth Jazz Is: Definitions and History

When delving into defining smooth jazz and mapping its history, one becomes immediately aware of why discussions concerning the style are so contentious. The problem begins with inclusion of the "j" word. Racially, socially, and economically charged definitorial arguments have abounded concerning the word jazz since it emerged as a delineated style. With every innovative step and/or stylistic change, there has been a contingency within the jazz community, which resisted the word's use as a label for designating the newest trend. Comments made by Louis Armstrong concerning bebop spring to mind. Smooth jazz poses no new issue here, but merely can be seen as this debate's most recent incarnation. However, what has changed is the amount of cultural capital at stake, due in part to the economic marginalization of jazz.

Smooth jazz first emerged in the 1980s as a separate, recognizable style. To fully understand its components, it is important to examine the historical factors that spurred this stylistic formation. With the advent of bebop in the 1940s, the commercial appeal of jazz declined and continued to do so for the next 30 years. No longer were the most novel styles of jazz accompanying the most recent dance crazes, and performances became introspective, with more emphasis on improvisation and new levels of dissonance, where personalized artistic expression explicitly superceded functions of mere entertainment. In the early 1960s, the popularity of jazz reached its lowest levels since its inception. It was the combination of the unpopularity of free jazz styles (largely due to their more hermetic and challenging qualities), the rock'n'roll invasion (Beatlemania in the mid-sixties), and the rise in popularity of R&B and soul among the African American communities—which challenged the commercial viability of jazz. For instance, even though musicians like Archie Shepp, Max Roach, and Sonny Rollins were extremely vocal about the civil rights movement, it was not their music that would serve as popular anthems for "the cause." Instead R&B and soul artists and their music, like Sam Cooke's "A Change Is Gonna Come," Curtis Mayfield's "People Get Ready," and James Brown's "Say It Loud, I'm Black and I'm Proud," served that purpose, thereby excluding jazz artists from lucrative protest markets and in some ways divorcing the music from the everyday lives of African Americans.

According to Stuart Nicholson, one of the few scholars who has written a book focusing on jazz rock and fusion (although smooth jazz is not explored to any extent), corporate strategies employed by record companies underwent a revamping in the 1960s, stemming in part from the unprecedented success of the Beatles. They dramatically changed how artists were marketed and they raised the level of expectations for sales.[11] Rock acts selling over 100,000 units became the industry's standard model, and one in which most jazz artists could not compete.

Companies sought only those jazz artists who had potential to cross over to, and share in, the new demographic that was purchasing rock records.

In such a climate, many jazz artists were forced to refocus their artistic direction along the lines of this altered socioeconomic reality. Early experiments by jazz artists who incorporated elements from rock were not, however, prompted by commercial pressures alone, but were a result of a long-term relationship between jazz and popular styles. *Down Beat* magazine's Dan Morgenstern comments,

> Today, in retrospect, there are musicians who may tell interviewers, if asked, that their erstwhile flirtations with what came to be known as fusion were in response to pressure from record producers, but most of them were not reluctant brides . . . jazz had become an extremely low recording priority in the 60s, and any musician with the chance to record naturally wanted to reach as wide a public as possible. Moreover, there were tunes and rhythms in popular music that appealed to jazz players—not just Beatles numbers . . .[12]

Since early jazz, musicians had been borrowing heavily from popular music and continuing in that tradition, musicians responded by recording covers of already successful popular tunes. And yet, there was a bit of a lag in terms of the actual success of those borrowings resulting in a plethora of misguided jazz-rock mixings in the beginning of this period. One need to look no further than Duke Ellington's 1966 recording of the Beatles "I Want To Hold Your Hand" on his *Ellington 66* release, or Count Basie's *Basie's Beatle Bag* released in the same year.[13] As a direct result of this new stylistic direction, on October 5, 1967 the cover of *Down Beat* (see figure 3) declared, "Jazz As We Know It Is Dead" and the magazine subsequently expanded their coverage to include rock.[14] Further, in 1969 George Wein responded to this change by including rock and R&B acts for the first time at the Newport Jazz Festival, a programming trend, which continues for many festivals.[15]

Even though rock and jazz mixtures had been going on for some time (early jazz rock experimenters were Larry Coryell, Jeremy Steig, Charles Lloyd, Keith Jarrett),[16] the release of Miles Davis's *Bitches Brew* recording in 1969 is still viewed as the galvanizing "fusion" event. Davis' stature as a trendsetter within the jazz community ensured wide exposure and solidified the direction that jazz would take for many years to come. Davis hired young musicians who could play rock,

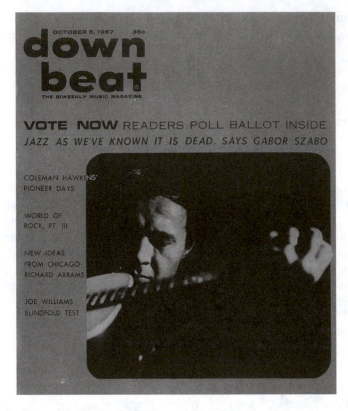

Figure 3   Cover of the October 5, 1967 issue of *Down Beat*.

added electronic instruments, replaced the swing feel with rock and funk grooves, used loud volumes in concert, and adjusted his dress and personal image accordingly. His innovations sparked a new commercially successful style called "fusion," "jazz rock," or "jazz-rock-fusion."[17] Despite harsh criticism by jazz purists, *Bitches Brew* and Davis' new groups brought rock listeners into the jazz world and set new trends in jazz experimentation and innovation—moreover the careers of many of his sidemen who would become influential in the fusion style were launched. Those included John McLaughlin, who formed the Mahavishnu Orchestra, Chick Corea and Return to Forever, Herbie Hancock's Headhunters, and Joe Zawinul, who formed Weather Report.

The commercial success of *Bitches Brew*, followed by Herbie Hancock's *Headhunters* (1973), prompted record companies to adjust their marketing and production strategies for these jazz-rock-fusion groups. By aligning jazz rock and fusion musicians with their rock and pop counterparts and supplying large production and promotion budgets, jazz-rock-fusion was taken from the margins and main-streamed by the mid-1970s. Columbia Records began to fill their rosters with artists whose stance was overtly commercial, such as, Walt Bolden, the Chris Hinze Combination, Jaroslav, and John Blair.[18] Press coverage also mirrored this strategic centralizing move. For instance, *Rolling Stone Magazine* declared 1974 as "the year of jazz-rock-fusion" and included articles on Herbie Hancock, Miles Davis, the Mahavishnu Orchestra, and the like.[19]

Serving as the standard model for innovation and change, the popular music industry often employs marketing strategies whereby music on and from the margins (cultural, political, and/or economic) is co-opted, appropriated, and transformed into the mainstream. This is nothing new. Indeed these strategies played a major role in the popularization of jazz in the early part of the twentieth century. However, what is significant about the renewed mainstreaming in the 1970s was that it directly set the stage for the emergence of smooth jazz. For the purpose of this chapter, I will briefly touch upon subsequent stylistic developments in order to construct a lineage that, I believe, leads us to Kenny G.

Save for Weather Report, most of the hard-edged jazz-rock-fusion bands formed in the late sixties and early seventies had disbanded by the mid-seventies. Representative of the next generation, roughly the mid-seventies to the mid-eighties, were groups such as Grover Washington Jr., George Benson, Pat Metheny, Chuck Mangione, Spyro Gyro, the Crusaders, and Jeff Lorber Fusion (Kenny Gorelick began performing with Lorber in 1977. Steeping the young saxophonist in the fusion style, Lorber's band provided a place for Gorelick to develop his smooth jazz sound). Along with this new generation came stylistic changes that reflected what was happening in the pop and rock worlds, where more slick, pop-oriented production techniques were employed and the rough edges of fusion (i.e., loud volumes, high energy, and raucous rock solos) were smoothed out, creating a more soft fusion sound.[20] Additionally, in the late seventies and early eighties soul influences were added which increased the already large African American fan base.[21] Examples of songs that reflected this change include Grover Washington's "Just the Two of Us" and George Winston's quiet piano music.

An even more polished sheen was introduced to the music in 1986, with the release of Kenny G's *Duotones*. As *Bitches Brew* galvanized the fusion style, *Duotones* did the same for smooth jazz. The album's unprecedented commercial success and the longevity of its popularity, it remained high on the charts through 1987, established a nonadventurous and highly accessible sound that would become known as "smooth jazz." Assisting in this process was the 1987 launch of "the Wave," KTWV 94.7 FM, a radio station in Los Angeles that programmed New Age music, instrumental and vocal soft fusion. Due in part to Gorelick's success, New Age music was slowly phased out and the station helped established what would become known as the "smooth jazz format." According to Ralph Stewart, assistant music director at the station, Kenny G's music defines what they do. "We play a lot of instrumentalists, but he [Kenny G] is the only one that is a household name. In fact, we often use him to explain what we do at the station to someone who has never listened in."[22] In the early 1990s WNUA in Chicago (1993) and KTWV in Los Angeles (1994) began to program smooth jazz exclusively and numerous stations across the country soon followed.

Even though, as my prehistory is meant to show, the music played by Kenny G stems from a long tradition of pop and jazz mixings, the label "smooth jazz" is a conspicuously fabricated construct that originated in consumer research studies conducted by Broadcast Architecture, a radio consulting firm. The company found that "smooth" was the most frequently used term listeners employed to describe this mainly instrumental musical style, whose defining elements include R&B, Latin, and soul-infused grooves, heavy use of synthesizers, easily recognizable melodies, slick pop-like studio productions, and jazz-like soloing. Guitarist Earl Klugh, further characterizes the style as "pop instrumental music." Dave Koz, smooth jazz performer, calls it "melodic music that doesn't have too many rough edges." And, jazz producer Michael Cuscuna views it in a less complimentary light: "It's smooth like a lobotomy flattens out the ridges on a brain."[23]

Such a radio friendly aesthetic provides few intellectual and emotional challenges to listeners, and smooth jazz musicians produce recordings that overtly cater to their fan base, creating a clear dividing line between making art and selling records. In fact, the music is so deeply entrenched with economics and its relation to radio airplay that Jay Beckenstein, saxophonist/leader of Spyro Gyra, comments

". . . smooth jazz isn't a musical style–it is a radio format . . ."[24] The format is sometimes referred to as NAC (new adult contemporary) and is dictated by companies, like Broadcast Architecture, whose executives construct play lists based off listener surveys and detailed market analysis of mass reception patterns. Commercial FM stations use these play lists to dictate their programming where a fixed listing of selections are played repeatedly. These are drawn from current *Billboard* charts mixed in with some classics and new releases. This list numbers around 30–40 songs. They are usually played in 6–8 hour cycles and typically 3–4 selections are added and subtracted per week.

Perhaps the most significant aspect of the smooth jazz phenomenon is that for the first time since the swing era a form of jazz is receiving wide exposure on commercial radio. In 2002 there were roughly 160 radio stations in the United States that had adopted the format. Arbitron ratings measure total listenership, which in turn dictate advertising prices. Throughout the late 1990s and early 2000s, smooth jazz stations garnered some of the highest Arbitron ratings. The top fifty smooth jazz stations had combined advertising revenues of over $190 million each year.[25] This is big business.

Since the history of jazz is coterminous with and inextricably linked to the history of radio, jazz musicians have always depended, to a greater or lesser extent, on this media for their survival. Airplay on jazz radio serves several economic functions for musicians. It advertises recordings, generates royalties, and it popularizes individual musicians, thereby establishing their marketability on the live performing circuit. What makes this smooth jazz format so significant in today's jazz scene is that since 1994, when KJAZ of Alameda, California went off the air, no commercial FM jazz radio stations remain which have not adopted the smooth jazz format. Additionally, many public radio stations have significantly limited or eliminated their jazz programming altogether. With their media outlets greatly reduced, jazz artists who do not play smooth jazz find themselves in a dire situation.

Musicians such as Thelonious Monk, Ella Fitzgerald, Duke Ellington, and even first generation fusion groups are deliberately omitted from smooth jazz play lists because, in research groups, they get a negative rating. Comments about these musicians range from "the music sounds old like my dad's music" to "it's too challenging." Or worse, "It's too jazzy." In fact, being jazzy is a downright handicap. David Neidhart, vice president of Verve Records commented that tracks receiving comments like "too aggressive," "too much soloing," and "too jazzy"are frequently rejected by radio executives.[26] To accommodate airplay on commercial radio, record companies, at times, will release two versions of the same song, one in its original form, and the other with the jazziness—extended soloing or overly dissonant sections—edited out.

What sets smooth jazz musicians apart from other jazz performers today, aside from obvious stylistic differences, is how companies are marketing these artists. Stemming from the 1960s Beatles/rock model, and since refined with jazz rock and fusion, companies have adapted economic and media strategies with the large budgets typically reserved only for money making pop acts. For instance, Kenny G's *Standards in the Key of G* (1999) release coincided with a television campaign featuring major talk shows (the *Oprah Winfrey Show* included), a PBS special, a satellite media tour, sales promotions at Starbucks, and a Barnes & Noble's Internet sales site with Kenny G as the first featured artist, just to mention a few. This wide exposure inevitably can, and for Kenny G does, translate into sales.[27] His media omnipotence bars access to other musicians and styles, and in general, serves to homogenize the smooth jazz sound (I am referring to the numerous copycat releases that emulate his productions from those banking on his formula for their own commercial success), and, most importantly, his high visibility serves to reinvent popular conceptions of what jazz is (for many, smooth jazz is the first, and at times only, jazz style to which they are exposed). Independent labels and artists cannot afford the same level of media visibility and access, nor do they enjoy the same opportunities through radio airplay. One result of this marketing inequity has been a deeper retreat of other jazz styles from the popular toward the art world, forcing jazz musicians to seek funding and support elsewhere. To the jazz community, Kenny G's sales numbers, along with the mass appeal of smooth jazz, are serious threats.

Further at issue is the interplay of racial politics. In its early stages, smooth jazz attracted mostly African American audiences, most likely due to its heavy borrowing from soul and R&B as well as the prominence of several black musicians who excelled in the style (e.g., George Benson and Grover Washington Jr.). Although the music's consumer demographic has broadened in the last few years, it still remains one of the best selling music styles within the African American community, especially with the black middle classes. Kenny G himself remarked, [my audience] ". . . used to be mainly a black [one] until I started getting a lot of radio airplay from mainstream pop stations in 1986. Before that, the only airplay I got was in the 'quiet storm' formats on the black stations."[28]

Attesting to his popularity among African Americans are comments made by Louis Farrakhan, a voice that has notoriously represented black separatism, among other things. In 1996 during an interview with Henry Louis Gates Jr., Farrakhan spoke of an epiphany he had during a Lionel Ritchie concert, which concerned the waning of both white cultural supremacy and myths of black superiority. "I see something happening in America . . . the myths of black superiority are . . . going by the wayside. Someone might believe that a white cannot play the horn . . . then Kenny G blows that all away . . . It used to be that white people listened to the blues but could never sing it . . . white people are experiencing that out of which the blues came . . ." Gates replies, "Joe Lovano, maybe, but Kenny G?! . . . The truth is that blacks—across the economic and ideological spectrum—often feel vulnerable to charges of inauthenticity, of disloyalty to the race. I know that I do, despite my vigorous efforts to deconstruct that vocabulary of reproach . . ."[29] This illustrates one cause for anxiety that some (both blacks and whites) feel about Gorelick's mass appeal within the black community at large; an appeal, which supposedly supercedes that of other more authentic (read black) jazz artists. On the one hand, Gorelick's economic success and popularity, I suggest, are reminiscent of previous generations of white musicians who, through the co-optation and appropriation of black music styles, were able to enjoy great financial benefits, more so than their black colleagues. On the other hand, Gorelick's position is a sort of double co-optation because not only has he appropriated the stylistic parameters of black music, but he has also appropriated a large black audience in the process. This raises issues of ownership and authenticity in a much more complex way than say, Benny Goodman or Elvis Presley did. Writers such as Francis Davis, Stanley Crouch, and Jerome Harris have all commented on, and at times lamented, the diminished role of jazz in everyday African American life. With black audiences dwindling for other jazz styles, Gorelick's popularity is then viewed as a double threat and highly problematic for some.

As demonstrated above, members of the jazz community strategically distance themselves from artists, such as Gorelick, by way of
derision or dismissal (I am sure some of that disdain comes simply
from economic jealousy as well). This type of dismissal, in and of
itself, has become a tradition within the jazz community. The institu-
tionalized disdain for pop oriented styles has been with jazz since its
early days. It is just the target of that contempt that changes over time.
At present, the recipient styles include fusion, jazz rock, and more
severely, smooth jazz. This was evidenced by filmmaker Ken Burns
and his associates, who chose to basically end their coverage of jazz
history just prior to the advent of fusion in their 2001 PBS *Jazz* series,
thereby ignoring the last forty years—close to half—of jazz history.
Additionally, writer Stanley Crouch characterizes Miles Davis as "the
most brilliant sellout in the history of jazz" due to his post-1960s fusion
and pop experimentations.[30] Dan Morgenstern, in his sage-like fashion,
comments on these traditions;

> Since when has jazz been a cloistered virgin avoiding contact with
> the great unwashed? This is the same attitude among critics that
> led to the 'dissing' of what's now called the Great American
> Songbook, tunes of Tin Pan Alley dross, unworthy of the great
> jazz artists, deprived by the evils of the marketplace, of their birth-
> right, of the blues and 'genuine' jazz tunes (whatever those might
> have been—mostly pop tunes of an earlier era patinized by the
> passing of time).[31]

Ironically, though, present strategies among jazz traditionalists view
that "dissed" popular music of the 1930s, that is Ellington, Armstrong,
and Goodman, as representative of the artistic highpoint of jazz, worthy
of preservation, canonization, institutionalization, and scholarly examination, thereby transforming the disdained popular of yesterday
into the esteemed art of today. The changes in society, along with the
music that have led to this shift, tend to be ignored by jazz scholarship. This is especially troubling in light of what Lawrence Levine
writes; "Exoteric or popular music is transformed into esoteric or high
art at precisely that time when it becomes esoteric, that is, when it
becomes or is rendered inaccessible to the types of people who appreciated it earlier."[32] To me, the disjuncture between the jazz tradition and
popular culture deserves close scholarly scrutiny. We need to find out
about our own cultural context, a context which enables Kenny G to

be so popular, and we need to scrutinize why his accessibility comes
at the expense of the exclusion of others.

Why Smooth Jazz Is Not Part
of Jazz Historical Narratives

Considering the explosion of popular music/culture studies, it is remarkable that smooth jazz has been excluded from jazz historical narratives and that it is rarely treated seriously in scholarly writing. Part of
the reason for its exclusion is the dynamics involved in the construction
of such narratives. As Scott Deveaux comments:

> I am increasingly aware of this narrative's limitations, especially
> its tendency to impose a kind of deadening uniformity of cultural
> meaning on the music, and jazz history's patent inability to explain
> current trends in any cogent form . . . The narratives we have in-
> herited to describe the history of jazz retain the patterns of out-
> moded forms of thought, especially the assumption that the progress
> of jazz as art necessitates increased distance from the popular. If
> we, as historians, critics, and educators, are to adapt to these new
> realities, we must be willing to construct new narratives to explain
> them . . .[33]

In other words, as it is, the conceptual language employed within jazz
discourses are insufficient for the challenge of understanding smooth
jazz, its historical baggage, and stylistic affiliations. What I am suggesting is that instead of marginalizing, yet again, a major popular influence on current jazz styles, we should aspire to refine and adapt our
historical conceptual lens through which we deal with these phenomena
and in the process align jazz scholarship with more cutting-edge popular
music/culture studies.

Even within the industry this issue is being consciously addressed,
demonstrating that record producers are adapting to these new structures
faster than current jazz scholarship. Chris Jonz, senior director of jazz
and urban AC music (that is, Urban Adult Contemporary, or, short for
the African-American demographic) for Warner Brothers relates, "One
of the problems we constantly face is breaking down the stigma of
what jazz is. Many people hear the word jazz and think of John Coltrane
or Louis Armstrong. But jazz encompasses much more."[34] To think

that some people view Coltrane and Armstrong as stigmas is unbeliev-
able. However, I would argue that this attests to the ossified definitions
of jazz that are oftentimes presumed, and to how the industry is acknowledging that we must re-evaluate the prescribed limits imposed
on the music and align them with what musicians actually do, as well
as with what consumers/listeners/fans do. Producer Quincy Jones provides us with a particularly apt example of the type of assumed limitations of jazz. He states, "What is a jazz record? Any record that sells
under 20,000 copies, once it sells over that, it is no longer a jazz
record."[35] This begs the question, "why can't jazz be popular and ob-
tain mass appeal?" And when it is, why is it considered either "bad
jazz" or not even jazz at all?

It comes down to how jazz is fundamentally defined, and this is a
political question. Jerome Harris has identified two definitorial stances:
the "canon position," where jazz is seen as a music defined by a specific
African American originated genealogy and socially constituted guild,
and the "process position" where jazz is viewed as the result of certain
African American originated processes and aesthetics manifested in
the music.[36] As I have discussed elsewhere,[37] the canon position defines jazz as a sort of endangered species whereby limitations are placed
on the constituent boundaries of the music, a high art status is affixed,
and the music undergoes an open-ended process of sacrilization. When
the jazz tradition is viewed more as an open-ended process, individual
musicians are empowered to innovate through a much broader spectrum of media forces than is the case within the strictly canon-based
self-conception of jazz as a fossilized establishment. In reality, most
musicians use both of these positions, and at specific times, locate
themselves on whichever side of this binary that serves them best.
Indeed, musicians such as Quincy Jones, Herbie Hancock, and Miles
Davis accentuate this fluidity and create real philosophical dilemmas
for those who uphold the canon position.

For an example of definatorial politics at work, one need to look
no further than at the *Jazz at Lincoln Center* program which provides
us with an archetypal manifestation of the canon position in today's
jazz scene. Wynton Marsalis and his associates have discovered that
this position opens access to large portions of public funds previously
reserved for Western Art music traditions. Narrowing their definition
of jazz allows them to claim ownership, thus establishing themselves
as the gatekeepers of the canon, and, it distances the music not only

from its popular music origins and roots, but also from today's popular music scene. Indeed, this distancing is an integral component of the sacrilization process. As Lawrence Levine writes, "The urge to depre-cate popular musical genres is an important element . . . The process of sacrilization endows the music it focuses upon with unique aesthetic and spiritual properties that render it inviolate, exclusive, and eternal."[38] With commercial resources dwindling for non-smooth jazz styles, a protectionist stance is taken by those who are currently funded. A rise in the popular appeal of smooth jazz raises a threat to the fragile jazz economy, creating even a greater need for the jazz community to dis-tance themselves from smooth jazz styles. In other words, why fund jazz as art if it is a commercially sustainable popular music? Can one imagine a *Rock at Lincoln Center* program? It is simpler and safer to deny smooth jazz its place under the jazz tradition umbrella.

Jazz, when viewed from the process position, inherently feeds off of a productive migration of styles and derives much of its innovation from these borrowings. Throughout its history, popular music styles have served as fertile sources for absorption into jazz, reinvigorating the style and its financial stability, and on occasion, transforming jazz into a popular music domain in the process ("Watermelon Man" and "Chameleon" spring to mind). Regardless of this openness to new sources of influence and its long relationship with popular musics, disdainful attitudes by the jazz community persist towards smooth jazz and smooth jazz musicians amounting to accusations that a parasitical economy is at work. Is smooth jazz not just the latest incarnation of the jazz tradition? Isn't smooth jazz jazz in its most commodified form, denuded, almost beyond recognition, to its most basic commercial es-sence? What is being lost by its omission into the historical narrative?

On to the Question: "Is It Jazz?"

If jazz requires an Albert Murray-esque, Amiri Baraka-ish blues aes-thetic, then Kenny G fits, right? Or, does smooth jazz borrow too heavily from soul and R&B to posit the music as jazz? Record stores stock Kenny G's CDs in the jazz section. Every single day, DJ's and fans make pragmatic choices as to the generic affiliation of his music when they position his tunes in this category. According to *Billboard*, Re-cording Industry Association of America (RIAA), National Academy of Recording Arts & Sciences (NARAS), National Association of

Recording Merchandisers (NARM), and many of his fans, Kenny G is a jazz musician, and so are the other smooth jazz artists.

This immediately brings to light the question of authority. Who has the right and ability to judge? In popular cultures, Simon Frith points out, "this isn't necessarily a problem—one could define popular culture as that cultural sector in which all participants claim authority to pass judgement . . . in practice though, there are people who do claim that their superior knowledge, experience, and commitment give their judgments particular weight."[39] This is why when Pat Metheny, a well-respected musician, spoke out in a tirade against Kenny G, the rest of the jazz community did not question his authority, rather, they rose in huge numbers to support him. Personally I received seventeen copies of his interview through email forwards by fellow musicians and researchers. This message was worthy of mass dissemination and it resonated as a testament of jazz truth![40]

Regardless of those presumably superior views put forth by Metheny and others, popular notions of what jazz is, are indeed profoundly reshaping what jazz is. This apparent tautology might be explained by means of the multi-directional dialectics at work, when complimentary levels of authority (coupled with pragmatic choices) interact with one another to produce the cultural capital that make up the raw material of historical narratives and canon-formations alike. The constant accumulation of cultural capital, in turn, circulates through what we might conceive of as fields of forces (economic, social, racial, etc.), and is encoded and colonized by the desires and needs of a multitude of different agents (musicians, listeners/fans, industry people, critics, educators, etc.). As a result of this dynamic process, jazz (as a distinct musical style) continues to undergo a number of aesthetic and stylistic transformations, which again feeds into the open-ended conversation about the extent to which jazz is cross-pollinated by different popular styles. In other words, marketing strategies, such as the ones employed for smooth jazz, may turn out to have a real impact on the actual aesthetic qualities of the music, and thus cannot be readily discarded as irrelevant by the self-pronounced jazz elite.

Kevin Gore, who runs the jazz marketing department for Columbia Records, commented that smooth jazz is actively shaping how companies are beginning to market jazz. "We're very happy about the success of our smooth jazz artists. If an average jazz album sells around 5,000 copies, a smooth jazz artist will be selling 125,000."[41] One instance where mass-marketing strategies, typically employed for smooth

jazz artists, were employed for more traditional styles was in conjunction with Ken Burn's PBS *Jazz* series. The series completed its runs on
January 31, 2001 and tallied over thirteen million viewers. Rigorous
sales campaigns were launched during its initial airing to promote the
sales of the accompanying CD compilations, video, and book. In January, Tower Records reported a 25 percent increase in cumulative jazz
sales (some other retailers were up by 40 percent). In February, CD
compilations released by Ken Burns occupied eighteen of the twenty-
five positions on the *Billboard* top Jazz Albums chart.[42] By the end of
2001, Ken Burns titles accounted for 31.7 percent of all traditional
jazz sales.[43] If that was not a wake up call to the jazz community as to
the benefits of smooth jazz marketing, then their slumber is much too
deep and their retreat to their sacred high art status too entrenched.

Further, the processes of educational institutionalization which
smooth jazz is presently undergoing demonstrate the influence that
popular notions of jazz are having on jazz. Since 1999, courses in
smooth jazz have been offered both at the Berklee School of Music in
Boston by smooth jazz saxophonist Walter Beasley, and at University
of Southern California's Thorton School of Music, offered by guitarist
Richard Smith. Smith comments, "It is career suicide for a young
musician not to be embracing contemporary music and styles . . . Music
colleges don't take the responsibility of training students how to make
a living."[44] Beasley, whose course is entitled "Smooth R&B/jazz," states,
"At first students taking the course would try to hide when entering the
classroom . . . students don't need to hide their longing to play music
with soul and groove. Not that traditional jazz doesn't, but it's difficult
to play that now for a living . . . we are where we are at because of
changes in society . . . People know when they put my disc on they're
going to be able to do two things: relax and procreate."[45] This formal
study of the music has spawned numerous instructional books, such as
John Novello's *The Contemporary Pianist*. The path toward such institutional study and formalized training is similar to that traveled by
all previous jazz styles, and, this trajectory has played a significant
role in their eventual canonization, I might add.

Conclusions

Does Kenny G play bad jazz? This is not really the point. As Simon
Frith writes, "What is at issue is not its immediate qualities of effect,
but the opportunities it offers for further interpretation, for a reading,

for a reading against the grain. And from this perspective even the judgment that something is 'bad' is really a political rather than an aesthetic assessment."[46] Judgment works in all cultural spheres with words such as "good" and "bad" used excessively. How can we turn this mundane act into a methodology in order to reveal and assess the ideological implications of these judgments? In jazz discourse, judgments of good and bad are deeply entangled with the academic notions of high versus low and art versus popular. The elitism that has been adopted by the jazz community accentuates this discourse of binaries. The antiquated models used for constructing historical narratives present real dilemmas and are insufficient for the task of unpacking the complex web of economic, racial, and other social forces behind this entanglement.

In this discussion, I have purposely confused the economic value of the commodity with its cultural value, because I believe that this is exactly what record companies seek to do (intentionally or not), and I believe this is how Gorelick views his music and his place within the jazz world. The economic value is obvious, but what cultural value does his overly commercial version of jazz have? In recent times, jazz in the popular imagination has experienced an affiliational shift whereby it can be representative of things quite distanced from its origins. As Krin Gabbard writes, "Advertisers no longer use jazz to connote the nightlife and slumming that can be purchased along with their products—jazz can now signify refinement and upper class status, once the exclusive province of classical music."[47] In line with this new-found association, smooth jazz provides an opportunity for the public to be sophisticatedly "jazzy" without having to delve deep into the jazz tradition. Even Gorelick recognizes the possible benefits his position may bring to the well-being of jazz at large, though his efforts may seem misguided and in poor taste, they ultimately may serve to revive less popular jazz styles in the more popular realms of culture. He wrote in the liner notes for his *Standards in the Key of G* recording, "If you like my interpretations, I would highly recommend your checking out the original masters who performed this great music many years ago. They are awesome . . . "

Gorelick's sentimental appeals aside, his music does serve an important purpose in relation to more well-defined and accepted jazz styles; it reinfuses the genre with a productive transformational power— both from within (as my historical genealogy will hopefully have shown) and from without (in the shape of marked forces and pragmatic framing-strategies). Innovation can come in many different forms, including marketing strategies, and the future of jazz may depend on those used for and by smooth jazz. If jazz is viewed more as process, as an aesthetic, as a culture, which in turn broadens its definition, smooth jazz can provide fodder for a productive reading against the grain of the great tradition. As Lawrence Levine writes, "Categories and classifications are not simply inevitable but also useful as long as they sharpen our vision and free us to rethink and redefine them. The cultural categories we live by can become vehicles of comprehension not mystification only insofar as we remember just how human and fragile, how recent and porous they have been and continue to be."[48]

Regardless of Gorelick's bad jazz, jazz-lite, or whatever you want to call it, distaste for his music does not justify his exclusion from the historical narrative, and thirty million records sold along with their consequential presence on the jazz scene are issues that need to be addressed. I believe smooth jazz is not a blip in jazz history, a mistake fueled by consumerism and mass market appeal that will be corrected any time soon. Rather, it is firmly rooted within a long-standing tradition located within the jazz tradition itself. The G force is with us whether we like it or not. It is troubling to me that we, as music scholars, choose to write about our own favorite music, searching for those Schuller-esque gems, while ignoring the mundane, the music that actually plays a role in the everyday lives of millions. I am not advocating giving up on those gems, rather, I am suggesting that if we seek to understand "jazz" in its entirety, gems and all, we must examine the wide variety of jazz styles and their myriad manifestations. Studies of smooth jazz may, in fact, reveal much about contemporary society and will definitely serve as an important backdrop in revealing why those gems are so special in the first place.

NOTES

1. http://www.leeharrismusic.com/kenny_g.htm
2. According to RIAA, jazz sales fluctuate between 1.9—3.3% of all music sales. Statistics are based on sound scans (1993—3.1%, 1994—3.0%, 1995—3.0%, 1996—3.3%, 1997—2.8%, 1998—1.9%, 1999—3.0%, 2000—2.9%, 2001—2.4%, 2002—3.2%) (www.riaa.com).
3. According to Scott Hanley of WDUQ, in 1999 total jazz sales were nearly 6.8 million units, contemporary jazz sales accounted for 4.7 million units. The top

two sellers were the Kenny G and Kenny G Christmas (#1) records and they accounted for 49% of all sold (http://www.jazzradioconsortium.org/Jazz%20CD%20Sales%202001.html).

4. http://www.kennyg.com
5. Peter Watrous, "The Jazz Is 'Lite,' the Profits Heavy: Radio Stations Enjoy Rising Ratings as Music Purists Fume," *New York Times* (June 5, 1997): C13.
6. George Varga, "Kenny G: Changing His Tune," *JazzTimes* 29 (May 1999): 53-54.
7. Personal communication, 2001.
8. Lee Mergner, "The G Force is With Us," *JazzTimes* (May 1999): 20.
9. Kenny G interview with Ted Panken, "G WHIZ: Kenny G Is Still the Smooth Jazz King," (http://music.barnesandnoble.com/features/interview.asp?NID=598266), 2002.
10. In the film, *Last of the Blue Devils*, the "Yardbird" nickname is explained as stemming from a road trip from Kansas City to Lincoln, Nebraska with the Jay McShann band. Parker saw a car hit a chicken (yardbird) and insisted that the band's vehicle stop and retrieve the carcass. Parker had it cooked for dinner that evening. "Yardbird" was eventually shortened to "Bird."
11. Stuart Nicholson, *Jazz Rock: A History* (New York: Schirmer, 1998).
12. Personal communication, 2001.
13. Other later examples include Chet Baker's "Blood, Chet and Tears" (1970) and Dizzy Gillespie's "Souled Out" (1970), and Benny Golson's disco release "Always Dancing to the Music" (1980), to name a few.
14. According to Dan Morgenstern, *Down Beat* editor, ". . . the magazine's rock coverage was in response to pressure from advertisers—and not the record labels, who after all had very few certain print outlets for jazz product, never a priority for majors and certainly not then, and who were by the late 1960s not a major advertising income source for *DB*. No, the pressure came from the key advertisers: musical instrument and accessory manufacturers, whose *DB* audience were high school and college kids who played instruments—in school bands or on their own. That was the main impetus, but some coverage of rock would have happened anyway, since those young readers wanted it as well (at least some of them), and even without that, there was a groundswell in the music itself" (Personal communication, 2001).
15. According to Wein, he decided to include rock acts because of their increasing popularity and the fact that the rock musicians he booked could really play their instruments. He found that the rock acts were willing to play at Newport because of its reputation for booking the best jazz acts. He said that he even received a personal phone call from Jimi Hendrix asking to play. "I didn't know Hendrix's music that well at the time and I was completely booked up, so I said, 'no.'" The rock concerts far surpassed his profits from ticket sales, but he also incurred tremendous clean-up bills after the performances, dwindling most of the profits (Personal communication, 2003).
16. Larry Coryell and Bob Moses formed Free Spirits. Their 1966 release, *Out of Sight and Sound,* was a seminal jazz-rock mixture. Jeremy Steig also led a jazz-rock group called Jeremy and the Satyrs. On the West Coast Charles Lloyd,

Jack Dejonette, Ron McClure, and Keith Jarrett appeared at the Fillmore Auditorium in 1967, San Francisco's premiere rock venue. And as early as 1966, Frank Zappa's groups experimented with rock and jazz mixtures.

17. *Bitches Brew* was not Davis' first attempt at recording rock-influenced jazz. *In A Silent Way, Miles In The Sky* and *Filles of Kilimanjaro* were released in 1968, however it was *Bitches Brew* that received the unprecedented record sales. It sold 400,000 copies in its first year, selling more than any other Miles Davis record at that time (http://www.pbs.org/jazz/time/time_sixties.htm).

18. Nicholson, *Jazz Rock.*

19. See Bob Palmer, "Jazz/Rock '74: The Plain Funky Truth," *Rolling Stone* (August 1, 1974) for an example.

20. Some of the commercially successful early soft fusion recordings include; The Crusaders' "Put it Where You Want It" (1972), Grover Washington's *Mister Magic* (1975), George Benson's "This Mascarade" from *Breezin* (1976), Chuck Mangione's "Feels So Good" (1977). Spyro Gyra's "The Shaker Song" (1978) and "Morning Dance (1979), and Pat Metheny's "Jaco" (1978).

21. Brian Soergel, "Brian Soergel on Smooth Jazz," *JazzTimes* 30 (September 2000): 67.

22. Carrie Bell, "Kenny G's first hits set due on Arista," *Billboard* 109/46 (November 15, 1997): 11, 83.

23. Eliot Tiegel, "Riffs: Smooth Moves on the Air," *Down Beat* 63 (December 1996): 10.

24. Jay Beckenstein, "Silver Anniversary and Still Sounding Good," *International Musician* (September 2001): 16.

25. Watrous, C13.

26. Don Jeffrey, "No Respect Dept," *Billboard* (June 28, 1997): 36, 38.

27. Another example of the benefits of a heavy marketing campaign can be demonstrated with his 1996 release *The Moment* (which has sold close to seven million units). Even though the record was released on October 1, during the week that ended May 4, 1997 the top 10 albums on *Billboard*'s (traditional) jazz chart sold a total 13,702 units, according to Sound Scan. The top 10 titles on the contemporary jazz chart sold 39,216 units. Kenny G accounted for 1/3 of those sales (Jeffrey 1997: 36–38).

28. Neil Strauss, ". . . And Two if by Seaplane," *New York Times* (January 8, 1997): C1.

29. Henry Louis Gates Jr., *Thirteen Ways of Looking at a Black Man* (New York: Random House, 1997): 125–27.

30. Stanley Crouch, *The All-American Skin Game* (New York: Pantheon Books, 1997).

31. Personal communication, 2001.

32. Lawrence Levine, *The Emergence of Cultural Hierarchy in America* (Cambridge, MA: Harvard University Press, 1988): 234.

33. Scott DeVeaux, "Constructing the Jazz Tradition: Jazz Historiography," *Black American Literature Forum* 25.3 (1991): 553.

34. Steven Graybow, "Jazz and the Urban Audience," *Billboard* 112 (June 3, 2000): 45.

35. "Quincy Jones In the Pocket," PBS Special, aired on November 19, 2001.
36. Jerome Harris, "Jazz on the Global Stage," in *The African Diaspora: A Musical Perspective*, edited by Ingrid Monson (New York: Garland Publishing, 2000): 121.
37. Christopher Washburne, "Latin Jazz: the Other History," *Current Musicology* 71–73 (2001-2): 409–26.
38. Levine, *The Emergence of Cultural Hierarchy in America,* 132,136.
39. Simon Frith, *Performing Rites: on the Value of Popular Music* (Cambridge: Harvard University Press, 1996): 9.
40. "What A Wonderful World" was not just a commercial endeavor for Kenny G and Arista Records; it was a philanthropic one as well, almost as a way to deflect the predicted criticism. Gorelick stated, "All the proceeds from that song will go to a new foundation I have established for at-risk children. The foundation will funnel the money to charities to purchase musical instruments and to supplement funding for the arts in schools. I've decided since the government has decided to cut back, it's time for me to give back." (Bouley, 1999: 14). Will the proceeds from his bad jazz buy the instruments for the next generation of jazz artists? What seems to have earned him such ire from the jazz community in their response to the overdubbing of the Armstrong cut, was that he reversed the established direction that borrowings usually take within the smooth jazz style. Rather than turning to the arena of pop music for innovation, he chose a jazz icon of an earlier era for material and inspiration, a musician that serves as the cornerstone of the jazz canon.
41. Watrous, C13.
42. Chris Morris, "Advent of a new jazz age?" *Billboard* 113 (Feb 10, 2001): 1, 82.
43. http://www.jazzradioconsortium.org/Jazz%20CD%20Sales%202001.html
44. Brian Soergel, "Smooth Educators." *JazzTimes Jazz Education Guide 2001/ 2002* (2001): 55.
45. Ibid, 56, 58.
46. Frith, *Performing Rites: on the Value of Popular Music*, 14.
47. Krin Gabbard, editor, *Jazz among the discourses* (Durham: Duke University Press, 1995): 1-2.
48. Levine, *The Emergence of Cultural Hierarchy in America,* 241–42.

REFERENCES

Beckenstein, J. 2001. Silver Anniversary and still sounding good. *International Musician* (September): 16–17.

Bell, C. 1997. Kenny G's first hits set due on Arista. *Billboard* 109/46 (November 15): 11, 83

Bouley, C. K. 1999. Kenny G takes on standards on 'Key of G'." *Billboard* 111 (May 29): 14, 19.

Bourdieu, P. 1984. *Distinction: A social critique of the judgement of taste.* London: Routledge.

Cole, P. 1992. Peer Pressures. *Down Beat* 59 (November): 22.

Crouch, S. 1995. *The all-American skin game.* New York: Pantheon Books.

Davis, F. 1996. Like Young. *Atlantic Monthly* 278 (July 1): 94.

DeVeaux, S. 1991. Constructing the jazz tradition: Jazz historiography." *Black American Literature Forum* 25.3: 525–60.

Frith, S. 1996. *Performing rites: On the value of popular music*. Cambridge: Harvard University Press.

Gabbard, K., ed. 1995. *Jazz among the discourses*. Durham: Duke University Press.

Gates, H. L. Jr. 1997. *Thirteen ways of looking at a black man*. New York: Random House.

Graybow, S. 2000. Jazz and the urban audience. *Billboard* 112 (June 3): 45.

Griffith, J. 1996. Spins: Business jazz reconsidered. *Pulse* (April): 27–28.

Harris, J. 2000. Jazz on the global stage. In *The African diaspora: A musical perspective*, ed. Ingrid Monson. New York: Garland Publishing.

Jeffrey, D. 1997. No respect dept. *Billboard* (June 28): 36, 38.

Levine, L. 1988. *The emergence of cultural hierarchy in America*. Cambridge, MA: Harvard University Press.

Mergner, L. 1999. The G force is with us. *JazzTimes* (May): 20.

Metheny, P. 2000. Pat Metheny vs. Kenny G. *JazzTimes* 30 (September): 23.

Milkowski, B. 2000. Fusion. In *The Oxford jazz companion*, ed. Bill Kirchner. New York: Oxford University Press.

Morris, C. 2001. Advent of a new jazz age? *Billboard* 113 (Feb. 10): 1, 82.

Moya, E. W. 1998. Kenny G! Dead Ahead! *JAZZIZ* 15 (July): 15.

Negus, K. 1999. *Music genres and corporate cultures*. London and New York: Routledge.

Nicholson, S. 1998. *Jazz rock: A history*. New York: Schirmer.

Reske, S. 1997. Smooth jazz springs to life on public TV. *JAZZIZ* 14 (June): 18.

Schwartz, M., Jr. 2000. Two turntables and Kenny G's saxophone. *JAZZIZ* 17 (January): 20.

Soergel, B. 2000. Brian Soergel on smooth jazz,. *JazzTimes* 30 (September): 67–68.

———. 2001. Smooth educators. *JazzTimes Jazz Education Guide 2001/2002*: 54–59.

Stewart, R. 2000. A tribute to Grover Washington Jr. *JAZZIZ* 17 (April): 38–42.

Strauss, N. 1997. . . . And two if by seaplane. *New York Times* (January 8): C1.

Taylor, C. 1997. Kenny G's first hits set due on Arista," *Billboard* 109 (November 15): 8, 83.

Tiegel, E. 1996. Riffs: Smooth moves on the air. *Down Beat* 63 (December): 10–11.

Varga, G. 1999. Kenny G: Changing his tune. *JazzTimes* 29 (May): 46–50, 52, 54, 102.

Washburne, C. 2001–2002. Latin jazz: The other history. *Current Musicology* 71–73: 409–26.

Watrous, P. 1997. The jazz is 'lite,' the profits heavy: Radio stations enjoy rising ratings as music purists fume. *New York Times* (June 5): C13.

7
The Flight from Banality

JAMES KOEHNE

Signs of Spenglerian decline are everywhere.[1] The bottom has fallen out of the Classical CD market, the honored recording labels of the past downsizing their output or closing altogether. Orchestras and chamber music presenters fret about the preponderance of grey heads among their audiences, and lament the lost days of patrons queuing eagerly for their subscription renewals. Classical music no longer figures as an essential element of our children's education. Radio stations devoted to classical music face closure or radical restructuring into "adult contemporary" formats.

In contemporary music, the remnant forces of the once fearsome avant-garde wander an undulating landscape, devoid of landmarks, indulging here and there in harmless and negligible skirmishes. Recalling the military origins of the term, one might say that the main forces this vanguard was meant to presage have forgotten them—indeed have even forgotten that some kind of revolutionary war is supposed to be going on at all.

On the bookshelves of thrift shops, voluminous tomes by the likes of Sigmund Spaeth, Hendrik van Loon and Bernard Shore, introducing the great masters and great music, sit unwanted month after month, even year after year. Once upon a time, it seems, not all that long ago, people regarded love of classical music[2] as something to aspire to, and would wade through fat books to learn about the stuff. The market for classical music was assured forever by its standing: not only (superficially) as a marker of social respectability, but also (genuinely) as a kind of moral force, an edifying power. Now it has become just one more entertainment option among a vast and impressive array, a specialization for an isolated minority.

It would be an overstatement to depict classical music as an edifice teetering on the edge of oblivion's abyss, but if that edifice is meant to be a lighthouse, its beacon shines none too brightly. The extent to which this light is flickering varies, perhaps, between different cities and national cultures, but the trends seen in those places where the status of classical music is less well established (i.e., outside of Europe) seem to be creeping in upon even the great nations of the classical tradition.

I've been engaged in my own mental struggle with these issues during the twenty years of my professional involvement with the Australian "Classical Music Industry" (as we now call ourselves, in deference to the new business-oriented models of our cultural funding agencies). As music adviser in the Arts Ministry of the government of the State of Victoria, as Policy Adviser to Symphony Australia based in Sydney and as Artistic Administrator of the Adelaide Symphony Orchestra, I've observed the quiet turmoil of the classical music world as it confronts changes it doesn't like and would rather not acknowledge.

Call me slow, but it's taken me this long to come to the recognition that classical music can no longer claim the moral, social or aesthetic authority which would give it the prestige it still expects to trade on. Indeed, I was wrong to believe that it ever had the right to do so, or that it should have wanted to. Undoubtedly, there is greatness in this music, but we have made a fetish out of this characteristic, lifting it out of the context of living, breathing social relations into an airless domain of reverential religiosity.

Unable to restrict my own musical curiosity to the confines of the classical repertoire, I have also been engaged during these years, in a broadening and diversification of my listening habits to include jazz, lounge music, so-called "world music," and occasional Sunday morning viewing of the local "Video Hits" on television. Within the ambit of my musical interests, classical music has become—like it is for the rest of the world—just one element within the mosaic of genres that makes up a rounded musical life.

Within the world of classical music itself, I fancy I can see some of the characteristics of a dysfunctional family: people don't talk to each other and they don't recognize each other's needs. Professionally, I find myself adopting different, even contradictory modes of communication in order to pull together a viable context in which my orchestra can operate. I commiserate with musicians who express their frustration at playing pops repertoire; I cajole conductors to perform pieces they disdain or to steer them away from choices I fear will put audiences off; I groan at the silly ideas marketers come up with to sell concerts; I bear good-naturedly the narrow-mindedness or aesthetic unsophistication of audience members. About the only thing these factions are united around is their disdain for Kylie Minogue, and that's just indicative of their remoteness from wider humanity. In those moments where I sense that bringing together the warring interests of all these sectors will be impossible, I frown and mumble to myself, "this is fucked." Perhaps there is a possibility of unfucking it. But one thing's certain: to do that, we will have to turn our attention away from finding external forces upon which to put the blame, and examine instead our own values to see how we ourselves might be at fault.

I remain a committed participant in this industry, and speak of it in terms in which I include myself—as "we" rather than "they." Unwilling to set myself outside of the world of classical music, I prefer to address the possible directions for its future development and character: I do not want to declare it dead, but to see it come back to life.

Keeping It Under Control

Warnings of the decline of the symphonic world aren't new, and it's the marketers who have led this charge. Worrying signs began to filter through from the investigations of marketers at the beginning of the 1990s.[3] The inclinations of the baby-boomer generation and of generation x, the studies showed, are fundamentally different to those of previous generations. They do not revere the classical canon in the same way that previous generations did. They will not naturally gravitate towards Brahms and Beethoven as they reach maturity, nor will they sit through a concert in the hope of being edified. They expect music to offer them spiritual uplift, pleasure and excitement, but are as likely to get that from The Beach Boys as they are from Beethoven.

In 1993, the American Symphony Orchestra League (ASOL) published *Americanizing the American Orchestra*,[4] a report urging a radical shift in the value system of the orchestral world, in acknowledgment of the changed make up of American society. No longer, the report argued, could orchestras shelter in their WASP-ish world view: they should acknowledge, attract and represent other musical cultures, like the African-American and Hispanic.

Where *Americanizing* specifically addresses issues about repertoire, it is tentative about interfering with the judgment of musical value. Instead, the report relies on conventional admonitions to include more music by contemporary (and American) composers, and a plea to embrace accessibility. This objective-sounding word, favored by bureaucrats, is readily scorned for its implication that music might be judged in some other terms than artistic merit: to apply this alternative criterion of judging value is simply giving in to the presumably easy pursuit of popularity.

The surprisingly controversial report was condemned as a piece of political correctness, a plan for employing music as a means of social engineering. Ten years on, one can point to an increased emphasis on things like educational and outreach programs along the lines urged by the report, but these harmless efforts are isolated within a context that has steadfastly resisted change.

For the majority of those with a stake in the classical music industry, the arguments put forward in both the ASOL report and the marketing analyses were never likely to succeed. Classical music itself is above and beyond the influence of demographics, social movements and earthly battles over such unmusical, unartistic concepts as empowerment and representation.

The resistance to *Americanizing* zeroed in on the report's use of social factors as potential motivators for altering the value system of classical music. Such arguments are not likely to break through the barriers of stylistic prejudice which constrain institutions like orchestras to their unbending views of worthiness and unworthiness. We believe in the aesthetic purity of our kind of music, and apply a subtle logic to defend it ideologically and practically from external challenges, relying, on the one hand, on abstract conceptions of musical value and, on the other, on internally reassuring hierarchies of musical decision making.

This is the attitude upheld by the two most outspoken repudiators of the *Americanizing* report, Edward Rothstein in the *New York Times*, and Samuel Lipman in the *New Criterion*, who contradicted the report's basic assumption that orchestras need to find ways of reintegrating into society, declaring that musicians:

> are not first of all members of their communities. They are musicians. Until recently, symphony orchestras in the United States and Europe existed—and knew they existed—primarily to pass on the masterworks of musical civilization by providing refined musical pleasure to a largely self-chosen audience. This was and remains the ideal.

> Doubtless music reflects the world of its origin. Because perfor-
> mance attempts to replicate more or less exactly an original text, it
> reflects the surrounding world in which it is performed to a vastly
> lesser extent. In the case of the greatest music, that world is un-
> doubtedly European; and because of the very meaning of the word
> "classic," the music comes from a bygone social milieu.[5]

In characterizing the aspiration of the classical musician as one of
devotion and dedication to a repertoire rather than one of creativity
and vitality, Lipman encapsulates the death wish of the classical music
world.

This constrained aspiration was shared by "The International
Conference of Symphony and Opera Musicians" (ICSOM), the symphony orchestras' arm of the American Federation of Musicians, which
took the report very personally. ICSOM urged its members to "disso-
ciate themselves" from the report, railing against it as:

> a project which is supposed to address critical issues facing the
> orchestral field today, but which has created a torrent of negative
> press about symphony orchestras and a document with a jingois-
> tic title that creates the erroneous impression that American sym-
> phony orchestras are non-American, racist, elitist organizations,
> subject to continuous and unrelenting labor strife, which present
> concerts for ever-diminishing audiences.[6]

The union joined Rothstein and Lipman in condemning the ASOL
for allowing the report to direct a critical gaze at the culture of classical music itself. Supporting the critics' challenge to the ASOL's very
right to exist, they wholeheartedly agreed with Lipman that the ASOL
"clearly does not have in mind either the interests of our beloved symphony orchestras and their audiences or the future of great music."

Perhaps I was the only one surprised by such reactions, but they
serve to demonstrate the pervasiveness of the belief that the perfection
of classical music, along with its presumed high moral purpose, make
it a thing to be defended and supported, but never questioned.

The symptoms and characteristics of classical music's problems
have not entirely escaped the attention of musicologists either. Among
those who identify with some version of "New Musicology" (ie, those
interested in the cultural study of music), questions about the supremacy
and borders of the canon of classical music have been a hot issue for at
least twenty years.

Robert Fink, for instance, proclaims the impending death of classical music and sees the updating of the marketing methods of the grand institutions (like symphony orchestras) as last gasp efforts to cling to their lost authority and prestige.[7] Where someone like Norman Lebrecht[8] sees the demeaning of classical music by marketing and corporate manipulation as the root of the genre's problem, Fink argues that this misses the point. With his "Cassandra-like" complaints against the intrusion of modern capitalist ways into classical music, Lebrecht deflects attention from the reality of the classical establishment's loss of control, the evaporation of its canonic power.

The loss of control is not just economic:

> For the first time in a century, classical music has lost even its symbolic or ritualistic power to define hierarchies of taste within the larger culture . . . Having long ago accepted loss of financial control (the final, bitter stages of this process are chronicled by Lebrecht), the institutions of classical music need to adjust to a much more disorienting loss of semiotic control. What they do is no longer Music-with-a-capital M.[9]

Most classical musicians will sympathize with Lebrecht's attribution of blame and almost find comfort in it. They will resist the implications of Fink's "brave new post-canonic world"[10] with all the vitriol and determination they showed towards *Americanizing the American Orchestra*. As Fink notes, "classical musicians have long complained, with voluptuous self-pity, that their position at the top of the hierarchy of musical taste was lonely, cold and poorly paid. They will now have to get used to ceding that drafty, if prestigious, position altogether."[11]

Classical musicians, and those who are implicated in their world, have too much invested emotionally, ethically, morally, spiritually and economically in the Classical World Order to admit that the paradigm has shifted around them. Despite the by now obvious realities of our post-canonic situation, we resist the fact with every mote of our being, and devote ourselves to the effort to sustain the old value system. One could perhaps prove this by undertaking some sociological analysis of the musical value systems that operate within, around, encircling orchestras.[12] But short of making that effort, I want to cite some examples drawn from my own recent experience—anecdotes, really—which illustrate the classical music industry's value system and the subtle ways in which it protects itself.

These events, though admittedly minor, are emblematic of attitudes that threaten slow starvation of the orchestral repertoire and the continued contraction of the industry. They demonstrate how we continue to emphasize the difference of classical music as a clearly identifiable category separated from (and elevated above) all the other musics out there. While not necessarily describing these other musics as outright *bad*, the internal culture of the symphonic world nevertheless works quietly to deflect them from serious attention. Admission is refused to music that is not clearly consistent with the ideological lineage of, the value system that defines the classical music repertoire.

Transgression of Inappropriate Sentiment

Almost a decade after Christopher Rouse wrote his Flute Concerto, the Adelaide Symphony Orchestra presented its Australian premiere.[13] Placed in one of our mainstream programs, I was nervous that audiences might be turned away by a contemporary piece being so prominent in the program, so it was cushioned with familiar Brahms and Sibelius (an old programmer's trick).

Thus, I was able to weave through the array of potential objectors to get the piece programmed. But during rehearsals I sensed the conductor's slight discomfort, specifically towards the concerto's tender elegy and the sections where the Celtic-sounding tune bounds along. When I asked about these misgivings, the term the conductor used to describe what felt wrong about the piece was that "sometimes it sounds a bit . . . *Hollywood*."

(It was not the first time I had heard the term used like this. For a little chamber music series back in 1990, I'd programmed Korngold's Piano Trio for a group of Conservatorium staff who rebelled angrily, retorting that "Korngold is a *Hollywood* composer").

Classical musicians often use this term to express their unease with music that is openly sentimental, or that uses some trace of the language we associate with either classical or contemporary Hollywood scoring. Demon Hollywood has become the personification of the forces in modern life which have undermined, if not destroyed, the classical establishment's faith in its own superiority. The Hollywood composer is by definition a failure, because he has succumbed to the lure of popularity, or relinquished his proper ambition to stand above the commercial and common world. Hollywood movie scores have given us—sometimes even still do give us—orchestral evocations of glamour, excitement, and emotional force, but we cannot consider these as relevant to our objectives and musical culture, because of the taint of evil or failure with which we have invested them.

There's really not much in Rouse's concerto that borrows from Hollywood film scoring, but the fact that it's inspired by and seeks to directly express the composer's own deep feelings (here responding to his horror at the murder of toddler James Bulger[14]) seems to be enough to bring it into disrepute. *Hollywood*, then, serves as a kind of byword for music that allows itself to indulge in emotive expression, provoking our inbred mistrust for what we take to be a manipulative approach to musical expressiveness.

Rouse's musical response to the sources of his inspiration is personal and reflective. Its surprising restraint communicates his anguish with heartfelt plainness, employing the sentimental and nostalgic as both a personal expression and an act of sharing grief. These qualities of common, universal subjective expression provoke discomfort in the classical musician, who values intellectual and learned objectivity as a signifier of his music's superiority over the ordinary world.

This tendency to view subjectivity and sentimentality as threatening ingredients lies deep at the core of classical music culture. One small but striking example of this occurs in the liner notes to one of my recordings of Webern's Six Pieces, op. 6.[15] In these notes, musicologist Arnold Whittall refers to the subjective personal reflections which inspired this work, namely Webern's intensely nostalgic memories of his mother and his grief at her death. But Whittall feels obliged to excuse these reflections since we are likely to find them "embarrassing, even distasteful" when coming from a composer "once regarded as the acme of austere abstraction."

To deflect the power of subjectivity in a work like Rouse's concerto (or the music of Korngold), the classical musician must discredit its musical language, and it is here that the term *Hollywood* takes on the purpose of providing grounds on which to preclude the music from acceptance. So finely attuned have we become to the infectious traces of *Hollywood* directness that the shudder of recognition and mistrust when such traces are identified is like a Pavlovian response.

Transgression of Inappropriate Style

For my orchestra's fledgling contemporary music series in 2000,[16] I programmed a concert of works by John Adams and Colin MacPhee, climaxing with Adams' *Grand Pianola Music*, a piece unaccountably neglected in concert programs (our performance was, again, the Australian premiere). The director Peter Sellars was in town at the time, working on his (ill-fated) 2002 Adelaide Festival, and I was thrilled when he agreed to speak briefly in introduction of the music.

I never doubted that *Grand Pianola* is a masterpiece of musical imagination, nor that it would be exciting and powerful for the audience. Sellars spoke persuasively, intelligently and beautifully about Adams' *Shaker Loops* and MacPhee's *Tabuh-Tabuhan*. So I was taken aback when he introduced *Grand Pianola* as "a work that has been widely despised . . . because it's in really, really bad taste."

As a rule, it's not a good sign for the audience when a new piece is introduced with an apology. But Sellars was being truthful. *Grand Pianola* has been condemned as kitsch-mongering from the moment it first appeared. Indeed, the story of the work's initial reception, amongst a hostile crowd of avant-gardists, verges on the level of the *Rite of Spring* debacle, only in reverse. "To this day," Adams' notes, *Grand Pianola Music* "has remained a weapon of choice among detractors who wish to hold up my work as exemplary of the evils of Postmodernism or—even more drastic—the pernicious influences of American consumerism on high art." Adams further admits that the piece "could only have been conceived by someone who had grown up surrounded by the detritus of mid-twentieth century recorded music. Beethoven and Rachmaninoff soak in the same warm bath with Liberace, Wagner, the Supremes, Charles Ives, and John Philip Sousa."[17]

These are the grounds on which *Grand Pianola Music* has been marginalized from the Repertoire. Based on the initial antagonism of the coterie that attended the premiere of the work, *Grand Pianola* has been tarnished by a bad reputation within the closed circle of decision makers who determine the repertoire that orchestras represent to the public.

Peter Sellars, of course, knows that art has to reignite its relationship with the vernacular. As he went on to describe the power and value of *Grand Pianola Music* to our audience, he observed that "the biggest problem with the classical music world in general is the tyranny of 'good taste'. John [Adams] has just burst right through that." *Grand*

Pianola achieves a level of ecstasy that reminds Sellars of the vernacular religious traditions of Mexico, Bali and Southern Italy, where "something deeply spiritual is expressed in the most vulgar, garish, outlandish out-of-control sort of way," achieving an "exuberance that cannot be contained by proper behaviour."

The work's final movement, Sellars went on to explain, "has the infamous 'big tune'. Now of course, one of the things about official High Art twentieth century music is that you weren't allowed to have a tune." But in *Grand Pianola Music*, the tune is at the center of the composer's effort to establish a communal feeling of celebration and sharing. Adams indulges "this very uncool thing of wanting to make the world better, bring all the people of the world together and surround everyone with love and joy." As Beethoven does in the *Ode to Joy*, Adams "takes a really, really tacky tune and repeats it over and over again until it becomes transcendent." In the final movement of *Grand Pianola Music*, "this tacky little tune just explodes into this The-Universe-is-Singing level of joy . . . The world will be saved by 'pop' music and 'bad' taste! Along the way, John puts in the whole history of classical music and the whole history of American commercial music and you can't tell where one begins and the other ends . . ."

There is more than a little defensiveness in Sellars' remarks, a defensiveness which only becomes necessary in the face of the judgments of experts. Where an audience member might be transported by the accelerating, upward rush and infectious melody of Adams' music (not noticing its alleged tackiness), an expert would know better. Astutely, the expert hears the cute tune and immediately identifies something common, a little invader from the everyday world, poking its way into the refined and superior business of classical music.

Such judgments are remote from the concerns of audiences, and in the case of the particular audience at the concert in Adelaide, Sellars' defensiveness was not necessary. The audience was neither aware of, nor influenced by the judgment that had been placed upon the work and naturally they responded enthusiastically to *Grand Pianola Music*.

In John Adams' case, the judgment of experts has worked effectively to undermine the composer's effort to establish a connection between vernacular forms of musical expression and the communal connection with the audience that derives from this. He sometimes receives grudging acceptance among the expert class because he possesses the technique and the musical imagination to transform material that might otherwise be judged banal into powerful and impressive large-scale compositions. This elaboration of the every-day, transforming the banal by means of aesthetic and technical so-phistication—yet without sacrificing or disrespecting the qualities which give the music it's immediate appeal—has long been an impor-tant element in classical composition, from Haydn to Tchaikovsky. Only in an expertised era would this be looked upon as an abrogation of artistic responsibility, or as a feature for which one would need to find excuses.

Turning of Backs

Programming a piece of music that does not wear the badge "This Is Repertoire" always provokes resistance from someone within the establishment. But over the objections of orchestral players, conduc-tors or marketers, I've managed it a few times: Mosolov's storming of the concert hall, *Iron Foundry*; an engaging little sinfonia concertante by the Chevalier de Saint-Georges; Raymond Scott's Bugs Bunny-inspiring *Powerhouse*; a piece of production library music called *Victory* by never-heard-of James Reichert (but immediately recognized by any Australian over a certain age as the theme from the 1960s Australian cop show, *Homicide*). Members of my orchestra kindly mock or loudly berate me for programming pieces like these, but audiences . . . well, they just love them.

From my experience, then, I have noted that audiences are highly likely to embrace music which has the following characteristics:

- Emotion and sentimentality
- Simplicity and directness
- Conviviality and cheerfulness

And these, of course, are precisely the characteristics which we in the classical music business conspire to deny them. They are char-acteristics of belonging to the world, precisely the thing which classi-cal music does not do—at least, not within the culture of classical music that we have created. In the case of the transgressions I've cited, someone plays the role of the boundary umpire or referee in a football match. When the ball falls or a player steps across the line, the whistle is blown or the off-side flag is raised. In classical music there is no official referee of course, so the keeping of boundaries becomes a matter of teamwork, requiring the collaboration of conductors, administrators, and orchestral players.

In the old days, conductors behaved as the voices of moral authority who could single-handedly make these delineations. In his history of British Light Music, Geoffrey Self recalls a story told by the (Australian) singer Peter Dawson. "Nothing so clearly illustrates," writes Self, "the division between popular taste and the trained musician's rejection of it as Sir Henry Wood's reaction when Dawson sang [his popular ballad, *Boots*, to a poem by Kipling] at the 1926 Promenade Concerts:

> I was about to take a bow because of the tumultuous applause when (Wood) stood in my way in a towering rage and shouted 'Don't ever sing rubbish like that here again. Boots, Boots . . . sing them songs that uplift them. Brahms or Schubert.'[18]

Critics and musicologists used to—heck, they still do!—adopt the umpire's role too, and the history of these professions is littered with diatribes against the banal, the vulgar, the trivial, the sentimental and the simple. Plucking one example from the millions available, I cite David Drew's invective against a composer named Jean Wièner. "Although wholly uninteresting as a composer," Drew takes a moment to point out that the "finale of the *Concerto Franco-Americain*—whose theme is of unsurpassed and unsurpassable vulgarity—makes its point by suggesting not so much a compromise between the *haute couture* of Paris and New York as between the plebeian joys of Margate Pier and the day-trip to Boulogne." Drew is pleased to observe, sneeringly, that "Wièner has recently achieved popular success with a song-hit, *Le Grisbi*. Once again a minor voice finds its proper *métier*."[19]

Drew's article is laced with interesting, deconstructable views of musical good and bad. Despite his contempt for Wièner, and most of Milhaud and Poulenc, Drew defends Satie, Henri Sauguet and Messiaen from accusations of badness. Sauguet should have found his *métier* as a composer of very superior light music, but France no longer possessed that category, since, paradoxically, the "Age of the Common Man has also been an age *against* the Common Composer."[20] Referring to a generation of French composers, including Sauguet, "whose talents were fundamentally similar to those of the *opéra comique* composers," Drew considers them failures because:

Instead of following their natural bent, they were forced by the trend of modern culture—which has degraded the popular until it has become synonymous with the commercial—to don the mantle of serious composers."[21]

The umpire calls "Off-side!" Bad luck, guys, you can't be admitted within these boundaries, and actually there is no field in which you are permitted to play. Speaking as an Artistic Administrator a generation or two later, I would suggest that more attention should have been paid to this discrepancy. If popular music won't have you, we will, could have been one response. When Howard Hartog, the editor of the volume in which Drew's essay appeared noted, in a throwaway line, that "In the flight from banality, music has moved some way from meeting the current popular taste . . .",[22] I would beg him to pause a moment and take that thought a bit further. What would be the consequences of that separation for the future of classical music?

In defending Messiaen, Drew notes that this composer's strangeness poses a challenge for the commentator, who must find a way of "ridding oneself of habits of taste that masquerade as aesthetic laws, and of attuning oneself to modes of thought and feeling that are in many ways contrary to the whole trend of modern culture."[23] Here, too, is a thought that, in hindsight, might have been examined a little further. Drew defends Messiaen against critics who damn his music "for its 'sentimentality', its 'naïvety' or its 'banality'," the words themselves enclosed in quotation marks so that we should not misconstrue these qualities as actually present in Messiaen's music. Perhaps, if the quotation marks were removed and these very qualities themselves admitted onto the playing field, we would find ourselves free to appreciate Messiaen's music in all its unrestrained glory.

Throughout the literature of the old musicology, and in the language of the keepers of classical music's flame, every sign of vernacular expression or feeling is unfailingly characterised as banal and vulgar. The words are used like weapons to defend the elevated concept of classical music from the incursion of the common and everyday.

It is worth reminding ourselves that the terms *banal* and *vulgar* are merely ways of characterizing the vernacular and the common. "Vulgarity," in my copy of the Shorter Oxford English Dictionary, is defined as "the quality of being usual, ordinary or commonplace," its pejorative sense of "unrefined or coarse" being a more recent form of use. "Banal," now meaning "commonplace; trivial," derives from an expression used in feudal England to describe property that was "open to the use of all the community" (in which case, I would suggest, banality would be the thing classical music needs more than anything else!).

These days, of course, neither critics, musicologists nor conductors enjoy the kind of authority that would make such baldly snobbish pronouncements acceptable in public. But the old attitudes have certainly not disappeared. To defend music from the interference of the ordinary, conductors, orchestra members and administrators now have to work together to uphold their constrained and exclusionist conception of classical music's heritage and continuing lineage. Words like banal or vulgar retain a surprising degree of currency within the closed circles of classical music decision making. The various parties of the conductor-orchestra-administrator circle reinforce each other's prejudices in order to defend a conception of classical music which is delivered from above.

The performance of orchestral music, where the conductor, his back turned to the audience, engages in secret and mysterious communication with the musicians of the orchestra, has a symbolic implication of closedness that is obvious. This example is not really anything more than symbolic, but the formation of closed or inward-facing circles is only too familiar a characteristic of the classical establishment's operating system.

For conductors, the audience is necessarily a factor of less importance than is the orchestra: they may spend a couple of hours with their back mostly turned to the audience, but they spend typically about twenty hours in close eye-to-eye, mouth-to-ear contact with the members of the orchestra. Accordingly, the relationship they share with their musician colleagues has far more influence than any notions of the audience. Working within the circle of musicians engaged in hours of rehearsal, it is an unpleasant prospect for a conductor to take on the role of advocate for music peripheral to the established repertoire.

It is true, also, that in choosing to adopt the career of a conductor, the motivations are hardly likely to be those of humility or modesty. The presentation of the masterpieces of the repertoire is embedded into the training of every conductor as an essential marker of their aspirations and achievement. Mastery of masterpieces becomes the ultimate goal delineating the fulfilment of a conductor's dreams.

The instrumentalists who make up an orchestra are among the most highly trained people on earth, spending little of their lives away from the shelter of the institutions in which they are educated and work. It is impossible to calculate the number of hours they spend in the company of the great masters and the great repertoire. These hours are dedicated to the development of a profound fetishism towards masterpieces and even the individual passages within those master-pieces which they come to know by heart as orchestral excerpts. These moments extracted from the established repertoire are the essential elements of every audition process. Performing one of them in concert represents a high point in an orchestra member's professional achieve-ment. With this recognition firmly inculcated into their minds (and hands), it is hardly surprising that these musicians instantly recognize the slightest lapse from Repertoire status or familiarity. The traces of the banal and the vulgar are recognised immediately upon hearing.

The "Rock Symphony" by the Estonian composer Imants Kalnins provides a pertinent example of the way that orchestra members con-strue value. Lan Shui, the conductor who revived the symphony after years of neglect, observed that during rehearsals, the orchestra was resistant to the allure of this rock-influenced music, with its melodic freshness, prominent drum kit part and quasi-pop vocal solo. His ex-perience demonstrates once more the divergence between the judgment of those within the classical establishment and those outside it: "To tell you the truth," the conductor admitted, " the orchestra found it a little bit too 'easy' at first—you have thirty bars only changing little things, one statement lasts for two minutes—but the audiences had a totally different reaction. They just went wild. We saw a lot of new faces because they had seen the title 'Rock Symphony'. When the orchestra saw the audience reaction they gradually changed theirs!"[24]

The administrator of orchestral programming shares, to a greater or lesser extent, the training of the professional musician and conductor. Placed at the center of the decision making circle, he might think of himself as a tightrope walker striving to balance the artistic views of the conductor and musicians against the countervailing force of the marketers' interpretation of audience demand. His ethical position, however, boils down to one of defending the conductor's and musicians' high ideals against the marketers' incessant advocacy of dumbing-down. In this situation, there is no way of knowing, really, the tastes and feelings of an audience: marketers pretend to have some understand-ing, but the devices they rely upon to measure these things don't even come close to identifying what or how people actually feel. It is, there-fore, a relatively easy battle to subdue the marketers' pleas with argu-ments of artistic excellence and value. But at no point is there any hope that the inner values and tastes of the audience will emerge as something we can approach with genuine understanding.

A circular pattern emerges: orchestra members want to play the kind of music they have been trained to play (replicate); conductors choose the repertoire which marks the achievement of their ambitions and respect; administrators defend the views of both against the ignorance and bad taste of the audience.

The attitudes and characteristics outlined above are admittedly highly generalized, but they do serve to indicate the broad outlines of a comfort zone for each of the elements engaged in constructing an orchestra's musical life. The boundaries of these comfort zones overlap sufficiently to ensure that the limits of an acceptable repertoire are not stretched too far. Moreover, the tastes and pleasures of the audience are kept at a safe distance from the circle. The process is one that can hardly be noticed, but nonetheless divergent selections of repertoire and different musical values are constantly being filtered out of consideration. The result is that we work together, as if abiding by some secret compact, to make sure that we stick with a repertoire and a set of judgments of value, that firmly resists external threat.

Turn That Frown Into a Smile . . .

If there is a philosopher who can be taken to speak for today's classical music practitioner, it is probably Theodor Adorno. Among musicologists and composers, he's a great champion. Perhaps acquaintance with Adorno's musical philosophy has been directly inculcated into conductors, composers, players, even administrators, depending upon the extent of their exposure to musicology. But even if that's not the case, Adorno was himself a trained classical musician, and it is arguable that his philosophical project was motivated by a desire to keep a place for this tradition in the midst of the onslaught of capitalism's demeaning tendencies. Perhaps even the fact that Adorno is so often discussed is a sign of just how much the practitioners of classical music rely upon his definition of an heroic status for the classical tradition.

Adorno laid the groundwork for a suspicion of the musically obvious: truth has to be excavated from beneath the immediate sensations of music by the pure force of intellectual watchfulness. The forces of capitalist domination not only exploit music for greedy purposes, but manufacture demand and constrain music to compliance by forcing it

into standardized forms and practices (commodification). Consequently, the only way of getting at the truth is to adopt a position of
hypercritical negativity, refined into the mode of philosophical inquiry
Adorno termed Negative Dialectics.

In his pursuit of dialectical tensions, Adorno set up the clash between popular and classical cultures as a battle for truth, where the
classical prevails morally over the popular. Even within classical music,
Adorno identified a dialectic to restrict the field even further, by casting
unpopular Schoenberg as the heroic seeker of true musical content,
and opposing him to relatively popular Stravinsky, the entertainer and
stylistic gadabout. Schoenberg, in Adorno's view, provides the almost
perfect illustration of the artist working autonomously from the structures of capitalist society, the only way in which it is possible to maintain
the critical, enlightening power of music.

Adorno articulates his own, highly original conception of musical
value, but one which in the end is as exclusive and exclusionist as the
most conservative canon. To accept Adorno's conclusions you have to
believe that there is, somewhere over the distant horizon, a pristine,
ideal higher moral state that would justify the sacrifice of all immediate
pleasures in order to one day attain the Ideal. From here, it only takes
a little forgetfulness to make Adorno's Marxist idealism appear to coincide with the idealized moral authority of classical music. Like David
Drew in the examples cited earlier, Adorno makes frequent recourse
to disparaging references to the vulgar and the banal. However unfair
it may be to Adorno, the appearance of elitism in his work is hard to
shake off. The similarity between Adorno's conception of value and
that of your common or garden-variety classical music snob is so close
as to be almost invisible.

Adorno has not gone unchallenged, however, and in the challenges
to his views we find clues as to how we might reorient our aesthetic
values to avoid the exclusionist trap. Andreas Huyssen summarises
the negative attitudes Adorno's philosophy has spawned within high
art:

> Only by fortifying its boundaries, by maintaining its purity and
> autonomy, and by avoiding any contamination with mass culture
> and with the signifying systems of everyday life can the art work
> maintain its adversary stance: adversary to the bourgeois culture
> of everyday life as well as adversary to mass culture and enter-
> tainment which are seen as the primary forms of bourgeois cul-
> tural articulation.[25]

High art thinks itself virtuous in its "resistance to the seductive lure of mass culture, abstention from the pleasure of trying to please a larger audience."[26] Writing in 1986, Huyssen hoped that by dismantling the great divide between high and low culture (the "two spheres" in Adorno's articulation), a new artistic/cultural future might be brought into being. Presumably, he would be disappointed that this new future has met such stoic resistance from the keepers of high culture.

The musicologist Rose Rosengard Subotnick, emerging from a long absorption with Adorno's thought processes, gradually began to seek a way of being "loyal to him in being disloyal."[27] The point, says Subotnick, is not to read Adorno for his definitive pronouncements of value (which are almost unsustainable in the current situation of Western society), but to understand his critical attitude, which can, in fact, lead one to quite different conclusions.

Subotnick takes notice of the lessons of her own experience to form a critique of Adorno's theoretical positioning of the artist as a being autonomous from society. We may choose to replace our faith in the trickle-down effect—where an elite's discoveries are passed on, over time, to the hoi-polloi—with a trickle-up effect, where the world of classical music admits lessons from the field of popular music. Suggesting a new way for contemporary music to operate, Subotnick urges composers "to renounce the ideal of complete structural autonomy in favor of values associated with community, including communication."[28] By forsaking the forward-looking historical role which Adorno gives to the intellectual force of individual compositional insight, composers might better consider themselves as participants in an "ongoing discourse, inseparable from interpretation on all sides (the listener's and also the speaker's) in terms of numberless concrete values, associations and needs." They have to "move toward a condition of music closer to process than to structure" in order to "reintegrate their music into a socially broader context of meanings and values."[29]

That Huyssen's and Subotnick's recommendations for a change of attitude in contemporary music have made such little progress since the 1980s shows that the problems of contemporary music have a deeper underpinning in the exclusionist value systems of the whole field of classical music. Only the institutional strength of classical music enables this value system to survive. Elitist conceptions of musical value are protected, and any attempts to counter them are suppressed so that we might avoid losing our treasured self-image of moral and aesthetic superiority.

One more critique of Adorno remains to be cited. In his *Critique of Cynical Reason*,[30] Peter Sloterdijk characterizes Adorno's philosophy as one:

> based on a reproachful attitude, composed of suffering, contempt and rage against everything that has power. It makes itself into a mirror of the evil in the world, of bourgeois coldness, of the principle of domination, of dirty business and its profit motive . . . Its basic prejudice is that only evil power against the living can come from this world . . .[31]

For Adorno, "Happiness can only be thought of as something lost, as a beautiful alien. It cannot be anything more than a premonition which we approach with tears in our eyes, without ever reaching it."[32] Adorno is the great nay-sayer. But his unrelenting denial of immediate pleasures flies in the face of our own experience which, even in our imperfect society, more often approaches joyfulness and ecstasy than Adorno is willing to allow.

Adorno's philosophy rejects the ordinary human functions which are actually the most powerful sources of social criticism, and which speak most eloquently of our genuine desires. To recover a more positive aesthetic attitude, Sloterdijk suggests we look to another musically-literate philosopher, in many ways the defeated rival to Adorno—Ernst Bloch. A theoretician of the "principle of hope," Bloch "knew the private secret of cheering up, trusting in life, letting expression flow, believing in development. It was his power to recover the 'current of warmth' . . ."[33] Sloterdijk takes up this theme again when discussing Science, warning that the "price of objectivity is the loss of closeness. Scientists lose the capacity to behave as neighbours of the world; they think in concepts of distance, not of friendship; they seek overviews, not neighbourly involvement."[34]

Instead of seeking rapport, of finding ways to belong in the world, "high art,"

> for more than a hundred years . . . has been retreating into the difficult, the artistic, and the painful, into refined ugliness, artful brutalities, and calculated incomprehensibility, into the tragically complex and the bewilderingly capricious.
>
> (. . .) So much fresh negativity is spewed out by the modern arts that the thought of an "enjoyment of art" vanishes. Only in

snobbery, for the elite of connoisseurs and for fetishists, does the pleasure in unenjoyability flourish . . ."[35]

To contradict the mood of cynicism, Sloterdijk seeks "to try to name a source of enlightenment in which the secret of its vitality is hidden: cheekiness [*Frechheit*, a word whose meaning lies somewhere between cheekiness and impudence—Trans.]."[36]

In the critiques of Huyssens, Subotnick and Sloterdijk, we find pointers to a new attitude for the arts—de-snobbified, communal (neighborly), open to influence from the popular and the everyday— which classical music badly needs. The critiques culminate, for me at least, in the freshness, warmth and playfulness of Sloterdijk, who goes on to suggest we could embrace notions like "nostalgic charm," "the belly-laugh," "sticking the tongue out" and "listening more to what one's arse has to say."[37]

Adorno's insistence on negativity and autonomy may have been a feasible choice if the great Marxist Enlightenment historical project had some prospect of being delivered. But in its absence, Sloterdijk's suggestion that we devote our efforts to laughing together, overcoming loneliness, and making the most of our humanity is a better way, a better prospect for hopefulness. In emphasizing spontaneous, physical responses it is an idea, by the way, that resonates with Robert Fink's groping towards the notion of an "Erotics of Music."[38]

"Ratbags" or "Custodians?"

The quality of cheekiness-impudence that Sloterdijk speaks of is immediately recognizable to me in the Australian concepts of the larrikin and the ratbag.[39] These are, however, hardly the kinds of notions that Australians ever like to associate with our high culture, the institutions of which have been built on the imitation of, and obeisance to an idealization of European civilisation.

The Australian symphony orchestras were established through the injection of substantial government funding during the 1930s, to replicate the musical culture of the mother country, England. For decades we mimicked Englishness and tried to overcome our natural proclivities to behave in an unruly, boisterous and uncivilized manner, so that we could match up to the role model which England established for us. With the decline of England's cultural power in the 1960s (when its popular culture overwhelmed the high), the orchestras began to shift their worshipful gaze to Europe, where it still remains today. Australia's official culture constantly seeks the approval of Europe, and tries to define itself by suppressing the miscreant element in the Australian character. Australia's classical musicians, whether they be instrumentalists, conductors or composers, either take pride in the approval of their European masters, or achieve serious regard only when they can be judged favorably by European cultural standards.

A uniquely Australian voice like Percy Grainger is only accorded recognition in so far as he conforms to the proper image of an English folklorist or an American Wind Band composer. But Grainger can be understood in a much more stimulating way. Almost from the moment he arrived in Frankfurt as a young student, Grainger knew that the German way was not for him, and commenced a life of unending curiosity and investigation of musical sources tangential and opposite to this tradition. The music of the common folk in Britain, Northern Europe, America and Asia; the freedom of pure sound and the physical act of making sounds became the stimulants for his unbounded creativity. Grainger provides a contentious legacy of democratic inclusiveness, imaginative fecundity and wicked pleasure-seeking that has hardly received the attention it deserves, even from the institutions of his native Australian culture.

During the numerous debates about the future directions (and the viability) of the network of the six Australian symphony orchestras in which I have participated over the last ten years, it has fallen to one of my colleagues—artistic administrator of one of the other Australian orchestras—to make a defense of that rock-hard object, surrounded by a mystical aura, known as the Repertoire. His argument is that orchestras exist because of the great music written by the great composers: the very existence of Bach, Beethoven, Mozart, Brahms, Tchaikovsky etc., is our justification for being. This lineage finds itself perpetuated in the work of contemporary composers who have achieved similar status as heroes of the canon. We are, says my colleague, the *custodians* of this heritage.

The argument against this custodian view goes like this: no, orchestras exist, or should only reasonably expect to exist, as long as they are being listened to, as long as they are really integral participants in our society or community. Our task is to engage with the people who live around us, to interact with them in ways that change them and change us. Even when we serve Beethoven, we are not doing it because he existed, but for the sake of the audiences who will enjoy his music now.

The custodian view of classical music casts a lineage of heroes, a pantheon in whose shadow the listener or musician might stand awestruck and subservient. The appeal of Sloterdijk's retelling of philosophical and cultural history is in its proposal of a post heroic view (I believe Sloterdijk has in fact used this term in his consideration of the political future), a concept which fits with Robert Fink's "post-canonic world."

In establishing a playful, neighborly relationship between the different sectors, we might just find a way to avoid our slow decline into market-driven programming. In the current state of panic which grips the classical music establishment, marketing is often seized upon as a means to salvation. But any answers which marketing may provide are at best short term, relying on clever persuasion rather than establishing a relationship of genuine rapport. Where short-term devices like audience surveys simply end up regurgitating the usual litany of best known pieces by best known composers, another, greater effort is required: to understand what audiences authentically feel as the basis for constructing a vital relationship. Good neighbors, after all, talk to each other over the fence, in a free exchange of gossip, opinions and judgments.

Recovering the lost sense of community requires a renewal of the values of classical music. It requires that we subject the repertoire to a process of revisionism in which ties to the vernacular are restored, both by expanding the boundaries to include music hitherto excluded from the Canon, and by restoring an awareness of the elements of commonness within the music of the beloved greats, rather than making a fetish out of their superior genius. A bit of healthy disrespect for traditional judgments will be helpful in setting us free from the entropic spiral of classical music's decline. The reconstruction of our value system will not restore orchestras to their former position of privilege at the top of the musical tree, but it may give them a reason to exist: as vital, vivacious contributors to the cultural and artistic future.

Those who develop the artistic direction of orchestras and classical music institutions should continue to advocate pieces and composers that are not known by audiences. We spend our lives, after all, listening to the stuff, so naturally we know more, in sheer quantity, than they do. But there is a mistake in believing (or even wanting to believe) that our knowledge is somehow qualitatively better than that of the ordinary individual.

We should not use our (supposedly) principled objections to criteria of accessibility or social justice to justify avoiding challenges to our attitudes and methods of valuing music. In the 1980s, French political theorist André Gorz made the startling gesture of urging socialists to bid "farewell to the working class," and now it's time for us to bid farewell to our old hierarchies of musical merit, too—perhaps even to the notion of classical music as a boundaried category itself.

NOTES

1. Oswald Spengler, author of *Decline of the West* (Allen & Unwin, London, 1922), was the first to utter a lament for the dying classical traditions of European culture.

2. Throughout this chapter, I use the term classical music to encompass the broad category or class of music that also goes by the name of "Western classical music," "fine music," or "serious music," and the range of institutions through which it is supported and maintained.

3. See Barbara Isenberg, "Marketing Music: 'Can you say Baby Boomer?'," *Los Angeles Times* (19 November, 1989); and National Endowment for the Arts Research Department (Richard A. Peterson, Darren C. Sherkat, Judith Huggins Balfe, Rolf Meyersohn), *Age and Arts Participation with a Focus on the Baby Boom Cohort*, Research Report no. 34, (Washington: National Endowment for the Arts, 1996). (Based on the NEA's Surveys of Public Participation in the Arts conducted in 1982 and 1992).

4. Americanizing the American Orchestra: Report of the National Task Force for "The American orchestra: An initiative for change" (Washington, DC: American Symphony Orchestra League, 1993).

5. Samuel Lipman, "Who's killing our symphony orchestras?" *The New Criterion* 12, no. 1 (September 1993).

6. Bradford D. Buckley, "ICSOM, ASOL, and Orchestras in Crisis" in *Senza Sordino: Official Publication of the International Conference of Symphony and Opera Musicians* 32, no. 1 (October 1993), 4.

7. Robert Fink, "Elvis Everywhere: Musicology and Popular Music Studies at the Twilight of the Canon," *American Music* 16, no. 2 (Summer 1998), 135–79.

8. Norman Lebrecht, When the Music Stops: Managers, Maestros and the Corporate Murder of Classical Music (London: Simon & Schuster, 1996).

9. Robert Fink, "Elvis Everywhere: Musicology and Popular Music Studies at the Twilight of the Canon," 138.

10. Ibid., 145.

11. Ibid., 140.

12. As represented, for instance, in the study by Robert R. Faulkner, *Hollywood Studio Musicians: their work and careers in the recording industry* (Chicago: Aldine-Atherton, 1971).

13. Adelaide Symphony Orchestra conducted by Arvo Volmer, soloist Geoffrey Collins (flute), (12–14 September, 2002).
14. CD Liner notes to the recording of the Rouse *Flute Concerto*, TELARC (CD 80452).
15. Arnold Whittall, liner notes to *Berg, Webern, Schoenberg: Orchestral Pieces*, Berlin Philharmonic Orchestra, conducted by James Levine, Deutsche Grammophon (CD 419 718-2).
16. Adelaide Symphony Orchestra conducted by Reinbert de Leeuw, soloists Michael Kieran Harvey and Bernadette Harvey-Balkus (pianos), (16 June, 2000). Recorded by ABC Classic FM Radio. Comments by Peter Sellars are transcribed from the broadcast tapes.
17. "John Adams on Grand Pianola Music" on the composer's Web site, http://www.earbox.com/sub-html/comp-details/gpianola-de.html.
18. Geoffrey Self, *Light Music in Britain since 1870: A Survey* (Aldershot: Ashgate, 2001), 71.
19. David Drew, "Modern French Music," in Howard Hartog, ed., *European Music in the Twentieth Century*, (London: Routledge & Kegan Paul, 1957), reprinted in paperback by Penguin, Harmondsworth (1961), 288. (Quotations and page numbers from the paperback edition).
20. Ibid., 292.
21. Ibid., 293.
22. Howard Hartog, "Introduction" to Ibid., 18. The phrase may have been borrowed from Adorno's "the flight from the banal" in his 1938 essay, "On the Fetish-Character in Music and the Regression of Listening", in Adorno, *Essays on Music*, Selected, with Introduction, Commentary and Notes by Richard Leppert, trans Susan H. Gillespie (Berkeley: University of California Press, 2002), 293.
23. David Drew, "Modern French Music," 306.
24. Imants Kalnin, *"Rock" Symphony (Symphony No.4)*, 1972. Recorded by the Singapore Symphony Orchestra, conducted by Lan Shui, soloist Jackie Short (soprano). Liner notes by Kingsley Flint (BIS CD-1052).
25. Andreas Huyssen, *After the Great Divide: Modernism, Mass Culture, Postmodernism* (London: Macmillan, 1988), 54.
26. Ibid., 55.
27. Rose Rosengard Subotnick, *Developing Variations: Style and Ideology in Western Music* (Minneapolis: University of Minnesota Press, 1991), 58.
28. Ibid., 291.
28. Ibid., 291.
30. Peter Sloterdijk, *Critique of Cynical Reason*, trans. Michael Eldred, (London: Verso, 1988). Originally published as *Kritik der zynischen Vernunft* (Frankfurt am Main: Suhrkamp Verlag, 1983).
31. Ibid., xxxiv–xxxv.
32. Ibid., xxxv.
33. Ibid., 125.
34. Ibid., 140.
35. Ibid., 109.
36. Ibid., 99–100.

37. Sloterdijk, op cit., these items are referred to in Chapter 6, "Concerning the Psychosomatics of the Zeitgeist," 139–154 and Conclusion, "Under Way towards a Critique of Subjective Reason," 534–547.

38. Fink, "Elvis Everywhere: Musicology and Popular Music Studies at the Twilight of the Canon," 171.

39. Larrikin: "a lout; a hoodlum; a mischievous young person"; Ratbag: "a rascal; rogue; a person of eccentric or nonconforming ideas or behaviour," *The Macquarie Dictionary*, Federation Edition, The Macquarie Library, Sydney, 2001.

8

The Good, The Bad, and The Folk

RICHARD CARLIN

As a sometimes folksinger, folklorist, and writer on traditional music, I have long been interested in how folk music is judged, not only by those outside the folk world but by its diehard partisans and practitioners. What makes for a "good" folk performance? Do you have to be "one of the folk" to play folk music? I always thought of Josh White's oft-quoted quip, "I never heard no horse play music" when some questioned why a Jewish, middle-class, suburban born-and-raised musician was playing Irish music on the concertina, as I was doing, or conducting field work recording older musicians. But, paradoxically, the recordings that I made—primarily my recordings of Irish musicians living in Cleveland—were criticized by (some) in the folk community for their lack of "professionalism": I included performances where musicians made "mistakes" and the recordings sounded like they were made in someone's basement—which, in fact, they were.

These critiques by folk performers, academic folklorists, and popular music writers led me to think about how folk music is defined; why some music is deemed "good" while other is thought to be "bad" or "impure"; and the ramifications this has on the performers themselves, both from within the folk tradition and those—like me—who are outsiders to it. My intention is not to denigrate folk revivalists for their sometimes contradictory statements about what makes folk music valuable and worth preserving; after all, I am a revivalist myself. Rather, I think these ideas need to be examined more thoroughly so that a new, perhaps more open and accepting standard can be developed for judging folk music performance.

Paradoxes and Problems in American Folk Music

If folk music can be performed by anyone who is a "folk," then how can we separate the "good" performers from the "bad?" Folk performers and their audiences have struggled with this problem for decades. Faced with the criticism of the classical (and to a lesser extent popular) music establishments—who often dismissed folk musicians as illiterates who could barely sing or play in tune—folk fans retaliated by developing their own criteria of goodness, i.e., taking what were formerly viewed as deficiencies and elevating them to hallmarks of the folk style. Some of the new ideas that the folk fans promulgated include: Classical music is aimed at a rarefied audience, and can only be performed by a talented few (that's *bad*); folk music is suitable for all listeners and can be performed by anyone (that's *good*). Popular music is sold by mighty musical conglomerates for profit (*bad*); folk music is free to all and owned by no one (*good*). Singing in tune requires years of specialized training and is artificial (*bad*); singing in a natural way requires no training (*good*).

However, in the process of elevating what was once perceived as "bad" music and making it "good"—and redefining other musical forms, previously seen as "good" and portraying them as "bad"—folklorists developed many false dichotomies between folk and other musical styles, exaggerating some aspects of folk music, downplaying others, to bolster their argument. In fact, there is not as much separating folk music from art or popular styles as was at first supposed. And ideas of what is good about folk music have changed, so that once bad musical styles are now warmly accepted as authentic folk ones.

The Establishment of a Folk Aesthetic

The first "folklorists" working from the late eighteenth through the early twentieth centuries defined "folk music" as music created by a native people, outside of the influence of "urban" ("popular" or "classical") styles. This music was said to have "survived" from "earlier times" among the folk because they were effectively cut off from the corrupting modern influences of newspapers or books, or travel beyond their native "community." Because the "folk" were deprived of written records of their music, folklorists determined that they must learn this music from each other, in a manner described as "oral transmission." Ideally, a parent would sing a song that the child might then learn; or a neighbor teach a friend a fiddle tune. The process of "oral transmission" led to some unintentional changes; just as in the game of telephone, words might be misunderstood or garbled or melodies inadvertently changed. This was all part of what came to be called the "folk process."[1]

Folk songs were not thought to be "composed" in the same sense that art or popular songs were written by individuals. Rather, the process of oral transmission enabled each singer to become, in a sense, a composer as well. Good versions of a song would survive because the community would learn them; bad versions would die because they wouldn't be as popular. This was essentially a democratic notion, allowing the "people" to build their own musical repertoire through self-selection.[2]

In the 1930s and 1940s when the first urban folk boom occurred in the United States, this definition was given a more political bent. Folklorists like Alan Lomax were disturbed by the mass merchandising of popular song through radio, phonograph recordings, and sheet music. Music was being imposed on the people, rather than welling up from among them. For Lomax, folk music represented the democratic "voice of the people," enabling them to express their views on politics, social conditions, and racial inequality.[3] Lomax and his cohorts were equally disturbed by the notion that music making was limited to a talented few. Anyone could be a folk musician in their view. Thus, polished performance became suspect because it indicated that the performer had been exposed to musical training. Technical proficiency was to be shunned in order to make music accessible to all.[4]

To summarize, folklorists essentially developed a set of rules or a folk aesthetic, if you will, in comparison with their understanding of what constituted popular music:

- Folk music grows out of the community and is supported by it; pop music is imposed by commercial interests on its audience
- Folk music can be performed by anyone, and talent (or lack of it) is no barrier to the folk performer; pop performers should be trained and meet minimum standards of musical capability

- "Good" folk songs are old; learned through oral means; and performed in a unique way; pop songs are new, learned from printed or recorded materials, and always performed in the same way.
- In folk music, *authenticity* is to be valued over popularity. Good folk performers are those who come out of a tradition, rather than learning the music second or third hand. Credentials such as these are unimportant to the pop performer.

However, if we examine each of these supposed dichotomies, we will discover that they are primarily based on mistaken ideas promulgated by folklorists who wished to carve out a special place for folk music. Furthermore, by adhering to these false definitions, the folk community has put its performers in a difficult, if not untenable position; they are part of the commercial world but are constricted by the rules governing their repertoire and its performance.

The Folk Music Community

The notion of a stable community that nurtures a musical style is based on the belief that in certain rural areas—the Appalachian mountains, for example—people are shielded from outside influences by the very inaccessibility of their homes. Thus, older traditions tend to survive because they aren't crowded out by more modern trends. While there may be some truth to this argument—the inhabitants of the Georgia Sea Islands, for example, have preserved their song and dance traditions, perhaps due to their lack of access to mainland Southern culture[5]—it is clear that as early as the mid-nineteenth century Southern mountain culture was influenced by outside forces.

The Civil War took many Southerners out of the mountains and exposed them to new musical styles. Fife and drum tune books from this era contain many of the fiddle tunes that were later collected from mountain musicians. After the war, traveling minstrel shows fanned out throughout the South, often visiting the smallest towns. Even as early as the 1840s to the 1850s, the banjo was spread by professional musicians, like Joel Walker Sweeney, working as traveling entertainers.[6] Instruction books were published and widely available on how to play the instrument by the 1870s, including notation of songs that were ideally accompanied by the banjo. A look at the recorded repertoire of early country performers like Fiddlin' John Carson or Uncle Dave Macon—both in their mid-fifties when they began to record in the 1920s—shows the vast majority of their material coming from printed sources, either sheet music, minstrel songbooks, or other nontraditional sources. Carson's first recording made in 1923 paired a popular sentimental song with a minstrel-show era fiddle instrumental, linking two key sources for old-time Southern music. In short, Southern musicians were exposed to a wide variety of musical styles and shared much of the same repertoire that Northern entertainers performed.

Further, folk music is not always proudly supported by the community out of which it emerges. As just one example, blues musicians of the teens and 1920s were not considered to be model citizens; many were unemployable (due to disabilities such as blindness). Blues was performed in places that were considered less-than-desirable by the African American community at large, such as edge-of-town jukè joints or whorehouses. Drunken brawls, acts of violence, and sexual promiscuity were all part of the blues performer's world. Clearly, the community at large shunned the blues.[7] Moreover, their popularity even among the less-desirable classes was short-lived; from about the turn of the century to the early 1930s, traditional blues performers flourished, but after that their style of music was considered hopelessly old-fashioned. The country blues revival of the 1950s and 1960s was limited to a small, primarily white and urban audience.

Finally, by the 1970s and 1980s, the notion of an insulated and supportive community as the natural source for folk music was belied by the brutal facts of mass communications (television, radio, cable television—and later the Internet) and mass mobility that made it possible for even the poorest members of society to leave home—or to be exposed to many different cultures without traveling around the world. Just one example comes from my own work as a folklorist. During the mid-1970s, I recorded musicians in one traditional enclave, the Irish community in Cleveland. The Irish tended to live in the same area, attend the same churches and schools, patronize the same dance schools, and support the same festivals. In short, they constituted nearly an ideal folk "community," as defined by folklorists. But, it was clear that those who valued traditional Irish music were among the minority, limited to a handful of performers.

Tom Byrne was an Irish flute player from Cleveland whom I recorded and played music with in the later 1970s. Although a handful of other musicians in the community appreciated his talent, even within his own family, his music was not highly regarded. His children were more interested in listening to Fleetwood Mac and other popular rock bands of the era than sitting in on the Irish sessions happening in their home. The sessions held in the basement of his home might consist of Tom with just one or two other musicians playing together; no one came to listen, and the group never played outside of Tom's home. While there were slightly more active musicians in the community, in general the Irish musicians in Cleveland gained little attention, even among the folk revivalists. The title of the record that I made of these musicians, titled *Irish Music from Cleveland*, was often greeted with humorous comments like, "*What* Irish music from Cleveland?"—even by natives of the city.[8]

The records that I made of Tom and his musical cohorts did not sell within the Irish community in Cleveland. I don't know of a single record store in the region that stocked them, and they attracted no local review attention. Meanwhile, the larger folk revival world also failed to embrace them. By this point in the folk revival, recordings of "pure" folk musicians like Byrne were themselves subject to criticism for being "bad" in comparison with the revivalists because they lacked the high polish of a commercial performance.[9] By the mid-1970s, folk performers were expected to entertain their audience, and display a level of virtuosity on a par with popular musicians. The popularity of Irish music—thanks to younger musicians incorporating rock and other popular musical instruments, stylings, and recording techniques into their records—had attracted a larger audience not interested in authenticity as much as high levels of virtuosity and showmanship. These folk musicians were considered crude in comparison.

Anyone Can Be a Folk Musician

The idea that folk musicians are "natural" performers who do not have any special musical abilities is belied by the fact that almost every musician "discovered" by a folklorist has in fact had exceptional talents, unusual repertories, and usually is a great entertainer, to boot. In fact, the very reason these musicians are chosen to be recorded—and later taken on tour to perform—is *because of* these exceptional abilities, not in spite of them—despite the fact that folklorists make every attempt to market their finds as natural or unspoiled commodities.

A perfect example is the prisoner/folksinger Lead Belly, "discovered" in Angola State Prison in Louisiana in 1933 by John and Alan Lomax.[10] The Lomaxes brought Lead Belly north to perform, wrote a book about his music, and oversaw his initial recording sessions, and so shaped how he was presented to his audience. They marketed him as a kind of folk primitive; in an early film, he was dressed in coveralls and seated on a large bale of hay while performing. In newspaper articles and in their book, *Negro Folk Songs as Sung by Lead Belly*, the Lomaxes constantly emphasized his past, rough-and-tumble life. Newspaper headlines announcing a Lead Belly performance, like "Sweet Singer of the Swamplands . . . To Do a Few Tunes Between Homicides," were not uncommon.[11]

But Lead Belly was an exceptional performer—clearly one of the best performers of the many prisoners that the Lomaxes recorded during their stay at Angola. He was an unusually inventive guitarist, incorporating a boogie-woogie bass line into his playing (showing clearly that he was influenced by current musical trends). He knew a wide range of songs, from personal compositions to hymns, children's songs, field hollers, and blues. Plus, he had been a successful songster—a traveling performer—in the Texas-Louisiana region before his imprisonment following a knife fight at a local dance (a not uncommon occurrence in the black musical world of the South at the time). Live recordings made in the late 1940s (admittedly after Lead Belly had been performing for Northern audiences for a while) show him to be an excellent performer, certainly not your typical nonprofessional musician.[12] The Lomaxes could have brought another performer north but clearly selected Lead Belly because of his exceptional talents as a performer.

Nonetheless, what made Lead Belly a "good" performer in the Lomaxes' eyes was his extra-musical value as an ex-convict from the South. As a musical curiosity, he was accepted by the folk audience; but no one in the "serious" (or even popular) music world would accept him as a performer, because his musical style was out-of-date. In fact, the first recordings he made for the commercial record label ARC, under Lomax's supervision, sold poorly.[13] Although he would later record for Victor and Capitol, he primarily recorded for the tiny Asch label, which catered to a folk audience, reflecting the fact that he had little commercial appeal.[14] The Lomaxes' book about Lead Belly did not focus on the performer's musical skills; the transcriptions were simplified melody lines with guitar chords and in no way reflected Lead Belly's intricate, blues and boogie-woogie influenced guitar playing. Moreover, the songs were presented as "authentic" outpourings of a folk performer; no attempt was made to trace them to their popular roots (because to do so would be to deny the genius of the folk and instead glorify the pop music industry).[15]

The Search for "Authentic" Performers

As the folk revivalists became more sophisticated, the search for *authentic* performers became more intense. Armed with portable tape recorders, an army of young folk fans combed the South in search of folk performers beginning in the mid-1950s. Just as the Lomaxes searched for unspoiled musicians who were unaware of modern commercial music, these devotees searched for older musicians who might still remember the traditional music of their youth (ignoring, conveniently, the fact that this traditional music was, in fact, the popular music of several decades earlier). The preference for older performers led to a somewhat skewed approach; many were in decline as musicians, and it was impossible to say with any certainty if their lack of skill (ability to sing or play in tune, rhythmic irregularities, etc.) was a product of age or an intentional, aesthetic choice.

A story that folklorist Mike Seeger tells illuminates this point. Like many other banjo players, Seeger is most interested in musicians who use unusual tunings or play in unconventional ways. He encountered a banjo player who tuned the fifth (or short) string lower than was usual, while tuning the other four strings conventionally. Fascinated by this highly unusual approach to tuning, he made a date to record the player. When he arrived to make the recording, he was surprised when the musician began playing, because now the fifth string was tuned in the conventional manner. When he asked why the banjo player had originally played using the unusual tuning, the musician replied, "Well, my tuning peg was broken; now it's fixed." Seeger, however, was less interested in the musician now that he realized he played in a normal way; the accidental, "bad" performance was more unique than the good one.[16]

Accidents such as broken banjo tuners can also happen to the physical body of the performer. Often, folk musicians work at physically taxing jobs, or can't afford proper health care, resulting in damage to their physical ability to sing and play. North Carolina banjo player Fred Cockerham claimed to have a high tenor voice in his youth. One night, as he related, he drove home during a snowstorm after drinking heavily and found himself trapped in his car. When he woke up, he claimed, his voice suddenly had dropped to a deep baritone.[17] The only recordings that exist are of this later, deep voice. What did he previously sound like? How did his style change? Despite the damage to his voice, Cockerham remained an expressive and talented singer; was he now a better singer? Did the damage in fact create an opportunity for him to create a new vocal style? Or was this simply a good story, one that Cockerham created as an amusing self-fiction to explain his unusually deep voice.

When older performers were rediscovered as part of the folk-revival movement, many were in their retirement years; several had not performed their own material for decades, due to lack of interest or downright hostility of their family and community. It was only when folk revivalists came on the scene that their music was valued. For example, Dock Boggs, who had recorded blues-influenced songs in the late 1920s and early 1930s, gave up banjo playing in the early 1950s due to the opposition of his wife and church. One of his early recordings, "Sugar Baby," an unusual, blues-tinged banjo song, was reissued on Harry Smith's landmark *Anthology of American Folk Music* collection in 1952, introducing Boggs's playing to a core of folk revivalists.[18] Determined to find Boggs, Mike Seeger made a trip to his home region in the early 1960s. Oddly enough, Seeger found him still listed in the local phone directory, called the number, and subsequently met and recorded the musician.[19]

Boggs probably would never have performed or recorded again in the 1960s if he hadn't been rediscovered; nor was he aware that his early recordings had been reissued and that there was a younger generation of (mostly urban) musicians copying his performances note-for-note. Because Boggs recorded in the late 1920s, and was then recorded again in the mid-1960s, we can compare his youthful performances to his later ones. As might be expected, judging from these recordings, the older Boggs was not as vocally or instrumentally adept as the younger musician. After all, he hadn't played for years, and it is natural for an older musician to lack the vocal or instrumental capabilities of a younger one. Could we then characterize Boggs's earlier recordings as *better* than his later ones? Moreover, if Boggs had never recorded in the 1920s and then been discovered in the 1960s, how would we judge his performances? His repertoire would have been much more limited: he might have been able to recall fragments of his youthful repertoire, but probably not to the extent that was made possible through the existence of the earlier recordings. Or, perhaps, he wouldn't have been heard at all; there's no reason why he would have taken up banjo playing again without the external stimulus of the urban revivalists.[20]

Folklorists as Arbiters of "Good" and "Bad" Music

If a ballad singer sang old ballads and newer pop songs, the folk collector would usually record only the older material. Material that is learned in a traditional manner—from a family member, passed down from generation to generation—is generally valued more highly by collectors than songs learned from songbooks, radio, or recordings. Thus, the more old/traditional material that a performer knows, the more "talented"/"good" that performer is judged to be by the folklorist/collector. Yet, there is ample evidence to suggest that the traditional musicians themselves rarely make this distinction.

I had the opportunity to record fiddle player Ward Jarvis in the mid-1970s. Jarvis played in a very archaic manner, resting his instrument on his forearm and angling his arm back and forth while bowing (rather than adjusting the angle of the bow) to hit the individual strings. However, his repertory ranged from unusual older tunes dating from the late eighteenth century to Civil War tunes, turn-of-the-century pop numbers, right up to bluegrass and contemporary country tunes he learned from the radio. Jarvis made little distinction; he played tunes that he liked, regardless of their age or how he learned them. However, when I played tapes for other folklorists, they were primarily interested in the oldest, most unusual tunes, and even somewhat disdainful of the newer tunes that Jarvis played.[21] Further, the more unusual tunes (less often performed by others) were more highly valued than the common ones, unless Jarvis played a common tune in an unusual way. But, as far as I could tell, Jarvis himself made no such value judgments.

Another example shows how evolving standards of "good" and "bad" among folk music collectors have changed how a performer is perceived is the career of guitarist/singer Arthel "Doc" Watson. Folklorist Ralph Rinzler first heard of the North Carolina musician from Clarence "Tom" Ashley, an older banjo player who had originally recorded in the 1920s and was rediscovered in the early 1960s by Rinzler. Watson was playing electric guitar at the time in a local club in a rockabilly cover band. Rinzler was unimpressed; he wasn't interested in hearing someone play lukewarm versions of Carl Perkins's songs. However, sometime later he happened to be with Watson when someone produced a banjo. Watson commented that he had played the instrument as a youth, and, picking it up, began to play in a traditional style. Suddenly, Rinzler's interest was piqued; and when Watson said that he also played traditional songs on the acoustic guitar, Rinzler immediately recognized his unique talent.[22]

The arc of Watson's career gives insights into his audience's changing expectations of what they wanted to hear from a folk performer. His initial recordings from the early 1960s were made for the folk label, Vanguard, and featured just himself and his son, Merle, on guitars. Watson's performing schedule focused on coffeehouses, clubs, college campuses, and the ubiquitous folk festivals of the era. However, Watson's career changed when, in 1970, he was invited to participate in a series of sessions in Nashville arranged by the country-rock band, The Nitty Gritty Dirt Band, resulting in the very popular 3-LP set, *Will the Circle Be Unbroken*? Signed to the major United Artists label, Watson began recording with electric bass and drums, accompaniment that would have riled his 1960s folk fans. After being dropped by UA in the later 1970s, Watson then recorded primarily for folk-bluegrass labels, but still with more accompanying instruments, including electric guitars, fiddles, electric bass, and drums. His son, Merle, was greatly influenced by the Allman Brothers, and introduced blues into Watson's shows. This broadening of musical styles was now considered acceptable by Watson's core audience, who no longer viewed either electric instruments or mixing blues, country, and other genres as a form of folk-music sin (as earlier folkies were apt to do). And, ironically, by the mid-1990s, Watson was back to performing the rockabilly music that he had played in the late 1950s. By this point, rockabilly was viewed as a roots music rather than a commercial pop one. It was considered as much a folk music style as the old ballads and songs that first attracted Rinzler to the musician.

The point is that our ideas of what is "good" and "bad" change over time, as the definition of what is traditional has changed. In the

1930s and 1940s, the original folk revivalists battled against the influx of jukebox music; today swing-era pop is itself a roots musical style, insofar as it influenced later musical developments in rock and R&B. The old dichotomies give way to new ones; and it is undoubtedly true that folklorists in the year 2050 will be studying today's pop as a traditional musical expression, just as folklorists in the 1950s studied turn-of-the-century pop as it was performed by country and blues musicians in authentic folk versions.

The Dilemma of the Revivalists

The folk revival has raised questions about what makes for "good" and "bad" performances. If you have to suffer to sing the blues, i.e., be an authentic, Southern field hand in order to perform this music, how can a white, middle-class performer like Dave Van Ronk or Paul Butterfield claim to be a bluesman? Can a white man sing the blues? And, if so, does the white man have the right to interpret the material, or merely to copy and pass on the earlier performances.

Sound recordings also have distorted the folk aesthetic. In the days of aural transmission of songs, one singer would learn a song from another. The process of learning and the vagaries of memory would color the new singer's interpretation. Verses would be substituted; local references changed; melodies and chords altered. This was all part of the time-honored folk process, and folklorists approved heartily of it—as long as you were one of the folk.

Folk revivalists, however, faced a different challenge. Not being folk themselves, they risked the universal condemnation of folklorists if they introduced musical elements from their own experience into their interpretations of traditional songs and tunes. The first popular folk revival groups, like the Kingston Trio, were unashamed in their introduction of pop harmonies, instrumentation, and rhythms into their cover versions of folksongs. The Trio's first major hit was "Tom Dooley," a composed song based on a real story of a 1920s-era love crime.[23] Folk purists universally were appalled by this record. This was partially due (ironically) to the group's success; the general feeling among diehard folk music fans is that anyone who achieves chart success can't be authentic. Alan Lomax and Pete Seeger spent years railing at the artificial sentiments of pop songwriters;[24] the folk crowd could not accept seeing their music turned into fodder for the commercial music machine. But it was also due to the group's willingness to introduce Four Freshman-styled harmonies and jazzy accompaniments into the world of toothless-old-banjo-music.

But how was this appropriation of an old folk song different from 1920s-era banjoist Charlie Poole introducing jazz-flavored elements and pop-influenced singing into his work? Poole is venerated by the old-time revivalists—indeed, his performances are often recreated note-for-note. Because seventy-eight recordings existed of his variations of traditional folk songs—and covers of pop songs of the day—revivalists could literally xerox his every inflection in their own performances. This kind of devoted carbon-copying was embodied in groups like The New Lost City Ramblers, the folk revival's own anti-Kingston Trio. The Ramblers were purists; they believed in the sanctity of the recorded document. In a time when seventy-eight recordings were not widely available through reissues, their performances helped inspire a revival of interest in the earlier artists like Charlie Poole and Uncle Dave Macon. But, in spite of these laudable results, one is tempted to ask why the Ramblers—three college-educated, urban-raised musicians—felt so strongly that they dare not reinterpret their material based on their own musical experiences.[25]

Unlike the New Lost City Ramblers, another old-time revival group, the Holy Modal Rounders, took a looser approach to their old-time music recreations, daring to meld Dada-esque and Beat-influenced poetry into their performances of stringband and country blues songs of the 1920s. Formed a few years later than the Ramblers—and coming out of New York's Lower East side mixture of avant-garde art and culture—the Rounders recorded two acoustic albums before succumbing to the allure of psychedelic music and mind-altering drugs. Never really enjoying a large following among diehard folk fans, the Rounders nonetheless pointed towards a different way of revering traditional roots. Rather than slavishly imitate, they were happy to introduce musical and lyrical references drawn from the contemporary scene.[26]

Blues recreators faced similar dilemmas. When Dave Van Ronk, popular Greenwich Village blues singer of the late 1950s and early 1960s, sang in a raspy voice, was he imitating earlier raspy-voiced blues singers—or was this his true singing voice? Were his note-for-note copies of seventy-eight recordings homages to the rich heritage of the blues (as undoubtedly Van Ronk and his fans would have believed) or minstrel-like appropriations, colored by his non-blues, non-black background (as some later scholars might assert). What's the difference between a blackface minstrel performer of the 1850s like Dan Rice copying a black rural musician's performance and Van Ronk's (or any other white blues revivalist's) later-day recreations? Is it merely the passage of 100 years and the lack of burnt cork that gives Van Ronk his validity? Why is Rice now viewed as a bad expropriator of traditional music, while Van Ronk is viewed as a good preserver of it?

The folk-purist trap was felt by those blues performers who dared to innovate as well. Paul Butterfield's Blues Band played electric instruments, which were traditional among the Chicago bluesmen from whom they learned their music, but not much liked by folk revivalists. (It was the Butterfield band that accompanied Bob Dylan at the infamous 1965 Newport Folk Festival show where Dylan went electric and the folkniks went berserk.) But, breaking ranks even further, the band introduced Indian-influenced sounds on albums like *East-West*, and in later incarnations incorporated pop-rock songs into their repertoire. The Butterfield Band played some folk events like major folk festivals, but were basically viewed by revivalists as a commercial, pop ensemble. They got no credit for stretching the boundaries of the blues.

Some would argue that the only valid revival recording of a folk performance is an exact copy—in the manner of the New Lost City Ramblers or dozens of blues revivalists. This was the working hypothesis for the original folk revivalists, although often they would unintentionally introduce their own idiosyncrasies into their performances. John Jacob Niles probably felt he was singing ballads in an "authentic" manner but his highly stylized vocals and classically flavored accompaniments were anything but traditional. Others would argue that because the folk process is based on musicians interacting with traditional material that revivalists should reflect their own musical tastes and backgrounds—this seems to be the dominant position today. The growth of sound recording has lead to an almost smorgasbord free-for-all where musicians feel they can pick and choose their favorite bits and pieces of various traditions, without worrying about exactly recreating any one style. Perhaps, this is the ultimate good end to decades of hand-wringing over authenticity. After all, the original folk performers were happy to perform any music that they heard and liked; thanks to the proliferation of sound recordings, today's musicians can sample an entire world of musical expression, spanning centuries of music as well as geographically encircling the globe. Perhaps, these subjective guideposts are the best ones for forming a new folk aesthetic, and ultimately settling—or at least setting aside—arguments over legitimacy and *goodness* versus *bad* performances.

NOTES

1. Abrahams & Foss (1968), 13–17; Filene (2000), 9–12.
2. Lomax (1947), in Cohen (2003), 91.
3. Lomax (1940), in Cohen (2003), 47.
4. See Calkins and Lomax (1960, in Cohen (2003), 203–06.
5. See for example *Been in the Storm So Long* (Folkways 3842) and Rosenbaum (1998).
6. B. Carlin (unpublished manuscript).
7. Calt (1994), 254–55 and Gussow (2002), 195ff.
8. These recordings, made between 1977–80, were originally issued on Folkways albums 3517, 3521, and 3523.
9. One example is Krassen's (1998) review.
10. Porterfield (1996), 200.
11. Wolfe and Lornell (1992), 139ff.
12. The Lomaxes and others in the folk revival community were upset by Lead Belly's increasing proficiency as a performer; for them, it spoiled his "pure, natural" style; see Filene (2000), 73.
13. Ibid, 159–60, 179–80. The actual ARC contract was with Lomax, not Leadbelly, but neither profited much from the deal because only one recording was issued at the time.
14. For Moses Asch's relation to Leadbelly, see Wolfe and Lornell, 224–27, also Young (1977), 5–6.
15. Lomax (1936).
16. Personal communication with Mike Seeger. Seeger was quite aware of the ironies in this story, and included himself in the implicit criticism of collectors who value oddities over more conventional performances.
17. Personal communication with Fred Cockerham. Cockerham told this story on many occasions to various collectors; see Alden (1992), [13–14].
18. Pankake, p. 19; O'Connell, 6.
19. Seeger 19–20
20. The posthumous reputation of Dock Boggs was given a major boost when Greil Marcus highlighted his music in his book, *Invisible Republic: Bob Dylan and the Basement Tapes*; see Marcus (1995).
21. I was introduced to Ward Jarvis by banjo player Dana Loomis. Jarvis lived outside of Athens, Ohio, and I visited and recorded him in winter 1978.
22. Rinzler (1994), [7–8].
23. Stambler and Landon (1983) Malone, 279.

24. See, for example, Lomax (1959), in Cohen (2003), 195–97.
25. Many in the folk revival held up the Ramblers as the perfect antidote to the "overly commercial" Kingston Trio, and indeed their recordings have held up much better than the Trio's work. Nonetheless, both groups were "revivalists," and each did reinterpret traditional music, albeit coming to the music from considerably different directions. See Malone, 280, 281.
26. Holy Modal Rounder cofounder Pete Stampfel tells the story of the early years of the duo in the liner notes to *The Holy Modal Rounders 1 & 2* (1998).

REFERENCES

Abrahams, R. D. and G. Foss. 1968. *Anglo-American folksong style*. Englewood Cliffs, NJ: Prentice-Hall.

Alden, R. 1992. Liner Notes to *Tommy and Fred*. Floyd, VA: County Records 2702.

Calkins, C with A Lomax. 1960. Getting to know folk music. Reprinted in Cohen, Ronald, ed. *Alan Lomax: Selected writings, 1934–1995*. New York: Routledge, 2003, 203–10.

Calt, S. 1994. *I'd rather be the devil: Skip James and the blues*. New York: Da Capo.

Cantwell, R. 1996. *When we were good: The folk revival*. Cambridge, MA: Harvard University Press.

Carlin, B. Joel Walker Sweeney: Minstrel banjo player. Unpublished manuscript.

Child, F. J. 1980. Ballad poetry. In *Johnson's new universal cyclopedia*, ed. F. A. P. Barnard, 361–68. New York: A. J. Johnson and Sons.

Cohen, R. 2002. *Rainbow quest: The folk music revival and American society, 1940–1970*. Amherst, MA: University of Massachusetts Press.

———, ed. 2003. *Alan Lomax: Selected writings 1934–95*. New York: Routledge.

Dixon, R., and J. Godrich.1970. *Recording the blues*. London: Studio Vista.

Filene, B. 2000. *Romancing the folk: Public memory and American roots music*. Chapel Hill: University of North Carolina Press.

Gussow, A. 2002. *Seems like murder here: Southern violence and the blues tradition*. Chicago: University of Chicago Press.

Keil, C. 1978. Who needs 'the folk'? *Journal of the Folklore Institute* 15 (Sept–Dec.): 263–65.

———, and S. Feld. 1994. *Music grooves: Essays and dialogues*. Chicago: University of Chicago Press.

Klein, J. 1980. *Woody Guthrie: A life*. New York: Knopf.

Krassen, M. 1998. Cleveland's musical eire. *Sing Out* 26(4): 46.

Lomax, A. 1940. Music in your own backyard. Reprinted in *Alan Lomax: Selected writings, 1934–1995,* ed. R. Cohen, 47–55. New York: Routledge, 2003.

———. 1947. America sings the saga of America. Reprinted in *Alan Lomax: Selected writings, 1934–1995,* ed. R.Cohen, 86–91. New York: Routledge, 2003.

———. 1959. The 'folkniks'—and the songs they sing. Reprinted in *Alan Lomax: Selected writings, 1934–1995,* ed. R. Cohen, 195–97. New York: Routledge, 2003.

Lomax, J. A. and A. Lomax. 1936. *Negro folk songs as sung by Lead Belly.* New York: Macmillan.

Malone, B. C. 1985. *Country music USA*, rev. ed. Austin: University of Texas Press.

Marcus, G. 1996. *Invisible republic: Bob Dylan and the basement tapes.* New York: Holt.

Nettl, B. and P. V. Bohlman, eds. 1991. *Comparative musicology and anthropology of music: Essays on the history of ethnomusicology.* Chicago: University of Chicago Press.

O'Connell, B. 1998. Down a lonesome road: Dock Boggs' life in music. Liner notes to Dock Boggs: His Folkways Years 1963–68. Smithsonian/Folkways CD 40108.

Pankake, J. 1997. Get into the graveyard. Liner notes to *Dock Boggs: Country Blues, Complete Early Recordings (1927–29).* Revenant CD 205.

Peterson, R. A. 1997. *Creating country music: Fabricating authenticity.* Chicago: University of Chicago Press.

Porterfield, N. 1996. *John Lomax: The last cavalier.* Champaign-Urbana: University of Illinois Press.

Rinzler, R. 1994. The background of these recordings. Liner notes to *Doc Watson and Clarence Ashley: The Original Folkways Recordings: 1960–62.* Smithsonian/Folkways CD 40029/30.

Rosenbaum, A. and M. N. Rosenbaum. 1998. *Shout because you're free: The African American ring shout tradition in coastal Georgia.* Athens: University of Georgia Press.

Sanjek, R. 1996. *Pennies from heaven: The American popular music business in the 20th century.* New York: Da Capo Press.

Seeger, Mike. Some personal notes. Liner notes to *Dock Boggs: His Folkways Years 1963-68.* Smithsonian/Folkways CD 40108, 1998.

Stambler, I. and G. Landon. 1983. *Encyclopedia of folk, country and western music.* New York: St. Martins Press.

Stampfel, P. 1998. Liner notes to *The Holy Modal Rounders 1 & 2.* Berkeley, CA: Fantasy Records 24711-2.

Wardlaw, G. D. 1998. *Chasin' that devil music: Searching for the blues.* San Francisco: Miller Freeman Books.

Wolfe, C. and K. Lornell. 1992. *The life and legend of Leadbelly.* New York: Harper Collins.

Young, I. 1977. Moses Asch: 20th century man. *Sing Out* 26(1): 2–8; 26(2): 2–5.

9
Film, Music, and the Redemption of the Mundane

GIORGIO BIANCOROSSO

Who knows why the memories of the mornings, afternoons, and evenings of our lives become so inextricably linked to the notes blown into the air by a silly radio broadcast or a little, vulgar orchestra.

—P. P. PASOLINI, "MY FASCINATION WITH THE JUKE-BOX"[1]

As a result of certain developments in twentieth-century art, most notably Dada and Pop art, common, functional objects, "mere real things"—to use Arthur Danto's words—have made their appearance not only in art museums and galleries but in critical and philosophical writings as well. Whenever critics and philosophers have discussed such artifacts as Duchamp's bottles or Warhol's famous "Brillo" box, this was primarily to discuss the difference between a mere artifact and a work of art, leading to the acknowledgement that the artistic status of a man-made work is the fruit of a negotiation between textual, intrinsic features, socially determined uses and expectations, and individual inclinations and circumstances of reception.[2] French sociologist Pierre Bourdieu has offered a socio-political reading of a cognate phenomenon, one that Dada and Pop Artists may be said to have brought to attention or parodied, namely "the capacity to confer aesthetic status upon objects that are banal or even 'common' [. . .], or the ability to apply the principles of a 'pure' aesthetic to the most everyday choices of everyday life, e.g., in cooking, clothing or decoration, completely reversing the popular disposition which annexes aesthetics to ethics."[3] Bourdieu claims not merely that aesthetic value is socially construed but also that the aesthetic disposition in general is not natural, as Kant and virtually all philosophers writing on the subject ever since have assumed, but rather the product of historical circumstances and the means to achieve a goal: to sanction and legitimize social differences. Conferring aesthetic status upon common, everyday objects is thus interpreted by Bourdieu less as complicating the philosophical question of what is aesthetic than as exemplifying the social roots of the aesthetic, for "nothing is more distinctive, more distinguished."[4]

Bourdieu's theory is of particular interest to musicologists because of the attention given to music in his discussion. Time and again he characterizes the cultivation of a certain kind of music not as a sign of one's sensitivity and proclivity toward its objective qualities but rather as a way of satisfying the need to identify or align oneself with a particular group. Taste in music thus mirrors—and validates—the existing social order. Music carries a particular weight in Bourdieu's model because it "is the 'pure' art par excellence. It says nothing and has nothing to say."[5] As such, it epitomizes the bourgeois aesthetic, its denial of representation, its distance from of any sort of naïve belief in what a work represents, and ultimately its moral agnosticism. To this, Bourdieu contrasts a popular 'aesthetic'—in quotation marks, one surmises, since he is redefining the areas of applicability of the term—based on the affirmation of the continuity between art and life, the active participation of an audience experiencing a work in the same way as they would an event occurring in their own life.

It is puzzling to realize how much Bourdieu relies on a heavily traditional—read formalist—view of the musical experience.[6] If I mention his theory here, however, it is less to mount an extended critique of the view of music listening that emerges from it than to point out that, for all its audacity, it shares with the philosophical tradition it allegedly breaks away from a conceptual framework wherein our modes of relating to an artifact, a text, or a piece of music are polarized: naïve participation vs. reflexive distance, use vs. contemplation, hedonistic play, or amusement, vs. aesthetic experience. This may be fine as far as a discussion of what is the aesthetic is concerned, but it leaves out a lot when the nature of our transactions with common, mundane artifacts is concerned.

Take the phenomenon described in the epigraph above by Pier Paolo Pasolini. Can one say that Pasolini's appreciation of the music is aesthetic? I would argue not, since he is not conferring aesthetic status upon what he generically and derogatorily calls a "silly" broadcast. But if it is not aesthetic, what kind of appreciation is it? Surely Pasolini is not referring to a strictly functional use of the music, nor to amusement, nor, finally, to a kind of absorption in the music, or its lyrics, that Bourdieu would likely associate with the "popular aesthetic." What seems to strike him, instead, is that the music has come to possess the power to make one recapture a whole phase of one's own life, functioning as the catalyst of a flow of memories. In fact, after Proust, one might say that the music *is* those memories. Now, in the context of an experience in which it is hard to separate the music's impact from the circumstances of one's own life at the time the music is heard, judging the music "good" or "bad" is beside the point, for that judgment would entail a distance from one's own existential sphere which is hard, and probably undesirable, to attain. Pasolini can call the music "silly" only by momentarily evoking in mid-sentence its status as an objective artifact. But the whole statement is in fact a concession that the music is imbued with the life of his consciousness to the point of being confused with a moment in that consciousness' life. Perhaps, it makes more sense to define the value of the music in dynamic rather than static terms by saying, for instance, that it is important to us or, more simply, that it "matters."

The process through which music takes on a value that is at once precious and highly personal would seem impossible to illustrate, given the breaking down of the boundary between subject and object that the assumption of that value necessarily entails. To show that this need not be the case, I would like to examine what I see as cinematic allegorizations of this phenomenon. In particular, I would like to explore some of the ways in which the strategic placement within a cinematic narrative enhances the significance of "mundane" music, which I define as music used for social occasions or intended as having a strictly utilitarian function: "café music," the muzak playing in lobbies or shopping malls, a temp-track used as "mood inducer" during the shooting of a scene, or the title-theme of a television show.

In the examples chosen, the music is either heard or sung by one or more characters. This is, to use film studies parlance, "diegetic" music: a sound event, be it a performance, a broadcast, or a recording, which is understood to be taking place within the fictional world of the film.[7] My exclusive focus on examples of diegetic music is deliberate. If the music is a sound event occurring in the world of the story, then the characters' response—or lack thereof—to it is an integral, and sometimes important, part of every scene in which it appears. This produces the intriguing possibility that the multiple meanings and functions the spectator hears in the music may not be available to the characters. Mundane music, for a character, often remains just that. Its very mundane quality, then, can be said to dramatize the gulf between character and spectator. The more poignant its presence, the more far-reaching its meanings for the spectator, the more apparent and palpable this gulf will appear.

If the characters cannot respond to the music the way a spectator does, this is not merely because they hear it only distractedly but, more importantly, because the possibility of hearing music as a function of an all-encompassing narrative—the narrative of their lives or the events they witness—is precluded to them, except in moments of self-reflection. For the spectator, on the other hand, even the most perfunctory incidental music is, like any other element of the represented narrative, potentially imbued with a function, a meaning in relation to the whole. In a well-known essay on narrative, Roland Barthes wrote that "[Art] is a system which is pure, no unit goes ever wasted, however long, however loose, however tenuous may be the thread connecting it to one of the levels of the story."[8] In a footnote to this statement, Barthes stated that this is true "at least in literature, where the freedom of notation [. . .] leads to a much greater responsibility than in the 'analogical' arts like cinema." I would contend, however, that it is the *experience* of narrative in general—irrespective of medium, degrees of authorial responsibility and control over the work—that entails that each element be capable of acquiring a function or meaning that rescues it from its incidental, seemingly secondary role (or even no role at all). This is a *process* and not something already present "within" the text, as Barthes' metaphor of the "thread" connecting detail to story may lead one to think. The observation has consequences, since it locates in the perceiving subject—not in the object—the reason why narratives seem so "saturated" with meaning, down to the minutest and seemingly most irrelevant detail. This, in turn, points to an inherent ability on the part of any spectator to integrate events, stimuli, and threads of information which must be at work in ordinary life as well as vis-à-vis the work of art.

Indeed, my claim here is that the transformation whereby in a film "mundane" music becomes a vehicle of great narrative import suggests an analogy between the musical experience at the movies and that of ordinary life. For the interests, dispositions, and skills which the spectator brings to bear on this transformation are the same he employs when, in everyday life outside of the movie theater, he forges a link between the music he hears and his own personal experience. The title of this chapter refers to the creation of this link as "redemption"; both in the sense of a rhetorical device and as an explicit reference to the Christian doctrine of redemption as an expression of love and grace meant to free sinners from the consequences of their sins. In the last analysis, then, it is the ever-present possibility of a new life for the music surrounding us which concerns me here. Acknowledging this possibility means neither to catapult the everyday into the spheres of high art—as is the case with Duchamp's empty bottles or Warhol's Brillo Box—nor to deny the aesthetic in order to develop a wholly functional theory of art—as Bourdieu would ask. Rather, it means to call attention to music's power of mediating between levels of reality, past and present, self and other, and even the split halves of a divided self; neither contemplation nor function, but mediation.

I begin with a scene from Antonioni's *Zabriskie Point* (1969), which I shall discuss here as a simple yet exemplary illustration of how filmmakers use diegetic music as more than a mere element of the setting. Halfway through the film, the female protagonist, Daria (Daria Halphrin), leaves Los Angeles for the desert to join her boss, a developer. During the trip she stops in a village for a drink only to find herself in a decrepit bar in the improbable company of a few old men. Snatches of conversation ensue when, as Daria makes her way out of the bar, Patti Page's "Tennessee Waltz" creeps into the soundtrack, presumably originating from an off-screen jukebox (see figures 1–2).

The song was an extraordinary hit in 1950, and one would be safe to assume that the jukebox in the bar dates back from around the same time. No matter how recognizable and charming in its unmistakable country mode and instrumentation, by the time in which the film is set—the late 1960s—this is music that hardly commands attention. The fact that no one in the bar seems to take notice of it only emphasizes this indifference. "Tennessee Waltz," it needs adding, is hardly specific to this region: thousands of miles separate California from Tennessee, the place famously evoked by the song.[9] Geographical inaccuracies notwithstanding, the example merits some scrutiny. It is significant that the sound level of the song remains the same even after the action moves outside the bar. This may be the result of an oversight on the filmmaker's part or a symptom of the fact that the song has captured the attention of Daria (if so, she hardly gives that away). Most likely, though, the constant sound level betrays the song's main

Figure 1   *Zabriskie Point*, 1969

Figure 2   *Zabriskie Point*, 1969

role in the scene: namely, the nuanced characterization of a milieu with the help of sonic means, in the best Hollywood tradition. The song is primarily there for the spectator to hear, as shorthand for the represented space in its geographical, social and temporal extensions; the perceivable element of an isolated, economically depressed outpost with an aging population, in stark contrast to urban, trend-setting L.A.

In the same film, there is another telling illustration of how incidental music, when woven into a cinematic narrative, may come to serve multiple functions. This occurs in a scene in which Daria's boss, Mr. Allen (Rod Taylor), enters the headquarters of his company (see figures 3–5). Though a transitional moment, it is realized with great care and subtlety. As Allen opens the door and enters the building, one suddenly hears Roscoe Holcomb's "I wish I were a single girl again," playing in the building in an instrumental version. Though the tune is not, strictly speaking, muzak, here it is used as such. The music appears just as the visuals shift in a straight cut from a silent, strikingly composed long shot of Allen as he approaches a building, to a tracking shot rendering his point of view as he enters the lobby (see figure 5). Because one hears music—as distinct from mere background noise— the contrast between the eerie silence in the first part of the sequence

Figure 3   *Zabriskie Point*, 1969

Figure 4   *Zabriskie Point*, 1969

and the presence of music in the second is greatly enhanced. This contrast, in turn, accents the transition from the objective, long shots in telephoto lens to a subjective, tracking shot. Besides being formally interesting in its own right, the transition from silence to music is suggestive of the awakening of Allen's senses after a moment of unseeing abstraction. If so, the silence preceding the appearance of the music could be understood not only as literal absence of sound but also as a representation of Allen's momentary obliviousness to his surroundings.

As is often the case in shopping malls, station lobbies, and other public spaces, marking the borders of the interior of a building seems to endow music with the power of encapsulating its essence (much like the way a façade often comes to stand for a building as a whole or, at least, its public image). This is, of course, an illusion, and one that can impoverish or flatten one's experience of a space, but it is also a stimulant, a catalyst of imaginary explorations of spaces and realms that are otherwise physically inaccessible. That is why I also hear the music as summoning up, in a single instant, images of the building as a whole—its lobbies, elevators, rows of offices, and vending machines—thus attenuating the need for establishing shots of the building's interior.

Finally, the music cannot fail to evoke the corporate world, which the film taken at large is so much at pains to stigmatize. This is facilitated by the wealth of visual information presented within the frame of this single shot (see figure 5). The clean, spacious lobby features familiar sights: a guard in his booth, an impeccably dressed woman—presumably a secretary—punching her card, glass panels, and a wall covered with large-scale reproductions of photographs of the founders of the company.

While maintaining its status as a diegetic element of the setting, as muzak playing at a certain time in a certain place within the represented story world, then, the music also behaves as a player in a network of formal, syntactical, and symbolic relationships. This is made possible by what Nicholas Cook has called a "transfer of attributes" between the visually depicted action and the music.[10] Wittingly or not, Cook talks about the transfer of attributes as a textual process. But it is the perceiving subject who must bring music and image to bear upon one another, thus creating the conditions for the production of potential meanings and the fulfilling of functions which the music in isolation would not be capable of inspiring. To take notice of these meanings

Figure 5   *Zabriskie Point*, 1969

and functions is the first, decisive step in what in the title I refer to as the redemption of the mundane.

The transfer of attributes between music and staged action is perhaps most clear in those type of film scenes in which a soloist or a performing group is heard playing, again from within the represented world itself, in close proximity to the main action. I have come across a moving instance of this kind in a scene from Bertrand Tavernier's *A Sunday in the Country* a film set in France in the years immediately preceding World War I. I am referring to a pivotal scene in which the old Ladmiral, a noted painter, candidly assesses his long career before his daughter Irene (see figures 6–8).

The setting, a dance hall *en plein air* in the French countryside, is rendered with great delicacy through very discrete lighting and shades of pale greens, browns, and yellows. In the soundtrack we hear the chatter of the other patrons, soon to be silenced by a local band playing a waltz. The band is seen just once, in a medium-long shot, after which it remains off-screen for the entire duration of the scene. After the accordion tentatively tries out a few chords and the suggestion of a melody, the whole ensemble joins in and begins the tune proper. With its staple accordion, chains of dominant sevenths, and moderate tempo,

Figure 6   *A Sunday in the Country*, 1984

Figure 7   *A Sunday in the Country*, 1984

this is music such as one hears, even today, in many of the countless cafes and bars catering to tourists in Paris and the surrounding countryside. At the sound of this music, the conversation begins:

Figure 8   *A Sunday in the Country*, 1984

IRENE (looking at the antics going on in the hall): That's what you
     should have painted!
LADMIRAL: Maybe. I painted the way I was taught. I believed my
     teachers: to respect the traditional rules. Maybe a bit too
     much. I saw originality in other painters' work.
          Cezanne's major exhibition—in '96 or '97—was in-
     teresting; but I thought "Where can that lead me?" Or
     take Van Gogh's work. I'd singled him out. I spent a
     summer painting in Arles with your mother. I'm boring
     you. Perhaps . . . I lacked courage. Some years ago, I con-
     sidered changing my style. I gave it a lot of thought. But
     it hurt your mother to see that at my age I was still . . .
     groping. I had just been decorated. Our future was assured.
IRENE: She was hurt . . .
LADMIRAL: If I had imitated what was original in other painters,
     Monet, Caillebot, Renoir, I'd have been even less origi-
     nal. I'd have lost my own melody. Not that I . . . I
     mean . . . at least it was mine. I painted as I felt—with
     honesty. Though I haven't achieved more I have at least
     been able to glimpse what I could have done. Earlier . . .
     when you woke me up I was dreaming—you'll laugh—
     about Moses just as he was going to die. He'd just seen
     the promised land and I realized that he could die with-
     out regret because he'd seen, understood, loved what
     he . . . loved. Do you understand? One can die for less.[11]

While the camera remains firmly focused on the two protagonists—first in a medium shot, then in alternating close-ups in reverse-
angle shooting—the music is a reminder of what lies outside of the
frame, bridging on-screen and off-screen space. But the music also
intensifies the effect of the visual framing: like a sonic frame or, better
yet, a spotlight, it isolates the two characters from any other element,
both visual as well as auditory, of the mise-en-scène. As the conversation continues, fragments of the melody—now in the accordion, now
in the clarinet—call attention to themselves, coloring the protagonists'
words with an unmistakably dark hue, reaching deep into the melancholy of the exchange between father and daughter and, in the last
analysis, signaling that there is a layer of unspoken—perhaps, unspeakable—feelings: regret and resignation on his part and profound empa-
thy for him, as well as anger toward her mother, on hers.

For the music to function in this way, one must be able to bring to bear upon one another two events that, except for their presumed simultaneity, are in principle unrelated: the off-screen band playing on the one hand, and the on-screen conversation on the other. The success of this integration is contingent upon the momentary refocusing of one's attention away from the process of sound production, the awareness of an ongoing performance, and onto an emergent, imaginary, new gestalt. And yet, since we never quite loose awareness of the fact that the music is being played by a group of performers within the scene, we may find ourselves referring it back to its source within the world of the story and the performance that gives rise to it. Rather like a gravitational force, the awareness of the off-screen band frustrates the music's flight toward a new existence, pulling it down repeatedly, back to its physical source in the story world. Like those ambiguous configurations that give rise to competing images alternating in the eyes of the beholder, the music restlessly switches status: now it is apprehended as anchored, realistically motivated sound, now as non-diegetic inflection. At stake in the alternation between these two entirely different modes of musical perception is the difference between music as evidence of a process or series of events and music as a mediator between a subject and his surroundings; put differently, between music as carrying information about a real, tangible event occurring in a specific portion of the physical world—a performance, for instance, or a broadcast—and music as a filter through which one apprehends that world as well as one's self.

I speak of "world" and "self," and not simply "story world" and "spectator," because I am drawing an analogy between our ability as spectators to let the music shape our understanding of a scene (however independent from it the music may initially seem), and our more general ability as humans to let music mediate between our selves and the external world. One way to bring home the analogy is perhaps to think of life as a loose, open-ended narrative in which visual and aural stimuli encountered in our everyday transactions with the world may give voice to, or induce, thoughts and feelings that otherwise lie dormant or latent in our consciousness; or, alternatively, to think of the film experience as two hours of our conscious lives, in which the entire world is reduced to the imaginary world of the story. Given this analogy, it follows that the spectators' ability to respond to non-diegetic music—some would say our leniency toward a patently source-less and intrusive stream of sounds—is not the product of habituation to a quintessentially modern apparatus. Rather, it involves the adaptation to the cinematic experience of a listening mode which people were already capable of prior to any exposure to the motion pictures, having exercised it not only upon attending other forms of spectacle and rituals, but also, if more haphazardly and under no scripted sequence of events, in their everyday lives.

A Sunday in the Country not only exemplifies this capacity for adaptation but also demonstrates the appeal of such use of diegetic music; the seemingly coincidental bond between the dance music and the dialogue between father and daughter makes it a far more effective, more poignant inflection than standard non-diegetic scoring would have been. The analogy between the film experience and ordinary life I have just drawn helps us, I think, understand why. By avoiding non-diegetic music, Tavernier presents us with a scenario that is strikingly similar to a situation we all experience in our lives when music which is accidentally playing in the street, at a subway stop or, as in the film, in a ballroom or cafe, suddenly enters the field of our attention and breaks through a layer of our consciousness, prompting a memory or a thought; measuring, intensifying, giving an edge to whatever state of mind in which we may find ourselves.

The simultaneity of the off-screen music and the dialogue between the two characters was, of course, carefully planned during the writing of the screenplay. But it is crucial to my analogy—and also to the effect sought by the filmmaker—that in the finished product the occurrence of the music seems absolutely natural, its capacity to echo the mood of the protagonists entirely unplanned.

The seeming serendipity of the match between music and dramatic action normally has the effect of diminishing one's awareness of the director's responsibility in the construction of a scene. In my next example, taken from Truffaut's *Day for Night*, the match is so transparent and precisely timed as to have the opposite effect. As students of French cinema will surely remember, *Day for Night* is a film about the making of a film in which Truffaut himself plays the director Ferrand. In what may be the most elegiac moment of the entire movie, Ferrand receives a phone call from George, a composer, whose voice is that of the actual composer for the film, Georges Delerue. George wants to know the director's opinion about a temp-track he has just finished recording for a love scene to be shot a few days later. Ferrand

Figure 9 *Day for Night*, 1973

is pleased to hear George on the other line and is shown handing an extra receiver to the producer so that the two of them can listen to the track together (see figure 9). The music is a sugary lento in duple meter, with two easily recognizable antecedent-consequent phrases, reminiscent of Mozart's "Voi che sapete che cosa è amor" from *Le Nozze di Figaro*. As the sound track begins, Ferrand opens a package sitting on the desk. Dutifully, the camera focuses in on the contents of the package: a pile of monographs about such filmmakers, among others, as Dreyer, Rossellini, Hitchcock, Hawks, Bergman, Bresson, and Buñuel (see figure 10). As the book covers roll out one after the other in medium close-up, the high-pitched, penetrating sound of the music (still emitting from the telephone receiver) lyrically underscores what turns out to be a touching homage to some of Truffaut's own favorite filmmakers. Through the combination of images and conveniently simultaneous music emerges the voice of the real, flesh and blood Truffaut—or at least his authorial persona. Like a fissure only temporarily open, the music offers a chance to dwell on the other, "subcutaneous" film which is also taking place, with Truffaut *lui-même*—not Ferrand—as protagonist.

Figure 10   *Day for Night*, 1973

Truffaut gives way to the fictional film director Ferrand only a moment later, however, as Ferrand quickly interrupts the phone conversation and thanks the composer for his good work (see figure 11). The matter-of-factness with which this lyrical interlude is brought to an end is representative of Truffaut's fondness for understatement, but it also helps convey the impression that all this was accidental, that it was almost not meant to be. It is at once a statement about the shameless adaptability of music to different contexts—the same tune will later be used as "mood-inducer" for a love scene—as well as its astonishing capacity to insinuate itself in perceptual cycles where it does not originally belong. I read the transformation of diegetic "telephone" music into an expression of Truffaut's own voice as a wonderful allegorization of how musical sound, encountered by chance, possess the ability to transcend its original raison d'être once it is referred back to our existential horizon.

My last example, from Stanley Kubrick's Vietnam film, *Full Metal Jacket*, represents the culmination of a progression within this essay, in that the full significance of the music emerges with reference neither

Figure 11 *Day for Night*, 1973

to a single moment nor scene, but only in relation to the film in its
entirety (and therefore also to a whole phase of the United States' recent history). Near the film's ending we encounter an unforgettable
moment in which the platoon, having successfully completed their
mission with the killing of a sniper, starts to sing the title-theme of the
"Mickey Mouse Club" television show in a strikingly coordinated fashion (see figure 12). To sing this tune in the midst of such carnage is
both a defiant and a cynical gesture on the soldiers' part. The frivolous, gay tone of the original song is turned on its head and, in a typical Kubrickian inversion, becomes its most disturbing feature. The
soldier's singing is also endearing, however, for it points to their still
very young age: these men were children when the "Mickey Mouse
Club" show was first aired and they are teenagers now in the film's
present time (set in the late 1960s).

Choreographed as a march—a clear reference to the first half of
the film, which is set in a training camp—this most unusual performance possesses a tremendous iconographic power. It presents us with
a rare moment of "togetherness" in the platoon, but the fact that everyone remembers the song by heart indicates that the annihilation of
these soldiers' individualities has started well before their Marine train-

Figure 12   *Full Metal Jacket*, 1987

ing, through continuous exposure to mainstream television and popular culture. It is the clearest expression in the entire film of a regression, not merely to childhood, but to a kind of prelogical, precultural, entirely instinctual phase of development, as is perhaps best indicated by the total lack of nuance, expression, let alone joy, in the way the soldiers deliver it. Numbed by murder, their repetitious, almost compulsive music making is symbolic of a collective, mental unraveling.[12]

The intensification of the expressive power of mundane music through the artful placement in visually depicted narratives is, of course, a manifestation of a phenomenon as old as representation itself. The "redemptive" potential of a representational frame has been amply anticipated in the classical repertoire. Consider the use of avowedly simple, sometimes even unabashedly vulgar, songs in opera, like "Deh, vieni alla finestra" in Mozart's *Don Giovanni,* or the brash, cocky "La donna è mobile" in Verdi's *Rigoletto*. The significance of these pieces emerges almost solely out of their friction with the narrative material that surrounds them. I am also thinking of many musical passages in less programmatically representational works: the use of untrimmed folk material in the beginning or middle section of some of Chopin's mazurcas, for instance; the intrusion of lullabies in Mahler's symphonies; the dull marches or childish tunes in Stravinsky's *Petrushka*; or the plentiful echoes of everyday music in many of Ives's works. These passages stand out for the layered, psychological experience they trigger, not for the complexity and sophistication of the musical surface per se.[13] They, too, allegorize "intrusions" of mundane music into our consciousness or, to paraphrase freely the Medieval philosopher Boethius, of *musica mundana* (music-of-the-world); music through which the outside world makes itself heard, noticed, present to our consciousness as listeners.[14]

In the cinematic examples I have discussed, music insinuates itself in the life of our consciousness by shaping our responses to the unfolding narrative. This process, as we have seen, can take a number of different forms: the marking of borders and articulation of shifts in time and space; the framing of a particularly significant aspect of the action, signaling the latent meaning of a verbal exchange, thereby capturing the meaning of a scene or an entire film. It would be a mistake, however, to insist that music's amazing potential for synergy is wholly emergent, for this would imply that, prior to its use in a film, the music existed in a contextual vacuum; a neutral, non-discursive, non-symbolic space. To the contrary, the modes of functioning described do far from entail the emergence of unprecedented meanings and functions, but rather their being teased out and showcased within a strategically constructed narrative. Put differently, films distill—and often crystallize for entire communities—meanings and modes of functioning that music possesses in the first place, as it circulates in the world and passes through people's everyday lives.

There is a suggestive and almost exaggeratedly poetic illustration of this intuition in a passage from a literary work that, significantly, predates our modern era of movie going. It appears in Chekhov's "The Steppe," published in 1888, the story of a long, frustrating search across the steppe for the entrepreneur Varlamov. There is a passage in this story in which Yegorushka, a young boy, takes advantage of a moment's rest to play with his imagination. He does so as he hears someone singing a melody which is "soft, lingering, dirge-like." The passage reads:

> While Yegorushka was watching those sleepy faces, suddenly there came the unexpected sound of quiet singing. A woman was singing, some way off, but where the song was coming from and from which direction was difficult to determine. That soft, lingering,

dirge-like song could be heard first to the right, then to the left, then up above, then from under the ground, as if some invisible spirit were hovering over the steppe and singing. As he looked around, Yegorushka could not make out where the strange singing was coming from. But then, when he had grown used to it, he fancied that the grass might be singing. Through its song, the half-dead, already doomed grass, plaintively and earnestly—and without any words—was trying to convince someone that it was guilty of no crime, that the sun had scorched it without reason. It insisted that it passionately wanted to live, that it was still young and would have been beautiful but for the burning heat and drought. Although guilty of no crime, it still begged someone for forgiveness and swore that it was suffering intolerable pain, melancholy, self-pity.[15]

Chekhov's words could serve as foundational myth for the history not only of the synchronization of sound and image, but also for the use of dramatic scoring in film. They suggest how the disposition to let music shape our responses to what we see, hear, or imagine, is part of our psychological endowment on a par with our capacity to create symbolic languages or decode images. Chekhov does not praise the melody for its beauty. He is content to describe its attributes and the outburst of imaginings it provokes. But there is little doubt that to Yegorushka the song possesses a value, no matter how little his experience of it may conform to more orthodox, scholastic ways of experiencing—and conceptualizing—musical value.

NOTES

1. P. P. Pasolini, "Quel che penso della canzone," in *Vie nuove*. I wish to thank Maiken Derno and Chris Washburne for their help in writing this article regarding matters both critical and editorial. Thanks also to an anonymous reader for several illuminating suggestions. Michael Beckerman, Elaine Sisman and Mark Swislocki offered valuable criticisms and suggestions on the occasion of an oral presentation of this essay at the Society of Fellows in the Humanities, Heyman Center, Columbia University in the Fall of 2002. I am grateful to the Board of the Society of Fellows in the Humanities, its Director, Walter Frisch, as well as the Society's Director, Marsha Manns, for providing time, resources, and moral and intellectual support to develop these ideas. Thanks, finally, to P. Adams Sitney for suggesting that I "write something up" about the ending of *Full Metal Jacket* as well as offering the key to its interpretation.
2. For a recent overview of the philosophical debate on the issue, see Gerard Genette, *The Aesthetic Relation*, 120–21. For Genette, the artistic relation to an

object is a special case of the aesthetic relation between a person and a natural phenomenon or man-made object. It obtains when "the subject of this relation, rightly or wrongly and to whatever degree, takes this object for a human product and ascribes to the person who produced it an 'aesthetic intention,' that is the aspiration to achieve an aesthetic effect[.]" (*The Aesthetic Relation*, 222).

3.   Pierre Bourdieu, *Distinction: A Social Critique of the Judgment of Taste*, 5.

4.   *Distinction: A Social Critique of the Judgment of Taste*, 5.

5.   *Distinction: A Social Critique of the Judgment of Taste*, 19.

6.   In general, Bourdieu reduces the aesthetic experience of a work to the experience of its formal features, as if the appreciation of the representational content of a work could not be of a contemplative, and thus aesthetic, kind. For instance, speaking of the popular "aesthetic" Bourdieu talks about the subordination of form to function as one of its defining features (*Distinction: A Social Critique of the Judgment of Taste*, 32). But form and function are not necessarily opposites. By the same token, functionality and representationality need not go hand in hand. It would seem that what distinguishes the "popular" from the "bourgeois" aesthetic is not the focus on represented content per se but rather, as Bourdieu sometimes observes, what "use" such content is put to.

7.   For the purposes of this essay, I will be content to treat the term "diegetic music" as synonymous with what studio executives, filmmakers and composers call "source music." I take both terms to refer to any music understood as being produced within the story world of the film, independent of whether its source is visualized (on-screen music) or not (off-screen). However, I should point out that some authors have persuasively argued that the two terms, aside from having very different histories, are not synonymous and that the semantic difference between them matters. See, for instance, J. Buhler, "Analytical and Interpretive Approaches to Film Music (II): Analysing Interactions of Music and Film," 40. For an illuminating discussion of the term "source music," see William H. Rosar, Editorial to *The Journal of Film Music*, 1, no. 1 (2002): 6–10.

8.   R. Barthes, "Structural Analysis of Narratives," 91. I suspect that in this paragraph Barthes inadvertently used the word "art" instead of "narrative."

9.   During a conversation following an oral presentation of this paper, Michael Beckerman pointed out that one should perhaps assume—not too jokingly—that from the industry's vantage point anything East of Hollywood looks and sounds the same.

10. N. Cook, *Analysing Musical Multimedia*, 70.

11. Transcribed by the author.

12. In Kubrick's *oeuvre* there are at least two more memorable instances of scenes in which compulsive acting signals, as it were, the beginning of the end: Jack Torrance's mindless typing in *Shining* and, of course, HAL 9000, in agony, singing "Daisy Bell" in *2001: A Space Odyssey*.

13. Though clearly intended as a polemical blow to Wagner and Wagnerism, this is perhaps what Stravinsky meant when he defended 'La donna è mobile' in these terms: "I regret having to say so; but I maintain that there is more substance and true invention in 'La donna è mobile', for example, in which this elite saw nothing but deplorable facility, than in the rhetoric and vociferations of the *Ring*." (I. Stravinsky, *Poetics of Music*, 61).

14. "Mundus" is the Latin word for "universe" or "world" and, by extension, also "mankind." In Boethius, *musica mundana* refers not to music as we conceive of it but to an all-pervading force determining the course of events such as the motion of the planets, the seasons of the year and the composition of matter ("Et primum ea, quea est mundane, in his maxime perspicienda est, quae in ipso caelo vel compage elementorum vel temporum varietate visuntur."). See Boethius, *De institutione musica*, I, 2, ed. by G. Marzi, 99.

15. A. Chekhov. "The Steppe," in *The Steppe and Other Stories*, 15. It is perhaps characteristic of a general lack of interest in music on the part of literary critics that Janet Malcolm, in her recent volume *Reading Chekhov*, delivers a penetrating reading of this passage of Chekhov's novella without, alas, mentioning the musical motive that is its precondition. See J. Malcolm, *Reading Chekhov* (New York: Random House, 2001), 142–43.

REFERENCES

Boethius. 1990. *De institutione musica*, ed. G. Marzi. Roma: Istituto italiano per la storia della musica.

Barthes, R. 1977. Structural analysis of narratives. In *Image/Music/Text*, trans. S. Heath, 79–124. New York: Hill and Wang.

Bourdieu, P. 1984. *Distinction: A social critique of the judgment of taste*, trans. R. Nice. Cambridge, MA: Harvard University Press.

Buhler, J. 2001. Analytical and interpretive approaches to film music (II): Analysing interactions of music and film. In *Film music: Critical approaches*, ed. K. J. Donnelly, 39–61. New York: The Continuum International Publishing Group.

Checkov, A. 2001. The steppe. In *The steppe and other stories*, trans. R. Wilks, with an introduction by D. Rayfield, 3–101. London: Penguin.

Cook, N. 1998. *Analysing musical multimedia*. Oxford: Clarendon Press.

Genette, G. 1999. *The aesthetic relation*, trans. G.. Goshgarian. Ithaca, NY: Cornell University Press.

Pasolini, P. P. 1964. Quel che penso della canzone. In *Vie nuove*, ed. G. Calligarich (October 8).

Rosar, W. H. 2002. Editorial to *The Journal of Film Music* 1(1): 1–18.

Stravinsky, I. (with Roland-Manuel and P. Souvtchinsky). 1970. *Poetics of music*, trans. A. Knodell and I. Dahl. Cambridge, MA: Harvard University Press.

10

A Moment Like This
American Idol and
Narratives of Meritocracy

MATTHEW WHEELOCK STAHL[1]

> *What is your definition of an AMERICAN IDOL?*
> Someone who represents the people.
> *Why do you want to be an AMERICAN IDOL?*
> So that I can show off my talents.
>   RUBEN STUDDARD, 2003 AMERICAN IDOL FINALIST[2]

In the summer of 2002, a musical talent contest-cum-reality television program snowballed into a multi-platform blockbuster megahit in a little over three months; by all measures, the 2003 and 2004 season has so far surpassed their predecessor.[3] Like previous radio and television talent contests, *American Idol* depended on audience voting for its selection of a winner. And, like the reality TV programs that have recently come to dominate American prime time, the show focused on the character development of an ever-dwindling pool of contestants. Combining the democratic principle of an audience vote and the narrative principle of the months-long competition, *American Idol* was a marketing phenomenon of unprecedented efficacy in the United States popular music industry. Telling captivating stories about its contestants and grueling audition process, the 2002 season produced a windfall for advertisers and a massive body of deeply invested fans for winner Kelly Clarkson and several of her runners-up.

Murray Forman has argued that from its emergence as a mass medium television has been a site of musically-themed discourses of opportunity; for musicians, appearance on television was "imagined as either a goal . . . as they advanced their careers or a portal to success on a larger scale in the entertainment industry."[4] Often culminating with a single "winner," sometimes positioned to convert his or her exposure into career advancement, talent and now reality show genres offer telegraphic stories of opportunity and social mobility.[5] In this chapter, to put into relief a dimension of the social meanings of "bad music," I analyze *American Idol's* strategic emphasis on and expansion of such narratives in the cultivation of a commercially exploitable relationship between audiences and contestants. The focus of *American Idol* narratives on themes of sincerity and pretense, training, evaluation, work, and social advancement, I argue, moved the show past mere legibility into both literal and utopian mappings of American character and opportunity structures, and played a decisive role in this talent/reality show's wide appeal.

Like the liberal market society that gave it its general form, *American Idol* was derived from a British institution. The hit British show of the previous year, *Pop Idol*, was a tremendous commercial success, and the Fox Network imported it virtually lock, stock and barrel to the United States. The setup: approximately ten thousand[6] wannabe pop music idols auditioned (in several U.S. cities) for a panel of three judges drawn from the upper reaches of the pop music industry. The first round resulted in a pool of 120 singers; this group was then brought to "Hollywood" (Pasadena) and further reduced to the thirty contestants who competed live on television for the phoned-in votes of the viewing audience. In each show, contestant after contestant sang a truncated version of a familiar pop song, was evaluated by the panel of judges, and then brought back into the Coca-Cola-sponsored 'red room'[7] with the rest of the contestants. Contestants were attended to (in their despair, joy, bewilderment or anger) by a pair of hosts, whose function it was to mediate between contestants, audience, and judges, constantly linking the various elements of the show back to the central story of the contest. Seven of these singing contestants were eliminated from the group following each of the first three weeks' programs. Each subsequent week, for the remainder of the series, the singer receiving the lowest number of audience votes was dropped from the contest, until, in the last moments of a two-hour finale, the American Idol was revealed, winner of a "one million dollar" recording and management contract.[8]

The show's commercial success was staggering. The voting audience, numbering in the millions,[9] demonstrated every week in certain, countable terms, their emotional investment in the singers. Aside from achieving audience numbers the likes of which Fox had not seen for years,[10] the CD single released just days after the announcement of the competition's winner in the early fall of 2002 gave audiences the chance to translate that investment into commodity purchases.[11] Written especially for the climactic final episode, Idol Kelly Clarkson's recording of "A Moment Like This" entered the *Billboard* pop charts at #52, and within a week it had leapt to #1; the closest rival for this sort of chart movement was the Beatles' 1964 hit "Can't Buy Me Love" which advanced from #27 to #1 in a single week.[12] That this level of audience investment could be sustained for months following the final show and the release of the CD single was demonstrated by the mid-April 2003 debut at the #1 position in the *Billboard* pop charts of Clarkson's debut album, appropriately titled *Thankful*.[13] The show has now become a franchise, already a hit in Poland and South Africa, and has been copied by regional networks and local stations (*Protagonistas de la Musica*, for example, on the American Spanish language network Telemundo).[14] A feature film starring Clarkson and first runner up Justin Guarini was scheduled for release in June 2003 (screenplay by *Idol* executive producer Simon Fuller's brother Kim, writer of the Spice Girls movie *Spice World*).

The above description of the show's mechanics, however, does not do much to specify the nature of *American Idol's* hybridization of and departure from its talent and reality show progenitors, though its ratings and marriage to music industry infrastructures gesture in that direction. What made this show so different from *Star Search*, for example (Ed McMahon's low-rated weekend daytime talent show of 1983–1995, now reformatted and reintroduced to capitalize on *American Idol's* success), was its protracted, intimate, reality-TV focus on the subjectivities and biographies of its contestants, their private relationships, and the rigors they were put through during the elimination process. What makes it so different from, say, *Survivor*, the turn-of-the-century reality show that subjected teams of contestants to highly scripted contests in exotic environments and compelled them to eliminate one another week-by-week, was its release of the contestants from direct competition by putting the audience in the position of reducing their number every week.[15] By foregrounding the biographies and moral trajectories of contestants as they audition again and again, and by reducing the pressure of intra-group competition, this hybridized talent/reality show behaves more like a dramatic series—albeit with an ever-shrinking cast—the plot of which is tied institutionally as well as thematically to the music industry. The character development that is so central to *American Idol*, however, suggests a more complex and compelling set of narratives than has generally been possible in talent and reality genres; it is the goal of this chapter to account for the show's appeal through the analysis of its two primary forms of narrative: stories of *authentication* (biographical and autobiographical vignettes), and of *humiliation* (dramatic punishment for poor auditions).

American Idol makes itself legible to its audience by drawing on television conventions, but its tremendous resonance points to a more complex relation to contemporary American society and culture than mere legibility. What might these stories of successful and failed approaches to the music industry tell us about our society in this historical moment? What can they tell us about the shared forms of life that make us legible and recognizable to each other? On the one hand, this show is about and aimed primarily at audiences in their teens and early twenties. What can we learn about the conditions and trajectories of American youth through their widespread identification with *American Idol* contestants and their mass consumption of and participation in the many forms of *American Idol* texts, from the TV show itself to the official and unofficial websites and chat rooms, CDs, DVDs, videocassettes, and the 2002 performance tour of the ten *Idol* finalists? On the other hand, the show's popularity extends far beyond that age cohort, sweeping the coveted 18–49 demographic and garnering large numbers in the advanced baby boomer set.[16] What can the show tell us about the shared concerns of viewers across these traditionally more segregated media markets? Finally—and this is a question more asked than answered in this chapter—how can we begin to understand, beyond (nevertheless useful) political economic analyses of multimedia marketing, the phenomenal resonance of pop music-related narrative at the turn of the century?

Frederic Jameson's insight into popular narrative is useful at this juncture.[17] Narrative, he suggests, is the preeminent cultural mechanism through which social relations are apprehended and negotiated. Mass cultural texts like *American Idol* are socially symbolic acts, 'individual utterance[s] of that vaster system . . . of class discourse'[18] that mediate between the social and cultural. It is through narrative that we activate ourselves and are positioned in society. Jameson acknowledges the ideological function of mass cultural narratives, their role in legitimizing and reproducing the social order, yet he suggests that by virtue of their very "massness" such narratives must contain contestatory, utopian strains. *American Idol*, to be attractive simultaneously to capital and audiences, must maintain a balancing act between these poles of "reification and utopia."[19] Following this logic, I approach *American Idol* narratives as social scripts produced to manage fan/idol subjectivities in the cultivation of the producers' desired (profitable) fan/idol relationship, that depend for their effectiveness in large part on suggested symbolic resolutions to widely shared social tensions.

Since *American Idol* viewership transcends traditional demographic boundaries, it is reasonable to ask what social tensions could be so widely shared. What is immediately apparent as a primary stake for contestants on this show is one that is indeed shared by vast numbers of people at this particularly unstable moment in the political and economic history of the United States: economic security and social mobility. All Americans feel and must deal either directly or indirectly with changes in the economy, public policy, the law and regimes of work. The widespread appeal of *American Idol* suggests we look in particular for lessons which the show might offer concerning the shape and negotiation of current occupational and social structures. Narrative, as Jameson points out, is a site where discourse takes on materiality by shaping the cultural conditions of practice; taken together, the two forms of *American Idol* narrative that I discuss in this chapter—*authentication* and *humiliation*—are part of a contemporary process of shaping work and enculturing workers in the *new* "new economy,"[20] quite appropriately incorporating the mass media of popular music and television, as well as ancillary forms such as magazines, computer games, and the internet. *Idol* narratives, as we shall see, work in varied and sometimes contradictory ways, nourishing the bonds between performers and audiences through reference to actual social positions of the fans- and the idols-in-training, as well as to a substantively level utopian "playing field."[21]

Why This Is Bad Music

Many of the individual performances by contestants, especially in the first weeks of the show, are demonstrably *bad* in terms of basic technical proficiency—the singers are still learning conventions of pop performance, as well as how to choose material which befits their vocal range, and many of the less expert among them have yet to be eliminated.

Beyond making fun of the first weeks' off-key performances, however, critics employ two primary arguments in their derision of *Idol* music. On the one hand, they argue that the music featured on the show is bland and derivative: 'The music and arrangements are trite, full of wannabe Whitney Houston and Stevie Wonder wails. Originality is a losing strategy', writes Caryn James of the *New York Times*.[22] More odious to critics than the music's blandness is the fact that the show makes visible a whole process of production that would otherwise be obscured—a highly rationalized process of selection, construction and marketing. As Pierre Bourdieu and Motti Regev have shown, artistic value often derives in large part from extra-textual discourses of production norms and practices that conform to ascendant (Romantic) models.[23] In other words, most of the show's mainstream critics cleave to criteria of value that privilege "individual," "original," and "disinterested" artistic production. In their opinion, the conditions of production and distribution significantly determine the music's value. "'Idol' . . . is a slick new step in music marketing," grumbles the *Boston Globe*'s Matthew Gilbert, "it's not some kind of altruistic attempt to give a young performer a chance at the big time; it's the first leg in a marketing campaign that will culminate in CD sales. We aren't the TV audience—we're the focus group."[24] The karaoke-style accompaniment is safe and dull—it often seems downplayed, as if too much attention to it would distract from what's really at stake: the contestants' presentation of themselves as worthy, creditable, authentic individuals.[25] According to this logic, no such obviously "inauthentic" musical product, conceived, manufactured and marketed in an openly rational and instrumental way, can carry other than commodity value.[26]

Joshua Gamson argues that legitimate stardom—celebrity that is clearly deserved by the celebrity—requires the development of a complex and paradoxical relationship with the target audience: aspiring idols must demonstrate both specialness and ordinariness, distance and closeness, similarity and difference, particularly regarding social position.[27] *American Idol's* narratives of authentication and humiliation balance these contrasting themes as they are deployed to cultivate and manage the fan/idol relationship. Stories told in these taped narrative segments describe the careers of contestants as they leave their prosaic pasts behind and confront representatives of the music business and the judgments of audiences.[28] (Leading characters in the humiliation sequences, however, usually only make it as far as the initial confrontation before they are sent home.)[29] These stories weave together material concerning contestants' moral and professional trajectories as aspirants struggle to demonstrate their qualifications to the on-camera judges and to the voting audience at home. At their most literal, they constitute both a set of claims about the morality, authenticity, and legitimacy of the aspiring idols, as well as a set of stories about entering the entertainment business. At their most political, they make up a set of guidelines concerning appropriate entry into and performance within the precarious (but still officially meritocratic) "new economy," appropriate attitudes toward its rewards and punishments, along with a utopian vision of a classless opportunity structure.

Narratives of both types feature the contestants in various "de-distancing" situations, i.e., situations that viewers can readily understand and, because of their familiarity, readily critique—at home; at work or play with friends and family or with other contestants; in the audition or professionalization process. While most audience members, it is safe to say, have never auditioned or professionalized in precisely this way before, the processes of having to present oneself to be judged, by a teacher, parent or employer, for example, while having to learn a new set of rules and behaviors, in school or at work, are homologous and provide a basis for legibility, identification, and engagement.

Authentication

These bio- and autobiographical vignettes concern individual aspirants and often follow patterns of surveillance, interview and direct address found in contemporary reality programming. Frequently on camera, contestants are typically placed in highly scripted contexts in which they are expected to perform themselves—visiting their hometowns, parents and siblings, their old schools, and places of work. Most of these documentary productions focus on contestants as *moral* individuals—emphasizing their family values, church and volunteer activities, devotion to friends, school, and community. Clips featuring such performances are a regular feature of the show and appear in several contexts—in most programs, for example, a video clip about each contestant, accompanied by her/his voiced-over narration, precedes each contestant's performance. One such sequence takes place during an outing in which the finalists are taken to "work" on a new home in an impoverished L.A. neighborhood with the non-governmental organization Habitat for Humanity.[30] The contestants wield hammers and carry boards; behind each foregrounded contestant several of the others can be seen at work. In one such vignette, Idol-to-be Kelly Clarkson is shown nailing a piece of siding to the house. She voices-over that her father is a contractor and that working on this house is the most at home she's felt since coming to L.A. Vignettes like these require contestants to produce and display personal characteristics, individualizing and authenticating, appearing as regular persons despite their growing celebrity.

First runner-up Justin's mother was taped for a "Coca-Cola Moment" (a series of sponsored segments featuring family members waxing sentimental) in which the mothers of the three remaining finalists say a few words about their progeny. As if to stave off an excess of ordinariness threatened by the display of his baby pictures, she declares from her sumptuous living room sofa that "there's just an aura around Justin. When you meet him you see it. From the time he was very small, when he was five and a half it was just evident that he was special."[31] Authentication narratives underwrite the paradoxical relation of difference and similarity between fan and idol. Whether articulated by contestants or family, friends or fans, they contribute to the ever-expanding backstory upon which all of their performances, musical and otherwise, build, as well as to the narrative self with which their on-stage utterances may be judged as consistent or contradictory.

Humiliation

Narratives of this type are drawn from the preliminary auditions that took place around the United States and are featured most prominently at the beginning of the series, when official and unofficial rules are being set out, and then during its final weeks when the finalists' legitimacy is being fortified.[32] The typical story goes like this: a singer enters the performance area and greets the three judges, all seated at a long folding table. The doomed auditioner, often dancing inexpertly, sings a few bars a cappella and is stopped mid-song by the judges (sometimes with a twinge of sympathy, but more often with an exclamation of worn patience or even outrage). The judges critique the auditioner's gestures, clothing, facial expression, and manner along with her/his voice, sometimes with deadpan sarcasm (especially by the panel's most aggressive male judge, Simon Cowell, coproducer and head of the label to which the winner will be signed). The critique is followed by reaction shots in which the auditioner either breaks down in tears, stares in disbelief, or verbally attacks the judges.

Consider the following snippet from a segment of the two-hour season finale, entitled "top five worst auditions." The narrator barks: "And the absolute worst, dead last out of ten thousand hopefuls, Jennifer's rendition of 'Genie in a Bottle' left us hoping that someone would put a cork in it!" Jennifer is shown singing a verse and chorus for the three judges. Cowell, dubbed "Mr. Nasty" by the British press during his tenure as judge on the first version of the show, says to Jennifer "That was extraordinary." Jennifer lights up, eager to hear more. Cowell continues, "unfortunately, extraordinarily bad." The camera zooms in on Jennifer's face as her look of joy turns to one of shock and grief.[33]

Keeping It Real

Idols have to be special, but they have to be ordinary too; images of the star as star are balanced by narratives of star ordinariness. *American Idol* constructs ordinariness: like other reality TV programs, through its surveillance and narrative installment/chapter logic, it allows and compels contestants' characters to develop over the course of a television season. Since the contestants are not professionals, not fully socialized into the entertainment industry, they are not as socially different from their audience as established pop music stars. Elizabeth Eva Leach argues that the quintessentially commercial Spice Girls enacted a form of authenticity distinct from the critically privileged rock'n'roll authenticity.[34] The Spice Girls legitimized themselves to their audiences exactly by weaving stories of their ordinariness into their music videos and feature film. Their authenticity, writes Leach, derived from their ability to suggest that "they think what we, the audience, would also think of this mad world of stars if we were suddenly translated thence, which, because their presence there implies that hard work and luck would be enough, they additionally reassure us we could be."[35] This kind of performance of authenticity, Leach suggests, implies an essential identity between idol and fan.

But whereas Simon Fuller (creator and executive producer of the Spice Girls as well as *American Idol*) kept the process of turning young women into Spice Girls hidden, *American Idol* invites audiences into this relationship by making visible a (highly edited) selection and training process.[36] Leach writes that the Spice Girls spoke not *for* but *as* their audience. Fuller has now advanced that principle a step further: he has drawn the aspiring idols *from* the audience in such a dramatically visible way that the democratic promise of equal *Idol* opportunity is held out to every singing person between the ages of sixteen and twenty-four and, by extension, the liberal democratic promise of equality of opportunity is likewise positioned within reach of viewers. Moreover, while authenticity alone is not enough to carry a contestant through to idolhood, without authenticity a contestant stands no chance. In the utopian meritocracy presented by *American Idol*, social class, race and gender are trumped by character;[37] and character is developed and demonstrated through the frequent biographical and documentary vignettes. Fans and idols are entwined by the telling of a story of success based on merit and character, of the hard work of honest folk rewarded, and of the hard knocks delivered by a tough but fair system. Widespread belief in the 'inherent star quality' of the aspirant, however, like belief in the natural (if unevenly distributed) inherent talents of those rewarded in a meritocracy, is also crucial to the legitimation of individual success and failure, the rhetorical victory of equality of opportunity over other possible regimes. The fan/idol relationship is thus made all the deeper through the representation of an initial social identity between performers and audience; contestants and viewers, assured at least of the *possibility* of being in possession of star quality or inherent talents, undertake this journey of social mobility together.

Back To Square One

Narratives of humiliation and attempted humiliation of poorly prepared losers are thus not out-takes or bloopers rolled in for mere comic relief or pathos. These narratives are instructive tableaux of punishment and vengeance that serve simultaneously as further legitimation and authentication of those in whom the desired talents inhere, and as graphic warnings to all those considering an attempt to breach a field for which their talents are not appropriate. William Ian Miller suggests that humiliation is the result of an insufficiently supported claim to enter a social territory in which one has no business being.[38] Unprepared, unworthy aspirants' pretences are exposed by lead judge Simon Cowell's rationalistic reciprocity: with his business-like lack of

patience, reinforced by his industry track record, he treats their auditions as insults, a waste of his time. Miller writes that while the violence of the humiliator "will shock and appall us when we feel the
perpetrator is predatory . . . [it] will provide catharsis and pleasure,
both aesthetic and erotic, when we feel the violator is justified, as when
he acts with righteous indignation and vengefulness."[39] *Idol's* strategy
of featuring the more aggressive dressings down is well suited to the
needs of the producers: it fills airtime with the entertaining foibles of
unpaid offender/victims, and, argues Miller, vengeance can make for
pleasurable narrative when audiences and humiliators share understandings of the rules and conventions that govern the desired position.[40]

Miller's argument points to the audience's familiarity with the
rules and boundaries governing social and economic mobility outside,
as well as inside, the entertainment industry. He highlights audience
capacity to draw narrative pleasure from the application of shared cultural conceptions governing success in the current Anglo-American
occupational structure, where most of them do or will spend most of
their time, to real people TV personalities whose positions at the gates
of the music business parallel those of employables pursuing social
advancement. The show is about and aimed at young people who are
in or close to their first jobs, on the borderline between subordinated
minority and emancipated majority, the private world of adult-
controlled home and school, mostly low-status, low-stakes work and
high-stakes leisure, and the public world of adult freedom, discipline,
responsibility and commitment. The show's appeal across age groups,
however, indicates that the nature of this boundary remains compelling to a very wide demographic, and suggests some further interroga-
tion. Youthful contestants, by trying out the role of pop star, and youthful
audiences, by doing so vicariously, are not just making adolescent bids
for freedom and identity—they are playing with a particular kind of
adult role that seems to offer a high degree of autonomy. Why is it that
the music industry is one "to which numerous young people aspire
and for which many train"?[41] One explanation is that facing entry into
McJobs "earmarked for youth or for other transient workers" in the
retail and service sectors, along with the bleak prospects for economic
security and social mobility in a recession economy, an alternate, if
riskier, tactic appears increasingly attractive.[42] To cross into adulthood
as an income property such as a pop music idol is a way to embed
valuable elements of the means of production *within* oneself. This move,
akin to attempts by downsized or downsizable professionals to refashion

themselves as consultants,[43] is a high-stakes bet, especially for adults, but holds out a promise of de-alienation as well as increased responsibility for and control over their own conditions of labor.

Bidding to be excused from conventional structures of employment—increasingly insecure at the turn of the century—auditioners in this position open themselves to scrutiny from evaluators and observers which threatens/promises to expose hubris and pretence. The humiliation of the pretentious dramatizes the harsh punishments awaiting those who do not take training and self-evaluation upon themselves with sufficient seriousness to underwrite their claims on these types of positions. Unpreparedness is also a lifestyle choice, not a structural problem; neither *American Idol* nor the eviscerated American welfare state is there to assist the unprepared.[44]

"A Moment Like This" b/w "Before Your Love"

Neva Chonin of the San Francisco Chronicle describes *American Idol's* culminating songs, the aforementioned "A Moment Like This," and its B-side "Before Your Love," as "a pair of faux-Whitney, wannabe-Celine power ballads so inoffensively generic they could carpet an elevator."[45] This reading of works specially commissioned for the two finalists to sing in the final hours of the contest, and to be released as a single immediately afterwards, overlooks both their context and their rhetorical thrust: the cementing of a broad and deep, multimedia fan/idol relationship with intimations of collective triumph. Taking advantage of the English vernacular's lack of a distinct second person singular/familiar, the finalists construct the objects of these songs as both individual lover and support group of well-wishing peers. "Before your love," they sing, "I wasn't really living," acknowledging the necessary participation of the fan-as-friend-as-lover in the social rise of the idol. After having been informed of her victory during the last moments of the finale, Kelly Clarkson, giving way to tears and apologizing mid-song for her lack of self-control,[46] sings "I can't believe it's happening to me . . . some people wait a lifetime for a moment like this," inviting those fans/friends/lovers to share in her authenticatedly humble, if highly scripted, joy and gratitude at her consecration.[47]

In conjunction with the narratives of individual effort, impartial/expert and democratic processes of evaluation and promotion, as well as humiliation of the pretentious and unprepared, these songs dramatize the essence of achievement in the new economy and a particular set of character traits that underwrite and justify it. Aspirants are entreated to learn all they can about the field they wish to enter, mobilizing all their resources, social and material, to prepare themselves for confrontation with the industry's gatekeepers. Finally, though they face the music alone and must, in order to justify their social rise, acknowledge their inherently unique value and capability, they must also be sure to acknowledge their sources of social and material support in such a way as not to alienate them—the operationalization of these sources will likely be necessary time and again throughout their careers. The music industry becomes a metaphor for the new economy: in recent decades, workers at all levels of the occupational structure have been learning first-hand some of the institutional realities faced by performers since the advent of mass culture: that employment insecurity and pressure constantly to expand skill sets in careers punctuated by regular, consequential auditions are the rule rather than the exception.

Conclusion: Narratives of Success and Failure

The contemporary expansion of communications media recalls the late 1940s television landscape described by Forman—an increased appetite for content drives the adaptation and hybridization of existing cultural forms. Meanwhile, music performance and contest genres again provide valuable resources for the production of what Lusted calls "light entertainment."[48] David Lusted argues that audience pleasure in such televisual material derives from performers' and audiences' shared sense of "the *risks* at stake" in the improvisatory and contingent nature of the light entertainment form; "part of the pleasure of game shows, quizzes and 'talent' contests," he writes, "is precisely that they foreground the risk of failure."[49] A shared sense of risk is indeed a powerful "contact point"[50] between fan and idol, one that enables identification through literal social homology. As the notion of the "secure individual"[51] becomes a thing of the past, more and more workers learn the currency of the old Hollywood adage that holds "you're only as good as your last picture."

In his discussion of the mid-20th century Hollywood musical, Richard Dyer suggests that entertainment is not merely the production of false consciousness and satisfaction of false needs—entertainment works, he argues, because "it responds to real needs *created by society*."[52] He locates the specificity of entertainment's utopia in the musical's "non-representational" communication of "what utopia would feel like rather than how it would be organized."[53] *American Idol*, responding to the real needs of early twenty-first century Americans, and looking "backstage" to social structures more effectively hidden in the mid-twentieth century, shows precisely how utopia would be organized. Jameson's analyses suggest that the show's appeal derives from its willingness to address core tensions of this historical moment, and to suggest a(n initially) classless society: anyone willing to stand in line for days is guaranteed the opportunity to audition.[54] From the start, however, *Idol's* narratives of individualism and meritocracy depotentiate and contain this utopian promise, even while enacting a critique of American occupational and social structure, and even while highlighting, by its democratic fairness and paced, graduated progression, the unfairnesses and risks of the new economy.

Representation of subjugated populations in the pluralistic group of *Idol* finalists suggests the potential fairness of the meritocratic system. However, increasing polarization and middle class instability associated with corporate and state restructuring, regressive taxation, and anti-affirmative action legislation strain the legitimacy of meritocracy and set up particular tensions to be dealt with in early twenty-first century popular culture. *American Idol* holds out a promise of individual recognition, but its focus on biography and relationship, along with the social and material support of family and community, points to the real necessity of social ties and support for success in the individualizing neo-liberal regime. *American Idol* deals with this tension by offering the representation of an ideal meritocracy. In this utopian society all participants, representing all social groups in a pop culture galactic federation, (re)present themselves as equally unknown individuals before impartial advisors and an entertainment demos, a liberal regime in which all participants share equal access to the most important resource: the rhetoric of coherent, authentic, individual selfhood.

Richard Sennett suggests that coherent selfhood in industrial society is enabled by a narrative framework that itself relies on stable economic and social structures.[55] A historical form of selfhood based on the long postwar boom that had become an important part of the rhetoric (and for many the reality) of the American dream, he argues, is threatened by late twentieth century economic restructuring. Downsizing and other corporate strategies regularly return vast numbers of workers to the entry level for another audition; "there is no narrative," he writes, "which can overcome [this regular] regression to the mean, you are 'always starting over'."[56] Like the 1990s workers Sennett writes about, *American Idol* contestants must audition again and again just to stay in the running; they have no apparent security. Yet, one solution that *American Idol* appears to suggest is that certain kinds of cultural work do offer more reliably certain forms of security and mobility. Forms of cultural work that depend for their products and for the success of their products on unique faces, voices, skill sets and expressive styles appear to promise a basis for strong claims for worker irreplaceability and increased worker control over working conditions. This is perhaps one reason why morality and character are so crucial in an audience-selected idol: in an era in which organized labor is widely considered suspect, even corrupt(ing), we must be careful whom we endow with such a voice.

An important question for future research is: why music? What is it about music—good or bad—that makes it such a compelling medium for the linking of work, narrative and the self? I will offer a tentative hypothesis. It is my sense that first, the idea of work is crucial to music; when we see musicians performing, even when they are lipsynching, we are seeing people at work. Second, the kind of work they do is shaped by an ideology of expression—something inner is made manifest; job qualifications for musical performers have more to do with the nature of this expression than with institutional credentials. Third, popular music is a field to which huge numbers of people can claim some expertise. Millions considered themselves expert enough to render judgment upon the *Idol* finalists—would a similar competition involving, say, doctors be imaginable? Fourth, unlike many other publicly performed professions, popular music performance is very often associated with pleasurable fantasy, autonomy, communitas, and joy. Perhaps, this is why narratives about performers' confrontations with industry institutions are so compelling: we see representatives of a utopian extreme of de-alienation facing rationalized, profit-driven challenges to their autonomy. And finally, the sensual, emotional, embodied, non-discursive aspects of music would seem to enable musical performance to convey finely nuanced stories of subjectivity in late capitalism. Representations of musical performers can be seen from this perspective as stories of work and selfhood with which we can identify particularly intimately.

Critical derision of the music on *American Idol* is not, in the main, misplaced: most of the performances, lacking technical mastery,

convincing accompaniment, and the technological studio manipulations that many singers rely on for the customary high-gloss finish of
their work, are not up to the standards of mainstream pop, and the two
songs specially composed for the finale are indeed safe reiterations of
the standard turn-of-the-century power ballad. Critics' focus on the
musical content, however, deflects attention from the socially symbolic elements of the show and its original compositions. My aim in
this chapter has been to investigate some of the social meanings of this
'bad music' by considering the ways *Idol* narratives model strategies
for negotiating contemporary economic conditions while laying out
compelling features of a meritocratic utopia. Just as dramatic stories
of success and failure in the new economy amplified the appeal of
American Idol's talent show, the musical performances around which
the show was built—however "bad"—provided the magnetic pole that
aligned the attention of an unusually wide audience to these stories.
Pop music, work and narrative are linked through the metaphor of the
audition; *American Idol* is all about auditions, successful and unsuccessful. On the last night of American Idol's second season, moments
before the 2003 Idol was announced, judge Paula Abdul offered some
final words of advice: "you know, life is an audition; you're going to
have to keep competing to stay on top."[57]

NOTES

1. Many thanks to the editors of this volume and the anonymous reviewers whose
   comments and suggestions were of immeasurable help in clarifying my argument. Many thanks also for the significant contributions of Allison Huber, Valerie
   Hartouni, and the University of California, San Diego undergrads who spoke
   with me about their love of *American Idol*.
2. http://idolonfox.com/contestants/rubenstuddard.htm (accessed 5/15/2003).
3. Ratings have climed steadily each season, from 13 to 22 to an average of 27
   million viewers per show as of this writing (late in season three). Because of
   this, advertising rates on *American Idol*, a steal at around $200,000 per thirty-
   second spot in 2002, are expected to crest to $1,000,000 during the season three
   finale in late May of 2004. Opportunities to sell increasingly valuable ad time
   have expanded significantly: the first season comprised about 22 hours of
   programming; the second and third almost 40. ("News Corp. Profit Up 69% in
   Quarter," *Los Angeles Times* May 7, 2004.) An unnamed Fox executive called
   the show "ratings crack." (Bill Carter "Fox Mulls How to Exploit The Mojo of
   'American Idol'," *New York Times*, May 23, 2003.)
4. M. Forman, "'One night on TV is worth weeks at the Paramount': musicians
   and opportunity in early television, 1948–1955," *Popular Music* 21, 3 (2002):
   261.

5. Reality show producers and contestants interviewed testify that reality shows also offer contestants opportunities for personal growth by way of constant surveillance. See Mark Andrejevic's "The kinder, gentler gaze of Big Brother: Reality TV in the era of digital capitalism," *New Media and Society* 4, 2, 251–270.

6. The *New York Times* reported 70,000 auditioners for season II. A. Stanley, "Here's Reality: 'Idol' Feeds Hopefuls to a Shaky Music Business," *New York Times* (January 23, 2003).

7. Though I will not be addressing this element of the show, it is important to note that *American Idol* has taken sponsorship to new heights. In addition to its innovative interweaving of Ford and Coca-Cola into *Idol* content, *American Idol* is itself a months-long commercial for its musical, cinematic and other associated products.

8. The recording and management contracts will be with the show's co-producers, creator and executive producer Simon Fuller, architect of the Spice Girls and the aforementioned *Pop Idol*, and Simon Cowell, lead judge, successful pop producer and record label chief in his own right. Cowell and Fuller also retain contract options on each of the ten finalists See Carla Hay, "'American Idol' Weds Reality TV And Music," *Billboard*, 3 August 2002.

9. "The voting-by-phone aspect proved popular, with more than 100 million votes by the time the show wrapped. That's more votes than were cast in the last U.S. presidential election, [Fremantle Media CEO Tony] Cohen pointed out." From P. Albiniak, "Ideal, not idle summer for Fox; American Idol turned into a surprising smash hit; now here come the copycats," *Broadcasting and Cable* (September 9, 2002).

10. "With more than one-fifth of American households tuning in to the finale *American Idol* last Wednesday, Fox's summer blockbuster garnered the biggest audience share the network has ever had in the 18–49 demographic" their largest viewership since the *Beverly Hills 90210* finale of May 1994. Albinak, "Ideal, not idle summer for Fox," 2002.

11. New digital encryption technology enabled "RCA and project team members dispersed across seven cities on two continents to securely share pristine, uncompressed audio files via the public Internet during the process of mixing, mastering, manufacturing, and radio distribution." This allowed producers to "take two singles from studios to manufacturing in an unprecedented nine days—weeks shorter than typical production cycles." From "DMOD Delivers 'American Idol' singles, CDs in record time, revolutionizes production processes for BMG's RCA singles," *Business Wire* (September 17, 2002).

12. F. Bronson "Chart Beat," *Billboard* (September 21, 2002).

13. Audience investment was sustained in part through the services of Fanscape.com, "the leaders in fan management," whose services include the coordination of fan "street teams"—virtual communities of fans exhorted by regular emails to vote for the contracting artists song on MTV's "Total Request Live," for example. "As part of our grassroots marketing," they write, "Fanscape utilizes our own technology and design to support fan community. We create marketing assets, street team member websites, fan-site enhancing tools and news rings. We often work directly with the artists to create and stream exclusive audio and

video content. We also enable fans to forward content to their peers virally." http://www.fanscape.com/marketing.asp (accessed 6/5/2003).

14. Hay, "'American Idol' Weds Reality TV And Music," 2002.

15. When asked by the host in the penultimate show of Idol's first season what it was like for the two finalists to compete against each other, Kelly Clarkson responded "we don't think of it like that, we're in support of one another;" Justin Guarini added "we go out and we compete against ourselves" (American Idol 9/3/2002).

16. "Although the show was intended for the young audiences Fox prefers, the last episode dominated the 8–10 p.m. ET time slot with a whopping 12.5 rating/21 share in households. It was first in all the key Nielsen Media Research categories as well—even adults 50-plus." Albinak, "Ideal, not idle summer for Fox," 2002.

17. F. Jameson, *The Political Unconscious: Narrative as a Socially Symbolic Act* (Ithaca: Cornell University Press, 1981).

18. Ibid., 85.

19. F. Jameson, "Reification and utopia in mass culture," *Social Text* 1 (1979) 130–48.

20. Though many contemporary authors use the term 'new economy' to describe the heady days of the internet boom/bubble era, I apply the term with a bit more cynicism, referring more generally to post-1960s changes in corporate organization and national economic policy, ensuing American economic decline, and the post-dotcom era and turn-of-the-century recession. For background on these elements of "new economy," see M. A. Bernstein and D. E. Adler, *Understanding American Economic Decline* (New York: Cambridge University Press, 1994); M. Castells, *The Rise of the Network Society* (Cambridge, MA: Blackwell Publishers 1996); D. Schiller, *Digital Capitalism: networking the global market system* (Cambridge, MA: MIT Press, 1999); and G. Neff, "Game over: with the collapse of the new economy complete, yesterday's dot-commers are only now beginning to understand the odds," *The American Prospect* (September 9, 2002).

21. *American Idol's* total content is distributed over DVDs, videos, books, tie-in magazine special issues, constant entertainment news coverage, official and countless unofficial Web sites, a CD-Rom game, and various branded clothing and accessories. A definitive work on the show would cover all these elements in detail; I limit my focus to the television show, understanding that evidence of the forms of narrative I describe is to be found across much of this range of products.

22. C. James, "On 'Idol,' the Only Losers Are the Audience's Ears," *New York Times* (September 1, 2002).

23. P. Bourdieu and R. Johnson, *The Field of Cultural Production: Essays on Art and Literature* (Cambridge: Polity Press, 1993) and M. Regev, "Producing artistic value: The case of rock music," *The Sociological Quarterly* 35, no. 1 (1994): 85–102.

24. M. Gilbert, "Idol' has the crass to make it must see," *Boston Globe* (September, 4 2002).

25. Evidence of this downplaying is offered again and again as the judges evaluate 'song choice' as well as performance. To them, an excellent performance can be marred by a poor song choice. While this would appear to reflect the importance

of the song, it points to the crucial importance of the singer's ability to read the context of the performance and judge her/his abilities and "style" against a given standard. It appears that the music can be either a well- or poorly-suited medium through which the singer makes her/his claim on judges and audience.

26. While middlebrow critics—(sometimes) unwitting promoters of the "cultural dupes" thesis—dismiss the music of *American Idol* on the basis of its apparent "inauthenticity," it is precisely authenticity that is a central theme in Idol narratives, and a central concern for finalists and fans.

27. J. Gamson, *Claims to Fame: Celebrity in Contemporary America* (Berkeley: University of California Press, 1994).

28. Such stories are not new with *American Idol*. Murray Forman writes that the repetition by contestants in early amateur TV talent contests of "an ideal image of success in show business is clearly measured against the descriptions of their actual vocations . . . described in terms of boredom and monotony." M. Forman, "'One night on TV is worth weeks at the Paramount'," 2002.

29. An exception that proves the rule is the recruitment of several of the more dramatic subjects of this kind of humiliation for a pastiche of off-key performances prepared for and presented during the finale of the 2003 season (*American Idol* 5/21/2003).

30. *American Idol* 7/23/2002. Thus, identifying the contestants with "new home construction" and "social service"—economic growth that leaves no one behind.

31. *American Idol* 8/27/2002.

32. In the second season, in response to audience demand—most likely registered via webboards—the percentage of each show taken up by these narratives has increased significantly.

33. *American Idol* 9/4/2002.

34. E. Leach, "Vicars of 'Wannabe': authenticity and the Spice Girls," *Popular Music* 20, no. 2 (2001): 143–67.

35. Ibid., 150.

36. For further discussion of the audition/selection process' place and value in contemporary televised popular music narrative, see M. Stahl, "Authentic Boy Bands on TV? Performers and Impresarios in *The Monkees* and *Making the Band*," *Popular Music* 21, no. 3 (2002): 327–49.

37. This is attested to by the removal of two season II finalists following discoveries of questionable moral behavior—one had posed nude, the other had been arrested.

38. W. I. Miller, *Humiliation* (Ithaca: Cornell University Press, 1993).

39. Ibid., 6.

40. Ibid., 50.

41. G. Fine, J. Mortimer, and D. Roberts. "Leisure, Work and the Mass Media," in *At the Threshold: the developing adolescent*, eds., S. S. Feldman and G. R. Elliotts. (Cambridge, MA: Harvard University Press, 1990), 232.

42. Ibid., 238.

43. R. Sennett, *The Corrosion of Character: the personal consequences of work in the new capitalism* (New York: Norton, 1998).

44. By contrast, when the good guys of the show—the thirty finalists—are subject to criticism, they have an another opportunity to demonstrate their worthiness

by taking that criticism graciously, and, if they disagree, to likewise do so graciously. A couple of young fans told me that the first thing they judge in a contestant is the graciousness with which she/he responds to criticism.

45. N. Chonin, "'American Idol' winner in tune with marketing," *San Francisco Chronicle* (September 17, 2002).
46. Dyer writes "Authenticity is established or constructed in media texts by the use of markers that indicate lack of control, lack of premeditation and privacy." R. Dyer, "*A star is born* and the construction of authenticity," in *Stardom: industry of desire,* ed. C. Gledhill (London: Routledge, 1991), 137.
47. *American Idol* 9/4/2002.
48. David Lusted, "The Glut of the Personality" in *Stardom: Industry of Desire,* ed. Christine Gledhill (London: Routledge, 1991).
49. Lusted, 253 (emphasis in original).
50. Dyer, op. cit.
51. J. Wallulis, *The New Insecurity: The End of the Standard Job and Family* (Albany: State University of New York Press, 1998).
52. Emphasis in original. R. Dyer, "Entertainment and Utopia," in *The Cultural Studies Reader,* ed. S. During (London: Routledge, 1993), 278.
53. Ibid., 273.
54. F. Jameson, "Reification and utopia in mass culture," *Social Text* 1 (1979).
55. Sennet, *The Corrosion of Character*, 1998.
56. Ibid., 84.
57. *American Idol* 5/21/2003.

REFERENCES

Albiniak, P. 2002. Ideal, not idle summer for Fox; American Idol turned into a surprising smash hit; now here come the copycats. *Broadcasting and Cable* (September 9).

Andrejevic, M. 2002. The kinder, gentler gaze of Big Brother: Reality TV in the era of digital capitalism. *New Media and Society* 4, 2, 251–270.

Bernstein, M. A. and D. E. Adler. 1994. *Understanding American economic decline.* New York: Cambridge University Press.

Bourdieu, P. and R. Johnson. 1993. *The field of cultural production: Essays on art and literature.* Cambridge: Polity Press.

Bronson, F. 2002. Chart Beat. *Billboard* (September 21).

Carter, B. 2003. Fox mulls how to exploit the mojo of "American Idol." *New York Times* (May 23).

Castells, M. 1996. *The rise of the network society.* Cambridge, MA: Blackwell Publishers.

Chonin, N. 2002. "American Idol" winner in tune with marketing. *San Francisco Chronicle* (September 17).

DMOD Delivers "American Idol" singles, CD in record time, revolutionizes production processes for BMG's RCA singles. 2002. *Business Wire* (September 17).

Dyer, R. 1993. Entertainment and Utopia. In *The cultural studies reader,* ed. S. During. London: Routledge.

———— 1991. *A star is born* and the construction of authenticity. In *Stardom: Industry of desire,* ed. C. Gledhill. London: Routledge.

Fine, G., J. Mortimer, and D. Roberts. 1990. Leisure, work and the mass media. In *At the threshold: The developing adolescent*, ed. S. S. Feldman and G. R. Elliott. Cambridge: Harvard University Press.

Forman, M. 2002. "One night on TV is worth weeks at the Paramount": Musicians and opportunity in early television, 1948–1955. *Popular Music* 21, no. 3: 249–76.

Gamson, J. 1994. *Claims to fame: Celebrity in contemporary America.* Berkeley: University of California Press.

Gilbert, M. 2002. "Idol" has the crass to make it must see. *Boston Globe* (September 4).

Hay, C. 2002. "American Idol" weds Reality TV and music. *Billboard* (August 3).

James, C. 2002. On "Idol," the only losers are the audience's ears. *New York Times* (September 1).

Jameson, F. 1979. Reification and utopia in mass culture. *Social Text* 1, 130–148.

———— 1981. *The political unconscious: Narrative as a socially symbolic act.* Ithaca: Cornell University Press.

Keightley, K. 2001. Reconsidering Rock. In *The Cambridge companion to pop and rock,* ed. S. Frith, W. Straw and J. Street, 109–42. New York: Cambridge University Press.

Leach, E. 2001. Vicars of "Wannabe": authenticity and the Spice Girls. *Popular Music* 20, no. 2: 143–67.

Lipsitz, G. 1990. *Time passages: Collective memory and American popular culture.* Minneapolis: University of Minnesota Press.

Lusted, D. 1991. The glut of the personality. In *Stardom: Industry of desire,* ed. Christine Gledhill, 251–58. London: Routledge.

Miller, W. I. 1993. *Humiliation*. Ithaca: Cornell University Press.

Neff, G. 2002. Game over: with the collapse of the new economy complete, yesterday's dot-commers are only now beginning to understand the odds. *The American Prospect* (September 9).

News Corp. profit up 69% in quarter; Rupert Murdoch sings 'American Idol' show's praises after it lifts Fox TV to third place among major broadcasters. 2004. *Los Angeles Times* (May 7).

Olsen, E. 2002. Slaves of celebrity. *Salon.com* (http://archive.salon.com/ent/feature/2002/09/18/idol–contract/) (September 18).

Regev, M. 1994. Producing artistic value: The case of rock music. *The Sociological Quarterly* 35: 85–102.

Schiller, D. 1999. *Digital capitalism: Networking the global market system.* Cambridge, MA: MIT Press.

Sennett, R. 1998. *The corrosion of character: The personal consequences of work in the new capitalism.* New York: Norton.

Stahl, M. 2002. Authentic boy bands on TV? Performers and Impresarios in *The Monkees* and *Making the Band. Popular Music* 21: 327–49.

Stanley, A. 2003. Here's reality: "Idol" feeds hopefuls to a shaky music business. *New York Times* (January 23).

Wallulis, J. 1998. *The new insecurity: The end of the standard job and family.* Albany: State University of New York Press.

PART III

Noise, Malfunction, and Discourses of (In)Authenticity

11

Extreme Noise Terror
Punk Rock and the Aesthetics of Badness[1]

ANGELA RODEL

They burst through your skull at an infinite velocity, turn your gray matter into slop, and flare out the other side leaving only spattered blood and shattered bone behind.[2]

—JEB BRANIN

While the above quotation may sound like the latest description of the weapons of mass destruction threatening world security, it does, in fact, describe something perhaps even more frightening to music lovers: a style of punk music referred to as *extreme hardcore*. To the mainstream music consumer and ethnomusicologist alike, punk, especially its more extreme, non-commercial varieties, has a reputation for being "bad music" par excellence: a music that seems to go out of its way to be terrible, offensive, unlistenable. To the reviewer who penned the above description, however, the sonic violence of the music is the source of its "goodness," as can be gathered from his effusive continuation: "It is totally refreshing to hear! One of the year's ten best seven-inch [records], without a doubt."[3]

In this chapter, I explore the ways in which what is heard from the outside as aesthetically bad makes the music so good to insiders, raising questions about how the concepts of "bad" and "good" music, as well as the precarious discrimination between "music" and "noise," are exploited in the struggle to create musical meaning and value. I wish to make it abundantly clear at the outset that when I discuss "badness" in punk, I am not making an evaluative judgment about the quality of punk music, which I grew up listening to and still listen to with pleasure. Rather, I argue that since punk's inception in the mid 1970s, punks have deliberately developed an aesthetics of badness as part of an attempt to retain control over punk sounds and images. To borrow a phrase from Pierre Bourdieu, in manipulating "badness," punks are taking part "in a struggle for the monopoly of legitimate discourse about the work of art [in this case, punk music], and consequently in the production of value of the work of art."[4] Extreme hardcore, a general term for death-metal-influenced genres of hardcore punk, can be seen as only the latest development of an ongoing struggle within punk to resist commodification in the commercial mainstream. I argue that extreme hardcore continues the punk tradition of using bad aesthetics to set itself apart from mainstream music production by introducing new dimensions to the idea of "badness" as a means of challenging the musical status quo. In my view, the aesthetics of badness in punk encompass two distinct yet related issues: "badness" defined as a low-level of technical proficiency and "badness" cultivated on a more purely aesthetic level. The first type of punk "badness," which I will characterize briefly in the first section, has already been explored to some extent in the scholarly literature.[5] In the remainder of the chapter, I will focus on the second—more complex—type of "badness" as articulated in extreme hardcore punk. I will argue that conceptions of "badness" in punk are developed and manipulated as part of a discourse of opposition to mainstream musical aesthetics and the political ideologies that such aesthetics are perceived as fostering. I will explore the ways in which punk "badness" can be theorized within various frameworks of artistic and social resistance, drawing on theories of the culture industry, noise, and cultural capital developed by Theodor Adorno, Jacques Attali, and Pierre Bourdieu, respectively. While all of these theorists provide valuable insight for understanding the dynamics of punk vis-à-vis the music industry, I will suggest that the true critical efficacy of punk's aesthetics of badness can be understood only when uniting their ideas with Hans-Georg Gadamer's ontology of the work of art, in terms of which extreme hardcore may be characterized as fomenting crisis through the bringing-to-presentation of apocalyptic sounds and imagery.

Detailed genealogies of punk, while beyond the scope of the present study, can be found in the works of Themis Chronopolous, Dave Laing, William Rice, and William Tsitsos.[6] It is nevertheless necessary to clarify my usage of the terms "punk" and "hardcore." In this context, I take punk to be a label for a general aggregate of musical styles and their associated subcultural ideologies that have developed over the past twenty-five years. While some branches of the punk family tree have blossomed into the mainstream media, I will focus here on non-commercialized "underground" styles that retain punk's traditionally oppositional stance to the corporate channels of music marketing and production. I understand "hardcore," and by the same token "extreme hardcore," to be broad labels for musical subgenres that have developed within punk. Following Tsitsos, I argue that most musicians playing hardcore still consider themselves to be "punks," which makes it necessary to discuss extreme hardcore in the larger context of punk.[7]

"They Can't Even Play Their Instruments": Badness as Technical Non-Proficiency

In attempting to untangle the aesthetics of badness in punk, the first question asked must be "bad in comparison to what?" Laing argues that it is crucial to discuss the development of meaning in punk in the context of mainstream rock music precisely because punk rock defines itself in opposition to meanings generated by mainstream rock music.[8] Furthermore, he argues that rock music in the 1970s was dominated by transnational supergroups like ABBA, The Who, and Led Zeppelin, whose albums made extensive use of the latest studio technology and whose live stage shows were increasingly costly in order to reproduce these studio effects in a live setting. Thus, the production and promotion of a rock album in this era required the kind of financial backing that only major labels can afford. Laing points out that punk, with its anti-status quo attitude, presented an alternative to these over-produced supergroups. In his view, meanings in punk rock are defined from both within and outside of punk, which defines itself in relation to the larger music industry. Indeed, punks themselves constantly examine and re-examine their relationship to the mainstream, the politics of selling out (i.e., entering the production and marketing channels of the commercial music industry in order to be able to profit from one's musical endeavors) being one of the hottest topics in fanzines. Also, punk's grassroots do-it-yourself attitude (usually abbreviated with the acronym DIY), which was reflected musically by the frequently low level of technical proficiency of performers, and practically by the rise of independent punk labels, fanzines, and distribution networks, flew directly in the face of mainstream rock, and empowered musicians without major label support to produce their own albums. This breaking down of the rockstar barrier and promoting an "everyone-can-and-should-do-this" attitude is best expressed in early fanzines, which frequently offered crude depictions of how to play powerchords, along with the message "Here's one chord, here's another. Now go start your own band!"[9] Keith Negus (1986) also characterizes the aesthetics of early punk as based on a "limited musical repertoire."[10] Laing argues that early punk's low level of technical proficiency and recording quality largely contributed to the rejection of punk by the mainstream music industry, leading to a "negative unity" among punks and an identity based on exclusion.

Given the importance of the DIY approach in the punk scene, it is not surprising that excesses of musical competence may be viewed suspiciously and considered pretentious, as well as implying a desire to sell-out. Even those punk musicians with a high degree of technical skill are constrained to a certain extent by punk's aesthetics of (technical) badness, especially guitarists, since extended and complex solos are seen as the ultimate sonic sign of aspiration towards mainstream rock stardom. In fact, I would argue that the downplaying of guitarists' virtuosity is the main musical characteristic that separates metal-influenced punk from metal, as the following excerpt from an interview with a member of the extreme hardcore band, Extreme Noise Terror, indicates:

> MATT WILLIAMS: Would you say that with this release you are headed in a more metal direction?

> PHIL VANE: I wouldn't say it's going definitely in a metal direction. I think it's just a relevant thing, if you learn how to play your instruments better you've got to go one way. I mean Punk and Hardcore is fairly restrictive in that sense. So yeah, I guess in some way the term metal could be applied, but I don't really see it as being a metal thing at all. . . . We've been sticking in some solos as you can probably tell off Retrobution, but it's nothing like the total two or three minute guitar wankin' shit or anything like that you know, it's like your straight forward blast in your face 20 second guitar solo like a typical Hardcore band. When you start playing guitar solos people start thinking of Heavy Metal music but it's not necessarily like that you know.[11]

Metal style "wanking" guitar solos are repeatedly mocked in the fanzine literature as "unpunk." Paradoxically, this problem of virtuosity does not appear to apply to drummers; in fact, in extreme hardcore, where unbelievably fast blast beats are crucial to the basic sound of the genre, the drummer is expected to display a certain level of virtuosity.

Recording quality is another important aspect of "badness" in punk and hardcore. "Slick" or overly produced sounds immediately raise suspicions of having commercial pretensions. In the following review, a *Short, Fast and Loud* reviewer humorously makes clear the importance of a somewhat degraded recording quality in extreme hardcore (and extreme metal) aesthetics:

> It is good to see these guys are not straying from the standard grindcore/death metal formulas. Repetitive, slightly generic grinding riffs that blaze in a mess of speed and fury? Check. A mediocre demo quality recording? Check. Harsh, throat-searing vocals that sound like they are being sung through a bottomless aluminum trashcan? Check. Wow, this is all key to putting out a great grind metal release, and they pull it off with no problem.[12]

Laing's description of the genesis of punk as a reaction to the economic and artistic stranglehold of the mainstream music industry immediately calls to mind Bourdieu's practice-oriented model of cultural production. In his *Field of Cultural Production,*[13] Bourdieu develops a model of competing hierarchies that can be applied to an analysis of a subaltern field of cultural production like punk. He argues that the field of cultural production is embedded within the field of power; the cultural field being organized by an *autonomous* principle of hierarchization that values symbolic capital, while the power field is organized by *heteronomous* principles that value economic capital. The following extended quotation enunciates the relationship between these hierarchies:

> the more autonomous [a field of cultural production] is, the more completely it fulfils its own logic as a field, the more it tends to suspend or reverse the dominant principle of hierarchization; but also that, whatever its degree of independence, it continues to be affected by the laws of the field which encompasses it, those of economic and political profit. The more autonomous the field becomes, the more favorable the symbolic power balance is to the

most autonomous producers and the more clear-cut is the division
between the field of restricted production, in which the producers
produce for other producers, and the field of large-scale production,
which is symbolically excluded and discredited.[14]

Although Bourdieu uses Symbolist poets as his example of an autonomous field, his description also describes very accurately the interplay
between punk as a autonomous field of cultural production suspended
within the very field of power which tries to distance itself from. The
discourses of DIY, selling-out, and what/who is punk, the main topics
of punk fanzines since punk's very inception, are critical to punk precisely because they help maintain the boundaries of the autonomous
field. Yet, as Bourdieu notes, while inverted, the hierarchies nevertheless
remain intimately interrelated, and it is often the case that symbolic
capital from an autonomous field can be transformed into economic
capital within the field of power. This is especially true in the case of
punk, which, with a few slight changes in musical sound, can move
(or be seen to move) into the mainstream of rock music's field of power.
It is no wonder, then, that many punks view their autonomous position
as highly precarious, ready to flip at any moment into its inversion.

Viewing punk through a Bourdieuian lens, as Laing's analysis
seems to encourage, however, reduces punk opposition to the musical
status quo to a struggle for symbolic capital and position-taking. Indeed, in such a picture, it is unclear how any true resistance could
challenge the logic of economies that rules such a system, as Bourdieu
himself notes:

> Because position-takings arise quasi-mechanically—that is, almost
> independently of the agents' consciousness and wills—from the
> relationship between positions, they take relatively invariant forms,
> and being determined relationally, negatively, they may remain
> virtually empty, amounting to little more than a *parti pris* of refusal,
> difference, rupture.[15]

From this vantage point, radical music genres like punk become little
more than weapons in the struggle for power and position, making
punks essentially as guilty of the same kind of instrumentalization of
culture as the record industry. While I do not reject Laing's observation
that to understand punk one must view it as being in tension with heteronomous fields of cultural production (i.e., the mainstream music

industry), I nevertheless would like to develop a view of punk (indeed, subcultural opposition as a whole) that recognizes the possibility for critical efficacy. At the close of this chapter, I will return to the question of the potential for meaningful resistance within extreme hardcore's bad aesthetics, drawing on ideas from the work of Adorno, Attali and Gadamer to rethink Bourdieu's bleak diagnostic of cultural opposition.

Badness as "Aesthetically Unbearable Style"

Although an aesthetics of technical "badness" perhaps gave the first generation of punks a fleeting sort of protection against commodification, this is certainly no longer the case. In fact, technical badness has proved not to be bad enough. As early as 1977, when The Sex Pistols exploded onto the British music scene, major labels realized that technical badness in music was no barrier whatsoever to mainstream popularity; rather, the rough, raw sound of punk has proven to add to its attractiveness as a commodity. As Theodor Adorno and Max Horkheimer note in their prescient observations on the adolescence of the culture industry, elimination of any genuine notion of style through mass repetition has paradoxically created a simultaneous demand for the possible recovery of style.[16] As a result, punk (subculture theorist Dick Hebdige's poster child of style [1979]) has had to struggle with the constant commodification of its sounds: almost every genre of punk sound has found its way into the mainstream, including old school punk, hardcore and melodic hardcore by bands such as The Clash, Green Day, and The Offspring. Also, punk clothing and visual styles have repeatedly been mined by the mainstream culture industry; for example, Rancid, cavorting on MTV with their towering mohawks and infinite spikes, look as punkly perfect as a "Greetings from London" postcard. Even punk's radical political ideology, based in anticapitalist, often anarchist beliefs[17] which might conceivably be too offensive to mainstream sensibilities to make the major airwaves, has recently been commercialized by bands like Rage Against The Machine[18] and Chumbawamba, ironically making punk's radical ideology itself a commodity for sale. Again, Adorno and Horkheimer recognized this commodification of the discourse of resistance as a particularly "diabolic" aspect of the culture industry, which makes the possibility of true resistance appear to recede even further beyond the horizon.[19] Thus, punks have had to resort to other methods (i.e., besides styles based on low levels of technique, poor recording quality or even overtly critical lyrical content) to keep their music out of the mainstream media; I argue that the development of extreme hardcore, a musical style that most non-punk fans (and even a fair number of punk fans, if reviews in *Maximum Rock N Roll* (*MRR*), non-commerical punk's über-fanzine, are any indication) find aesthetically unbearable, is an example of an attempt by punk to escape commodification by creating a style of music which, through its very aesthetics, is absolutely immune to appropriation.

Since the late 1990s, there has been a renewed interest in forms of "extreme hardcore," a fast (or, more precisely, alternation between extremely fast "thrash" parts and slow, heavy "sludge" parts) metal-influenced punk genre. This genre first arose in the 1980s, when punk-metal "crossover" bands such as Amebix began cropping up in the hardcore scene.[20] Indeed, it was only a small musical step to move from the quick tempos, shouted vocals and aggressive sounds of hardcore to the warp-speed double-bass drumming and growled vocals characteristic of death metal and other forms of extreme metal that had been concurrently gaining popularity as a separate global counter-culture. Indeed, many punks had been fans of metal before discovering punk (this was certainly the case with me), thus it is not surprising that during the 1980s many metal-influenced groups gained popularity within punk. In discussing the current wave of punk and metal cross-over genres, *MRR* columnist Felix von Havoc echoes Lemmy Kilmister, the vocalist of seminal metal band Motorhead, when he says that "'When the punks learn to play their instruments, they will play metal' and often this has been the case."[21]

Extreme hardcore includes sub-genres that go by various category names such as thrash, fastcore, noisecore, grind(core), and power violence. Instead of teasing out subtle musical differences in sub-genres, I will here discuss what I see to be the most basic identifying musical features of extreme hardcore, which are in fact succinctly summed up by the title of the genre's flagship zine: *Short, Fast and Loud.*[22]

The "loud" refers to the instrumentation of extreme hardcore, which is basically the same as in other genres of punk and hardcore: vocals, guitar, bass, and drums, although the drums are usually enhanced by double-bass pedals.[23] Guitars are normally heavily distorted, and may be tuned down (i.e., tuned lower than standard guitar strings), as is customary in many metal styles. Vocals are often distorted as well, and tend to be either screamed at a high pitch or grunted/growled at a low pitch; the vocalists provide a more timbral and rhythmic effect, instead of "singing" any kind of a melody. Words, which were the crucial vehicle for oppositional content in earlier forms of punk,[24] are generally unintelligible, a problem that is remedied by the customary inclusion of extensive inserts containing all of the lyrical material in CDs and records.

The "short" refers to the length of songs, which tend to be less than a minute (unless they alternate between fast and slow tempos). This brevity is understandable, given the genre's typically breakneck tempo; I doubt that even the best of drummers could physically maintain such a barrage of sound for a substantially longer period. In the tradition of pioneering extreme metal bands such as Napalm Death, some groups have songs that are exceedingly short, lasting only a few seconds. Such songs are so short and unstructured (basically just a blast of drumming and a barrage of screaming and guitars) that they push the limits of the typical boundary between music and noise. Indeed, even insiders are surprised by the way bands push the envelope of noise, as one reviewer humorously notes, "As soon as the first song started, I was convinced that this was playing at the wrong speed. You know, the sound of a 45 rpm record being played at 33 rpm. But as soon as I remembered that this is a CD and not vinyl, I could only marvel at the fact that these guys are so gol-darned HEAVY [author's emphasis]."[25] In an interview with the now-defunct influential extreme hardcore band Lärm, a band member recalls an incident in which the band's definition of music collided with a sound engineer's more mainstream ditto: "The sound check of our first concert ever was funny, the PA guy kept asking us when we were actually going to play a song…we already played three, we said. He shut down the PA and left . . ."[26]

"Fast" is the essential description of this genre: the speeds of most extreme hardcore bands defy my metronome's attempts to clock them. However, many bands not only play fast, but alternate tempos frequently, in order to create an interesting rhythmic texture (which seems to be more crucial in the aesthetics of this genre than vocal or even guitar melodies). Many groups compose songs with rhythmic modulations of extreme complexity; the band Dillinger Escape Plan, for example, has a few songs that seem to be rhythmically through composed, a series of starts and stops in which a certain rhythm will be held only very briefly before modulating into a new pattern of accent. The focus on rhythmic, rather than melodic, complexity tends to be a general feature of much extreme hardcore, as witnessed by the following comment of a *Short, Fast and Loud* reviewer: "Onto a framework of grinding thrash discordance and mayhem they weld two embellishments you don't always find. The first is melody. Buried under their wall of noise is an oddball sense of melody . . . almost jazzy sometimes, albeit jazz being run through a blender on puree."[27]

Such complexity of rhythm and texture inverts the notion of technical badness discussed above. Unlike early genres of punk, which anybody could (and should) play, I argue that in order to play extreme hardcore, musicians must have a relatively high level of technical proficiency due to the high speed and rhythmic complexity of many of the compositions. In the Dillinger Escape Plan example, the guitarist and bassist are following the complex non-cyclical rhythmic patterns of starts and stops highly accurately. Thus, while punks may have previously cultivated a lack of technique in order to make their music unappealing to the commercial mainstream, extreme hardcore musicians are cultivating relatively high levels of technique in order to make music that mainstream listeners will find unlistenable; that is, aesthetically bad while technically proficient. The same basic goal of avoiding appropriation underlies both strategies of "badness," although the strategies themselves are almost diametrically opposed in their cultivation of musical technique.

Rethinking Theories of Musical Resistance

Here, I will return to the question posed in the introduction: do the bad aesthetics of extreme hardcore offer a form of resistance that can be understood in terms that transcend the "Bourdieuian trap" into which badness as technical non-proficiency apparently falls? Attali's notion of "noise" and Adorno's concept of "autonomous music" offer theoretical frameworks that help enunciate the relationship of aesthetics and resistance to the question of mass commodification. Neither Adorno[28] nor Attali[29] presents a rosy picture of the effect of the music industry on the possibility for creative cultural opposition. Nevertheless, their theories do hold out the hope for a productive opposition that could lead to change.

Attali's theory of "noise" suggests a way to move past Bourdieu's vicious circle of position-takings via a deliberately self-imposed alien-ation.[30] Attali's view of the development of the political economy of music is based on four "networks" or potentially overlapping phases that musical production tends to pass through historically. The first phase is that of (sacrificial) "ritual," in which music equals power itself, the power to produce both order and violence. The second phase is that of "representation" (corresponding to the bourgeois audience), in which music presents a passive spectacle. The third phase is that of "repetition," which characterizes the current state of mass-produced music, in which music becomes an industry and "enters the general economy as a material object of exchange and profit."[31] In the current network of repetition, music becomes a weapon of disguised violence, used to silence people through the illusion of choice and the banalization of any oppositional messages. Attali's third stage corresponds in many ways to Bourdieu's model of cultural production, which is based largely on the covert violence of struggles for control of economic and symbolic capital. In contrast to Bourdieu, however, Attali admits the possibility of moving past such economic logic to a fourth stage, that of "compo-sition," in which music is played for self-enjoyment alone, an inher-ently egotistical and non-commercial act. Such music is in a sense no longer music, but *noise*. Since this noise-music is an inherently private and non-communicatory act, it is able to escape absorption into even a symbolic economy (since for Bourdieu capital is always public). Finally, Attali suggests that individual composers, having voluntarily alienated/liberated themselves from repetitive music, would then be able to form new "networks of composition," ostensibly not on an economic model.

Although Attali himself is far from clear about what the nature of such post-repetitive networks would be, Susan McClary, in her afterword to Attali's *Noise*, identifies "New Wave" (including punk) and art music as the two genres that demonstrate the best potential for developing into Attali's projected network of composition.[32] Indeed, it could be argued that with respect to creating a non-commercial style which specifically excludes the majority of the population with its "unbearable aesthetics," twentieth century art music employs many of the same strategies as punk. As Milton Babbitt argues in his aptly-titled piece "Who Cares If You Listen?," the general public's distaste for modern art music, along with its tendency to dismiss music it does not like as "non-music," is a boon for composers: "to assign blame is to imply that this isolation is unnecessary and undesirable. It is my contention that, on the contrary, this condition is not only inevitable, but potentially advantageous for the composer and his music."[33] Many punks would celebrate this sentiment: we don't care if you listen; in fact, we hope you don't! By freeing their music from the constraints of mainstream "good aesthetics," punk musicians and art composers alike are able to "recognize the possibility, and actuality, of alternatives to what were once regarded as musical [and by extension, social] absolutes."[34]

However, there are some important differences between Babbitt's art manifesto and punk ideology, most notably their relationship to community. Babbitt appears to recommend that the composer follow an Attali-style self-alienation from society as a whole in order to achieve this freedom of possibility: "I dare suggest that the composer would do himself and his music an immediate and eventual service by total, resolute, and voluntary withdrawal from its public world to one of private performance and electronic media, with its very real possibility of complete elimination of the public and social aspects of musical composition."[35] Attali sees such withdrawal into oneself, as well as the creation of a musical code that does not communicate, as the only way to transcend the cycle of repetition.[36] He further encourages this alienation as the first step away from repetition towards the desirable state of composition: "by getting rid of the communicatory function of music, the goal of music is no longer to communicate with an audience, but to perform for one's own sake."[37] Elsewhere, he claims that "in the extreme, music would no longer be made to be heard."[38] One could point to the same compositional intent in extreme hardcore, especially the shortest, most "noisy" examples: such songs are no longer meant to be heard, but rather to be experienced as a physical assault (as the opening quote of this article implies). In this view, alienation is a prerequisite, indeed the mechanism for, change.

While Attali lauds this deliberate refusal to communicate as liberatory, the alienation imposed by creating an "unlistenable" music could also be seen as essentially self-defeating. As he explains, "in a society in which power is so abstract that it can no longer be seized, in which the worst threat people feel is solitude, not alienation [because you cannot get away from it even if you try], conformity to the norm becomes the pleasure of belonging and the acceptance of powerlessness takes root in the comfort of repetition."[39] In this view, radical, self-imposed alienation (if it is even possible) can be viewed as a last-ditch attempt to resist the all-encompassing power of repetitive culture. However, it is difficult to imagine how such a scenario would not result in a downward spiral of self-destruction and nihilism. The nihilistic tendency of self-imposed alienation has long been recognized in punk, since The Sex Pistols' first cries of "no future" were heard echoing from Britain's slums. Indeed, there remain today sub-factions within punk, most notably drunk punks and gutter punks, who are indeed nihilistic.[40]

Despite punk's nihilistic reputation in the mainstream media, I would argue that this bleak, self-alienating attitude is far from dominant within punk as a whole. As Laing notes,[41] the tension between nihilism and radical leftist utopianism is one of the ongoing tensions within punk. Since radically political punks tend to be the ones who are organized enough to control the "means of production" within the underground scene, i.e., zines, bands, clubs, etc, the non-nihilistic utopian viewpoint tends to dominate the subculture. In punk, probably owing to its egalitarian, grass-roots aesthetics, music is in many cases essentially a pretext for communication, for an enactment of shared beliefs and ideologies.[42] Thus, while I recognize that punks may be employing an Attalian strategy of noise to break the cycle of "repetitive" music and to effect a certain self-imposed alienation from mass-culture, I would reject a characterization of extreme hardcore "noise" as ultimately cultivating self-alienation and nihilism, since extreme hardcore, despite its noisiness, does still communicate—at least to other punks, if not to mass culture at large. Thus, while Attali offers a radical strategy of self-alienation to break out of the cycle of repetitive music, this is not the approach which most punks seem to be taking. Therefore, I suggest turning to Adorno, another critic of mass-mediated music, in search of another way of conceiving of artistic resistance to mass commodification.

Adorno's theories on art and the culture industry, too, offer a unique view of how discordant music is able to critique society and hold out the hope for change. In his negative dialectics, Adorno argues that the apparent identity achieved through dialectical synthesis is in fact ideological dissimulation that conceals contradictions and antagonisms. The main thrust of Adorno's critical project is to reveal the moments of non-identity within identity, that is, the moments of discord and contradiction that are masked by an apparently harmonious whole. In terms of society and art, Adorno argues that ideological art conceals antagonisms in social reality by offering a harmonious and pleasant representation of the world, when this representation is, in fact, ideological, a propaganda of sorts for the "degraded utopia of the present." Vis-à-vis this "ideological" art, Adorno posits the possibility for autonomous art, an art that does not merely perpetuate the ideology of the dominant members of society, but rather is able to reveal the moments of nonidentity in identity, that is, the moments of discord and social antagonism which that ideology conceals. A "true" artwork preserves the tension between the part and the whole otherwise collapsed by ideological art.

The music to which Adorno points as the most "autonomous" and capable of revealing the truth about social discord is modern art music (i.e., composers such as Arnold Schoenberg and Anton Webern); such twentieth-century art music, in all its atonality and experimental structure, is able to negate the pleasantness of mass music, exposing its untruth or its concealment of societal antagonisms. Extreme hardcore could arguably represent a type of autonomous music, given that its frequent lack of a clear melody, rhythmic complexity and irregularity, the unintelligibility of its text, etc. all confound the listener who has been socialized to expect popular music to feature such stock ingredients as catchy tunes, memorable words, a recurring verse-chorus structure and danceable beats. It may just be that extreme hardcore's lack of easily grasped "idioms" is what saves it from what Adorno deems "fetishization" and "regressive listening."[43] It is not entirely clear, however, that music such as extreme hardcore actually preserves the tension between the part and whole at the core of Adorno's concept of autonomous music. Perhaps, a more accurate assessment of the critical efficacy of extreme hardcore is that its disjunctive and noisy aesthetics explodes the tension between part and whole, thereby destroying any notion of a coherent whole by fetishizing the discordant parts in the extreme. The "bad" aesthetics of extreme hardcore, then, share the critical potential of autonomous music more completely than the "badness" of technical non-proficiency, which is easily commodified. Adorno argues that in mass culture, "pleasure is the flight from the last remaining thought of resistance."[44] By creating a sound as harsh and "unpleasant" as possible, proponents of extreme hardcore attempt to reestablish a sense of resistance to the seemingly inescapable stylistic poaching of mainstream music. By redefining punk in musical terms completely incompatible with mainstream music aesthetics, extreme hardcore is sonically striving to "make punk a threat again," to steal the by-line of the well-respected punk news-zine *Profane Existence*.

Although some members of the punk community appear a bit offended when their music is dismissed as "noise" by critics, at the same time many seem to revel in the creation of "sonic chaos," as is reflected in band names and album titles such as "Extreme Noise Terror" and "Total Noise Chaos." I argue that by stretching the definition of music and blurring the distinction between music and noise, punks attempt to create a space from which it is possible to truly critique and oppose hegemonic definitions and appropriations of "music." Attali states that "what is called music today is all too often only a disguise for the monologue of power";[45] thus, by creating "noise," or a new kind of music outside the traditional bounds of music, punks can be viewed as trying to get outside the silencing scope of hegemonic power. Likewise, Adorno notes that the culture industry effectively silences critique by creating the illusion of the inevitability of the status quo. If music has become a means of silencing people, does one not have to go beyond music to noise to be able to speak? Creating "noise" rather than "music" is in a certain sense advantageous, in that it gives sound a chance to regain the power taken away from music by commodification. Spreading noise is, in essence, the same as spreading resistance; a sonic critique of the traditional structures of music and traditional structures of power.

The Potential for a Productive Moment in Punk

If Attali and Adorno's models point to ways in which musical badness or noise can oppose and critique repetitive, ideological music, it is certainly not true that all "bad music" or "noise" has the same effect on the listener, nor the same critical efficacy. To understand the nature of the critique offered by extreme hardcore and how it could have any critical purchase beyond oppositional position-taking, we need to touch briefly on Hans-Georg Gadamer's ontology of the work of art, which addresses the way in which an artwork structures the experience of the perceiver. By focusing his aesthetic theory on the experience of the work of art, Gadamer argues for the ability of the artwork to affect the self-understanding of the perceiver, "the work of art has its true being in the fact that it becomes an experience that changes the person who experiences it."[46] To this end, he develops the idea of "play" as the mode of being of a work of art, since art exists in performance, that is, it has its mode of being in being played. Gadamer further identifies the mode of being of a work of art as a bringing-to-presentation of what the work is.

In the case of extreme hardcore, we can ask, what is extreme hardcore bringing to presentation? It is certainly not accidental that fans of this genre have coined the alternate term "power violence" to describe the style; although tongue-in-cheek, this label captures the overwhelming aesthetic quality of the music. Indeed, the record reviews of extreme hardcore in fanzines are full of descriptions of bands as "brutal, crushing, killer"; for example, one reviewer praises a group in the following graphic terms: "Whoa . . . Rawness to the max. Uplifting song titles like "Life Burns Me Out" and "I've Had Enough." Put NEGATIVE APPROACH's "Ready to Fight" on top of this and you've got yourself a perfect soundtrack for violence. This record is just hardcore. Raw, fast, basic, angry, mean, loud, terrifying. . . . Rush out on the street and find this piece."[47]

Following the rhetoric of insider reviewers, I would argue that extreme hardcore is a highly mediated and cultivated form of sonic violence. In claiming that the fundamental nature of this music is "violence," I am not implying that the musicians or their fans are prone to physical violence (in fact, in my experience, physical violence of any kind at punk shows is relatively rare), but rather that its mode of being is violence and aggression. In Attali's terms, the openness of violence expressed in extreme hardcore is less detrimental than the "hidden violence" of repetitive music and mass culture, which, as Adorno points out, is insidious in that it gives the listener the false impression of preserving her choice and free will.

Responding to one kind of violence with another, extreme hardcore is a music style that brings violence and aggression to presentation in order to "unmasks false consciousness"[48] and fight the covert violence perpetrated by mass-mediated music. Indeed, at the level of what Attali calls "composition" of music (which underground punk, in its melding of production and consumption, seems to embody), he argues that "violence ceases to be channeled into an object [and thus hidden and mystified], but rather becomes invested in the act of doing."[49] Punk's radical musical aesthetic potentially furthers its political program through its very sound; in essence, the "oppositional force" in punk has been removed from the visually or verbally symbolic back to the structure of the musical sounds themselves.

If the aesthetics of extreme hardcore bring "power violence" to presentation, it could be asked how it is possible to critique covert violence with overt violence. I believe the answer to this question lies in understanding the violence of extreme hardcore as a form of apocalypticism. (Indeed, much of the gory iconography of extreme hardcore record jackets and CD artwork includes post-apocalyptic scenes of nuclear annihilation, war and famine.) Punk's focus on apocalyptic imagery, along with the destructive "noise" of the extreme hardcore sound, can be seen as intensifying a sense of crisis, which, rather than being a pessimistic capitulation to the inevitable, could also lead to the positive outcome of forcing the exercise of thought and judgment. Indeed, Attali recognizes the power of extreme music to provoke crisis in order to clear a space for change, "Noise only produces order if it can concentrate on a new sacrificial crisis at a singular point, in a catastrophe, in order to transcend the old violence and recreate a system of differences on another level of organization."[50] The apocalyptic aggression of extreme hardcore is more "positive" than the pleasantness of mass produced music, since in fomenting a crisis through the presentation of violent sounds extreme hardcore holds out the hope for real change, while mass-produced music "forsakes promises of future happiness in the name of a degraded utopia of the present."[51]

If we accept as valid my characterization of extreme hardcore punk as a form of music that escapes the Bourdieuian trap of endless position-taking and represents a true critique of the culture industry, then we may want to ask whether the punk movement also holds out the potential for a productive moment. While I cannot offer a definitive answer to this question, I suggest that if punk anywhere harbors the potential for productive change, such potential lies not in the music (which nevertheless fulfils a crucial role in bringing about the conditions for change through aesthetic critique), but in the organization of the punk scene into a "global community." Somewhat akin to global networks of non-governmental organizations, the global punk network is basically a non-hierarchical web of musicians, writers, activists, and organizers from various local scenes, who often attempt to organize modes of production and habitation as egalitarian collectives.[52] While using the global "flows" to spread their music, literature and ideology, punks (as well as other underground music networks) may be the best example yet of the "embarrassing new potentials for equity" that Arjun Appadurai suggests with his idea of "grassroots globalization."[53] While far from ideal, sectors of the underground punk scene are nevertheless experimenting with new systems of economic and social organization, which, even if they do not themselves succeed in refiguring social and economic reality, nevertheless may clear a path for subsequent trans-figuring movements (the close links between the punk community and the anti-globalization movements indicate this may already be happening). Insider historians such as Marc Bayard, Mark Anderson and Mark Jenkins note that in the twenty-five years of its existence, punk has moved away from a nihilistic community based on merely oppositional, "negative unity" towards a self-understanding of punk that is neither self-destructive nor alienating, but rather community-forming.[54] If punk truly is able to create a community of listeners who recognize in the music, as well as in its webs of distribution and dis-semination, the possibility for political action, then punks may very well be able to construct a self-understanding that is not merely oppo-sitional, but productive.

NOTES

1. I would like to express my gratitude to Roger W. H. Savage, whose seminars in critical theory were crucial to the development of many of the ideas in this chapter. Thanks also to Timothy Rice, Chris Washburne, Maiken Derno, and an anonymous reviewer for their insightful comments on earlier drafts.
2. Jeb Branin, Review of *Strong Intention* (musical recording), *Short, Fast and Loud* 7(2001): 66.
3. Ibid.
4. Pierre Bourdieu, *The Field of Cultural Production* (New York: Columbia University Press, 1993), 36.
5. See Dave Laing, *One Chord Wonders: Power and Meaning in Punk Rock.* (Milton Keynes: Open University Press, 1985), and Keith Negus, *Popular Music in Theory.* (Hanover and London: Wesleyan University Press, 1996)
6. Themis Chronopoulos, *A Cultural History of Punk, 1964-1996* (master's thesis, San Jose State University, 1997); Dave Laing, *One Chord Wonders*, 1985, William Thomas Rice II, "The Geography of Punk Music" (master's thesis, University of California, Fullerton, 1998), and William Tsitsos, "Rules of Rebellion: Slamdancing, Moshing, and the American Alternative Scene," *Popular Music* 18, no. 3 (1999): 397–415.

7.   Tsitsos, op. cit.

8.   Laing, op. cit.

9.   Tricia Henry, *Break All the Rules: Punk Rock and the Making of a Style* (Ann Arbor: UMI Research Press, 1989).

10. Negus, op. cit.

11. Matt Williams, 2002, "Enterview [sic] with Phil Vane of Extreme Noise Terror," (available at http://get.to/ent).

12. Rob Coons, Review of *Malignant Tumor* (musical recording), *Short, Fast and Loud* 7 (2001): 61.

13. Pierre Bourdieu, *The Field of Cultural Production* (New York: Columbia University Press, 1993).

14. Ibid., 39.

15. Ibid., 59.

16. Theodor Adorno and Max Horkheimer, *Dialectic of Enlightenment,* trans. John Cumming (London: Verso, 1979), 130.

17. Craig O'Hara. *The Philosophy of Punk* (San Francisco and London: AK Press, 1999).

18. An acrimonious debate arose in *HeartattaCk,* issue 30 (May, 2001) fanzine as to whether Rage Against the Machine should still be considered "punk" given their popularity, since they had at least not sold out their political rhetoric when signing to a label.

19. Adorno and Horkheimer, *Dialectic of Enlightenment,* 129.

20. Felix Von Havoc, "Fin de Siecle Angst," *Maximum Rock N Roll* 218 (July 2001).

21. Ibid.

22. Any attempt to map out the subtle differences between extreme hardcore sub-genres is an endeavor beyond the scope of this discussion, as such divisions and labels are being continually disputed and redefined by musicians and re-viewers within the scene; indeed, to create a new sub-genre of extreme hardcore, one apparently need only attach the suffix "-core" to any descriptive element, as frequently happens on the pages of fanzines: in one issue of *Short, Fast and Loud*, reviewers produced various neologisms, such as vomitcore, blistercore, mincecore, etc., whose usefulness as markers of any tangible musical or ideological difference was at best dubious.

23. Recently, certain groups have been experimenting with adding keyboards and other electronically synthesized sounds, leading some insiders to joke about the "keyboardization of hardcore;" previously, keyboards (with the rare exception of their rather subtle use by bands like Amebix) had been for the most part disregarded as too "New Wave" or pop-inflected for hardcore. Yet, any inclusion of instruments besides guitar, bass and drums is still considered somewhat experimental (one reviewer remarks on a band's use of "exotic" instruments: flute and saxophone!).

24. Laing, op. cit.

25. Chris Dodge, Review of *Systral* (musical recording), *Short, Fast and Loud* 7 (2001): 66.

26. Rudolph Everts, "What Ever Happened to Lärm?" *Short, Fast and Loud* 6 (2000): 37.

27. Jeb Branin, Review of *Shikabane* (musical recording), *Short, Fast and Loud* 7 (2001): 65.

28. Theodor Adorno, *The Culture Industry* (London and New York: Routledge, 1991).

29. Jacques Attali, *Noise: The Political Economy of Music* (Minneapolis: University of Minnesota Press, 1985).

30. Attali, op. cit.

31. Ibid., 87.

32. See Susan McClary, Afterword to *Noise: The Political Economy of Music*, by Jacques Attali (Minneapolis: University of Minnesota Press, 1985). Although McClary uses the term "New Wave" exclusively, I would argue that the phenomenon she is describing is in fact "punk," since she points to The Sex Pistols and the subsequent grass-roots (i.e., DIY) ideology that has spread (which is more characteristic in punk than New Wave, in my opinion, as well as in Laing's [op. cit.]). She nevertheless refers to such music as "New Wave," as if the term "punk" and the associated music were still too vulgar to be given such praise in the academic literature.

33. Milton Babbitt, "The Composer as Specialist" in *Classic Essays on Twentieth-Century Music*, edited by Richard Kostelanetz and Joseph Darby (New York: Schirmer Books, 1996), 161.

34. Ibid., 162.

35. Ibid., 166.

36. Attali, *Noise*, 118.

37. Ibid., 142.

38. Ibid., 32.

39. Ibid., 125.

40. Tsitsos, op. cit.

41. Laing, op. cit.

42. Angela Rodel, "The Globalization of Punk" (Unpublished manuscript, University of California at Los Angeles, 2002).

43. Adorno, *The Culture Industry.*

44. Ibid., 11.

45. Attali, *Noise*, 9.

46. Hans-Georg Gadamer, *Truth and Method,* 2nd revised ed., trans. and revised by Joel Weinsheimer and Donald G. Marshall, (New York: Continuum,1991), 102.

47. Jeb Branin, Review of *Suicide Party* (musical recording), *Short, Fast and Loud* 7 (2001): 66.

48. Attali , *Noise*, 42.

49. Ibid., 144.

50. Ibid., 33.

51. Adorno, *The Culture Industry*, 9.

52. See Rodel, op. cit. and Alan O'Connor, "Local Scenes and Dangerous Crossroads: Punk and Theories of Cultural Hybridity," *Popular Music* 21, 2 (2002): 225–36.

53. Arjun Appadurai, "Grassroots Globalization and the Research Imagination," *Public Culture* 12, 1 (2000): 1–19.

54. Marc Bayard, Introduction to *The Philosophy of Punk*, by Craig O'Hara (San Francisco and London: AK Press, 1999); and Mark Anderson and Mark Jenkins, *Dance of Days: Two Decades of Punk in Our Nation's Capital* (Winnipeg, Canada: Soft Skull Press, 2001).

REFERENCES

Adorno, T. 1989. *Introduction to the sociology of music*, trans. E. B. Ashton. New York: Continuum.

———— 1991. *The culture industry.* London and New York: Routledge.

Adorno, T., and M. Horkheimer. 1979. *Dialectic of enlightenment*, trans. J. Cumming. London: Verso.

Anderson, M., and M. Jenkins. 2001. *Dance of days: Two decades of punk in our nation's capital.* Winnipeg, Canada: Soft Skull Press.

Appadurai, A. 2000. Grassroots globalization and the research imagination. *Public Culture* 12(1): 1–19.

Attali, J. 1985. *Noise: The political economy of music.* Minneapolis: University of Minnesota Press.

Bayard, M. 1999. *Introduction to the philosophy of punk*, ed. C. O'Hara. San Francisco and London: AK Press.

Babbitt, M. 1996. The composer as specialist. In *Classic essays on twentieth-century music*, eds., R. Kostelanetz and J. Darby, 161–67. New York: Schirmer Books. (Orig. pub. as "Who Cares If You Listen?" in *High Fidelity,* 1958.)

Bourdieu, P. 1993. *The field of cultural production.* New York: Columbia University Press.

Branin, J. 2001. Review of *Strong intention* (musical recording). *Short, Fast and Loud* 7: 66.

———— 2001. Review of *Shikabane* (musical recording). *Short, Fast and Loud* 7: 65.

———— 2001. Review of *Suicide party* (musical recording). *Short, Fast and Loud* 7: 66.

Chronopoulos, T. 1997. *A cultural history of punk, 1964–1996.* Master's thesis, San Jose State University.

Coons, R. 2001. Review of *Malignant tumor* (musical recording). *Short, Fast and Loud* 7: 61.

Dodge, C. 2001. Review of *Systral* (musical recording). *Short, Fast and Loud* 7: 66.

Everts, R. 2000. What Ever Happened to Lärm? *Short, Fast and Loud* 6: 35–38.

Gadamer, H.-G. 1991. *Truth and method.* 2nd rev. ed., trans. and rev. J. Weinsheimer and D. G. Marshall. New York: Continuum.

Hebdige, D. 1979. *Subculture: The meaning of style.* London: Methuen.

Henry, T. 1989. *Break all the rules: Punk rock and the making of a style.* Ann Arbor: UMI Research Press.

Heylin, C. 1993. *From velvets to voidoids: A pre-punk history for a post-punk world.* New York: Penguin Books.

Laing, D. 1983. *One chord wonders: Power and meaning in punk rock.* Milton Keynes: Open University Press.

McClary, S. 1985. *Afterword to noise: The political economy of music*, ed. J. Attali. Minneapolis: University of Minnesota Press.

Negus, K. 1996. *Popular music in theory*. Hanover: Wesleyan University Press.

O'Connor, A. 2002. Local scenes and dangerous crossroads: Punk and theories of cultural hybridity. *Popular Music* 21(2): 225–36.

O'Hara, C. 1999. *The philosophy of punk*. San Francisco and London: AK Press.

Rice, W. T., II. 1998. The geography of punk music. Master's thesis, University of California, Fullerton.

Rodel, A. 2002. The globalization of punk. Unpublished manuscript, University of California at Los Angeles.

Tsitsos, W. 1999. Rules of rebellion: Slamdancing, moshing, and the American alternative scene. *Popular Music* 18(3): 397–415.

Von Havoc, F. 2001. Fin de siecle Angst. *Maximum Rock N Roll* 218 (July).

Williams, M. 2002. Interview [sic] with Phil Vane of Extreme Noise Terror. http://get.to/ent

12
Glitch —
The Beauty of Malfunction

TORBEN SANGILD

You are sitting in a cafe on a Tuesday afternoon. People are seated in small groups, chatting, drinking, smoking, eating. In the background a pop record is playing—probably supplied to the cafe by one of the major labels. People are paying little attention to the tune, even though they will recognize it later when they hear it on the radio. The record serves its purpose as soothing ambience and commercial strategy. People are having a good time. Everything is normal.

Suddenly the CD in the cafe begins to stutter: Tchuck-tchuck-tchuck-tchuck. The cafe guests interrupt their conversations and frown impatiently, annoyed, disturbed. For a few seconds the sound of CD glitch invades the space of afternoon relaxation. This state of tension will not subside until one of the waitresses, stressed by the crowd's expectations to move quickly to stop the annoyance, although she is serving a costumer, hurries to the stereo and puts in a new CD. Now, people are able to relax again.

About

This chapter is about the other side of technology, about CD players and computers not functioning, about the homogenization of the music and computer industries. It is about fragile sensibility, avant-garde experiments and a different kind of beauty. The beauty of computers crashing and CDs skipping, of clicks and cuts and bleeps and stutters. It is about contemporary electronic music, about music often vaguely referred to as "glitch," but rarely treated systematically as a genre concept. It began in the mid-1990s and has spread as a musical virus to become one of the most significant aspects of today's electronica with a sound and aesthetic of its own.

It may be discussed whether "glitch" is an appropriate genre term, as it accentuates certain technical aspects over purely musical ones and, therefore, is in danger of over-emphasizing the conceptual perspective. I do not see a conflict between the sensuous and the conceptual, however. Glitch artists in general tend to be conceptually self-conscious; the technical means seem to lead to a certain musical sensibility, and "glitch" remains the most common term applied to this music.

In this chapter, I examine "glitch" as a meaningful concept, rather than as a casual label. This will be accomplished by exploring the conceptual implications of the genre term.[1] I will suggest some subgenres, each stressing a certain quality of glitch. And, I will claim musical fragility and techno-critique[2] as common denominators, and hint at the aesthetic experience of glitch as an oppurtunity for relating to technology in everyday life. All this is tentative, suffering from a general lack of overview that goes with mapping and reflecting a contemporary phenomenon.

What Is Glitch?

A glitch is a minor malfunction or spurious signal, often related to a system or an electronic device. It is not a collapse of the machinery. The machinery is still running, but the performance is poor—either annoying, problematic, or downright useless.

The word "glitch" derives from Yiddish "glitshn," to slip, slide or glide. Something glitchy is slippery and out of control. The first recorded usage of the term associated with technical malfunction was by astronaut John Glenn. He and his crew adopted the term to refer to electrical power problems encountered on the first U.S. manned spacecraft.[3] Later the term has been employed in referring to mishaps and malfunctions, such as sudden changes in the period of rotation of a neutron star, problems in navigational systems, the disruption of a process or project, a power surge, a loss of network service, a transient bug in a computer program, the horizontal noise bar moving vertically on a video screen due to frequency interference, etc.

Today, glitch is commonly used to describe errors in computer software (more or less synonymous with "bug") or hardware, computers crashing, or, specifically, the sound of a CD or sound file skipping and stuttering. A glitch, also when not connected to audio technology, is often accompanied by some noise, reminding us that something is wrong.

Glitch music incorporates these and related sounds. Apart from damaging CDs, glitch artists collapse software processing, for example, by overloading processors, reducing bit rates and by reading files from another file format (text files, picture files, program files) as if they were audio files. The results are sampled and composed into a specific musical context depending on the aesthetic preferences of the composer.[4]

Fragments of a Prehistory

One day in the early 1940s, French radio engineer, Pierre Schaeffer, who was later to become the famous creator of *musique concréte*, put an Edith Piaf record on his turntable. The record was worn and scratched—it stuttered and jumped uncontrollably. Instead of pulling off the record, Schaeffer began varying the speed of the turntable. The combination of analogue glitches and a constant glissando created a strange musical expression reminiscent of a surrealist collage.[5]

There has always been an urge among composers and musicians to experiment with and expand upon the conventional sound possibilities of established instruments. This has been an important part in the development of new instruments, timbres and sounds. In the twentieth century the avant-garde has taken this strategy in a radical direction, exploring the sound qualities very far from the original intention for the instrument. John Cage's invention of the prepared piano provides a significant example, as it goes against the grain of the piano sound to explore the percussive possibilities of piano strings attached with rubber, screws and other objects. Additionally, Cage used two record players as instruments for his work *Imaginary Landscape no.1* (1939). Even before Cage, composers such as Darius Milhaud and Paul Hindemith experimented with turntables, however without preserving these experiments in official works.[6]

There is a difference between such mere trying out of different possibilities inherent in instruments and objects in general and a more specific, consistent adoption of the sounds of error in technological equipment. When rock musicians of the 1960s started using feedback and distortion as an integrated part of the music they actively transformed unwanted noise into signal. Feedback and distortion were originally undesirable side effects of amplification of electric guitars. Within a few years, however, the employment of guitar noise became so common that the music industry began producing different noise effect pedals.[7]

Another important point of reference for a pre-history of glitch is the British conceptual rock band, Throbbing Gristle, whose label *Industrial* coined the genre of the same name. At live performances they would experiment with malfunctioning tape recorders (sometimes destroying them on stage) with the result of unpredictable sounds of tapes running defectively. Rap music hinted at vinyl glitches with the invention of the scratch effect. More direct vinyl damaging was featured in the works of Christian Marclay who released his *Record without a cover* in 1985, where the explicit instruction written on the vinyl itself was to *not* protect the record, but instead let it be damaged and scratched. That same year, the technique of CD glitch (if not the musical style itself) was born with the experiments of Yasunao Toné.

Styles and Subgenres

Even though style classifications always represent a violent abstraction of concrete particulars and therefore must be understood non-substantially, they may still serve as preliminary concepts for mapping a new field, enabling overview and reflection. I will suggest the following three types of glitch music:

1. *Conceptual glitch*: Sound artists working with glitch as a primarily conceptual phenomenon, often as part of art installations.
2. *Oceanic glitch*: Electronic music is basically "cool," working with the sounds of technology. However, the oceanic glitch artists work from that base towards a rich and "warm" harmonics inspired by rock music as does My Bloody Valentine, although quite distinct from rock in their gestures and sound-work. Whereas Oval, Andreas Tilliander, Microstoria and others create complex textures of diverse sonic material, Fennesz, Nobukazu Takemura and others work with fewer elements in an equally luscious melodies.
3. *Minimal click*: Ryoji Ikeda, Alva Noto, Pan Sonic and others work minimally with dry, repetitive movements of the tiniest, sometimes almost inaudible, clicks of computer and sound technology,

thereby exposing these sounds musically, often without adding melodic material.

Of course, these broad generic tendencies overlap each other in various instances, and it should be stressed that the conceptual aspect is always a conscious part of glitch. Likewise, not all glitch records fit easily into these three categories.[8]

Yasunao Toné, the Pioneer—Conceptual Glitch

In 1985, the Japanese-American sound artist Yasunao Toné performed *Techno-Eden* together with dancer Kay Nishikawa.[9] Here, and in his solo work *Music for 2 CDs*, he prepared music CD's by slicing them with razor blades or attaching scotch tape filled with pinholes. The result was unpredictable chunks of sound as the CDs glitched and skipped—fragments of the original music (classical works by Beethoven and Tchaikovsky) combined with noises from the CD players, trying in vain to read the digital information on the damaged discs. Apart from making chance music in the tradition of John Cage,[10] Toné also revealed the new CD technology to be more fragile than commonly assumed at the time. What Toné could not know was that he anticipated a technique that would be refined and used for sonic evolution by young laptop composers in the 90s, coining the genre now known as "glitch."

In 1997, Toné returned to what was now known as the glitch method on his *Solo for Wounded CD*, where he used only one prepared CD, his own work *Musica Iconologos*,[11] which is very high-pitched. The result is a harsh attack on the nervous system, a high frequency noise collage of pure glitch sounds. The title of the work suggests the literally wounded CD "screaming" and glitching in pain as the cause of these squeaking sounds. In a certain sense, the screaming CD is more "human" than the violent person inflicting the wounds. Of course, a CD is not able to feel pain, being only a disc with binary codes on it, but by employing the metonymy of the wound and by stressing the erratic nature of CD technology, the dialectics between supposedly "cold" technology and "warm" humanity is artistically played out in Toné's work.

Toné, among the founders of the fluxus movement in the early 1960s, conceives of himself as an artist rather than a music composer, and refuses to construct anything reminiscent of synthesis, melody or development. Rather, his work may be described as sound art conceptualism in the tradition of Marcel Duchamp and John Cage. He explores the ideologies of technology through sound-making, and makes de-skilled art with experiments that anyone could reproduce. The sensuous qualities are not at the core of the experiment. They are, however, as in all interesting conceptual art, not without significance. As the case with Lou Reed's *Metal Machine Music* (1975) and Merzbow's numerous CDs prove,[12] even extreme and abstract noise has aesthetic qualities, although it requires a lot of receptiveness and accommodation from the listener. Listening to extreme noise requires tolerance. The reward is an expanded sense of differentiation between qualities of sound.

The young laptop composers who have taken up glitch in the 1990s are well aware of the conceptual implications connected with this approach.[13] Yet, most of them are not satisfied with random unmediated glitch, but try instead to synthesize the sounds; to actually construct music out of the clicks, squeaks and fragments. They are often preoccupied with media critique and aesthetic qualities as part of the same creative process.

Oval—Oceanic Glitch

Probably the most important name in glitch is German Oval. Oval more or less invented glitch as a constructive musical technique with *Wohnton* in 1993, and he is still the most influential glitch-composer, combining art installations, critical manifestos and highly developed musical textures. Oval began as a trio, but since 1996 the name has been a pseudonym for Markus Popp alone, collaborating with different individuals from project to project.

On the debut album, *Wohnton* (1993), the glitches provide a noisy background to naïvely melodic vocal songs. In the catchy lyric pop song "Allesin Gedanken" the harmonic structure is constituted from two interchanging CD glitches looped repeatedly, combined with a guitar chord accompanied by a single repeated piano note.[14] "Theoriebahn" is more complex, based on rapidly changing sounds made from fast-forwarding the CD, causing it to skip fragmentarily. These randomly produced sound patterns are interwoven into a surprisingly coherent collage. The glitches and skips are not just new and conceptually interesting ways of creation—they also endow the music with a different sensibility, with textures, phrasings and sound material of an innovative and contemporary character.

After *Wohnton*, Oval's music has been devoid of vocal melodies, instead gradually refining the glitch aesthetic. In 1994 the trio made a reputation for themselves by creating a whole album, *Systemisch*, made primarily from a destroyed version of Aphex Twin's trendsetting *Selected Ambient Works vol. II*, still considered a masterpiece of early electronica. By drawing lines on the CD bottom with a felt-tipped pen, the unpredictable sonic results were recorded and selections sampled and looped with a rich variety of sounds available.

Systemisch almost amounts to a concept album with track titles such as "Compact Disc" and "The Politics of Digital Audio." Here, Oval sets the agenda for glitch. The typical *Systemisch* track is constructed from a glitch loop with clicks accentuating a beat with rumbling, distorted tones floating above. Some of the tracks, though, notably "Oval Office" and "Compact Disc," delve deeper into a purely ambient, meditative style of distorted oceanic waves of sound.

On *Szenariodisc* (1999) Oval refined his compositions by using a greater variety of sounds, synthesized into a more complex texture. These refinements point towards the most elaborate and subtle glitch-record to date, *OvalProcess* (2000), the epitome of what I call oceanic glitch. Here is the evidence of where glitch may end up if it is worked through compositionally, synthesizing seemingly incompatible and unmusical noises into coherent music with its own unique sound. The sound material still consists of noisy glitches, rumbling distortions and bleeping sine tones. Working on the borderline between noise and tone, Oval uses his skilled ear for harmony to transform the annoying into beauty.[15]

There is a sense of fragility and porosity in Oval despite the richness in texture, due to an intricate web of elements found in the timbral aspects as well as in the musical structure. I will now briefly try to hint at just a few of these elements, encouraging the reader to listen to the music for further understanding.[16]

Digital sound equipment typically employs upper level threshold limiters to control the volume power and to prevent distortion caused by clipping of loud sound signals. When you take a sine tone right to the subtle edge between an allowed and a censured signal, the result is a sound with irregular, clipped "holes" in it, a porous tone on the verge of crumbling, almost like a nervous alarm breaking down. Oval combines this "fragile alarm" effect with glitch loops, different noises and clicks. This is just one of numerous examples of how important the sound processing is for the overall emotional gesture of the music.[17]

The traditional ideal in acoustic and electric music alike (classical, jazz, folk, rock, etc.) is an organic rhythmic flow as opposed to the metronomic, mechanical beat associated with techno and electronic dance music. All electronica share the inorganic basis of techno. In oceanic glitch this premise is taken in a quasi-organic direction, softening the rigidity towards a sensibility of its own. Oval's music often surprises the listener with unpredictable, sudden bursts of sound, stumbling chaotically into the music before finding its place in the complex overall flow, with or without a beat. Where a beat is present, it is always the clicking sound of the stuck CD, struggling to move on, randomly skipping from one sound fragment to another. It is equally far from the firm, rigid pulse of techno and from the elastic phrasing of classical music. Its gesture would be considered a non-gesture in acoustic music, a secondary sound, a touch or strike too vague to be taken seriously. And it would not even be heard in techno.

There are many other elements constituting the peculiar style of Oval, which deserves to be analyzed further elsewhere. Suffice it here to say that the result is a warm, rich sound, a gestural flow torn between repetition of loops and chaotic unpredictability, between coherence and fragility, between tone and noise.

Ryoji Ikeda and Alva Noto—Minimal click

If less is more, then the Japanese composer Ryoji Ikeda's music is overwhelmingly rich. He is not afraid of exploring one single sound for eleven minutes, while slowly changing its timbre through digital processing, as if performing a phenomenological reduction. The sound may be a sine tone or something that sounds like a helicopter rotor. The track titles on +/– are as stripped down and mathematically systematic as the music itself: "+," "+.," "+..," "–," "–.," "–.." etc. Like the Finnish duo, Pan Sonic, Ikeda belongs to a style of extreme techno minimalism, investigating the beauty of single sounds, or sometimes, when indulging in sensuous orgies, the combination of two or three sounds. His sound material consists of sine tones from stereo test records, fax connections screeches, radio static noise, humble techno-logical clicks and ticks, bad speaker connection hums, and the like. The title track on +/– consists of nothing but ultrasounds.[18] Here, the importance of playback device quality comes into focus. With normal or poor speakers one almost doesn't hear anything until this last track on the album stops and a sudden release of tension is felt. What you hear is the sound ending, not its presence. Unless one presses the fast-forward button on the CD player, that is, which makes it play a variety of fast changing sounds—only skipping brings you music. With great quality high fidelity speakers, a painful assault of high frequencies will burst out at high loudness, and few people with intact hearing abilities will be able to endure the track, even at a fairly low volume. In both cases, the track points at the stress of unnoticed sounds in technological environments.

On *0°C* Ikeda is less minimal in terms of sound, if not in terms of exploring distinctive features one at a time. "Cacoepy," with its de-composed computer voice, sounds like a robot or talking computer infused with a virus, and "Cuts" resembles a maltreated drum machine running amok. Two tracks ("Cadenza" and "Canon") are CDs with classical music skipping and occasionally playing a few seconds before continuing the fragmented patterns with their own, impatient harmony. "Coda" is almost dramatic; a simple ding-tone, first sounding alone, is later accompanied by sinister synth chords and a ticking sound, suggest-ing a time bomb. Almost inaudible, low distorted singing voices add to the gloomy atmosphere of this atypically moody track.

There is a sense of abstraction in Ryoji Ikeda's music, an almost inhuman gesture, as opposed to Oval's quasi-organic syntheses. Like a sonic scientist, Ikeda explores the micro-semantics of isolated sounds, carefully and gradually combining them to create a minimal gesture. Consequently, every tiny inclination toward tension or struggle in Ikeda's music is perceived as highly expressive. The micro-semantics is also a question of micro-affects.

Alva Noto (aka Carsten Nicolai[19]) draws his sound material from the same clicking, beeping world of electronic devices as Ryoji Ikeda. He is, however, more focused on developing rhythmic patterns. He records the slightest sounds from electronic equipment, even flimsier than Ikeda's, and creates the frailest dance beat ever heard. The typical track begins with a few sounds discreetly disturbing the silence—some crackles and a high frequency buzz, for instance. They seem to be non-periodic, i.e., not forming a pattern. A few more sounds are added—bleeps and clicks. Suddenly you realize that you are hearing a beat, even though you are not able to figure out exactly when it started. The gestalt of a rhythmic beat pattern in Alva Noto's music is a gradual process for the listener—it happens without being consciously noticed. And the beat is not just some regular metronomic repetition—it is funky. It has the groove of dance music without any hint of a melody and with a beat only audible in a quiet room, even when the volume is turned up high.

Minimal click focuses on sounds that are rarely recognized in everyday life; the forgotten secondary sounds of electronic equipment. They are withdrawn from their concrete environment and inserted in an abstract, empty sound space, where they are endowed with a new relative autonomy, and perceived as music. These sounds will only be heard through abstraction, frail and fragile as they are. Precisely through the decontextualization and micro-acoustics, minimal click has the ability to influence our perception of microsounds in daily life. The experience of *minimal click* provides the opportunity to relate more consciously to the sounds we are involuntarily exposed to in our techno-environments, and to become aware of the stress they inflict upon us as well as the potential beauty they posses.

Téchne

Glitches are the sounds of technology not working; the sounds of the grit in the machinery of sound-making. Few things in everyday life are more annoying than malfunctioning technology. The sound of malfunction is far from neutral; it becomes a disturbing sign which reminds us that things are not right. The sound often enhances the annoyance, as if scorning our impotence in relation to advanced technological equipment. The impotence of the machine is projected on to us, as we are the ones who suffer. But at the same time, this is where technology reveals its téchne—its material, structural and ideological foundations which in everyday life have become transparent, invisible.

Martin Heidegger's theory of technology focuses on téchne as a way of being in the world. Technology is never neutral. It is a way of dealing in and with life, and the important thing is to have a free relation to technology, which implies not merely regarding it as a tool. A tool (e.g., a hammer) is transparent in the sense that we think of it as purely functional. When it breaks, however, we become aware of its construction and design; the tool becomes unfamiliar, no longer an unquestioned extension of ourselves, and its téchne is revealed.[20] Theodor Adorno seems to have had the same idea already in 1928 in specific relation to music technology, when he wrote, "There is only one point at which the gramophone interferes with both the work and the interpretation. This occurs when the mechanical spring wears out . . . only when gramophonic reproduction breaks down are its objects transformed. Or else one removes the records and lets the spring play out in the dark."[21]

The common digital technology of today is governed by "user-centered interface design,"[22] which is geared towards making things as smooth, easy and uncomplicated for the user as possible. The ideal is a minimum of interpretation and a maximum of transparency. This, of course, is desirable and convenient for us all, in so far as we behave as mere users. However, from a Heideggerian perspective, being nothing but a user is exactly the problem. We should also be interpreters and creative agents. This implies a higher awareness of the materiality and structure of the hardware and software to which we are exposed. The software corporations design their user interfaces in ways that not only make things as easy as possible, but also predisposes the user to specific actions, commitments and metaphors. The most obvious examples, of course, are the companies which preinstall specific commercial links in the Web browser or pop-up invitations to use a specific program from a sponsor. Beneath this surface of clear manipulation lie endless ideological choices of structures and metaphors, images and defaults, non-available options and settings, etc.[23]

The important metaphor in this chapter is, of course, the representation of music. The common audio software is designed to produce commercial and standardized forms of music. The conception of music is often traditional—tones, functional harmonies, metric rhythms, instrumental layers, and spectral diagrams. One way of critiquing these standardizations is for the composer or producer to change the parameters, the quantitative thresholds or the allowed input data.[24] In order to do so it is necessary to have an interpretative knowledge of and a creative interaction with the technology in question—be it software, hardware, or reproduction technology. The artist is then no longer merely a user, but becomes a creative techno agent, a deconstructionist of sorts. He speaks the language of technology rather than being spoken by it, as Heidegger would have said.

Together with structures of ideology and standardization, the creative techno agent also explores the material and semiotic aspects of music technology, going against the everyday notion of computers as being somewhat immaterial, virtual spaces of action, sensation and communication or of CD players being perfect, neutral actualizations of musical material—despite the fact that we know better. There are very concrete ("dirty") material foundations underlying these mirages—mechanical, electrical machinery reading codes. Codes are read and interpreted, and sometimes misread or at odds with one another. This becomes the material for the heretical media artist. Technology becomes more tangible, "it shows up the fake immateriality of the electronic media, collapses the clean, evanescent streams of data back into sensible dirt and grit; pulls the media themselves out into the material world, into temporal, kinesthetic and affective experience."[25] Glitch music is a heretical media art in this vein. And even on the level of critical import, it is still a question of *sensibility* towards technology. The conceptual and the sensuous are intertwined. The deconstructive disenchantment of technology becomes at the same time an aesthetic reenchantment.

The Ghost in the Machine

"In science fiction, ghosts in machines always appear as malfunctions, glitches, interruptions in the normal flow of things. Something unexpected appears seemingly out of nothing and from nowhere. Through a malfunction, a glitch, we get a fleeting glimpse of an alien intelligence at work," writes Janne Vanhanen,[26] pointing to how glitch also gives us a sense of something living, something conscious, even though we know this is not the case.

Glitch displays the fragility and vulnerability of technology. It points to the dialectic moments of irrationality embedded in rational computers. When people say that only humans, not machines, can be irrational, they employ a limited idea of what irrationality is. They focus on rationality as either something belonging to self-conscious intelligence (human life) or to strict calculation. In the first case, computers are neither rational nor irrational; in the second case, computers are perfectly rational. However, computers are interactive and thus not restricted to their "inner," binary calculations, just as human beings are not just molecules moving in the nervous system. Computers have a communicative interface that is an essential part of their practical being.[27]

And rationality is not just about following rules. There is something irrational about following rules slavishly. Rationality is also about efficiency and practicality, about doing things the easiest and most economical way. Computers that crash or display absurd behavior are, in a certain sense, irrational, even though the reason behind it may, in principle, be explicable.

Glitch music focuses on these dialectic moments of irrationality, inefficacy and absurdity in digital technology, finding a delicate beauty there. The luscious loops of oceanic glitch and the tiny ticks of minimal click share this fragile sensibility.

Progress and Biology

In general, we want things to be efficient and smooth. The ideology of Western society relies upon efficiency and productivity as a driving force. The sounds of malfunction are unwanted, as malfunctions seem to stop progress. In reality, though, glitches can also become the occasion for a break, a step back from the habits of everyday life. And employed creatively, it can contribute to artistic development in all of the arts.[28]

In nature, genetic "glitches" occur when the copying of genes from one generation to the next is imperfect. Something goes wrong and a butterfly gets a different color or a bird is born with a slightly different beak. We call these *mutations*. They are genetic errors or imperfections, and most of them are unimportant, while some are downright handicaps. Once in a while, though, a mutation turns out to be beneficial for the species in a given biological environment. Through natural selection this mutation becomes dominant. An evolutionary step has taken place. Evolution depends on errors and imperfections.

Digital technology allows for cloning, for perfect copying of digital information. When bugs and glitches occur, such perfection is disturbed. Imperfections are often annoying, some would say downright "bad," but they can also be used aesthetically to create new sounds and textures, causing music to evolve further.

This may only be a metaphor. However, such metaphors go both ways, from music to biology and back.[29] The point is that errors and malfunctions are not only to be viewed as unproductive setbacks, but also as creative energy sparks, sometimes providing a non-conformist progress. Therefore, patterns of biological selection and evolution are used in computer technology for developing computer programs—an example of so-called "artificial life." On the level of models, a triangle connection between music, technology and biology is established.

The Oyster

An irritant—a grain of sand or a parasite—finds its way inside the shell of an oyster. As a way to defend itself from the irritant, the oyster covers it with layers of protective substance to form a barrier. The glitch in the oyster is thereby transformed into a pearl. This is another biological metaphor for glitch music.[30] It speaks of annoyance turned into beauty.

Back at the Cafe

You are sitting in a cafe on a Tuesday afternoon. In the background a pop record is playing. Suddenly the CD stutters. You have listened to glitch music for quite a while now. Your reaction has changed. Instead of the usual frustrated response you lean back and enjoy the random loops and skips of the CD, finding it more beautiful in its simplicity than the commercial hit from which it derives. You hear how well it goes with the cappuccino-maker's noise, the cell phone ringing at another table and the chiming from tablespoons on teacups and of forks on plates. When the waitress changes the CD everything is almost back to normal.

NOTES

1. Early treatments of glitch as a genre can be found in Kim Cascone, "The Aesthetics of Failure: "Post-digital" Tendencies in Contemporary Computer Music," *Computer Music Journal* 24.4 (2000); Kenneth Goldsmith, "It was a bug, Dave—The Dawn of Glitchwerks," 1999; Rob Young, "Worship the Glitch," *The Wire* 190/191, 2000.

2. Techno-critique is not the same as opposing technology—it is the self-critique of technology from within.

3. Gene Gurney, *Americans Into Orbit* (Random House, 1962) 86.

4. I use the word "composer" not in the narrow sense of academically educated sheet music composers. To compose means literally to put together, to construct music. This is what self-taught laptop musicians do.

5. Schaeffer recounts this in Pierre Schaeffer, "Pierre Schaeffer," *Ljudkonst*, ed. Peter R. Meyer (Stockholm: Proprius, 1992). I have found no English translation of this essay.

6. See Roger Sutherland, *New Perspectives in Music* (London: Sun Tavern Fields, 1994) 36. It should be noted that neither of these composers explored scratches and errors in the records as Schaeffer did.

7. The techniques of feedback and distortion and the history of guitar noise are treated briefly in Torben Sangild, *The Aesthetics of Noise* (Copenhagen: Datanom (also published online: www.datanom.com/noise), 2002) 8–15. A longer version is found in the Danish book: Torben Sangild, *Støjens æstetik* (København: Multivers, 2003).

8. In this chapter, I have chosen to focus on a few seminal glitch-artists instead of providing an exhaustive overview of the many composers and bands working on the glitch scene today. I will, however, mention the most important ones, dealing partly or exclusively with glitch in their music: Skinny Puppy (on Last Rights), Farmers Manual (on Explorers_We), Disc, Txture, Kid 606, Farben, Vladislav Delay, Kit Clayton, Matmos, Florian Hecker, Frank Bretschneider, Massimo, Pole, Mikael Stavöstrand, Otomo Yoshihide, Beautyon, Marc Behrens and SND. Some independent record labels have specialized in glitch, notably Mille Plateaux, Mego, Touch and Thrill Jockey. Equivalents to the glitch has occasionally been used in pop music such as Madonna's hit "Don't Tell Me" (2000). That does not make it glitch music as it is theatrically staged as a momentary effect.

9. Alan Licht, "Random Tone Bursts," *The Wire* 223, 2002.

10. On this occasion, Cage was among the audience, laughing out loudly and joyously during the whole performance. Cage and Toné worked together on several occasions. Licht, "Random Tone Bursts," 32.

11. In this work from 1992, Toné also proved himself a pioneer, being one of the first to directly translate digital images (of Chinese characters) into music, exploiting the fact that both consist of binary codes. This technique is common now, as software (such as Metasynth, Coagula and Goldwave) has been created to facilitate this operation. See Phil Thomson, "Atoms and Errors: Towards a History and Aesthetics of Microsound", 2003.

12. See Sangild, *The Aesthetics of Noise* 13, 20–21.

13. In recent years, Toné has worked with young New York laptop composers like DJ Spooky and Jim O'Rourke.

14. I will not go into detail with the harmony, as it cannot be abstracted from the parameter of timbre in glitch, where each chord is usually made from one or more looped samples, often with very uneven sonorous qualities. A harmonic analysis would miss the point, especially with regard to the later Oval. Here, on *Wohnton* traditional pop harmonies may still be traced.

15. When I speak of beauty in this chapter, I use the term not in any specific philo-sophical (Kantian) sense as opposed to the sublime. Rather, I speak of beauty as opposed to ugly, annoying, "bad," focusing on the tension between the two and the point where they meet.

    It is ironic how Markus Popp (Oval) always denies being interested in the aesthetic qualities and in making music, being one of the most skilled glitch composers from an aesthetic point of view. He frequently denies music as any-thing but a metaphor for critique.

16. I must thank Jakob Weigand Goetz for inspiring input and dialogue. Nobody has a better ear for Oval than him.

17. In Torben Sangild, "Sensitive electronics," *Look at the Music—SeeSound*, ed. J. W. Goetz (Ystad/Roskilde: Ystad Art Musem/Museum of Contemporary Art, Roskilde, Denmark, 2002). I attempt to explain how electronic music can ex-press an emotional and bodily gesture, even though the indexical traces of a bodily activity (significant in acoustic music) is absent. This points toward a more object-oriented concept of emotions in art in general.

18. Ultrasounds are frequencies above normal human hearing ability, convention-ally over 20.000 hz. Some animals hear them clearly. They are used by bats to navigate and by humans to explore flaws and defects in solid material. At high intensity ultrasound can be extremely stressful and can be used to kill insects.

19. Like Markus Popp (Oval) Carsten Nicolai is an installation artist dealing with music CDs as one media among others.

20. A reading of Heidegger's concept of téchne in a critical perspective is per-formed by Feenberg, Di Scipio and Hamman. The argument is more complex than my account here, as Heidegger did not draw the conclusions of a material-aesthetic techno-self-critique. Martin Heidegger, "The Question Concerning Technology," trans. D. F. Krell, *Basic Writings* (New York: Harper & Row, 1977 (German: 1953)). Michael Hamman, "From Technical to Technological: Interpreting Technology Through Composition", 2000; Agostino Di Scipio, "Interpreting Music Technology—From Heidegger to Subversive Rationaliza-tion," *Sonus* 18.1 (1997). Andrew Feenberg, "Subversive Rationalization: Tech-nology, Power and Democracy," *Technology and the Power of Knowledge*, ed. A. Feenberg and A. Hannay (Bloomington: Indiana University Press, 1995).

21. Theodor W. Adorno, "The Curves of the Needle," *October* 55, 1990 (German: 1928) Originally published in *Musikblätter des Anbruch #10*. For a refreshing and vital account of Adorno's often progressive thoughts on music technology (despite the rumours), see Thomas Y. Levin, "For the Record: Adorno on Music in the Age of Its Technological Reproducibility," *October* 55 (1990).

22. Hamman, "From Technical to Technological".

23. I am not talking about conspirations. Often the structures on this level are not manipulations, but well-meant, well-crafted and fine design. The impact on our behaviour is nevertheless significant.

24. Another is of course to produce one's own software accommodating pre-for-mulated conceptions from the composer. This is common in the field of electro-acoustic music, and it is a constructive rather than deconstructive approach.

Reaktor and the IRCAM developed *Max/MSP* are the most established meta-programmes in this vein designed for extreme flexibility, where the composer builds his/her own patches from scratch with innumerable possibilities.

25. Mitchell Whitelaw, "Inframedia Audio," *Artlink* 21.3 (2001): 52.
26. Janne Vanhanen, "Loving the Ghost in the Machine," 2001.
27. This is one of the reasons why techno theorist Bruno Latour refuses to call machines non-human. Bruno Latour, "Where Are the Missing Masses?," *Shaping Technology/Building Society*, ed. W. Bijker and J. Law (Cambridge, MA: MIT, 1992).
28. Examples of visual glitches can be found at http://www.beflix.com/html.
29. An example of this speaks of glitch in DNA strings: "The system that copies the genetic blueprint message in sperm cells sometimes slips and stutters, like a stuck record, when it handles certain groups of three "letters" in the four-letter chemical alphabet of DNA. When this happens, these triplets are copied over and over, so that they repeat themselves ten, twenty, even hundreds of times in the DNA of affected persons." (Eric Mankin: "NIH awards researchers $3.6 million to study genetic glitch", *HSC Weekly* January 21 (2000)).
30. Cf. Philip Sherburne, "Click/," (Cover notes to the CD "Clicks and Cuts 2": Mille Plateaux, 2001).

REFERENCES

Articles and Books

Adorno, T. W. 1990. The curves of the needle. *October* 55, 48–55. (Orig. pub. 1928. *Musikblätter des Anbruch #10.*)

Cascone, K. 2000. The aesthetics of failure: "Post-digital" tendencies in contemporary computer music. *Computer Music Journal* 24.4 (2000): 12–18.

Feenberg, A. 1995. Subversive rationalization: Technology, power and democracy. In *Technology and the power of knowledge*, ed. A. Feenberg and A. Hannay. Indiana University Press.

Goldsmith, K. 1999. It was a bug, Dave—The dawn of glitchwerks. http://www.wfmu.org/~kennyg/popular/articles/glitchwerks.html

Gurney, G. 1962. *Americans into orbit*. Random House.

Hamman, M. 2000. From technical to technological: Interpreting technology through composition. http://www.shout.net/~mhamman/ as of June 2003

Heidegger, M. 1977. The question concerning technology. In *Basic writings,* trans. D. F. Krell. New York: Harper & Row (Orig. pub. 1953. *Vorträge und Aufsätze.*)

Latour, B. 1992. Where are the missing masses? In *Shaping Technology/Building Society*, ed. W. Bijker and J. Law, 225–58. Cambridge, MA: MIT.

Levin, T. L. 1990. For the record: Adorno on music in the age of its technological reproducibility. *October* 55: 23–47.

Licht, A. 2002. Random tone bursts. *The Wire* 223: 31–32.

Sangild, T. 2002. *The aesthetics of noise.* Copenhagen: Datanom (also published online: www.datanom.com/noise).

———— 2002. Sensitive electronics. In *Look at the music—SeeSound*, ed. J. W. Goetz, 20–28. Ystad/Roskilde: Ystad Art Musem/Museum of Contemporary Art, Roskilde, Denmark.

———— 2003. *Støjens æstetik*. København: Multivers.

Schaeffer, P. 1992. Pierre Schaeffer. In *Ljudkonst*, ed. P. R. Meyer. Stockholm: Proprius.

Di Scipio, A. 1997. Interpreting music technology—From Heidegger to subversive rationalization. In *Sonus* 18(1): 63–80.

Sherburne, P. 2001. Click/. Cover notes to the CD "Clicks and Cuts 2": Mille Plateaux.

Sutherland, R. 1994. *New perspectives in music*. London: Sun Tavern Fields.

Thomson, P. 2003. Atoms and errors: Towards a history and aesthetics of microsound. http://www.sfu.ca/~pthomson/Thomson.Phil-Atoms.and.Errors-Towards.a.History.and.Aesthetics.of.Microsound.pdf as of June 2003

Vanhanen, J. 2001. Loving the ghost in the machine. www.ctheory.net as of June 2003

Whitelaw, M. 2001. Inframedia audio. *Artlink* 21(3): 49–52.

Young, R. 2000. Worship the glitch. *The Wire* 190/191: 52–56.

Discography

Clicks + Cuts, Mille Plateaux, EFA 8079, 2000.
Clicks & Cuts 2, Mille Plateaux, EFA 8098, 2001.

ALVA NOTO
Transform, Mille Plateaux, EFA 23102, 2001.
RYOJI IKEDA
+/–, Touch 30, 1996.
0°C, Touch 38, 1998.
OVAL
Wohnton, Thrill Jockey 3761, 1993.
Systemisch, Mille Plateaux, Thrill Jockey 32, 1994.
94 Diskont, Thrill Jockey 36, 1995.
Szenariodisc, Thrill Jockey 64, 1999.
OvalProcess, Thrill Jockey 81, 2000.
OvalCommers, Thrill Jockey 103, 2001.
YASUNAO TONÉ
Solo for Wounded CD, Tzadik 7212, 1997.

13

Glitches, Bugs, and Hisses:
The Degeneration
of Musical Recordings and
the Contemporary Musical Work

ELIOT BATES

In a local music store, I recently picked up a copy of *In Memoriam Gilles Deleuze*, a two-CD set of experimental electronic music recordings influenced by the French philosopher by that name. The rare pair of CDs was quite cheap, and a tag on the package explained the reason: "The surface of this disc is scratched." The irony is that this particular CD was one of the first to bring critical attention to the glitch artist Oval, whose contribution to contemporary music consists entirely of the sounds of skipping CDs. Though the economic value of the music was lessened because of a presumed defect, the aesthetic value of the CD inhered in its artful usage of this very same defect. Such apparent double standards expose the discrepancy between concepts of "high fidelity" and the type of music representation made possible by the technology behind the tapes and discs to which we listen. However, it also shows that the creative work of contemporary composers does not echo the fidelity criteria honored by music stores. What in one context is considered a poor representation of music, in another, becomes music itself.

This chapter explores the transformation of glitch—the malfunction in music playback technology—into a music genre in its own right. The music industry has spent over a hundred years creating devices that allegedly have higher and higher fidelity, but new technologies have merely introduced new glitches, and the end result is that we cannot help but be exposed to non-intentional sounds. Aesthetic critiques of the mass-produced work of art have argued that listening is always a repetitive experience. I argue that because of the inevitable presence of glitches in playback technology, and the ways in which recordings come to be changed by their sonic environments, each listening experience must be understood as a unique event. In fact, it is precisely this unique characteristic of glitches that has inspired composers to recycle them as building blocks in new musical compositions—these artists work at subverting the nature and function of glitch. Glitch, which once presumably worsened the musical work, is now transformed into something aesthetically productive, but this is only a partial transformation, since a scratched CD consisting of "glitch music" is still considered worthless within the context of the used music store.

Literature addressing the effect of the recording process on the representation of the musical work has tended to rely on four key assumptions. First, there exists such a thing as an "authentic" or "real" musical work, and that the composer's intent or unique expression of the artist's voice (perhaps even a divine vision) is knowable. The second assumption concerns the "work of art in the age of mechanical reproduction," where a dichotomy is created between the *original* (the real work) and the *copy* (an imitation of the real work).[1] This extends the first assumption, requiring a real work of art to exist before identifying its copies. The third assumption creates a dichotomy between representation and repetition: "In representation, a work is generally heard only once—it is a unique moment; in repetition, hearings are stockpiled."[2] The fourth assumption is that the act of listening to music has been affected by our repeated listenings to recordings. Referring to such repeated listenings, Theodor Adorno states, "It is contemporary listening which has regressed, arrested at the infantile stage. Not only do the listening subjects lose . . . the capacity for conscious perception of music . . . but they stubbornly reject the possibility of such perception."[3] The elaboration of these four assumptions has often occurred in tandem with discussions on the development of recording technology and the music industry itself, framed by a desire for "higher fidelity" recordings, or perhaps, the desire for a more pure representation of the musical work.[4]

However, these four assumptions miss a key detail—namely, that playback of recorded sound-tracks always takes place in a *new* acoustic environment (a bedroom, a dance club, a car stereo, a shopping mall), mediated by particulars of the playback technology, and juxtaposed with environmental sounds and experiences.[5] As I will suggest, a study of malfunction offers us insights into the ways in which these mass-produced recordings are actually received by listeners, and the ways in which music recording and playback exposes people to unique listening experiences that contain much stimuli that are not part of any accepted "work of art." The highly distinctive analog scratches and pops of the twenties, or the digital skips and pops of a CD in the nineties, become sonic markers of the level of fidelity and the quality of sound characteristic of each era. With all the variables in the act of listening, we may conclude that each listening experience is a unique musical moment and not a repetition of a prior performance.

What are the implications on definitions of the musical work when we consider machine-additions, the inevitable degeneration or playback malfunction, along with environmental interpretations? Should unique interpretations of a given musical work (due to the mechanics of playback technology) still be considered part of the milieu of the musical work, or rather as separate entities? If we assume that the goal of "live" recordings is the truthful documentation of a particular event, and if we further acknowledge the inability of recording technology to capture any such event without distortion, are live recordings then by definition *bad music*?

A glitch is that which betrays the fidelity of the musical work— the skipping CD or record, the mangling cassette tape, the distorting PA system. There is something striking in the power of glitch, and musicians have recently seized upon this opportunity to use glitches as compositional elements in their music. In the 1990s, a popular production trend known as "lo-fi" valorized antiquated technology, *amplifying* the features that exposed the non-transparency of the machine.[6] An entire style of music known as "glitch" is formed of the sounds of skipping CDs, defective records, cellular phone scans, computer bugs, and blown speakers. To see how lo-fi and glitch musicians view these "defects" as musical influences requires an analysis of a key transformation—the historical moment when the glitch *became desirable* and no longer represented that which was bad in music.

The first three sections of this chapter explore glitch in the context of fidelity issues and the deterioration of "the musical work." Starting with a history of the concept of fidelity, I will show how recording and playback idiosyncrasies and malfunctions have had a profound effect on musicians and listeners, and how glitch simultaneously worsens the work of art, yet helps make listening to recordings a unique experience. The final sections focus on the transformation of glitch into a positive compositional element of contemporary music. Rooting glitch music in a body of practices that extend back at least to the beginning of electronic music, I will explore several composers and the ways they have reconciled their practices with the inevitable malfunctions of audio technology.·

1. (In)fidelity

Emily Thompson creates a compelling early history of how "fidelity" was conceived with regard to recording technology. In 1877, the term related to the phonograph's ability to accurately represent musical speech, and hence "fidelity, or faithfulness to the source, was the goal."[7] The phonograph was remarketed in 1887 to businesses as a tool for creating "aural letters" that represented *truth*. Thus, a definition of fidelity "now referred to the retrievable truth of the message; an oral contract or agreement, committed to wax, was rendered permanent and therefore indisputable."[8] In 1890, phonographs equipped with a coin-operated slot became a popular entertainment fad in New York.

> As the phonograph took on the role of a purveyor of music rather than simply a transmitter of words, standards moved beyond audibility and intelligibility. "Quality of tone" was the new criterion, and advertisements began increasingly to point to "the sweet tone for which the Edison is famous."[9]

Since 1890, quality of tone has been a selling feature of new media and playback technologies. The digital compact disc (introduced in 1980) and DVD-Audio (introduced in the late 1990s) are just the most recent technologies marketed for their quality of tone. With each new playback and media standard comes a host of novel recording equipments and practices. Despite the increasing rigors of high fidelity standards, advances in the digital recording process do not facilitate an easy representation of art, as the recording process is riddled with unintentional noises and sonic artifacts that dominate the tracking, mixing, editing, and mastering processes. In the act and art of recording, then, there is an increasing antagonism between what is technologically demanded (fidelity) and what is artistically desired. Though great albums are still created, each stage of the recording process presents its own unique "enemies" of the musical work that are essential to understanding the aural influence on contemporary musicians.

In the recording or tracking stage, the primary enemy is ambient sound and noise. Extra-musical sounds come in the forms of street noises, water pipes, airplanes, ringing phones, buzzing fluorescent lights, or even rodents in the walls. Instruments have their own noisy imperfections too: guitar amps and pedals emit hum; strings buzz, keyboard and amplifier volume pots pop as you turn them; and saxophone valves click or leak air. Musicians themselves are a noisy bunch, emitting extraneous noises while they record; coughs, sneezes, chair squeaks, and out of time foot tapping are encountered in most recording sessions.

In the editing stage, the challenge is maintaining the simulacrum of a continuous performance. Bad edits and splices are audible, and with hundreds of edits per song errors are prone to happen. Over-editing can lose the continuity of a melody or rhythm, leading to a feel musicians often describe as "inhuman."

In mixing, the primary enemy is distortion, and there are three major kinds of distortion. Frequency distortion consists of two (not mutually exclusive) possibilities: frequencies are lost, or frequencies are gained (as in second and third order harmonics, from tube or tape saturation). Amplitude distortion, most commonly, means that the original dynamic range (difference in volume between soft and loud sounds) is lost, lessening the subtlety or nuance of the recording. One type of audio gear, known as a compressor, is designed specifically to reduce the dynamic range of the incoming signal (and raise the overall volume of the signal), but compressors are prone to producing their own artifacts known as "pumping and breathing," and, when used in extreme ways, remove the attack (beginning of the sound) of notes or beats altogether. The worst sort of distortion is clipping, containing both frequency and amplitude distortion. In the analog domain this is sometimes desired, but in digital recording clipping causes a squaring of naturally curved waveforms, audibly resulting in harsh screeching noises. The third type of distortion happens in the phase domain, and is a result of sound leakage between tracks (in multi-track recording) or from improperly wired equipment (a reality in the majority of studios). This form of distortion can cause "phase cancellation," or the disappearance of frequencies because they were "cancelled out," or "standing waves" that are exponentially louder than other frequencies.

Finally, in the mastering stage of recording, the enemy is softness. One common goal of mastering is to make the loudest possible interpretation of an album. Though some mastering engineers don't subscribe to this philosophy, radio broadcast demands loud products, and a quorum of really loud recordings dominate the marketplace, effectively defining a paradigm of obligatorily loud releases. Compressors and limiters are used (again) to raise the volume, introducing yet more amplitude and frequency distortions. Mastering amplifies the background and machine-added noises that the first three stages of the recording chain attempted to minimize, subsequently requiring the intervention of "noise reduction" circuits (devices that delete much of the original high frequency information and replace it with synthesized and reconstructed noise). In this sense, the true enemy of mastering is the entire recording process.

2. Playback Idiosyncrasies

One aspect of recordings that has been underestimated is degradation. Though critics notice that vinyl records are imperfect renditions of the musical work to begin with, they tend to focus on the "copy" aspect of media and repetitive playing of those copies, thereby implying that the copies are static entities. However, as with any media, even supposedly flawless digital media, each successive playback includes the potential for loss of musical data. As individual copies increasingly degrade, and playback technology displays increasing difficulty in sounding the recording (the scratched record or CD, for example), what we end up with are skips, pops, and glitches that express not the voice of the composer, but rather the voice of technology itself. The worsening of the musical work, then, happens with the increase in extra-musical stimuli (those not intended in the "work") at the expense of the genuine musical stimuli; in short, noise instead of sonority. The aesthetics of recorded art, therefore, are somewhat different from the "aesthetic distancing" described by Pierre Bourdieu, where "good art" maintains a detachment from the mode of representation and the differentiation between form and function.[10] In this case, the new form of the work is even more detached from the original function, yet the work of art worsens.

> A similar analysis of recorded music might be made: i.e., that it is alienating but not yet alienated . . . And yet there's a lot to be said for scratchy old 78s played over distant radio stations late at night—

a flash of illumination which seems to spark across all the levels of mediation and achieve a paradoxical presence.[11]

As listeners we tend to be highly aware of the unique sound each type of media exhibits with increasing degradation. 78s and wax cylinders are immediately evocative of the 1910s through the 1940s.[12] 45RPM and 33RPM records have their own unique sounds, depending on the quality of vinyl and the density of the grooves, but the rumble, the pops, and the turntable's responses to large dirt mounds (the skipping record) are all highly distinctive. After the 1950s, magnetic tape introduced hiss and hum into the sonic picture, and a succession of noise reduction systems patented by Dolby Labs reduced hiss (at the cost of distorted high frequencies). Tapes stretch when they become too hot, and the sound of warbling tape is familiar to anyone with a cassette car stereo.

Finally, digital media, touted for its perfect sample-accurate rendition of the musical work, is nevertheless easily damaged, too. The sound of digital skipping and clipping is unique to the realm of CDs, and is one of the most arresting sounds of the 1990s and 2000s. The skipping CD is one of the only sounds that can truly destroy the ambience of a restaurant, articulating a process whereby the background (music for ambience) is suddenly foregrounded (the skip must be stopped), suggesting that the CD player itself has a potent voice. Even streaming digital media is not immune to this phenomena, as mp3s often end early, hiccup from buffer underruns, or, at the worst, crash the computer altogether, ending in a triumphant eternal loop of noise comprised of the last 20–30 digital samples played before the computer died. The substantial difference between analog and digital media is the suddenness and violence of the distortion. While records gradually become noisier, CDs suddenly showcase irrevocable skips, immediately becoming useless as valid representations of a given work of art.

This analysis, however, only addresses the sonic issues present in physical media. The broadcast of media through stereos, on radio, TV, film, video, and the Internet, imparts a whole separate set of characteristic distortions, particularly when the broadcasting equipment does not function properly. Record players are prone to wear of the platter-spinning motor, resulting in an erratic variance of the playback speed. Styli wear quickly, progressively dulling the sound. Tape players epitomize "disposable technology" with an estimated lifespan of two and a half years. Many parts are prone to malfunctioning, including motors, capstans, and tape heads (which become magnetized, dirty, and mis-aligned), leading first to loss of frequency range, followed by inconsistent speed playback and destructive tape munching. CD players rely on a specific rotation speed, and when the motor wears, the CD will either not play at all or incur additional skips (unrelated to scratches on the discs). Early portable CD players were prone to damaging the discs, too, becoming creators of unique and useless artifacts. Regardless of the playback technology, electrical amplification is a necessity, and amplifiers and their outward manifestation (headphones or speakers) are prone to wear, too—blown speakers, worn amplifiers, and static from poor wiring. Even when the amplification system is not mal-functioning, there are a variety of ways a listener can alter and individualize the playback experience, including EQ settings, speaker placement, "spectral enhancers," and the dreaded "loudness" button, all ensuring that the listener's experience may be very different than the "original" sonic character envisioned by artists, engineers, and producers.

3. What is the Work of Art in the Age of Mechanical Reproduction?

The reality of the modern aural environment, particularly in cities and urban areas, is one of constant noise bombardment. Much of this noise is produced by machines—construction and demolition equipment, air conditioners, power generators, motorized vehicles—but a certain portion of this "noise" comes to us in the form of broadcast music. Music fills almost every store, restaurant and office, is piped into elevators, airports, and even underwater in swimming pools, or is mobilized by individuals via boom boxes, Walkmans, and car stereos. Thus, the urban sound environment is filled with a mix of unintentional machine-produced sounds (byproducts of the industrial era) and intentional machine-produced sounds (byproducts of commercial audio recording and distribution networks). At times, the intentional and unintentional sounds are indistinguishable, interchangeable, and even nuance the hearing of each other. At other times, the intricate system of music broadcast breaks down—the CD playing in the restaurant skips, the speaker in the elevator is blown, thereby sonically mangling, say, a Beach Boys song. The mechanical reproduction of music, then, finds the same piece of music interpreted into hundreds of unique environments, each time juxtaposed on a new sonic background.

Though many recordings are studio-created, a large number are constructed to be a "truthful" representation of a particular concert moment. In the case of classical music, however, there is usually a discrepancy between the recording and the actual concert experience, where movements of works are separated by concert hall sounds—audience noises and page turns on stage. Some recordings attempt to simulate the concert experience, but remove the context from the concert hall by removing the hall's sounds. Others keep the audience noise between tracks, preserving the mythology of the concert experience, but amplifying sounds that are not generally thought to be part of the composers' musical work (paper rustling, etc.) Machines add their own "overtures" and "codas" to the musical work, creating unique technology-specific simulations of the spaces between works or movements of the work, either through (unnaturally) pure silence, technologically derived noise (tape hum and record pops), or samples and simulations of the sound of the noisy twentieth and twenty-first century concert hall. It cannot be said that this type of distortion is unique to the classical music score in its technological realization; even works that were conceived with recording in mind suffer the same "overture" and "coda" problems. Another technologically mediated distorter of musical works is *sampling*, an electronic music technique that involves storing and repeatedly playing a sound fragment known as a "sample." Though the first samplers were analog, the technique wasn't widely used until the early 1980s with the advent of digital samplers.[13] In contemporary computer-based audio recording, every moment of recorded sound is essentially a "sample." Thus, rock 'n' roll, country, blues, and classical genres not traditionally associated with sampling—are now sample-based musics. Though sampling is associated with "musical theft," copyright infringement, and the less creative aspects of dance music production, sampling is vital to the study of a musical object's lifecycle, as it freezes in time a fragment of a recording, documenting all the glitches that brought it to that point in its history. The fragment often becomes better known than the complete original work—a signifier of the whole. But, sampling isn't always concerned with the part of the record that documents the "musical work," as contemporary recordings often sample the machine-made overtures and codas of tapes and records, making loops out of glitches.

4. The Electronic Music Palimpsest

Histories of electronic music have largely followed historical models of other Western Art musics (Classical, Baroque and Romantic, for example), by charting a lineage of "great" musical works and composers, or perhaps by establishing a sequence of key events.[14] Even contemporary popular music writing continues this quest for sequential influences (John Cage influenced Brian Eno who influenced the Orb's Alex Patterson). However, the mechanics of the music industry, simultaneously maintaining a system of rapid obsolescence of popular recorded hits and continuously reissuing formerly popular (or unpopular) music, suggest that the commercialization of music is at once progressive and regressive. Listening to Direct Stream Digital[15] reissues of Pink Floyd's *Dark Side of the Moon* (1973) or Miles Davis' *Kind of Blue* (1959) is hearing these classic albums transformed into the sonic aesthetics of the twenty-first century, while in sample-based practices, obscure 1970s funk is reconstituted as "downtempo," and 1960s musique concrète is mixed into drum and bass. Since contemporary listenings no longer appear to be historically situated moments, perhaps electronic music "history" would benefit from an alternative history structured like a *palimpsest*, where elements never disappear but are constantly overlaid.[16] The palimpsest presented here charts the creation and transformations of futurist machine-music manifestos and subsequent obsessions with naturalness and found sound.[17]

In 1916, an Italian artist named Luigi Russolo penned the *Art of Noises* manifesto, ushering in the Italian futurist movement.[18] He then created a number of music-making machines (the *intonarumori*, or symphony of noise-makers), onomatopoetically named after their particular sounds. Around the same time in Paris, George Antheil's *Ballet mécanique* (1924) called for an airplane engine amongst other noisemaking "instruments." There is a striking contrast in these two approaches to machine-music—the Italian approach involved the creation of new machines, while the French approach involved new uses of non-musical technologies. Both met with hostile audience and critic responses, perhaps because people weren't yet ready to discover the possibilities and pleasures of the voice of technology.

A chance intrusion on bedroom listening and the ensuing scratch of a record needle on vinyl in 1981 led Grandmaster Flash to discover "scratching," a practice of using records as sources for percussive, expressive sounds:

> After [Grandmaster] Flash, the turntable becomes a machine for building and melding mindstates from your record collection. The turntables, a Technics deck, become a subjectivity engine generating a stereophonics, a hifi [sic] consciousness of the head, wholly tuned in and turned on by the found noise of vinyl degeneration that hears scratches, crackle, fuzz, hiss and static as lead instruments.[19]

Chance also figured in the discovery of the warped psychedelic sounds Roland never intended in their TB-303 "bassline" machine.[20] This device, part of a series of technologies designed to replace rock bass players and drummers, failed miserably in its original intent (rock was still fairly technologically conservative), but found its niche in techno— a new dance music aesthetic that preached science fiction, space travel, and cybotrons. The instruments of techno (drum machines, sequencers, and turntables) were not originally developed for that purpose (like Antheil's airplane engine), but were designed to simulate "natural" instruments. Likewise producers were not aware of previous transformations of the same technologies—John Cage's "Imaginary Landscapes I," written in 1939, called for two variable-speed turntables:

> The novelty of our work derives therefore from our having moved away from simply private human concerns towards the world of nature and society of which all of us are a part. Our intention is to affirm this life, not to bring order out of chaos nor to suggest improvements in creation, but simply to wake up to the very life we're living . . .[21]

In the palimpsest model of electronically generated music, composed musique concrète has equal weight to sounds of the everyday. As Robert Rauschenberg's white canvases drew attention to the shadows created by the viewers, and John Cage's "4:33" focused attention on the musicality of environments, 1980s British experimental artists including :zoviet*france:, Muslimgauze, and Rapoon found extensive interest in broadcast as well as found sounds and field recordings. By looping moments in the recordings, they focused attention on aspects of these former historical archives that had hitherto been overlooked. By broadcasting the found sounds through ghetto blasters into new spaces and re-recording the sounds, they emulated the PA distortions in the sonic environments of Bombay and Cairo, expanding definitions of the "natural" environment to include technologically-modified sound spaces. Additionally, their creative re-use of broken and malfunctioning equipment for mixing purposes challenged contemporary proper mixing techniques, signaling a sort of revolution against technological determinism.

Robin Rimbaud (aka Scanner) explores a different set of modern environmental phenomena—the abundance of broadcast radio waves, particularly cellular phone signals. "I take small samples, small snatches from the atmosphere, from the radio waves around us."[22] His work combines obvious everyday sounds (conversations) with unexpected "glitches"—unique sounds picked up by the cellular phone scanner from the din of broadcast radio waves. The scanner becomes a metaphor for a radio wave "ear," and Rimbaud's compositional process includes selecting and arranging the sounds. Most reviewers of Scanner's work have focused on the legal issues of recording conversations with a police scanner, but this misses the point (i.e., that Rimbaud is mapping the radio waves in his home city of London), offering a new look on the sound already in the public domain but inaudible without the appropriate interface.

Naturalism and simulation continue to have a push and pull in electronic music practices. In the 1990s, techno fragmented into hundreds of specific musical practices. Some trajectories aimed for pure machine-music, others for increasing naturalism, incorporating acoustic instrument samples, nature sounds, and the like. Similarly, some practices focused on the making of danceable products, while others headed towards abstraction—non-dance dance music. IDM ("Intelligent" Dance Music) is one such movement, glorifying the computer-as-instrument and giving rise to laptop "bands." Perhaps, due to music press critiques that non-danceable IDM was lacking substance, producers strove to connect their music to respected lineages such as dub and musique concrète, in an attempt to discover ways to reconcile the alleged sterility of digital music with a love of analog recordings and practices. The natural and machine-music patterns in the electronic music palimpsest were resurrected in a twenty-first century way. "Glitch," "microsound," and "post-digital" epitomize these discoveries, a Y2k vindication of the futurists.

5. Glitch ideologies

Markus Popp is the audio designer behind the Oval moniker.[23] Audio designer is his preferred title (over composer or artist), as he doesn't directly control the generation of musical material himself, but instead designs systems and processes in which technology derives the sounds. He later functions as a selector and arranger of the interesting results produced by his process compositions:

> Instead of trying to inscribe ourselves into some "musical" heritage, Oval rather relies on the irrelevance of even trying to provide "groundbreaking" artifacts. Instead, we produce transitory, "just-in-time" by-products of our accommodation process with the given operating systems and user-interface-technology of digital (music) media. Therefore, any assumed eventual "historic" dimensionality embedded in our musical outcome is negligible, rendered obsolete by the sheer development speed of digital media components in general and their mediation.[24]

Oval's discovery that CD players tend to treat scratched and damaged CDs in unpredictable ways led to the creation of a device known as Oval Process, which in turn generated "new works by Oval." The Oval Process machine was made public, allowing users other than Popp to create new works "by Oval." Though process-generated music is not new (Xenakis used mathematical theories to derive elements of musical scores as early as 1954), the open-source nature of the interface reflects contemporary concepts of intellectual property born from computer programming ideologies (i.e., Linux and GNU).[25] Oval's work references the electronic music palimpsest, drawing in part on Satie, Antheil, and Cage's experiments in transforming everyday sounds into music, but most specifically in encouraging listeners to hear technological function and malfunction as music.

Composer Kim Cascone shares a concern with Markus Popp, namely that the musical work should not be limited to the constraints of the compact disc media:

> Our minds have become nodes in the expanding space of the Internet, connecting freely with other nodes in a rhizomatic manner. Comparing this fluidic, smooth space with the linear space of the audio compact disc, we find that a linear model of time has been imposed onto an inherently non-linear medium.[26]

He describes compositions as processes that may be enacted in many ways. Rather than creating physical technology to illustrate this process, Cascone designs software algorithms in the computer music environment known as Max/MSP, thereby producing works that explore the nature of "artifacts," or bugs in digital audio. "These artifacts form a critique of the perceived perfection of digital audio in that it exposes the flaws and illusion of 'perfect reproduction'."[27] Subsequently, repeat performances of the same piece by Cascone result in unique-sounding actualizations.

Glitch music may appear to be new, since the label was coined only in the late 1990s, but it echoes paths of compositional exploration already taken by musique concrète, dub, drum and bass, as well as acid house composers. Talking to three Berkeley based electronic music composers (Ryan Francesconi, David Wessel, and Phil Lockwood), I found that all of them had made music that would "fit" in the glitch category, though none of the composers were aware that a genre distinction such as glitch had yet been defined. Francesconi (referencing his compositions as "rf") intimated that the process of developing new computer music software, one of the most challenging forms of software programming to date, exposed glitches in operating system code that could produce unpredictable sonic results.

> The weirdest feature in Spongefork [software created by Francesconi] is "Noise Spork"—an experiment in recording to memory. I discovered this strange dialog that was part of System 6 [legacy code in the Macintosh computer operating system]. This produced these unbelievable noise things, essentially just scrambled memory. Listening to it by itself, it sounds like scrambled noise, but it's derived from what is coming in the input.[28]

The process of composing with Spongefork involves "getting some sources, essentially destroying them with Spongefork, and then rebuilding them in Logic [computer recording software]."[29] The glitches in rf's music, as well as many other electronic music artists, demonstrate that working with imperfect technology, whether it be legacy operating system code or scratched CDs, automatically subjects the composer to unintentional sounds, which in some cases appear to be more aesthetically interesting than intended ones.

6. Conclusion

If, as a point of departure, we define "high fidelity" concerns in recording as *the pursuit of truth*, then in this context the glitch is *the betrayal of the simulation*. When a glitch comes to dominate (i.e., if a

CD or LP is irrevocably scratched, or if the playback technology fails), music moves beyond the aesthetic position of "bad" to a category of non-music, and hence the commodity loses its use-value. The odds are against any particular artifact, particularly digital media (CDs are simultaneously light and scratch sensitive, with an estimated life of 10–100 years for an unplayed CD). Thus, recordings' medias fall into the category of disposable commodities.

In light of this disposability (of media, playback and recording technology, respectively), some musicians have engaged in what I call "musical commodity recycling programs." Instances include: 1970s dub reggae production, where King Tubby and Lee Perry found interest in dubbing out mistakenly recorded noises on original source tapes (pops, mechanical noises, hisses, hums); groups such as :zoviet*france: and Rapoon, with their interest in recycling imperfect field recordings; and late 1990s glitch composers, who practice and perfect the art of salvaging valueless CDs, 78s, and computers. In one context, glitch is considered bad—that which arrests the flow of music; whereas in certain subversive and manipulated contexts, glitch is considered good—the arresting quality of music itself.

In listening to recently released popular albums, I hear glitch aesthetics materializing in works by non-glitch artists. Producers Mark Bell, Howie B., and Adrian Utley introduced glitches into Björk and Portishead, while Madonna's 2003 release "American Life," produced by Mirwais Ahmadzai, contains backing tracks of 78RPM record noise. Meanwhile, groups like To Rococo Rot, Pan Sonic, and Plaid have glitch elements worked into their live and studio efforts. Thus, the musical commodity recycling programs have turned out to hold currency as an arresting feature of popular music, and in multi-million dollar studios pops, hisses, clicks, and record noise are now routinely added to "dirty up" otherwise pristine digital recordings.

Glitch composition is a meta-discursive practice: rather than writing new music inspired by older recordings, it constructs new music inspired by the technological conditions and limitations in which those recordings emerged. For those listeners who aren't particularly interested in technology theories, such music is particularly alienating—an in-joke that one doesn't get. When glitch becomes pop, it loses its theoretical savvy, replacing the "synth pad" in a contemporary pop song. Glitch's subversion of the bad value judgment placed on damaged media is only a partial one—as scratched CDs (whether they be glitch ones or not) remain economically worthless commodities.

NOTES

1. Walter Benjamin, "The Work of Art in the Age of Mechanical Reproduction,"in *Illuminations*, trans. Harry Zohn (New York: Schocken Books, 1968).

2. Jacques Attali, *Noise: The Political Economy of Music* (Minneapolis: University of Minnesota Press, 1985), 41.

3. Theodor W. Adorno, "On the Fetish-Character in Music and the Regression of Listening," in *The Essential Frankfurt School Reader*, eds. Andrew Arato and Eike Gebhardt (New York: Urizen, 1978), 286.

4. Michael Chanan, *Repeated Takes: A Short History of Recording and its Effects on Music* (London: Verso, 1995) and Simon Frith, *Performing Rites: On the Value of Popular Music* (Cambridge: Harvard University Press, 1996).

5. "Environmental" sounds are defined as background sounds perceived in any actual acoustic setting, whether they be sounds of nature or those of machines.

6. The lo-fi production aesthetic (at least in name) was made famous by the post-rock group Tortoise and electronica act Portishead in the mid 1990s, though precedents existed in 4-track cassette recordings, "garage," and DIY punk rock.

7. Emily Thompson, "Machines, Music, and the Quest for Fidelity: Marketing the Edison Phonograph in America, 1877-1925," *Musical Quarterly* 79, no. 1 (1995): 135.

8. Ibid., 137.

9. Ibid., 138.

10. Pierre Bourdieu, *Distinction: A Social Critique of the Judgment of Taste* (Cambridge: Harvard University Press, 1984), 34.

11. Hakim Bey, "Radio Sermonettes" (1992): http://www.hermetic.com/bey/radio_se.html

12. One example of the authenticity accorded to 78s comes from the 1970s San Francisco band The Cheap Suit Serenaders, who performed covers of music learned off old jazz 78s and decided to record their own 78s, thereby situating their music in the aural environment of their roots. These were released by Ordinary Records and include "A High Standard of Standardness," and "Party Record."

13. The mellotron, developed in 1966, was a 35-note keyboard with a magnetic tape loop for each key. It was used by British progressive rock groups (Genesis, King Crimson) and American experimental rock bands (Captain Beefheart), but required too much maintenance to be a practical instrument for touring bands. The first digital sampler was part of the $25,000 Fairlight CMI Series I keyboard (1979), but the more affordable E-mu Emulator II (a modest $8,000 in 1982) was the first widely used one.

14. See David Cope, *New Directions in Music,* 7th ed. (Prospect Heights: Waveland Press, 2001); Michael Nyman, *Experimental Music: Cage and Beyond* 2nd ed. (Cambridge: Cambridge University Press, 1999); and Jon Appleton and Ronald Perera, eds., *The Development and Practice of Electronic Music* (Englewood Cliffs, NJ: Prentice-Hall, 1974).

15. As of the writing of this article, the "highest fidelity" format yet marketed.

16. This approach to history has been suggested by Hakim Bey: "A palimpsest is a manuscript that has been re-used by writing over the original writing, often at

right angles to it, and sometimes more than once. Frequently it's impossible to say which layer was first inscribed; and in any case any 'development' (except in orthography) from layer to layer would be sheer accident. The connections between layers are not sequential in time but juxtapositional in space." Hakim Bey, "The Palimpsest," (1996): http://www.hermetic.com/bey/palimpsest.html.

17. To explore the electronic music palimpsest further one should consider many other patterns: chance and stochastic systems, the changing conceptions of composition and improvisation, and the art/ popular music dichotomy, to name a few.

18. Luigi Russolo, *The Art of Noises,* trans. Barclay Brown (New York: Pendragon Press, 1986).

19. Kodwo Eshun, *More Brilliant Than The Sun: Adventures In Sonic Fiction* (London: Quartet Press, 1998), 14.

20. Italian disco composer Alexander Robotnik is credited with the first acid house track (1983). See Simon Reynolds, *Generation Ecstasy: Into the World of Techno and Rave Culture* (Boston: Little, Brown and Company, 1998), 32.

21. John Cage, *Silence: Lectures and Writings by John Cage* (Cambridge, MA: M.I.T. Press, 1966), 95.

22. Scanner, quoted in Kurt Reighley, "Downtempo: Lost in Music," in *Modulations: A History of Electronic Music: Throbbing Words on Sound,* ed. Peter Shapiro (New York: Caipirinha Productions, 2000), 184.

23. Popp also has a significant glitch collaboration with Jan St. Werner known as Microstoria.

24. Markus Popp, quoted by Thomas Palermo, "Random Operations." *XLR8R* 25 (2000): http://www.xlr8r.com/archive/25/25FEAT.oval.html.

25. The open source movement in computer software arose in the 1990s as a direct challenge to the monopoly control Microsoft and its Windows operating system had on the computer industry. It provided both an operating system and the code needed to write software for free, challenging the for-profit motives of much of the computer industry. It should be noted that although Oval purports open-source style ideology, the Oval Process machine has publicly appeared only at art galleries and museums.

26. Kim Cascone, quoted in David Toop, "The Generation Game," *Wire: Adventures in Modern Music* 207 (2001): 45.

27. Kim Cascone, "Deleuze and Contemporary Electronic Music," *Intersects* (December 2001): http://www.iisgp.ubc.ca/whatsnew/intersects/issues/dec01/cascone.htm.

28. Ryan Francesconi, personal communication with author, 25 November 2003.

29. Ibid.

REFERENCES

Articles and Books

Adorno, T. W. 1978. On the fetish-character in music and the regression of listening. In *The essential Frankfurt School reader*, eds. A. Arato and E. Gebhardt. New York: Urizen.

Appleton, J. and R. Perera, eds.1974. *The development and practice of electronic music*. Englewood Cliffs, NJ: Prentice-Hall.

Attali, J. 1985. *Noise: The political economy of music*. Minneapolis: University of Minnesota Press.

Benjamin, W. 1968. The work of art in the age of mechanical reproduction. In *Illuminations*, trans. H. Zohn. New York: Schocken Books.

Bourdieu, P. 1984. *Distinction: A social critique of the judgment of taste*. Cambridge, MA: Harvard University Press.

Cage, J. 1966. *Silence: Lectures and writings by John Cage*. Cambridge, MA: MIT Press.

Cascone, K. 2001. Deleuze and contemporary electronic music. *Intersects* (December): http://www.iisgp.ubc.ca/whatsnew/intersects/issues/dec01/cascone.htm.

Chanan, M. 1995. *Repeated takes: A short history of recording and its effects on music*. London: Verso.

Cope, D. 2001. *New directions in music*, 7th ed. Prospect Heights: Waveland Press.

Deleuze, G. and F. Guattari. 1998. *A thousand plateaus: Capitalism and schizophrenia*. Minneapolis/London: University of Minnesota Press.

Eshun, K. 1998. *More brilliant than the sun: Adventures in sonic fiction*. London: Quartet Press.

Frith, S. 1996. *Performing rites: On the value of popular music*. Cambridge, MA: Harvard University Press.

Hakim, B. 1996. The palimpsest. http://www.hermetic.com/bey/palimpsest.html
———— 1992. Radio sermonettes. http://www.hermetic.com/bey/radio_se.html

Nyman, M. 1999. *Experimental music: Cage and beyond,* 2nd ed. Cambridge: Cambridge University Press.

Palermo, T. 2000. Random operations. *XLR8R* (25): http://www.xlr8r.com/archive/25/25FEAT.oval.html.

Reighley, K. 2000. Downtempo: Lost in music. In *Modulations: A history of electronic music: Throbbing words on sound,* ed. P. Shapiro. New York: Caipirinha Productions.

Reynolds, S. 1998. *Generation ecstasy: Into the world of techno and rave culture*. Boston: Little, Brown and Company.

Russolo, L. 1986. *The art of noises*, trans. B. Brown. New York: Pendragon Press.

Tagg, P. 1979. *Kojak—50 seconds of television music: Toward the analysis of affect in popular music*. Goteborg: Musikvetenskapliga Institutionen.

Thompson, E. 1995. Machines, music, and the quest for fidelity: Marketing the Edison Phonograph in America, 1877–1925. *Musical Quarterly,* 79(1): 131–71.

Toop, D. 2001. The generation game. *Wire: Adventures in Modern Music* 207: 38–45.

Discography

VARIOUS ARTISTS
Clicks and Cuts. Mille Plateaux CD mp79, 2000.
In Memoriam Gilles Deleuze. Mille Plateaux CD mp22, 1996.
Modulation and Transformation II. Mille Plateaux CD mp15, 1995.

CASCONE, KIM
Dust Theories. C74 CD 004, 2001.
MICROSTORIA
snd. Thrill Jockey CD thrill035, 1996.
MUSLIMGAUZE
Vote Hezbollah. Soleilmoon CD Sol17, 1993.
OVAL
Systemisch. Thrill Jockey CD thrill032, 1994.
POLE
3. Matador CD Ole 428-2, 2000.
RAPOON
Tin of Drum. Staalplaat CD STCD130, 1998.
RF
Interno. Odd Shaped Case CD osc2000-2, 2002.
SCANNER
Mass Observation. Ash International CD ASH 1.7, 1995.
TO ROCOCO ROT
Veiculo. Emperor Jones CDTO ROVEIC, 1997.
:ZOVIET*FRANCE:
Shouting at the Ground. Charrm CD12, 1989.

14

Rock Critics Need Bad Music

DEENA WEINSTEIN

> *"Whenever a phenomenon is given blanket dismissal, you can be
> sure something deeper is at work."*
> —MIKAL GILMORE, *ROLLING STONE* [1]

"**I** like bad music."

That's my usual response to people who ask me about my musical taste. It's my fault that I'm constantly being queried on this. I bring the question on by my incessant exploration of the musical preferences of almost everyone I meet, no matter how casually. The mailman, the computer tech support guy on the phone, the dozens of students who come into my office for one reason or another each quarter, and the people whom I meet at parties. After exploring the range and history of their musical predilections, I'm invariably asked about my own. It's a subject that I have no interest in discussing, because I can anticipate the response. But after all of my nosiness, it seems only polite to address it.

Of course, I don't really think that I like bad music. When I say that I do, the statement is dripping with irony. But unlike sarcasm, irony is silent and invisible.

I get a lot of puzzled looks or laughs from my oxymoronic response, followed by: "That's impossible. If you like it, how could it be bad?" Or, "No really, what kind of music do you like?" In either case, I then have to own up to my preferred soundscape.

I never give that "bad music" response when I'm surrounded by others who share my musical tastes. Their queries are always answered without irony; I readily admit to my favorite subgenres and provide names of specific bands.

But there is another class of persons to whom I don't know what to say: rock critics. They are a species that I've been studying for more than a dozen years. I've met scores of them, from the most famous to young zine-sters. For them, taste in music is the *sine qua non* of their presentation of self and their judgment of others, somewhat like junior high school kids with their attachment to special brands of clothing.

My taste in music sets me outside the rockcrit pale, but they don't quite know what to make of me. I can talk rock as well as they can and also know its history as trivial pursuit. Even more challenging is my tendency to discuss all things rock within philosophical, literary, political and cultural theory discourses. That the critics can't square this with my musical preferences, and my demographics—a middle-aged female professor—only increases their discomfort. I'm not of the age, gender or social class of a typical fan of the music that I seriously appreciate.

I like metal. And most mainstream rock critics have labeled metal as *Bad Music*.

I've always felt pangs about putting the critics into this uncomfortable position. In the late 1980s, I quickly let them know that I also didn't like what they meant by metal, MTV's version. Personally, the music that MTV and commercial radio called heavy metal, the Poisons and Warrants and Guns N'Roses and Bon Jovis, were not my cup of tea. This music was hard rock, and although I'd never choose to listen to it, I wouldn't walk across a bed of coals, or across the room, to turn it off. (There are so many other forms of popular music, an infinite number of songs, for which the burning coals would be a small price to pay for getting out of their range.)

MTV metal is called many unflattering names by those who share my musical tastes. Some of the phrases are more descriptive than derisive: "Hair metal," the most common, references the musicians' gravity defying, ozone depleting, curly shagged coifs. (Those who play the stuff I like have long hair too, even longer than hair metal musicians, but their hair is unstyled and unsprayed.) Another term is "lite metal," which informatively distinguishes the lack of a big bottom sound, as well as the color of the singer's (usually blonde) hair.

The term MTV metal is fitting because the cable channel was responsible for the style's massive popularity and its look. According to *Billboard Magazine*, "MTV 'discovered' metal in 1984. Metal's market share was eight percent in 1983, and then rose dramatically to twenty percent in 1984."[2]

There were other less descriptive, rather scornful, terms tossed about by metal fans who resented the conflation of their music with this commercialized form, and resented too, perhaps, its enormous popularity. The most useful one is the expression "pop metal." It neatly distinguishes the style from the underground forms of thrash, death and black metal, and references its massive popularity. Like pop punk, the phrase calls attention to a blending in of generic pop features (melody, vocals put high in the mix, and singing styles in which lyrics can be understood).

The critics didn't refer to it as pop metal, or lite metal, nor did they use any of the metal subculture's put-downs: hair metal, poser metal, etc. They, like MTV, called it "heavy metal."

By the time I began speaking with them, pop metal was, and it still largely is, the metal most critics know and reference, aside from seventies-era Black Sabbath and Led Zeppelin, and those bands were not the ones that I listened to. They got their albums from the major labels and listened to some of them because of publicists' phone calls. Indie metal labels may send some critics the other sorts of metal, but, for the most part, they service only the segregated species of rock journalists writing in metal magazines. (Throughout much of the 1980s, I bought my metal second hand. New releases were easily found in stores, having been discarded by the rockcrits.)

I'd always felt a bit dirty about denouncing MTV metal to the critics, because it was like putting down a relative, and a relative that they'd generally associate me with anyway.

Critics Despise Metal

Reading rock criticism in non-metal publications, from mainstream outlets like *Rolling Stone* and daily newspapers, to a host of indie 'zines, I was impressed by the constant references to heavy metal, even though there were few reviews of albums by metal bands. Initially I thought that I noticed these allusions in the way that one tends to notice all the cars on the road that are of the same model as the one you just bought. But when I did research for a cultural sociology book on the genre and began to collect these references, I saw that there was a pattern.

That pattern, in sum, was that heavy metal was *bad music*. The critics, no matter what their age, gender, or publication, disliked it. Really disliked it. They'd had their knives out for metal since its inception.

This nearly blanket dismissal of a form of music that I appreciated not only viscerally but reflectively led me to explore why critics
took the stance that they did. The discussion that follows is the result
of that inquiry. As a first step, I document the case that mainstream
criticism has tended to denigrate metal. Then I suggest that genera-
tional, class, and subcultural differences separating critics from metal
fans are in great part responsible for the critical animus. Finally, I try
to make sense of why rock critics need their demons.

Even before heavy metal was named, in 1971 a *Rolling Stone*
reviewer, Chet Flippo, decried the

> trend that may yet rule rock for another year or so: the heavy re-
> naissance, as exemplified by Bloodrock and Grand Funk and Black
> Sabbath. Critics agree they're putting out dreadful music but such
> groups, by appealing to the basest instincts of teens and subteens,
> are drawing sellout crowds everywhere.[3]

Other critics concurred; it was dreadful music. A year later *Creem*
critic Paul Battiste, deploying that magazine's over-the-top literary
style, wrote about Black Sabbath: "The group performs with all the
restraint and sophistication of four CroMagnon hunters who've
stumbled upon a rock band's equipment after a bad day chasing meat."[4]

The metal put-downs continued throughout the decade. Writing
in his hip zine *Trouser Press* in 1977, Ira Robbins scoffed: "Heavy
metal has always been the preserve of (a) those musicians incapable
of creating melody and then committing it to vinyl; and (b) those riff
bands who lack the necessary technique to solo endlessly."[5]

I wasn't the only academician to notice the critical tirade. "The
response of American rock criticism to Heavy Metal in the early-mid
1970s was consistently a negative one," wrote Will Straw in the
Canadian University Music Review.[6]

During metal's rise to massive popularity in the 1980s, the song
may have not remained the same, but the critical disdain did. A *Chicago
Tribune* reviewer in 1988 identified metal with nihilism:

> Metal pretends to challenge but offers only a carefully manipu-
> lated aura of mindless hedonism in place of fun, and virulent sex-
> ism instead of love. It is as though there were nothing left to rebel
> against but value itself. And that is what remains with metal
> nothing.[7]

Vituperation towards metal went into over-drive as the genre hit its sales peak in 1990. *Rolling Stone*'s review of pop metal Warrant is typical:

> Ultimately, these guys are about nothing more than their yearning for wealth and sexual power. Virtually every grunt, every shriek, every sixty-fourth-note triplet guitar figure, every pout and tattoo and pelvic thrust in their OEUVRE seems calculated to induce white suburban teenagers to marvel and yell, 'Rock and ROLL!' and to spend more money on Warrant product. In short, Warrant is New Kids on the Block with nipple-length hair and Marshall amps.[8]

Classic heavy metal stalwarts, Judas Priest, fared no better in David Fricke's nose-holding review of *Painkiller* in *Rolling Stone*. The album received uniformly high praise from metal critics, but for Fricke: "It's just more of the same cartoon bikerfantasy thunder the band has been peddling for years. Rob Halford's voice rarely drops below a banshee soprano, and the content of the lyrics is a hoot."[9]

Denouncing all things metal also meant de-metallizing the music that the critics championed. When critical faves Nirvana hit the top of *Billboard*'s chart in early 1992, the rhetorical scrubbing was obvious:

> Yet another misunderstanding surrounding Nirvana is that the band plays, or even embraces, heavy metal. "Metal's searching for an identity because it's exhausted itself, so they're going to latch onto us," says Novoselic. "We're not metal fans. There's a lack of insight into anything higher on any level. When you think of heavy metal, you think of sexist innuendos and pseudo Satanism. A lot of heavy-metal kids are just plain dumb," he says.[10]

What's Bad About Metal?

Maybe metal IS bad music. Has my irony been fully misplaced?

Metal was denounced as bad music from various American pulpits, bully and otherwise, during the second half of the 1980s. New York's Cardinal O'Connor and a host of Protestant ministers from the more conservative denominations echoed the accusations of a famous congressional hearing orchestrated by the wives of (then) Senator Albert Gore and Ronald Reagan's Treasury Secretary James Baker—the PMRC (Parents Music Resource Center). The allegations were that the genre recruited for satanism and induced suicide among its listeners. These charges were taken up by the Parent Teacher Association, American Medical Association and the national news media. Not bothered by the absence of evidence, these moral critics tarred and feathered metal. And, of course, they increased the sales of the genre.

Rock critics, in general, didn't take up cudgels against these denunciations, but they didn't support them either. There was no love lost between the rock critics and the long line of rock's moral critics who'd been denouncing the music since its inception.

Through a wide variety of rock styles, from early rock'n'roll in the mid-1950s through folk-rock, psychedelic rock, and, of course, heavy metal, coalitions of politicians, clergymen and parent groups have stepped up to put down the music of America's youth. It's interesting to note the wide variety of aspects of "the music" in various styles that they've seen as problematic. At first the drum roll was against the beat. It was viewed as dragging white teenagers into animalism and vulgarity.[11] The race of many of the musicians seemed to be behind that accusation. Some years later, there were attacks on lyrics. Folk-rock in the sixties was judged as advertisements for communism,[12] while psychedelic rock's words, and its musicians' life-styles, were seen to turn youth on to drugs.[13] What all these diverse charges against different features of different styles of rock had in common was the similarity of their accusers—all social conservatives.

Each of rock's external detractors had an interest in denouncing the music or its fans. Politicians, for example, spoke out most strongly when youth groups opposed their policies. Religious leaders felt that their message was in competition with the music's. In *The Triumph of Vulgarity*, Pattison contends: "Protestant fundamentalists have been quick to identify rock as 'the Devil's diversion' because it encroaches on the emotional territory where charismatic religion does its business."[14] Parents denounced "the noise," fearing social change that would take their kids out of their sphere of influence, values and behavioral standards.

Lipsitz concludes that:

> the musical censors of the 1950s (like their New Right counterparts in the 1980s) raised the specter of sexuality and its threat to youth as a cover for their real concerns the "transgressions" perpetrated by middleclass white youths when they embraced "prestige from below" and undercut the ideological hegemony of their own race, class, and family.[15]

Rock critics may be accused of many things, but sociopolitical conservativism isn't one of them. They are, by and large, on the other side of the divide, some further to the left than others. Conservatives' enmity toward them isn't subtle: "For the most part, rock critics are a dreary and dullwitted bunch of guys with rumpled clothes, dirty tennis shoes," the *National Review* declared, adding that they are "gimps and failures who've found a way to hang out with the guys whose posters used to adorn their bedrooms when they lived at home. In common parlance, they're groupies."[16]

Most rock critics were, in their teens, fans of music denounced by the conservative anti-rock camp. One would expect their understanding of metal as bad music to be different than that of the moral critics and it is. The music critics have little truck with charges that metal causes satanism and suicide. So what is it about metal that gets their goat?

Unlike the moral rock bashers, rock journalists haven't centered on some specific feature of metal to justify their collective contempt. Summing up their critique of metal: What's not to dislike?

Many of the critical barbs sound strangely familiar, echoing campaigns damning rock'n'roll of the 1950s. Frank Sinatra said in 1957: "It is sung, played and written for the most part by cretinous goons." He added, "and, by means of its almost imbecilic reiterations and sly, lewd—in fact, plain dirty—lyrics, it manages to be the martial music of every sideburned delinquent on the face of the earth."[17]

Echoing Sinatra's sentiments, *Los Angeles Times* writer John Mendelsohn denounced metal's "complete lack of subtlety, intelligence, and originality." It's all noise to him: "new songs are as indistinguishable from its old songs as its old songs are from one another."[18]

More importantly, metal's lyrics tend to fall outside the critics' two preferred attitudes: an "authentic" auteur posture and general statements upholding some progressive policy. Early on, the "dean" of rock critics, Robert Christgau, wrote of his "steadily increasing disaffection with rock's male chauvinism. I am acutely uncomfortable with songs of cock-pride (Led Zeppelin's 'Whole Lotta Love' for instance.)"[19] Metal, especially the forms played on MTV, is, as critics never tire of pointing out, sexist. "But sexism is certainly part of the blues and reggae," reminds Philip Bashe,[20] noting the pass given to those styles by the same critics who bash metal.

Complaints about metal's vocals focus on its "banshee wailing." Reviewers prefer the personal, not only as revealed in words, but also as expressed in intimate or quirky vocals (e.g., P. J. Harvey, Bjork, Dylan). In contrast, metal privileges powerful vocals.

The most frequent attacks on metal, however, have nothing to do with music or elements of performance like the spandex pants (with or without the cucumber), but with metal's audience. The critics seem to grasp the genre through its fans and they definitely don't identify with these folk. Their disdain for metal fans more than borders on hostility. As Bashe puts it:

> Especially among rock journalists, those arbiters of what's in and what's out, heavy metal has been handled only at arm's length. It has been scorned for its alleged musical primitivism (the same quality inherent in the mid Seventies punk rock so hailed by critics), and its participants, both musicians and fans, have been ridiculed as living contradictions to the theory of evolution.[21]

Metal's fans were radically Other to the critics in several ways. Attempting to grasp their long-standing contempt, Bashe noted the difference in age between metal's audience and the journalists: "They no longer have an interest in a music that is directed at a younger, adolescent audience."[22]

In his *Record Guide: Rock Albums of the '80s*, the then over-forty Robert Christgau put down AC/DC's *Back in Black* with reference to the youth of those who like the band: "Fresh recruit Brian Johnson sings like there's a cattle prod at his scrotum, just the thing for fans who can't decide whether their newfound testosterone is agony or ecstasy."[23]

More than just registering an age gap, the otherness of metal's audience expressed an education divide, which is one of the determining factors of social class differentiation. The majority of the critics, and especially the first generation that set the parameters of the profession, were college educated—Greil Marcus at Berkeley, John Rockwell at Harvard, Jon Landau at Brandeis and Robert Christgau at Dartmouth. In sharp contrast, metal's fanbase, since its inception, tends to come from the working class and its post-industrial version, the para-professional and service-sector lower-middle class; they have not attended elite universities.

In addition to age and class, a historical factor entered into the critics' distance from the metal audience. In the 1970s, after the suppression of the protest movements of the sixties, youth ideology changed and adapted to a reactionary social and political environment, leaving rock critics stranded with their no longer vital ideals. The general demise of the counter-culture was reflected in the fate of its music.

As Lipsitz remarks in *Time Passages*:

> The hippie counter culture confronted its own demise most dramatically in the deaths of Hendrix and Joplin. With the breakup of the Beatles, the murder of a participant in the 1969 Altamont Rock festival . . . the degeneration into drug-ravaged slums of . . . Haight-Ashbury and New York's East Village, it became clear even to its adherents that "the dream" was over.[24]

As early as 1967, "Critics no longer spoke for a monolithic body of fans as they had during the days of Beatlemania." Led Zeppelin was the symbol of the incipient rupture between "popularity and quality."[25] The band "was loud, flashy and 'raunchy' in the eyes of most critics. They were seen as 'heavy' in the most negative respect possible. Critical judgment notwithstanding, Zeppelin was an enormous commercial success . . . Other performers and fans, seeing their favorite acts ignored or panned, joined in the chorus, 'What do we need critics for?'"[26]

Underlying the changes in audience sentiment were the deadly blows to the counter-culture's political aspirations, including the police-riot at the Chicago Democratic Convention in 1968 and the Kent State murders in 1970, which altered cultural alliances and brought latent class divisions to the surface. The audience for metal and hard rock in the 1970s, according to the editors of *Rock of Ages: The Rolling Stone History of Rock & Roll*:

> "represented a union that could not have been predicted in the sixties—a mating of the hippie and working-class ethos, the two united in their feeling of being despised outsiders in the increasingly gentrified world of popular music." They continue: "a line was being drawn; the late-sixties notion of rock-culture-as-pop-culture was coming to an end. Youth had spoken, and many of them had decided to secede from Woodstock Nation."[27]

The political traumas inflicted on sixties progressivism bled into rock criticism. Joe Carducci contends that "Rock writers have ignored the reality of rock—the music—in an attempt to promote their sociopolitical hegemony over the intellectual life of the pop medium."[28] Similarly, Steve Jones acknowledges the prevalence of non-musical elements in rock criticism, especially themes such as "groping for an end to racism and decrying the pollution of 'pure' music by commerce, to searching for redemption and transcendence in 'authentic' rock and roll."[29] Assessing the work of "Paul Williams, Greil Marcus, and Richard Meltzer," the profession's first, "sixties," generation, of rock reviewers, Fred Goodman states that they "frequently seemed obsessed with elevating rock by placing it in a broad social context or emphasizing its philosophical and mythmaking capabilities."[30]

Carducci sums up the gulf between the critics and the youth audience, describing the former's "insensibility rooted in class and age resentment. The aging sixties critics resent that white kids of the middle and lower classes are able to party with music of their own choosing and design without the benefit of Tracy Chapman or Bruce Springsteen—that is, without submitting to the class tenets of the rock crit establishment."[31]

Here Carducci identifies a condition that applies generally to the formation of taste; preferences in the arts not only function to reflect and reinforce invidious social distinctions, they serve to constitute them. As the sociologist Pierre Bourdieu notes: "To the socially recognized hierarchy of the arts, and within each of them, of genres, schools or periods, corresponds a social hierarchy of the consumers. This predisposes tastes to function as markers of 'class.'"[32]

Although Carducci is generally right, the rock critics' animus was more than simply a clash of class-based cultures. As students, the future critics had absorbed from counter-cultural gurus, such as Herbert Marcuse, the dictum that commercial forms of popular culture were the antithesis of authentic transformative art, and that the former were directly responsible for corrupting the "mass."

Authenticity has remained a central term in the discourse of rock criticism ever since its inception, taking a variety of meanings from connection with folk, minority and outsider musical traditions, through oppositional political stances and novel and/or unpopular musical styles, to supposedly genuine personal expression. Generally, however, it has been placed in opposition to commercially successful music, preserving the critic's position as uncorrupted and as the member of a select, hip group, still linked to the counter-cultural past.

The contradictions within the notion of authenticity are obvious. For example, music can be both novel and contrived, oppositional and hackneyed, based on non-commercial traditions and imitative, and so on. The status of "authenticity" as a floating signifier has been helpful for rock critics in the post-sixties decades, allowing them to adjust to cultural changes and emerging musical styles without appearing to surrender their counter-cultural aura.

Consider, for example, what happened in the 1970s after political protests had been crushed and rock rose to mass popularity. The critics retreated to the eccentric, holding fast to their auteur avant-garde which excluded metal:

> Provincial art [indie rock] is the search for the authentically eccentric: that which can never be reified as glamorous style. It is only in and through such eccentricity that art can retain its role as the sanctuary of the alternative, which is what . . . was really meant by the old avant-garde conception of it as the zone of opposition and rebellion.[33]

There was an irony in the critics' retreat to the margins of popular culture. As Adam Gopnik points out: "The transgressive Romantic gestures that the rock critics credited their heroes with were being advanced through exactly the same commercial system that had advanced the old ersatz culture."[34] Gopnik is correct, but to be fair to the critics, in a hegemonic culture it is very difficult to avoid being co-opted and nearly impossible to refrain from entering the commercial system, unless one wants to renounce dissemination of their music.

Why Do Critics Need Bad Music?

In the early 1990s, metal underwent a decline in popularity, displaced by the rise of "alternative." After two decades of having a reliable Other to kick around, critics no longer had a paradigm of bad music. It was not long before they found other targets—Hootie and the Blowfish, rap, boy bands and, more recently, Britney Spears—proving that they needed something to bash and that metal had only been their first and most convenient bête noire.[35]

There are many ways of being a critic, not all of them involve confirming one's own judgments of taste by tearing down another's. Walter Benjamin defined the standard of "immanent criticism," in which the critic's role is to enter the art object of whatever medium or genre, and to understand it in its own terms and its own standards of success. José Ortega y Gasset and Clement Greenberg are examples of noted critics who practiced an advocacy criticism, advancing a particular art form by describing its virtues and its relevance to their contemporary circumstances, without denouncing other forms. Rock critics, in contrast, are adversarial critics; they seem to need an Other to detract from and are not content with either sympathetic appreciation or passionate advocacy.

In order to understand rock critics' need to define their taste against a negation of it upon which they pile abuse, it's necessary to understand that they are not free-floating intellectuals, but journalists working for businesses that make their profits selling audiences to advertisers; they must satisfy their audience and their editors if they want to keep publishing. It helps, in the case of rock critics, that they usually come from the audience that they serve and share its taste prejudices.

The requirement that rock critics affirm their audience's taste should not be underestimated. As Charlie Bertsch observes, "the music we listen to plays a significant role in stabilizing our identities" and "'fixes' us in a particular place within the social order." He notes that audiences are "pleased" with criticism that confirms their preferences, but get upset when it challenges them, because they are forced not only to question their tastes but their identities. Bertsch concludes, "Music fans find it distinctly unpleasureable to read criticism that runs counter to their own taste-preferences."[36]

The fact that rock critics dare not challenge their audience's musical prejudices does not yet explain why it is necessary for them to affirm the taste of their audience through the denigration of one form or another of bad music. The explanation cannot be found in the realm of aesthetic criteria or the domain of individual psychology, although wherever there is resentment (and it is pervasive in contemporary society), beating a scapegoat is sure to win applause. There is nothing that all of the targets of critical abuse have in common but their popularity. And, as argued above, not all art critics construct demonized Others and confirm their taste against them. Something else is going on than aesthetic debate or the operation of psychological laws, and that something is culture wars based on social conflict.

It is useful to remember that rock originates as youth music and carries the stench of the high school lunchroom with it even as it passes into a style that can be appropriated by consumers of all ages.

Adolescence is notorious for its status anxiety, which is expressed in the formation of rival cliques that affirm themselves at the expense of the others. In the final decades of the twentieth century, after the birth of rock in the sixties, music became a badge of adolescent identity and sometimes, in music subcultures, became the definition of that identity, to be raised up and defended against all comers.

The rock critics and their readers originate in the cliques that affirm themselves by being "hip" and "cool," superior in their sophistication and depth to the benighted jocks, nerds, dips and burnouts surrounding them. More than music counts even in a music subculture; its members are fighting a status war within themselves and against rival taste groups, which represent clashing social groups, cultural attitudes and life-styles. The weapon of the hipoisie indie crowd is the tried-and-true approach of those with pretensions to refinement, intellect and superior discernment—snobbery. The hip and discerning snob finds members of the out groups to be unenlightened, naive, politically incorrect, simple-minded and utterly undiscerning (cultural dopes); they are objects of contempt.

The normal status anxieties of adolescence are compounded for the cool crowd by the fact that it is, after all, some forms of rock, rather than "high culture," that they are elevating to a superior rank. This added tension carries over into rock criticism, whose practitioners are aware that their very enterprise is not accorded legitimacy by aficionados of high culture who scorn them and their musical tastes, just as they denigrate what they despise. Rock critics must overcome the judgment that they are engaged in a trivial pursuit and they do so by differentiating good from bad music, defining their superior taste by contrast to the forms that they brand debased. Since many critics have been schooled in high culture, they are particularly sensitive to charges that they are simply hyping commercial dross. If they defended all kinds of rock music, they would not have any prospects for gaining credibility in the general culture.

Even more important than their bid to be taken seriously is the fact that rock criticism has never developed self-conscious and reflexive standards defining the characteristics of good music. In the absence of a tradition and a discourse of cultural theory, rock critics experience acute anxiety about making independent judgments about new music and freely admit to their insecurity. In place of consensual or contested standards, they try to anticipate what their colleagues will esteem, setting off a ceaseless quest to tap into the "buzz." Bill Wyman, former critic of the *Chicago Reader*, remarks, "You're always scared when you're going through tapes because you never know who is going to be the next Nirvana or Liz Phair."[37] The *Chicago Tribune*'s Greg Kot observes, "I talk to people in the Chicago music community every day. When a name comes up three or four times in the span of a week, you know that some people are hearing things here."[38]

In the throes of anxious anticipation, rock critics find some safety in being able to use bad music as a negation of whatever they decide to call good; at least they can all agree on something and be sure of corroboration.

Rock critics also want their audience to take them seriously. In light of their root insecurity about their affirmative judgments, they rely on bashing bad music to ingratiate themselves with their readers.

Academician and longtime rock critic Simon Frith concurs:

> For most rock critics . . . the issue in the end isn't so much representing music to the public . . . as creating a knowing community, orchestrating a collusion between selected musicians and an equally select part of the public—select in its superiority to the ordinary, undiscriminating pop consumer.[39]

The primary reason why rock critics need bad music is that the status anxiety and resentments of youth persist in their readers and themselves. Critics and their audience, in common with many other adults, have never fully grown up; they persist in their youthful snobbery and need it confirmed continually. The critics choose as the objects of their detraction forms of music that the status claims of their audience are sure to reject and that are enjoyed by groups for which their audience has contempt. Related to status anxiety and reinforcing the need for a despised Other are concerns for cultural credibility and the lack of a critical tradition.

Bad music isn't about music at all; it's about status for the audience, money for the mediator, and status and money for the critic. It's too much to expect rock critics to be generous appreciators or to be only passionate advocates.

NOTES

1. Mikal Gilmore writing about disco in *Rolling Stone* in 1977, cited in Reebee Garofalo, *Rockin' Out*, Upper Saddle River, NJ: Prentice-Hall 2002, 253.
2. *Billboard* reference (April 27, 1985) cited in Linda Martin and Kerry Segrave, *Anti-rock: The Opposition to Rock 'n' Roll*, Hamden, CT: Archon Book, 1988, 232.

3.   Chet Flippo, "Review of Bloodrock 3," *Rolling Stone* (June 24, 1971):44.

4.   Paul Battiste, *Creem* (1972), cited in Philip Bashe, "Black Sabbath: Rock's Dinosaur dogs its detractors," *Circus* (March 31, 1981): 29–30.

5.   Ira Robbins, "Heavy Metal: Down But Not Out," *Trouser Press* (September 1977): 20.

6.   Will Straw, "Characterizing Rock Music Cultures: The Case of Heavy Metal," *Canadian University Music Review* 5 (1984): 113.

7.   Chris Heim, "Whitesnake offers chapter from a heavy-metal manual," *Chicago Tribune* (February 12, 1988): sect.2, 8.

8.   John Mendelssohn, "Review of Warrant's Cherry Pie," *Rolling Stone* (October 18, 1990): 104.

9.   David Fricke, "The Year in Records: Review of Judas Priest's Painkiller and 2 Live Crew's Banned in the USA," *Rolling Stone* (December 13, 1990): 218.

10. Chris Mundy, "Nirvana," *Rolling Stone* (January 23, 1992): 40.

11. See Trent Hill's discussion of the reaction of the White Citizen's Council of Birmingham, Alabama to the music. ["The Enemy Within: Censorship in Rock Music in the 1950s" *The South Atlantic Quarterly* 90, #4 (Fall 1991): 686.]

12. R. Serge Denisoff, *Solid Gold: The Popular Record Industry*, New Brunswick, NJ: Transaction Books, 1975, 385.

13. Linda Martin and Kerry Segrave, *Anti-Rock: The Opposition to Rock 'n' Roll*, Hamden, CT: Archon Books, 1988, 199–202 and Denisoff, op. cit., 388–89.

14. Robert Pattison, *The Triumph of Vulgarity: Rock Music in the Mirror of Romanticism*, New York: Oxford University Press, 1987, 184.

15. George Lipsitz, *Time Passages: Collective Memory and American Popular Culture,* Minneapolis: University of Minnesota Press, 1990, 123.

16. Stuart Goldman, "Gimme A Break," *National Review* (May 5, 1989): 45.

17. Mikal Gilmore, "An Appreciation of Frank Sinatra," *Rolling Stone* (June 25, 1998): 64.

18. Cited in Garofalo, *Rockin' Out*, 243.

19. Robert Christgau, *Any Old Way You Choose It* (1973), cited in Garofalo, *Rockin' Out,* 243.

20. Philip Bashe, *Heavy Metal Thunder: The Music, Its History, Its Heroes,* Garden City, NY: Dolphin, 1985, 24.

21. Bashe, op. cit., 6.

22. Bashe, op. cit., 24.

23. Cited in Mark Coleman, "Review of Christgau's Record Guide: Rock Albums of the '80s," *Rolling Stone* (November 29, 1990): 113.

24. Lipsitz, *Time Passages,* 130.

25. The mainstream media have, in general, hailed Led Zeppelin's recent DVD release. This does not mark a change in the general attitude of the media toward music, but is an attempt to appeal to their aging boomer constituency.

26. Denisoff, *Solid Gold,* 305.

27. Ed Ward, Geoffrey Stokes and Ken Tucker, *Rock of Ages: The Rolling Stone History of Rock & Roll,* New York: Rolling Stone Press/ Summit Books, 1986, 486.

28. Joe Carducci, *Rock and the Pop Narcotic: Testament for the Electric Church Volume 1*, Chicago: Redoubt Press, 1990, 61.

29. Steve Jones, "Re-viewing Rock Writing: Recurring Themes in Popular Music Criticism," *American Journalism* (March 1992): 159.

30. Fred Goodman, *The Mansion on The Hill: Dylan, Young, Geffen, Springsteen, and the Head-On Collision of Rock and Commerce,* New York: Times Books, 1997, 33–34.

31. Carducci, *Rock and the Pop Narcotic*, 61.

32. Pierre Bourdieu, *Distinction: A Social Critique of the Judgement of Taste.* Richard Nice trans. Cambridge: Harvard University Press, 1984, 64.

33. Donald Kuspit, *Signs of Psyche in Modern and Postmodern Art*, Cambridge: Cambridge University Press, 1993, 289.

34. Adam Gopnik, "Carry that Weight: Why do the Beatles endure?" *New Yorker* (May 1, 1995):84.

35. Metal isn't the only style that the critics have regularly held "beneath contempt." In his analysis of rock criticism in North America, Kembrew McLeod details their disdain of "feminine 'prefabricated' pop music" (Kembrew McLeod, "3½': A Critique of Rock Criticism in North America," *Popular Music* 20, #1 (2001):47). His data compared artists on the top of the annual Village Voice Pazz & Jop critics' poll to those on the same year's best selling *Billboard* charts. "Artists like Nelson and The Spice Girls, whose most visible fans are eight to thirteen year-old girls, are regularly dismissed," McLeod concludes (McLeod, op.cit., 52).

36. Charlie Bertsch, "Autobiography in Music Criticism," *Bad Subjects* 44 (June 1999) (http://eserver.org/bs/44/bertsch.html:5-6).

37. Eric M. Roth, "Chicago's Rock Critics: More Than Just Reporters?" *Tail Spins Magazine* 13 (March 1994):6.

38. Roth, op. cit, 6.

39. Simon Frith, *Performing Rites: On the Value of Popular Music*, Cambridge, MA: Harvard University Press, 1996, 67.

REFERENCES

Bashe, P. 1985. *Heavy metal thunder: The music, its history, its heroes.* Garden City, NY: Dolphin.

———— 1981. Black Sabbath: Rock's dinosaur dogs its detractors," *Circus* (March 31): 29–30.

Bertsch, C. 1999. Autobiography in music criticism. *Bad Subjects* 44 (June) http://eserver.org/bs/44/bertsch.html.

Bourdieu, P. 1984. *Distinction: A social critique of the judgement of taste*, trans. R. Nice. Cambridge, MA: Harvard University Press.

Carducci, J. 1990. *Rock and the pop narcotic: Testament for the electric church volume 1.* Chicago: Redoubt Press.

Coleman, M. 1990. Review of Christgau's Record Guide: Rock albums of the '80s. *Rolling Stone* (November 29): 113.

Denisoff, S. 1975. *Solid gold: The popular record industry.* New Brunswick, NJ: Transaction Books.

Flippo, C. 1971. Review of Bloodrock 3. *Rolling Stone* (June 24): 44.

Fricke, D. 1990. The year in records; Review of Judas Priest's Painkiller and 2 Live Crew's banned in the USA. *Rolling Stone* (December 13): 217–18.

Frith, S. 1996. *Performing rites: On the value of popular music*. Cambridge, MA: Harvard University Press.

Garofalo, R. 2002. *Rockin' out*. Upper Saddle River, NJ: Prentice-Hall.

Gilmore, M. 1998. An appreciation of Frank Sinatra. *Rolling Stone* (June 25): 64.

Goldman, S. 1989. Gimme a break. *National Review* (May 5): 45.

Goodman, F. 1997. *The mansion on the hill: Dylan, Young, Geffen, Springsteen, and the head-on collision of rock and commerce*. New York: Times Books.

Gopnik, A. 1995. Carry that weight: Why do the Beatles endure? *New Yorker* (May 1): 80–85.

Heim, C. 1988. Whitesnake offers chapter from a heavymetal manual. *Chicago Tribune* (February 12): sect. 2, 8.

Hill, T. 1991. The enemy within: Censorship in rock music in the 1950s. *The South Atlantic Quarterly* 90, no. 4 (Fall): 675–707.

Jones, S. 1992. Reviewing rock writing: Recurring themes in popular music criticism. *American Journalism* (March): 142–62.

Kuspit, D. 1993. *Signs of psyche in modern and postmodern art*. Cambridge: Cambridge University Press.

Lipsitz, G. 1990. *Time passages: Collective memory and American popular culture*. Minneapolis: University of Minnesota Press.

Martin, L. and K. Segrave. 1988. *Antirock: The opposition to rock 'n' roll*. Hamden, CT: Archon Book.

McLeod, K. 2001. 3½': A critique of rock criticism in North America. *Popular Music* 20(1): 47–60.

Mendelssohn, J. 1990. Review of Warrant's *Cherry Pie*," *Rolling Stone* (October 18): 104.

Mundy, C. 1992. Nirvana. *Rolling Stone* (January 23): 39–41.

Robbins, I. 1977. Heavy metal: Down but not out. *Trouser Press* (September): 20–23.

Pattison, R. 1987. *The triumph of vulgarity: Rock music in the mirror of romanticism*. New York: Oxford University Press.

Roth, E. M. 1994. Chicago's rock critics: More than just reporters? *Tail Spins Magazine* 13 (March): 5–6, 20–21.

Straw, W. 1984. Characterizing rock music cultures: The case of heavy metal, *Canadian University Music Review* 5:104–21.

Ward, E., G. Stokes, and K. Tucker. 1986. *Rock of ages: The Rolling Stone history of rock & roll*. New York: Rolling Stone Press/Summit Books.

15

Much Too Loud and Not Loud Enough:
Issues Involving the Reception of Staged Rock Musicals

ELIZABETH L. WOLLMAN

The significance of magic is that people believe it.
—SIMON FRITH

Rock music has always had an uneasy relationship with the American musical theater. Although the critical and commercial impact of the 1968 Broadway production of *Hair* led many members of the theater industry to believe that rock would revolutionize the American musical, there have since been few successful rock musicals staged. Over the last thirty years, Broadway and Off-Broadway have been littered with flops, the creators of which attempted to blend the performance aesthetics of rock with those of the American musical. For every critically and commercially successful attempt at this combination—*Hair,* for example, or *Rent*—there have been so many highly publicized, costly failures that most theater industry members view a successful rock musical as a contradiction in terms.

A primary factor that has influenced this negative reception of staged rock musicals is rock's association with discourses of authenticity, which emerged as 1950s rock 'n' roll developed into the more socio-politically aware rock of the 1960s. The resultant ideology implies that despite its strong commercial moorings—which are often downplayed by the music industry, denied by the rock press, and ignored by fans—rock is a transgressive, rebellious genre that is stylistically comparable, but ideologically superior to, "pop" music. While the line dividing rock and pop is impossibly blurred and regularly contested, pop is generally seen to be more obviously commercialized

311

and commodified than rock, and thus less representative of the "true" emotional state of the performer. In comparison with pop musicians, rock musicians are often viewed as uncompromised artists who bare their souls in composition and performance, who share their "true" selves more completely with their audiences, and who thus transcend the influences of the music industry. While many writers on rock argue that this putative authenticity exists largely in the collective imagination, most acknowledge that it is nevertheless a powerfully influential factor.[1]

Rock's failure to lend itself effectively to the musical theater lies not necessarily in the genres' performative differences, but instead in their ideological ones. Such conflicting ideologies—which result, more often than not, in the commercial and critical rejection of rock musicals as "bad"—thus deserve closer investigation. In the following pages, I discuss some of these conflicts, with emphasis on the ways they have affected the musicals *The Who's Tommy*, *Bright Lights Big City*, and *Hedwig and the Angry Inch*.

In the first place, the musical theater is more comparable to pop than to the rock sphere in that it is not particularly preoccupied with notions of authenticity. Rather, it traditionally celebrates the self-conscious blend of high and low cultures, revels in artifice and kitsch, and has been closely and comparatively unflinchingly associated with commercialism from its inception. Further, like those in the pop realm, musical theater composers write music for other people to perform. They are thus often required to be more open to collaboration than their rock counterparts, since musical scores are regularly, and sometimes drastically, altered during the staging of a piece. Such compromises are not usually as acceptable in the rock sphere, where singer-songwriter-musicians seen to maintain artistic control over their work are traditionally held in highest esteem.

Compounding the ideological rift between the two genres, then, is the fact that rock has never been fully respected or understood in the musical theater world, and vice-versa. When rock 'n' roll was introduced in the United States in the mid-1950s, most of those who were then creating American musical theater dismissed the new genre as a noisy, vulgar fad. Yet, by the end of the decade, rock 'n' roll, which was far more suitable to sound recording than the musical theater, had surpassed Tin Pan Alley to become the dominant American popular music genre. By the early 1960s, rock had become associated with an increasingly powerful youth market, while the American musical the-

ater became associated with a rapidly aging—and thus rapidly shrink-
ing—audience.[2] The interest in adapting rock for the musical stage
was thus one borne of a perceived necessity, not any particular fondness
for, or interest in, the genre.

More than half a century later, the creators of musical theater
continue the struggle to regain a foothold in American popular culture
by emulating stylistic trends that have since developed in other, more
wide-ranging and influential types of media. Such a struggle has resulted in the absorption of many current popular genres—for example,
rhythm and blues, country music, and middle-of-the-road pop—all of
which have lent themselves relatively well to the musical theater. Yet,
despite repeated attempts, and a small handful of successes, rock musicals prove particularly difficult to develop.

Because they draw on both rock and musical theater traditions,
rock musicals are usually deemed not enough of either, or too much of
one at the expense of the other. In trying to appeal to musical theater
and rock fans, they generally fail to attract either, which is why they
are considered particularly risky among theater producers. The rare
commercially and critically successful rock musical is celebrated as a
work of genius that has managed to breathe new life into the musical
theater without negating the raw energy and excitement that makes
rock appealing in the first place—hence a primary reason why anyone
attempts them at all.

Nevertheless, rock musicals are almost always criticized, ridiculed, or simply dismissed as "bad" by both camps. Many rock critics
and fans view rock musicals as laughable efforts on the part of theater
composers to appeal to larger audiences by referencing a musical tradition that they do not understand or respect. Not helping matters is the
fact that the American musical, as well as the industry around it, have
proven remarkably conservative and resistant to change. Thus, while
theater industry members, critics, and musical theater aficionados continue to covet rock's access to broader audiences and its relationship
to American popular culture, many simultaneously continue to view
rock as a necessary evil: repetitive noise that is only worth experimenting with because its inclusion occasionally succeeds in appealing to
the larger, younger audiences which, most agree, are needed to keep
the business thriving.

This helps explain why critically and commercially successful
rock musicals are often heralded by theater industry members, critics,

and musical theater fans as lending legitimacy to their "corny" or
"uncool" genre. As theatrical press agent Tom D'Ambrosio notes:

> For me, there's always been a little shame involved with liking
> musicals. Buying a show-tune CD is like buying pornography. You
> buy a Prince CD too, just so you can be like, "I'm cool—*that's* for
> my mother." There's a legitimizing feel with *Rent* [and] *Hedwig
> and the Angry Inch*. If I sent a CD of *Hedwig* to my brother, who
> doesn't go to the theater, he'd like it. So there's part of—"Oh, I
> can finally like rock music like I'm supposed to," for me at least.[3]

Ironically, though, even the most successful rock musicals tend to be
regarded by rock journalists, industry members, and audiences as
"corny" and "inauthentic," simply as a result of their association with
the musical theater.[4]

Part of the problem lies in the subtle and often overlooked distinction between *theatricality* and *theater*. Rock's ideology of authenticity
dictates that an interest in theatricality—as reflected in the use of costumes, choreography, innovative lighting, or short skits—may be used
to great effect. For example, Alice Cooper, David Bowie, and Marilyn
Manson have built careers that highlight a flair for the dramatic. Yet,
while their concerts may borrow from them, they would nevertheless
not be confused with Broadway musicals, especially since rock shows
do not tend to rely, as musical theater almost always does, on linear
narrative.

Conversely, while many rock musicals are designed to evoke the
excitement and raw energy of live rock spectacles, they would never
be mistaken for actual rock concerts. *Rent*, for example, was dismissed
in the rock press, and continues to be viewed by many rock fans, as
too musically sugary and structurally stiff to function as a "real" rock
show.

Despite all attempts by Pete Townshend and director Des McAnuff
to remain true to the Who's 1969 concept album *Tommy*, the Broadway
adaptation was criticized in much the same way. When it opened in
1993, *The Who's Tommy* earned the glowing praise of theater critics,
and set a box office record by selling almost $500,000 worth of tickets
in a single day.[5] Despite an opening that held the critical and commercial promise of such long-running shows as *The Lion King*, *The Who's
Tommy* surprised many theater industry members by closing after barely
two years and earning its investors a slim 10 percent profit.[6]

Part of the problem lay in the fact that in attempting to appeal to rock and theater camps alike, *The Who's Tommy* alienated both. On the one hand, many rock critics and fans objected to the musical adaptation's enhanced linear narrative, muted references to sex and drugs, newly upbeat ending (in which Tommy reconciles with his abusive family), and musical arrangements, which were perceived as too tame to rival the energy of the original album.[7] On the other hand, many theatergoers who were unfamiliar with the original concept album—and with rock in general—came away feeling that the music was too loud and the linear narrative too unstructured, and that the show was thus difficult to follow.[8] Despite its promising start, then, *The Who's Tommy* ultimately fell flat after being transformed from a rock product that utilized theater into a theatrical production that utilized rock.

This distinction helps explain why performers who are embraced by one camp often suffer disastrous results when they tip the balance too far toward the other. In this light, Pete Townshend was relatively successful: many non-narrative rock explorations that appeared on and Off-Broadway in the 1970s drew memorably hostile reactions from audiences and critics, who grew frustrated at the emphasis on spectacle and volume, as well as the lack of plot. Rock musicals like *Dude* and *Via Galactica*, both from 1973, remain some of the worst critical and commercial disasters in Broadway history.[9] Conversely, all but the most established rock musicians tend to shy away from appearing in musical theater productions or otherwise revealing too much of an interest in the genre, since doing so is believed to damage their credibility and careers.[10] Due to such perceptions, Don Summa, the *Rent* press agent, remembers that despite the musical's monumental success, he failed to generate interest when he tried to shop the show's songs around to rock recording artists in the hope of promoting the musical via radio airplay.[11]

The ideological rift between rock and the musical theater is manifested in the genres' differing performative approaches. While rock concerts and musical theater productions are both staged and rehearsed, there is ultimately more emphasis on accuracy and precision—and thus, less on spontaneity—in the latter than the former. Rock concerts are often carefully designed to seem like ecstatic events: performers exert and emote; audience members cheer, applaud, dance, and otherwise commune emotionally with the performers and one another.[12] While

the musical theater may be just as emotionally engaging for its performers and spectators, emotionalism is nevertheless typically held in comparative reserve: actors are expected to perform carefully rehearsed
lines and choreography in more or less exactly the same way each night,
while audience members are expected to sit quietly, emoting only at
designated intervals so as not to disturb the performers or other spectators.

This distinction is intensified by the relative spatial permanence
of live events, which affects the sense of spontaneity audiences receive
in viewing them. Staged musicals usually run a number of times per
week in an unchanging location over a given time period. In contrast,
rock concerts are rarely as permanent in terms of space and location.
Rather, rock acts typically perform in many different places during a
national or international tour. At most, a rock act might play a few
concerts at the same site before moving on to the next one. This comparative ephemerality adds to the perception of rock music and its
practitioners as more spontaneous, and thus more emotionally genuine,
than the musical theater.

The relative emphasis on authenticity as a guiding ideal also influences the relationships between audiences and performers of these
two genres. While performers in the rock realm are often romanticized
as uncompromised artists who reveal their true selves to their audiences, musical theater performers, while certainly capable of earning
fans' adoration, are nevertheless rarely idealized in quite the same way.
Simon Frith is correct in arguing that "*all* live performance involves
both spontaneous action and the playing of a role";[13] nevertheless, actors
and musicians tend to approach role playing very differently.

An actor draws from personal experience in creating a role, but
then immerses herself so deeply in that role that dual recognition—
that of character *and* actor—fades, allowing spectators to focus on the
character. This skill allows one actor to play different roles, and different actors to interpret the same character. Therefore, while the departure
of a specific performer from a theatrical production might result in
slumping ticket sales or the occasional closure, most successful shows
tend to outlast their original casts.

Like actors, many rock stars develop public personae that are not
necessarily consistent with their private ones. Nevertheless, due in part
to the authenticity with which rock has been saddled, there is an absence
of dual recognition in the rock realm, and the distinction between what
is real and what is an act tends to get more muddled. While a rock
musician might play a character every time she appears in public, the

character is not as separable from the person creating it as one might be in the theater, where actors follow a memorized script and direction. Because rock musicians do not play characters that are as fully developed and enacted as those in the theater, their personae are more likely to be read as "real," and their emotions more nakedly exposed. Frith argues that the blurring between private and onstage personae is precisely what makes rock musicians appealing to audiences.[14] Thus, while one theater role may be performed by countless actors, no audience would accept an understudy in place of a rock star.

Rock musicians seldom involve themselves with musical theater projects, since the risks in doing so far outweigh the benefits. Adding to the many ideological distinctions between the two genres is an important economic one: as Pete Townshend notes, "the prospect of going onto Broadway and being paid $50,000 a week to do eight shows is not [one] that the modern wanky little [rock] star thinks he wants."[15] Rock musicians who do perform in or collaborate on musical theater projects do so for one of two principal reasons: either their careers have slowed significantly—as in the case of Joan Jett and Sebastian Bach, who recently appeared on Broadway in *Jekyll and Hyde* and *The Rocky Horror Show* respectively—or they are in the late stages of long, fruitful careers, and are thus in little danger of harming their images—as in the case of Pete Townshend, Paul Simon, and Elton John. Yet, the presence of such performers helps reinforce the idea that Broadway—often nicknamed "the Fabulous Invalid"—lags hopelessly behind the times, a site for the aging and the outmoded.

Exacerbating the rift between the two camps is the fact that journalists and industry personnel who specialize in one camp do not necessarily involve themselves with the other. In this light, theater critics may not be best adept at ruling what is or is not a successful use of rock music on the stage, just as their rock counterparts are not ideal evaluators of musical theater. Yet, rock musicals are almost always covered by theater critics, in large part because the rock press typically shows no interest in them. Michael Cerveris, who originated the title role in *The Who's Tommy* and appeared in the title role of *Hedwig and the Angry Inch*, argues that rock journalists' hesitancy is the result of their collective insistence on rock's authenticity:

> The rock press are slow to give the nod to any rock [musical], partly because they'd never want to look like they were being establishment, or condoning the marketing of rock into old people's

culture, which is how theater is perceived. Part of it is that rock pretends to be so much about authenticity . . . The truth is that it's all business, [but] the press has so much invested in pretending it's *not* a show that it's really hard for them to embrace something that *is* a show.[16]

As a result of this attitude, theatrical press agents often find themselves working to convince members of the rock press to attend rock musicals, which usually proves a futile exercise, albeit one deemed necessary by those who hope to attract wider audiences to the musical theater.[17]

The tidbits that do appear about rock musicals in the rock press are often the results of hard work, mixed with sheer luck. Asked, for example, about a photograph in *Rolling Stone* of him and Townshend backstage at *Hedwig and the Angry Inch*, Cerveris notes:

That "Random Notes" photo? There was nothing random about it. It was the result of a lot of hard work from the show's publicist, and a friend of mine who is also a publicist who has friends at *Rolling Stone*, and who worked very hard to get them to see the show. They were dragging their heels until Pete [Townshend] was coming, and *then* suddenly it was worth checking out.[18]

In keeping with the notion that rock musicals are "inauthentic," and thus undeserving of rock fans' attentions, the coverage of rock musicals by rock and theater journalists alike is often notably defensive. Emphasis tends to be placed on convincing both camps that the piece in question is worth seeing, even though all other representatives of the subgenre are not. Favorable comparisons of a specific rock musical with its predecessors are ubiquitous, as are proclamations like "Broadway finally got a rock musical right,"[19] or "at long last the authentic rock musical that has eluded Broadway for two generations . . ."[20] Coverage of *Hedwig* in the rock press was no different: in *Billboard,* Jim Bessman dubbed *Hedwig* the "rare rock musical that works";[21] David Fricke of *Rolling Stone* insisted that in the "whole, long, sorry history of rock musicals, *Hedwig* . . . is the first one that truly *rocks*," and that it "was born a million miles away from the Broadway sugar of *Rent*";[22] and Zev Borow wrote in *Spin* that *Hedwig* was "glammy, rock-inspired theater for people who think glammy, rock-inspired theater sucks."[23]

Because staged rock musicals tend to be aimed at two camps that do not share the same values and do not always understand one another, it is unsurprising that rock composers and performers who get involved in musical theater productions find themselves caught between two worlds, neither of which fully accepts them. Two examples are the singer-songwriter-musicians Paul Scott Goodman and Stephen Trask, whose musicals, *Bright Lights Big City* and *Hedwig and the Angry Inch,* opened in New York City in the late 1990s. Despite their musicals' very different receptions, both men found themselves in the same double bind, since the work methods and performance approaches that are celebrated as marks of authenticity in the rock camp are often dismissed as laughably unprofessional in the theater camp.

Of the two, Paul Scott Goodman encountered greater difficulties in trying to bridge the gap between rock and the musical theater. Despite his respect for both forms, he was rejected by the musical theater and rock camps when he appeared onstage at the New York Theatre Workshop (NYTW) in 1999 as a performer in his own musical. Goodman, a Scotland native, moved to New York City in the 1980s to enroll in Broadcast Music, Inc.'s Lehman Engel Musical Theater Workshop. After writing a few small-scale, one- or two-person musicals, he began adapting Jay McInerney's 1984 novel, *Bright Lights, Big City*, for the stage in August 1996.[24] Three months later, Goodman sang through a version of his musical for James Nicola, NYTW's artistic director.[25] Impressed, Nicola saw Goodman's project through a few readings, and then tapped Michael Greif, director of *Rent*, to stage a workshop and, later, the finished piece.[26]

In developing McInerney's novel for the stage, the creative team was faced with a number of challenges. First, Goodman cannot notate music. This touches upon yet another important distinction between rock and the musical theater: the former is ideologically rooted in oral tradition, and the latter is not. While composers from the popular music world who are not musically literate—Frank Wildhorn, for example— are slowly becoming more present in the musical theater, they remain exceptions to the rule. Goodman's compositional process was thus distinctive: he wrote the entire score in his head before committing a version to tape.[27]

In an attempt to compensate for his inability to put notes to paper, Goodman enlisted the help of Richard Barone, a popular music composer, producer, and musician, who became *Bright Light*'s musical director. Yet, Barone was no more adept at notating music than Goodman. Rather, he orchestrated the show by taping Goodman as he played through the musical, and then overdubbing the instrumental parts.[28]

While such practices might be the norm in the popular music realm, the lack of written music proved problematic; Barone's tape proved useless when the time came to teach the score to the cast and pit band of *Bright Lights*. Thus, Joe McGinty, the musically literate director of the concert series Loser's Lounge, was brought in as the conductor. During the first weeks of rehearsal for the musical, McGinty worked furiously to transcribe the score from tape to paper.[29]

The number of people working on the score of *Bright Lights* was no more challenging than the unorthodox approach Barone took as musical director. Interested in attaining the best sound for each number, Barone had a habit of tinkering with the tempi and instrumentation of songs, even after the director had set them.[30] While such practices may be expected of a studio producer, they proved confusing and annoying to the cast and crew during rehearsals for the musical theater production.

A greater problem lay in working with Goodman, who was not only the writer of *Bright Lights*, but also a featured actor. Goodman's presence in his own piece was the result of decisions made by the creative team, who hoped to effectively translate the novel's distinctive voice for the stage. Set in New York City in the early 1980s, *Bright Lights, Big City* is narrated by an unnamed young writer, whose mother has recently died and whose wife, a successful model, has even more recently left him for another man. The narrator enters a self-destructive spiral of drinking, drug abuse, and club-hopping, which costs him his job at a respected literary magazine. The novel, which follows the writer from the depths of Gatsbian despair to emotional health, is distinctive because it is one of very few written in the second-person singular: the protagonist addresses himself throughout as "you." In the project's early stages, it was decided that Goodman would serve as the alter-ego to the main character, thereby bringing the novel's distinctive voice to the stage. Goodman thus became a guitar strumming narrator who "delivers most of the novel's descriptive passages and conveys unwelcome insights to the protagonist."[31]

Goodman's acting abilities, however, proved problematic. During rehearsals and through the run of the show, he regularly demonstrated an unwillingness or inability to shed qualities that befit rock musicians, but are considered inappropriate in the theater. Onstage for most of the musical, Goodman had a penchant for verbal and musical improvisation, which frequently threw off the rest of the company.[32] He also regularly failed to follow stage directions. Accustomed to a slightly greater degree of improvisational leeway after years of performing as a solo singer-songwriter, Goodman admitted that acting was much too repetitive for his taste.[33] Yet, doing the same things in the same way each night is important in the theater world, where company members rely on one another for cues. As assistant director Leigh Silverman remembers:

> There is a discipline that goes along with the theater that has to do with consistency and a focus on keeping your performance fresh every night, but keeping it exactly the same. Paul [didn't] understand that. He [did] something different every night. For everything.[34]

Goodman's habit of ignoring his lines and blocking thus frustrated the rest of the company, members of which regularly complained about his onstage behavior during the run of the show.[35]

Finally, while a singer-songwriter-musician in the rock realm is allowed the luxury of a distinctive performing style, Goodman's flair for the dramatic did not translate onto the musical theater stage. With his shaggy mop of hair, reedy and occasionally unintelligible singing style, and penchant for black nail polish, Goodman often seemed to occupy a different stage from the rest of the obviously trained, carefully groomed cast.

When *Bright Lights* opened on 24 February 1999, it was typically ignored by rock critics and harshly panned by theater critics. Most compared it unfavorably with NYTW's previous rock musical, *Rent*, and Goodman's presence was almost universally cited as the musical's biggest shortcoming. For example, Peter Marks wrote in the *New York Times* that Goodman was so miscast as to be "pointless."[36]

While critical and commercial reception do not always reflect one another, they did in this case. Ticket sales for *Bright Lights* slumped after the reviews came out, and the negative reactions to the show only worked to make Goodman's onstage behavior even more idiosyncratic.[37] *Bright Lights* closed on 21 March 1999, less than a month after it opened.[38]

One might argue that Goodman's inability to meld with the rest of the cast was not his fault, but that of the creative staff who attempted to force him into the mold of a professional actor. As one cast member argued:

> Paul was neither here nor there. Either use him like he is, or don't use him at all. Because he's not an actor. And his energy you could really harness, or you should leave it out. He ended up in the middle. They tried to take away that he was eccentric, but a little bit crept out, so then people had the reaction of, "What's that? Who's that? He's some Scottish guy on the stage."[39]

In the rock realm, authenticity is bound up with the notion of a songwriter performing his or her own music. But the singer-songwriter is comparatively nonexistent in the musical theater, where to perform one's own music onstage—especially poorly—can be perceived as the epitome of egotism. While Goodman's behavior in the musical was rejected as inappropriate by theater critics, spectators, and fellow members of the company, one might argue that the only thing wrong with Goodman's performance was the setting.

Like Goodman, the rock musician, composer, and lyricist Stephen Trask, who teamed with stage actor John Cameron Mitchell to create the rock musical *Hedwig and the Angry Inch*, experienced difficulties in trying to unite rock and the musical theater. This is somewhat surprising, since *Hedwig* was far more successful than *Bright Lights*. After opening at the Jane Street Theatre on 14 February 1998, *Hedwig* enjoyed a long run, was praised by both theater and rock critics, and has since been mounted in cities around the world and adapted into a film that won awards at the Sundance Film Festival before opening nationwide in 2001.

In many respects, *Hedwig* offers the most successful blend of rock and musical theater elements to date, in part because the creators made no attempt to fully integrate the divergent genres, but instead allowed them to exist side by side. More a monologue with songs than a fully-fledged musical, *Hedwig*—which focuses on a young East German man who is left, after a botched sex-change operation, with an unsightly mound of flesh where his penis had been (hence the "Angry Inch" of the title)—borrows from Plato's *Symposium* in depicting its title character's search for love and emotional completion.

Set in a bar where Hedwig and his/her band (also called the Angry Inch) are ostensibly playing, Hedwig delivers the monologue as a series of drunken ramblings between songs, which are far more aggressively amplified and rendered than most songs on the theatrical stage. Freed from narrative trappings, in that they are not used to further the plot, the songs punctuate the title character's changing moods. In structuring the show this way, Mitchell and Trask sidestepped a number of problems "by saying, 'You're coming to a gig to see a singer and her band,' so you don't have to pretend they're not singing to you. . . . T]he narrative comes as onstage patter between songs, as if you're watching a concert. . . . [The] structure sets up the freedom to have it feel like an authentic rock event."[40]

The show's careful balance of rock and musical theater elements is a result of the unique collaboration between its creators. Mitchell and Trask met on a flight to Los Angeles, and after discovering that they had mutual passions (rock and the theater) and dislikes (all extant rock musicals), they decided to collaborate on "a play that translated the visceral charge of live rock into theater that wasn't watered down or sanitized."[41] Mitchell developed the title character, while Trask wrote music and lyrics. As the piece developed, Trask's rock band, Cheater, was enlisted to play the Angry Inch.

An early version of *Hedwig* enjoyed a short run at New York's Westbeth Theatre Center in 1997, after which its creators began to shop for a more permanent venue.[42] Unable to find a site that offered a proper mix of theater and nightclub aesthetics, Mitchell finally stumbled upon the dilapidated Jane Street Theatre in the Hotel Riverview, a former seaman's hotel and current haven for backpackers, located in the far reaches of the West Village.[43]

The rundown, hard-to-reach location hurt ticket sales before the reviews came out, but ultimately served the production well. Accepted venues for rock concerts may be far larger than those for the musical theater—it is, after all, more likely that one would see the Rolling Stones at Shea Stadium than the cast of *Rent*—the musical theater's presentational style tends to drive a wedge between performer and audience that is not as pronounced in rock performance.[44] As a result, rock musicals that premiere on Broadway tend to be less successful than those that first open in smaller theaters before moving to Broadway, where the presentational style is deeply engrained: because intimacy is easier to cultivate in smaller, alternative performance spaces, theaters

Off Broadway have proven more nurturing than those on Broadway for staged rock musicals. The Jane Street Theater's sense of exclusiveness and intimacy thus benefited *Hedwig*. As press agent Tom D'Ambrosio remembers, once it had opened to strong reviews, "the location didn't stand in your way of going, and if it did, then you were square and that's *your* problem."[45]

Adding further to the sense of exclusiveness that *Hedwig* exuded was the interest that many rock musicians took in the show. As noted above, the rock press took interest in the show after Pete Townshend attended a performance; interest increased with the attendance of denizens like David Bowie, Lou Reed, Laurie Anderson, Bob Mould, and Joey Ramone.[46] These celebrities' presence at performances helped add to *Hedwig*'s legitimacy in the rock press, as well as among rock fans: one audience member, who noted that he typically "avoids rock musicals like the plague," stated that "*Hedwig* . . . is the only musical I've ever seen that made me want to stand up, raise my fist, and yell."[47]

For all its success, however, *Hedwig* was not without internal complications. In the first place, although *Hedwig* arguably captured the spirit of live rock more competently than most rock musicals, the performances were nevertheless compromised. Trask and his band were onstage for the entire show, but remained largely silent and motionless during the lengthy segments of monologue between songs. Given little to do during these interludes, the band often seemed stiff, uncomfortable, and bored. These feelings were compounded by the fact that when they were playing, the band members had to take precautions so as not to distract attention from the title character: careful not to disrupt the mix, which was amped at lower levels than those at rock clubs tend to be, the band had to learn to play in a way that Trask remembers was "unnatural" and "terribly constraining."[48]

Second, Trask was given short shrift in the media. Tom D'Ambrosio remembers that "for a rock musical, all anybody cared about was John Cameron Mitchell from a press point of view."[49] The flamboyant, quick-witted Mitchell-as-Hedwig likely proved somewhat more appealing, from a media perspective, than Trask, who played a less ostentatious role onstage as the bandleader. Although he was cited as an "authentic" rock musician who composed an "authentic" score, even the rock press ultimately showed more interest in Mitchell.[50] Such media emphasis is typical of the musical theater: lead actors often receive more attention than those in supportive roles. Yet, the opposite

is usually the case in the rock world, where performers are traditionally lauded for their musicianship and the originality of their
songwriting.

Making matters worse for Trask was the fact that the cast recording of *Hedwig* failed to cross over into the rock market. After *Hedwig*
opened, Trask began negotiations over the cast album, and eventually
signed with Atlantic Records. Aware that most cast albums are recorded in one day, which struck him as "a ridiculous way of recording,"
Trask grew interested in creating a concept album that would stand
apart from the show. He enlisted indie-rock producer Brad Wood and
commenced work on the project. The result was a cast recording put
together in a studio, more in the manner of a rock album.[51]

Hoping that the cast recording would move beyond its musical
theater moorings, personnel at Atlantic Records attempted to market it
to a broad audience.[52] Such efforts initially seemed to pay off: like the
show itself, the cast recording earned rare accolades in the rock press.
In keeping with the habit rock critics have of justifying what little
attention they give to rock musicals, Barry Walters of *Rolling Stone*
wrote that while "rock rarely makes it to the theatrical stage with balls
intact," the *Hedwig* album "makes for the brainiest, catchiest concept
album since Liz Phair's *Exile in Guyville*."[53] The musical even enjoyed
airplay on a rock radio station, which is rare: the late-night DJ Vin
Scelsa, then broadcasting from WNEW-FM in New York, invited the
cast of *Hedwig* to perform on his show, mentioned the production frequently during broadcasts, and played songs from the recording.[54]

The recording nevertheless failed to cross over to a larger market.
Cerveris argues that the fault lies with divisions imposed by a music
industry obsessed with target audiences and niche marketing: "[it]
comes down to the music business' resistance of anything performance
oriented, or its distrust of it. So if anything comes from the theatre, it's
automatically fake, artificial."[55] In the end, the attempts that were made
to divorce the songs from the show seemed futile: the recording never
even made it to the "popular music" section of most major record stores.
Rather, it was grouped with other musicals in the "soundtrack" section.

Although, unlike Goodman, his rock musical was embraced by
the theater world and awarded an unprecedented amount of respect by
rock critics, Trask found his dreams oddly compromised. His songs
ultimately failed to transcend their status as parts of the score to a
successful Off Broadway production, and his dreams of becoming a

rock star were quashed when his songs became closely associated with a fictional character. There is no aesthetic reason why the show's music, with its catchy hooks, moody lyrics, and aggressive delivery should not have won the interest of rock audiences. Yet, by nature of its association with the musical theater, *Hedwig* became a specialty item that was tolerated and even respected, but ultimately never fully embraced in the rock world.

The differences between Paul Scott Goodman and Stephen Trask are thus not as vast as their experiences might make them seem. Both experienced similar difficulties in crossing from the rock to the theater realm. These difficulties reflect inherent tensions between the two worlds, especially those that arise when rock's connection to authenticity fails to resonate within the theatrical sphere. Goodman's passion for the spontaneous, the improvisational, and the rebellious ultimately hurt him in a setting where such qualities are viewed as laughably unprofessional. Trask and his band made the transition from one camp to the other more gracefully, but their success came at a price: Cheater went from laboring in obscurity as an actual rock band to winning praise as the fake Angry Inch, and had to drastically alter their onstage behavior and performance style in the process. Trask's personal goals were similarly compromised: while he joked publicly that "it's weird after trying to be a rock star myself to be in the Dave Stewart half of this very Eurythmics relationship,"[56] he acknowledged privately that his success in the musical theater realm did not help him to feel like less of a failure in the rock realm.[57]

Resistance to staged rock musicals emanates from both the rock and theater realms, yet members of each camp tend to dismiss rock musicals as "bad" for conflicting reasons. Rock resists absorption by the musical theater because of its aesthetics and ideology, which include an emphasis on loud volumes and an interest in the aggressive- or extreme-sounding; performance styles that are decidedly less formal than those typical of the musical theater; a lack of interest in the narrative structure to which the musical theater closely adheres; and a strong interest in maintaining a veneer of artistic authenticity and anti-commercialism, despite evidence to the contrary. Yet, the ways in which these aesthetics and ideologies are manifested by rock's practitioners are often dismissed as unprofessional in the musical theater realm.

While divergent aesthetics, performance styles, and ideologies certainly work against attempts to merge rock and the American musical, it is possible that the biggest problem inherent in attaining such a union lies in the fact that the popular music world tends to be ephemeral and forward-looking, while the musical theater realm seems forever to be trying to step forward with one foot while keeping the other rooted in its canonized, celebrated past. A problem that the musical and its surrounding industry face, then, is how to rectify its history with its need to remain fresh and relevant. The current solution—emulating trends in the dominant popular culture—can also be a problem: as long as it continues to chase aesthetic developments introduced by more dominant media, the American musical will forever be seen as derivative and anachronistic, and Broadway, its spiritual home, will forever be saddled with its nickname, "the Fabulous Invalid." This is especially the case since stage musicals often take many years to be produced, and thus run the risk of appealing to audiences with stylistic trends that have long since passed out of the dominant popular culture. The resultant perception of the American musical as a corny and aging art form is, perhaps, even more of a deterrent to those interested in creating rock musicals than is their divergence in aesthetics or ideology.

NOTES

1.　See, for example Frith, Simon. "The Magic That Can Set You Free: The Ideology of Folk and the Myth of the Rock Community." *Popular Music* I. Edited by Richard Middleton and David Horn. Cambridge: Press Syndicate of the University of Cambridge, 1981; Sanjek, David. "Pleasure and Principles: Issues of Authenticity in the Analysis of Rock 'n' Roll." *Tracking* 4 no. 2 (1992); Goodman, Fred. *The Mansion on the Hill: Dylan, Young, Geffen, Springsteen, and the Head-on Collision of Rock and Commerce*. New York: Vintage Books, 1998; and Gracyk, Theodore. "Valuing and Evaluating Popular Music." *The Journal of Aesthetics and Art Criticism* 57 no. 2 (1999).
2.　Gottfried, Martin. *Broadway Musicals*. New York: Abradale/Harry Abrams, 1984, 287. For early identification and discussion of the youth market, see "A Young $10 Billion Power: The US Teen-age Consumer Has Become a Major Factor in the Nation's Economy." *Life* magazine (31 August 1959), 78–84.
3.　Personal communication, 17 July 1998.
4.　Personal communication with rock critic Evelyn McDonnell, 30 September 1999.
5.　Fox, Margalit. "Not the Usual Broadway Crowd: Audience Who's Who at 'The Who's Tommy'" *Newsday*, 30 April 1993.
6.　Morehouse, Ward, III. "Who Killed 'Tommy'?" *New York Post*, 21 June 1995; Personal communication with Jujamcyn Creative Director Jack Viertel.
7.　Morehouse, Ward, III, "Who Killed 'Tommy'?"; DeCurtis, Anthony. "Opinion: Broadway Production of 'Tommy'." *Rolling Stone*, 24 June 1993.
8.　Personal communication with theater historian Ken Mandelbaum, 3 August 1998.

9.   Bosworth, Patricia. "'Dude' . . . An $800,000 Disaster: Where Did They Go Wrong?" *New York Times*, 22 October 1972; Kerr, Walter. *"Via Galactica."* *New York Times*, 10 December 1972.

10. Orgill, Roxanne. "From Hard Facts Comes Comfortable Music." *New York Times*, 18 April 1999: 23.

11. Personal communication, 6 October 1998.

12. Frith, Simon. *Peforming Rites: On the Value of Popular Music*. Cambridge, MA: Harvard University Press, 1996: 216.

13. Frith, *Performing Rites* 207.

14. Ibid., 214.

15. Wild, David. "Who's on Broadway? Pete Townshend Discusses Bringing the Rock Opera to the Great White Way." *Rolling Stone*, 18 March 1993: 21.

16. Personal communication, 28 August 1998.

17. Personal communication with Don Summa, 6 October 1998, and Tom D'Ambrosio, 17 July 1998.

18. Personal communication, 28 August 1998.

19. Winer, Linda. "Time Warp Redux: 'Rocky Horror' Is Original Again, on Broadway." *Newsday*, 16 November 2000.

20. Rich, Frank. Capturing Rock-and-Roll and the Passions of 1969. The *New York Times*, 23 April 1993: C1.

21. Bessman, Jim. "On Stage: *Hedwig and the Angry Inch."* *Billboard* 10 no. 4 (1998): 66.

22. Fricke, David. "Sex & Drag & Rock & Roll: 'Hedwig and the Angry Inch' Is the First Rock Musical that Truly Rocks." *Rolling Stone*, 10 December 1998: 55.

23. Borow, Zev. "Glam Slam: The Star of the Hit Musical *Hedwig* Muses on Previous Rock Opuses." *Spin*, January 1999.

24. Personal communication with Paul Scott Goodman, 14 March 1999. The title of the musical omits the comma that appears in the book title.

25. Smith, Wendy. "Turning a Touchstone of the 80's Into a Musical for the 90's." *New York Times*, 21 February 1999: 14.

26. Nicola, program notes, 7.

27. Personal communication with Paul Scott Goodman, 14 March 1999.

28. Personal communication with Richard Barone, 25 March 1999.

29. Personal communication with Martha Donaldson, 15 January 1999.

30. Personal communication with stage manager Martha Donaldson, 25 March 1999.

31. Smith, Wendy. "Turning a Touchstone," 14.

32. Personal communication with Richard Barone, 25 March 1999.

33. Personal communication, 14 March 1999.

34. Personal communication, 11 March 1999.

35. Personal communication with stage manager Martha Donaldson, 25 March 1999.

36. Marks, Peter. "The Clubs! The Snorts! The Rhymes! (Last Resorts)." *New York Times*, 25 February 1999: 7.

37. Personal communication with Martha Donaldson, 25 March 1999.

38. Personal communication with Leigh Silverman, 11 March 1999.

39. Personal communication with Annmarie Milazzo, 31 March 1999.

40. Kendt, Rob. "Rocks in His Hedwig: Most Rock Musicals Are a Drag—Actor/ Singer Michael Cerveris Headlines Ones That Actually Rock." *Backstage West*, 21 October 1999.

41. Eisenbach, Helen. "Pretty Boy: Cavorting Onstage in Pumps and a Fright Wig, John Cameron Mitchell Has Become One of the City's Most Wanted Leading Men." *New York Magazine*, 11 May 1998.

42. McDonnell, Evelyn. "The Angry Inch Monologues: How John Cameron Mitchell and Stephen Trask Created *Hedwig*, the Rockingest Musical Since Nothing." *The Village Voice*, 10 March 1998: 51.

43. Marks, Peter. "Briefly, a New Hedwig, but the Same Self-Discovery." *New York Times*, 24 July 1998.

44. Representational and presentational theater styles differ in the following ways: With representational theater, or realism, an attempt is made to create an illusion of real life. The presentational style features characters, plot, and dialogue that are clearly fictitious. Acting styles in presentational theater are thus more exaggerated, and the expression of emotions more formulaic when compared with representational theater. While the distinction between the styles is not absolute, and the American musical borrows from representational theater, it is primarily a presentational genre.

45. Personal communication, 17 July 1998.

46. Personal communication with Stephen Trask, 29 July 1998; personal communication with Tom D'Ambrosio, 17 July 1998.

47. Personal communication with Jacob M. Rye, 23 June 2001.

48. Personal communication, 29 July 1998.

49. Personal communication, 17 July 1998.

50. See for example Fricke, David, "Sex & Drag & Rock & Roll."

51. Dansby, Andrew. "Hedwig Unleashed: The Creators of the Groundbreaking Glam Rock-Opera Are Getting Miles Out of Their Angry Little Inch." *Rolling Stone*, 18 February 1999; personal communication with Stephen Trask, 29 July 1998.

52. Galtney, Smith. "Double Fantasy: Can an Off Broadway Musical About a Transsexual Prostitute Become a Classic Rock Album?" *Time Out New York*, January 28–February 4, 1999: 13.

53. Walters, Barry. "*Hedwig and the Angry Inch*: Original Cast Recording." *Rolling Stone*, 18 February 1999: 58.

54. Personal communication with Stephen Trask, 29 July 1998; Broadcast of Vin Scelsa's *Idiot's Delight*, 7 February 1999, 10:00 p.m.

55. Kendt, "Rocks in His Hedwig."

56. McDonnell, Evelyn. "The Angry Inch Monologues."

57. Personal communication with Evelyn McDonnell, 30 September 1999; personal communication with Stephen Trask, 29 July 1998.

REFERENCES

Bessman, J. 1998. On stage: *Hedwig and the Angry Inch. Billboard* 10, no. 4: 66.

Borow, Z. 1999. Glam slam: The star of the hit musical *Hedwig* muses on previous rock opuses. *Spin*, January.

Dansby, A. 1999. Hedwig unleashed: The creators of the groundbreaking glam rock-opera are getting miles out of their angry little inch. *Rolling Stone*, 18 February.

DeCurtis, A. 1993. Opinion: Broadway production of Tommy. *Rolling Stone*, 24 June.

Eisenbach, H. 1998. Pretty boy: Cavorting onstage in pumps and a fright wig, John Cameron Mitchell has become one of the city's most wanted leading men. *New York Magazine*, 11 May.

Fox, M. 1993. Not the usual Broadway crowd: Audience who's who at "The Who's Tommy." *Newsday*, 30 April.

Fricke, D. 1998. Sex & Drag & Rock & Roll: 'Hedwig and the Angry Inch' is the first rock musical that truly rocks. *Rolling Stone*, 10 December.

Frith, S. 1981. "The magic that can set you free": The ideology of folk and the myth of the rock community. *Popular Music* I, eds. R. Middleton and D. Horn. Cambridge: Press Syndicate of the University of Cambridge.

———— 1996. *Peforming rites: On the value of popular music.* Cambridge: Harvard University Press.

Galtney, S. 1999. Double fantasy: Can an Off Broadway musical about a transsexual prostitute become a classic rock album? *Time Out New York,* January 28–February 4.

Gottfried, M. 1984. *Broadway musicals.* New York: Abradale/Harry Abrams, 287.

Kendt, R. 1999. Rocks in his Hedwig: Most rock musicals are a drag—actor/singer Michael Cerveris headlines ones that actually rock. *Backstage West*, 21 October 1999.

Nicola, J. 1999. Program notes for *Bright Lights Big City.* January–March.

Marks, P. 1999. The clubs! The snorts! The rhymes! (Last Resorts). *New York Times*, 25 February.

McDonnell, E. 1998. The Angry Inch monologues: How John Cameron Mitchell and Stephen Trask created *Hedwig*, the rockingest musical since nothing. *The Village Voice*, 10 March.

Morehouse, W., III. 1995. Who killed 'Tommy'? *New York Post*, 21 June.

Orgill, R. 1999. From hard facts comes comfortable music. *New York Times*, 18 April.

Rich, F. 1993. Capturing rock-and-roll and the passions of 1969. *New York Times*, 23 April: C1.

Smith, W. 1999. Turning a touchstone of the 80's into a musical for the 90's. *New York Times*, 21 February.

Walters, B. 1999. *Hedwig and the Angry Inch*: Original cast recording. *Rolling Stone*, 18 February.

Wild, D. 1993. Who's on Broadway? Pete Townshend discusses bringing the rock opera to the great white way. *Rolling Stone*, 18 March: 21.

Winer, L. 2000. Time warp redux: "Rocky Horror" is original again, on Broadway." *Newsday*, 16 November.

PART IV

Historical Afterthought

16
Trivial Music (Trivialmusik)
"Preface" and "Trivial Music and Aesthetic Judgment"[1]

CARL DAHLHAUS

translated by Uli Sailer

Introductory Comments by Walter Frisch

*arl Dahlhaus (1928–1989) was one of the most prolific histori-
cal musicologists working in the second half of the twentieth
century, and also probably the most influential. His impact on
Anglo American scholarship grew exponentially as his major works,
all written in German, were translated beginning in the 1970s.
Dahlhaus became admired for his penetrating insights into musical
aesthetics, historiography, the history of music theory, and the music
of Beethoven, Wagner, and Schoenberg.*

 *Dahlhaus worked for most of his career in Berlin, the geographi-
cally and ideologically circumscribed capital of cold-war West Germany, where he was Ordinarius at the Technische Universität. He died
just before the Berlin Wall fell. Much of his writing has as its goal to
rescue the music he cared most about—the music of the Western canon,
especially from Bach through Schoenberg—from the Marxist-Leninist
viewpoints which dominated East German scholarship in the 1960s
and 1970s, and which interpreted artworks through an overtly
sociopolitical lens. Dahlhaus drew his intellectual sustenance from a
wide range of German thinkers, including Hegel, Max Weber, Theodor
Adorno, Hans-Georg Gadamer, Hans Robert Jauss, and Jürgen
Habermas.*

 *Dahlhaus's magnum opus was his history of nineteenth-century
music, which he completed in 1980 and which appeared in English as*
Nineteenth-Century Music *in 1989 (translated by J. Bradford Robinson;
University of California Press). In one sense, most of his other earlier*

writings were preparatory to that work, each addressing a problem that he felt he needed to solve—or broaching a perspective he wanted to master—before tackling a large-scale history in a responsible manner. The central books are: Esthetics of Music *(1967; Eng. trans. 1982),* Analysis and Value Judgment *(1970; Eng. trans. 1983), and* Foundations of Music History *(1977; Eng. trans. 1983).*

The broad cultural sweep of Dahlhaus's writings, together with their philosophical rigor, restored to musicology an intellectual dimension that had been largely eclipsed since about 1950 (at least in the United States), when much scholarship had fallen into what has been characterized by Joseph Kerman as a "positivist" phase. Dahlhaus's articles and books came as gusts of fresh air at a time when musicologists often worked in tiny corners of music history, with what were seen by some as narrowly specialized philological concerns.

Dahlhaus's deeply dialectical mode of thought can make his writing difficult to understand. He was rarely interested in finding a single truth, or in establishing historical facts. He sought rather to characterize a phenomenon or period through a juxtaposition of opposing notions. With the concept of "trivial" music, Dahlhaus confronts head-on the dichotomy between high and low art, which he felt had to be addressed by any music historian working on the nineteenth century, when popular genres occupied an enormous slice of what he calls the "musical reality."

In the essays included here, Dahlhaus provides no survey or outline of trivial music in the nineteenth century, but instead refracts the concept into many facets. Dahlhaus seems to work with two broad categories of trivial music. One is based on social function or origin: trivial music is the "repertoire of dance halls and proms, of salons and variétés." This is the music that Heinrich Besseler dubbed umgangsmäßig (roughly, suited to its context). Second, the label of trivial music can also be applied to melodies by opera composers like Meyerbeer, Hérold, and Pacini. These meet the criterion of "emphasizing detail without being original"; they are mechanical, or, to paraphrase Wagner on Meyerbeer, reduce music to "effects without causes."

Dahlhaus understands that "bad" music, whether popular in origin or banal in taste (or both), cannot be analyzed with the same techniques that one does the music of Beethoven. How to make appropriate "aesthetic judgment" is for Dahlhaus the key issue, and is often tantamout to assessing value. Throughout these essays, we sense

Dahlhaus constantly (and often, it seems, heroically) seeking to balance the aesthetic with other forces coming from "outside" the music— from history, politics, religion, or society. Trivial music offered him one opportunity to explore those dialectics.

Carl Dahlhaus: Preface[2]

The nineteenth century's trivial music, the repertoire of dance halls and proms, of salons and varietés, is as well-known to us as it is unknown. The fact that everybody knows more or less what to expect from titles like *Alpenglühn* [The shining of the Alps], *Cloches du monastère* [Bells of the monastery] or *Gebet einer Jungfrau* [A virgin's prayer] has impeded reflection about the nature and the mysterious popularity of such creations. Also, the sheer quantity and monotony of the musically banal have a paralyzing effect. No matter how colorfully alluring this music may present itself to the fleeting glance—it reaches from the vulgar *Gassenhauer*[3] to the stilted salon piece, and from the disciplining march to the anarchic cancan—the discovery of the stereotypical nature of its musical means is sobering. Indeed, Hans Mersmann described the banal as music whose compositional technique defies analysis.[4]

The word "trivial music" [*trivialmusik*] implies an aesthetic judgment that may be suspicious to historians or sociologists because it smacks of prejudice. The principle of "impartiality" suggests the use of a neutral term; and there is no lack of alternatives. More common than "trivial music" are expressions like entertainment music, *gebrauchs-* or *umgangsmusik*,[5] light and popular music. Yet, none of the expressions that are less strongly characterized by intellectual arrogance than "trivial music" is more appropriate to the phenomenon at hand. To entertain was the function of the eighteenth century's *divertimenti*, but nobody would consider these equivalent to the nineteenth century's salon pieces. While neutral, the term *gebrauchs-* or *umgangsmusik* is too comprehensive and thus unspecific; it includes all liturgical church music. It would be more appropriate to speak of "light music"; yet that expression suggests a lightheartedness that is not typical of all products of trivial music—a sphere in which sentimentality plays no smaller role than that kind of merriness which, from a distance, is so disturbing. Finally, it is hardly necessary to spell out the fact that the concept of the popular is too vague a criterion: Not only works of unspeakable banality, but even some works [or at least fragments of] great music are popular—and, vice versa, most of the rubbish that is produced lacks success just like the majority of those works claiming to be art.

The ambivalence of the term "trivial music," expressing a difference both in kind and in quality towards works of an artistic nature, may be disturbing for logicians, yet it is adequate for the characteristics of the music at hand. In general: The music that Heinrich Besseler called *umgangsmäßig* tends toward the banal in the nineteenth century. On the one hand, nobody would deny that marches, *couplets*[6] and even *gassenhauer* exhibit specific qualities that distinguish a small number of successful creations from the mass of failed ones; mere advertising, poorly developed in the nineteenth century anyways, does not suffice to impose a piece on an audience. First, it is uncertain whether the properties of a hit—which by the way are astonishingly hard to determine—should be considered aesthetic. Second, this categorical split (which is simultaneously experienced as a qualitative split) is a historical and socio-psychological fact—regardless of which perspective one takes: Whether low music is brushed aside as bad or, vice versa, high music as pretentious, is unimportant. Both judgments are based on the separation of these areas that shape concert programs and musical listening. A rare degree of independence from established reaction patterns would be necessary in order to allow one to perceive the triviality of a string quartet or the artistic nature of a *couplet*.

Low music has existed at all times, yet its earlier stages of development are separated from the trivial music of the late eighteenth and the nineteenth century by a qualitative leap that is apparent in the ways judgments about this scorned genre are justified. Up until the early eighteenth century, three motivations drove polemics against the practices exercised in the musical *souterrain*, among beer fiddlers[7] and mendicant musicians: Musically, it was their breach of rules, morally, their alluring indecency and socially, their low status that triggered contempt, whether genuine or feigned. The privileged musician was outraged by the disenfranchised one, the guild-shaped craftsman by the outsider who was suspected of bungling even if he was a virtuoso. These ambivalent feelings, the mixture of fascination and contempt with which itinerant musicians were confronted, are still apparent in the nineteenth century's criticism of virtuosity.

One may, from two centuries of distance, doubt the justification of judgments about low, unprivileged music. One characteristic, however, that distinguishes earlier criteria—to their advantage—from those of the nineteenth century, is that they were firm and unequivocal. Rules of the craft and social stratifications were rough, yet on secure legal grounds. In contrast, under the rule of the aesthetic criteria that gained acceptance in the late eighteenth century, judgments were increasingly in danger of becoming vague and intangible. The concept of art of Romantic theory became the highest authority. Along with low music, it also excluded functional music; and any functional music that is disdained tends to indeed become as lousy as it had been presupposed to be in the first place. The reproach it faced was not that it broke the rules, but that it was epigonic and prosaic. The concept, however, during the aesthetic epoch that brings together functional and low music, is "trivial." Trivial music is an historical category.

1.   In terms of stylistic history, it is based, according to Eva Eggli, on two phenomena that came into existence independently, but then grew into one: sentimentalism and the discovery that modern compositional technique—predominant from around 1730—could be mechanized. The eighteenth century's composed or (on the clavichord) improvised "confessions from the heart" are distinct from the ars movendi of musical rhetoric—the tradition of which extends up to Bach—by means of their emphasis on naturalness and immediate experience, as well as their contempt, or denial, of the artificial. Johann Mattheson writes in his 1739 *Vollkommener Capellmeister* that music is the art which "should, through the tools of the ears, please the sense of hearing that lives in the soul and touch and stir the heart or the emotions." "Touching" [*Rührung*], an expression in which sensual and emotional factors converge, was the key word of popular music aesthetics. At the same time, however, recipes for the composition of dances were published for the benefit of ambitious amateurs: polonaises and minuets could be pieced together arbitrarily from tables consisting of prefabricated measure-long motives. These mechanical practices, however naive, are indicative of a characteristic of eighteenth century compositional technique: the temptation to fall back into a second primitivity. Melodies are often nothing more than paraphrases of chords, the number of which has been reduced to two: tonic and dominant.

Trivial music has, as a paradoxical crossing, been the outcome of the eighteenth century's extreme tendencies, sentimentalism and mechanization. It is shallow, yet does not do away with the pretense to be expressive; it wants to be understood immediately and, thus, remains fully within the narrowest limits of convention while attempting to appear as spontaneous outburst; it presents itself as intentional and instinctive, artificial and natural at the same time. The banal masks itself as poetry—even if it may be merely by means of a title—because the effects of the poetic in a world that becomes increasingly prosaic have been recognized.

However, an interpretation that denounces trivial music as mere deception would be insufficient. While the mechanics that pursue the stirring of emotions are half-hidden, they are at the same time half-visible. And the poetic titles are understood, by silent consensus, to be framed with imaginary quotation marks. Expressing it with some exaggeration: the listener may enjoy and contempt simultaneously. He is spared the self-denial required by great art; he feels superior to the music. Cynicism, relying on sentimentality, is answered by a sentimentality that may at any time switch over into cynicism.

2.   As previously mentioned, breaches of rules contradict the Romantic concept of art less than the worn out and banal does. An artistic sensibility whose highest authority is the concept of the poetic, does not struggle against manifest technical deficiencies of the composition—however irksome these may often be—but against aesthetic shortcomings that are hard to pin down. Triviality hurts taste, which is the aesthetic equivalent to social sense of tact and against whose judgments there is no appeal. Triviality is a fact that relates less to the musical profession than to aesthetic reflection—i.e., to a reflection that is required of the composer as long as he claims the title of tone poet.

It seems that Robert Schumann was one of the first people to realize that the existence and dissemination of a music that is not badly composed in a technical sense, yet that still cannot be considered art, is an aesthetic problem. The diametrical opposition of "poetry" and "prose"—of fundamental importance to his aesthetics—expresses this insight in the language of Jean Paul. Schumann refers to the "mantellied" *Schier dreißig Jahre bist du alt* [You're almost thirty years of age][8] as prosaic; musical prose is then nothing else but trivial music. In the *Neue Zeitschrift für Musik* he writes that the decade from 1820 to 1830 had been a time "when half the musical world pondered over Beethoven, while the other half lived for the day." Music breaks apart into two areas; that of art, and in Schumann's words, that of the "Juste-Milieu."[9]

Poetic music, the contrasting foil of trivial music, presupposes originality. The employment of musical formulae and topoi, legitimate in the early eighteenth century, became suspect in the late eighteenth century. Rather than providing prestige, traditionalism (i.e., reference to models) aroused the suspicion of being a mask behind which epigones sought to hide their weakness. The origins of the idea of originality in intellectual and social history are so well-known that there is no need to restate them here. It should be mentioned, though, that immanently musical, compositional reasons are, in fact, possible. Speaking in rough formulae, a shift in emphasis from counterpoint to harmony and from vertical construction to melody is characteristic to the development of composition in the eighteenth century. It became easier than ever to master the rudiments of music, yet artificial composition became harder in the same measure. The simplicity of compositional fundamentals, of harmonic models and phrase construction, meant that originality in melodic and rhythmic detail, as well as in the relationship of the parts to each other and to the whole, was necessary in order to avoid monotony. Those who mastered no more than the basics described in Mattheson's *Vollkommener Capellmeister* ultimately succumbed to banality. The difference between the works of Haydn and Pleyel, apparently small, is decisive.

3.   Schumann also called the "Juste-Milieu" composers (whom he despised) as "moderns" that fulfill the needs of the day—in contrast to the "reactionaries" or "classics" who are backward-looking, and the "romantics," who are directed towards the future. "Modern" in 1830 meant "to be in keeping with the times," or pejoratively speaking: subject to fashion—the latter, however, was justified and praised in its fleetingness and contingency by none less than Baudelaire.

That trivial music is linked to the present distinguishes it, according to a widely held opinion, from folk music, whose characteristic is survival: the tenacity with which melodies are passed on for decades or even centuries. The pattern is rough, it is not difficult to discover exceptions; and it is even possible that we are dealing with a difference in terms of the consciousnesses of time rather than with a difference, in principle, in terms of the actual lifespan of melodies. While folk music does not, from the outside, lack history, it still seems as if it were experienced in unbroken traditions, independent from the passing of time. That whatever is traded down is old means less that it wears the color of the past, than that it is taken for granted and thus reaches back into time immemorial. In contrast to this, the raison d'être of trivial music—classified by Schumann as "Juste-Milieu"—is to be contemporary and current in the awareness of its audience, or—expressed in the fashionable term for fashion—to be in keeping with the times. As soon as it becomes out-of-date, it is generally recognized and dismissed as trivial, in particular by the previous year's enthusiasts: nothing is more ridiculous than yesterday's fashion. The trivial reveals its nature the moment in which it looses its form of life, currency.

4.   The boundaries between the classes or strata of music are not fixed but permeable, so to speak. Musical triviality has sometimes (and not unjustly) been explained as trivialization, as solidification and descending of genres and compositional techniques. Yet the opposite development, ascendancy out of the musical *souterrain* into high literature is hardly rarer. The piano etude, a banal functional form for Cramer, has been ennobled by Chopin. And it seems as if Romantic opera had developed less as a reaction to classical opera than with reference to traditions that had previously been neglected.

5.   For centuries low music has been transmitted without notation. Only around 1750, and initially in England, did the wider dissemination of trivial music begin through print, reaching industrial dimensions in the nineteenth and twentieth centuries and triggering the interdependent mechanism of ever-increasing need and production. At the same time, the mass production of printed songs and romances, pseudo-virtuoso piano pieces, and opera arrangements would not have been possible without the eighteenth century's pedagogical efforts, laying the foundations of a musical culture that could then be industrially exploited and deprived of its humanitarian purpose.

Socio-psychological and economic motives coincided. Around 1800, piano playing and singing became status symbols that were quickly picked up even by the middle- and lower-bourgeoisie. "She should also play the piano," Hermann's father expects from an acceptable daughter-in-law in *Hermann und Dorothea*.[10] Still, it is difficult to attempt a more precise sociological description, to assign different types of music to certain classes or strata. Facing the challenge to formulate assumptions that initially sounded plausible as empirically verifiable hypotheses, one quickly becomes embarrassed. In a sketch on the sociology of literature, Matthew Arnold defined—not without malice—the culture of the upper class as consumption for prestige, that of the middle class as trivial, and that of the lower class as rubbish. Yet, whether the audience that helped Brahms gain success represented a different class than the consumers of banal salon pieces is doubtful, and even improbable.

Similarly hard to disentangle, although more accessible by empirical methods, is the relationship between institutions and repertoires. During the century's second half, the separation of programs into those categories for which the language of radio has invented the ciphers *U* and *E* gradually gradually gained acceptance[11] during its first half, however, the same pieces were often played both at the opera and in the symphony concert, as well as at the fair and in the beer garden. And it was not the overture to the *Magic Flute* but that to *Zampa* under whose sign was united what custom had strictly divided. Trivial music is the distorted image of the universal music that the Enlightenment had dreamed of.

Carl Dahlhaus: Trivial Music and Aesthetic Judgment

The audience's favor is my only lottery.

—SIR WALTER SCOTT

That guy writes for money!

—LUDWIG VAN BEETHOVEN

I

"Trivial music" is not a neutral term. A judgment is inherent in the expression, and it is uncertain whether this judgment is legitimate, or whether it betrays a detached arrogance that misses the case at hand. Also, the judgment's meaning is ambiguous: it may be based primarily on moral grounds, or on aesthetic and compositional ones.

"Trivial" means "common, shallow, quotidian, worn." Hans Georg Nägeli was outraged in 1826 about a couple of measures in the *Jupiter Symphony* whose solemn simplicity he found to be worn out.

With regard to the first issue, the departure from the main key, pay
attention to measures 19–21 in the first Allegro and compare them
with measures 49–54; furthermore, do the same in the second section, measures 87–89 and 117–122. Such a mere alternating between a triad and a six-four-chord based on the exact same note is
already trivial per se, indeed, it is one of the most worn-out and
common commonplaces that typically is used only by the most
common composers in orchestral compositions to facilitate the
entrance of the French horns into the tutti. Here, however, this
triviality appears analogously twice (i.e., four times in the very
same piece).[12]

Nägeli's reproach is narrow-minded, yet telling. It betrays a way of
listening that focuses on minutiae and expects originality on the level
of detail. The simple harmonic formula appears banal to Nägeli because
he neglects the context that accounts for and justifies it. A lack of
connection, however, is characteristic of trivial music. And buried in
Nägeli's misguided judgment—distorted by his lack of understanding
of symphonic form—is an insight into the nature of the trivial: "Trivial"
refers to a music that emphasizes detail without being original.

When aesthetic judgment approaches the musical *souterrain*, it
is almost always morally colored or even morally determined. Ethical
arguments are excluded from the realm of the high arts as obsolete
and irrelevant, yet they survive within the low arts. With a kind of
indignation that the merely worn and miserable are hardly ever able to
induce, the assertion is made that trivial music is low and bad,[13] that—
as kitsch—it represents "evil in the value system of the arts."[14] It is the
primitively tempting and the garishly and colorfully enticing that is
rejected.[15] Religious distrust against profane pleasure, pragmatic distrust against absent-minded daydreams and an aesthetic sensitivity that
detests dullness and lack of differentiation combine in the verdict of
"trivial."

II

The judgment expressed by the term "trivial music" is not inviolable.
One could object that trivial music is functional music;[16] and that aesthetic and technical methods of analysis distort its meaning. This argument must be taken seriously. Examining functional music as if it
were autonomous is, so it seems, a contradiction in terms.

Yet, it is doubtful whether this contrast between functional object and art work constitutes a limit to analysis. The counterargument is that trivial music is a deficient mode of music that is simultaneously functional and artificial and represents the residue left over after autonomous music split from functional music.

According to Heinrich Besseler, the appropriate "way of accessing" functional music is "experiencing along" [*mitvollzug*].[17] He argues that functional, *umgangsmäßig* music is not perceived as an autonomous object, but as one partial aspect of an event that is determined by extra-musical factors. The behavior of a dancer is a case in point. "He does not listen, but behaves like an active, radiating subject, without explicitly perceiving the music as objectively existing. For him, it is not there as an object... In this case, we cannot speak of listening in a concert-like sense. The way the dancer is guided in his own musical-dancing activity might at most be called 'listening along' [*mithören*]."[18] An aesthetic judgment that presupposes distance would be inadequate in this case. Since music is not appreciated as an object, "the value of dance music as such is determined solely in terms of the extent to which it satisfies the demands of the society for which it is played."[19] Other kinds of music that we should consider *umgangsmäßig* (the opposition of *umgangsmäßig* and "objective" music is reminiscent of Heideggers distinction between "ready-to-hand" equipment and "present-at-hand" things) include work songs, sociable song—"the way of accessing the music is always by 'singing along' [*mitmachen*]"[20]—and liturgical music. "Here also, the music is merely decorum and serves to intensify a frame of mind that is produced by an extra-musical activity, praying, and the appropriate way of accessing this music is by "experiencing along" this fundamental frame of mind—it is 'praying along' [*mitbeten*]."[21]

Besseler takes advantage of the ambivalence inherent in the term *mitvollzug* ["experiencing along"][22] when, in one stroke, he arranges as opposites the passive nature of listening vis-à-vis the active nature of musical practice, the isolated individual vis-à-vis the collective group, and autonomous music vis-à-vis functional music. Yet the distinction between *umgangsmäßig* music and objective music—the antithesis between function and object by means of which all functional music evades aesthetic judgment, including the claim that it is trivial—is a construction of "ideal types" (whose heuristic value is undeniable) rather than a description of musical reality.

1. The functions of *umgangsmäßig* music, dance, sociability, and liturgy mentioned by Besseler are subject to historical change. In the seventeenth and eighteenth centuries, these functions unmistakably tend to be of a representative nature. As ceremonial, however, they become "objective," i.e., taken together with the music (that equally assumes a representative nature), they open up to aesthetic judgment. Provoking further historical analysis is the fact that categorizing liturgical music as art has not always been possible. An attempt to describe the prerequisites for the artistic character of church music would need to consider not only the history of liturgy and piety, but also the development of musical technique and aesthetic consciousness. While these different factors converge in fortunate periods of a musico-liturgical genre, they gape enormously in its destitute ones—it would be an illusion to expect that the "zeitgeist" maintained them all constantly at one level. Adjudicated with reference to its potential of being art, however, liturgical music which is not art falls prey to the verdict of triviality.

2. Pure functionality is an extreme case. A large part of musical reality lies between music that serves as mere contraption and is trite per se, and its polar opposite, strict autonomy. If, however, function and artistic nature are not mutually exclusive, then the functional examination of music must be complemented by the reverse procedure, i.e., by an analysis of functions from a musical perspective.

In rough and schematic terms, we can set out from the hypothesis that the artistic nature of functional music is endangered when, on the one hand, the function is of minor importance (its social status or, in Hegel's words, its "substantial content" is insignificant) and, on the other, when the purpose the music is supposed to serve dictates its confinement within narrow boundaries. Dance music is generally of poor content, and, at the same time, formally restricted by fixated rhythmic patterns, structure and scope—a fixation that equally affects melody and harmony. A church mass, in contrast, is elevated by the high status of its function, and is formally bound by nothing except the text and a few norms of church style which have rarely been rigorous.

For music whose value is purely functional, it may be that judgment based on aesthetic distance is irrelevant or misguided. However, if one is ready to accept that differences in functional status (such as that between dance and church masses) often coincide with musical differences, then taking the function into account will support, rather than thwart or wipe out, the aesthetic judgment that a piece of music is trivial.

3.   Functional music would be suitable as subject of an "art history without name," because of its indifference towards the origin of the melodies it is using. Methods of appropriation—parody and contrafactum, adaptation and arrangement—are more typical of it than those of creation; decisive is not the original purpose of a work, but its useability.[23]

This *umgangsmäßig* behavior becomes questionable when it touches music that is conceived as an autonomous work. Originality and integrity are fundamental concepts of nineteenth century aesthetics—the theory of art that presupposes and creates awareness for the distinction between autonomous and functional music. Using music in a manner that is unconcerned about the original form and meaning of a work is, according to aesthetic norms, a distortion or trivialization. Breaking pieces out of their context (the transformation of Schubert's *Lindenbaum* [The Linden Tree] into a folk song is a paradigmatic example), interfering with the musical text, and changing the orchestration are suspicious within the realm of aesthetics.

One could object that aesthetic judgments about *umgangsmäßig* music—the verdict "trivial"—are inadequate despite the fact that functional music lives parasitically off the works and means of autonomous music. And one could argue that a music's "mode of being" [*daseinsweise*] is decisive; that it would be inappropriate to judge one form of existence by the norms of another—and the inviolability of the text is undeniably a norm of "objective" music.

If followed through to its extreme, this thesis leaves no other recourse than to relinquish the concept of the identity of the musical work: Severed from its symphonic context and used as dance music, the *Minuet* of Mozart's *Symphony in E flat major* is no longer the "same" work; it is transformed into an anonymous piece of functional music. At the same time, the idea of identity is a fundamental premise for the aesthetic judgment that rejects adaptation as trivialization: In order to appear distorted, the *Minuet* must be the "same" and not "another" piece.

This conflict seems unresolvable, because the concept of "mode of being" [*daseinsweise*] is abstracted from functional music and that of the identical work from autonomous music. Thus there is no neutral authority. (It would be a mistake to think that "objectivity" could also only be explained as a "mode of being" [*daseinsweise*]. The identity of musical works cannot adequately be captured by "mode of being" [*daseinsweise*]; it is one of the fundamental categories of the aesthetic of autonomous music. The concept of "mode of being" [*daseinsweise*] thus cannot provide a solution.)

Umgangsmäßig music, according to Besseler,[24] is "more primordial" than "objective" music. If history, however, tends towards objectification, the aesthetic categories that have been developed for autonomous works ultimately take precedence. The method of publishing arrangements as texts that bear the name of the arranger just as if he were an author, expresses, even if unconsciously, the subjugation of functional music to the current norms of the aesthetic—i.e., to the concepts of identity, inviolability, and originality. *Umgangsmäßig* practices purport to be objective music; especially as parvenus, however, do they become trivial.

The fact that aesthetic norms prevailed as authorities for judgment, and that it seems justified to dismiss functional music as trivial, therefore needs to be understood historically. Aesthetic judgments are simultaneously historical.

4. In the case of some forms of music making, it is doubtful whether the *umgangsmäßig* behavior existed earlier than "objective" behavior. It does not seem as if "experiencing along" [*mitvollzug*] predated objectification, but rather that a unified way of listening predated their separation.

The musical recital, whether by a virtuoso or a mendicant musician—where the appeal of music turns into its negation, becoming a nuisance—is probably hardly less old than *umgangsmäßig* music making. "Going along" [*mitgehen*] with the performer's person and performance cannot be separated from the attention given to music as an object; and—as with storytelling—it would be inadequate to distinguish a primary factor from a secondary one. A musician submitting himself—as interpreter—to a work that has been transmitted in written form, is historically a recent phenomenon. However, this same split between object and presentation has also bred virtuosity, where music sinks to the level of an almost meaningless and intrinsically worthless substrate of technical and gestural-mimic display.

Sociable music making, the highest forms of which are the sixteenth century's multi-part song and the late eighteenth century's string quartet, has repeatedly been compared to a conversation, with which it equally shares the characteristic of it being indeterminable whether the subject is the substance of sociability or vice versa. It would be inadequate to try and distinguish between means and aim. The music as work, or the sociability as "mode of being" [*daseinsweise*], move into the foreground only if the state of vagueness that is actually characteristic for sociable music making is destroyed. (Relative to conversation, both a topic-oriented discussion and empty small talk whose function is exclusively social, are forms of decay.) The *kommerslied*,[25] described by Besseler as *umgangsmäßig*,[26] is a deficient, rather than an "original," mode of sociable music making.

Bach's Inventions are not études. (The idea, prevalent in the nineteenth century, to turn creations that are not art into artworks was alien to earlier centuries.) The étude was created by splitting the spielstück into "objective" works and *umgangsmäßig* exercises. The type of perception that accompanies practicing is "listening along" [*mithören*], and in the extreme case of a technically useful, yet musically absurd étude, it tends towards non-listening. "Listening along" [*mithören*], however—just like "going along" [*mitgehen*], in the case of a music that appears as mere function of sociability—represents a form of decay of musical perception.

The split of "experiencing along" [*mitvollzug*] from objectification is one of the origins of the musically banal. All that is left after autonomous music separates from functional music—the virtuoso piece, the kommerslied or the étude—decays into triviality.

5.   Trivial music is, to a considerable extent, functional music that presents itself as object, as a piece for a recital or concert; and this quid pro quo is one of the characteristics of the musically banal. The original function of a dance or march fades into an image of memory, yet even in its watered-down, secondary existence, it is at least as crucial for the piece's effect as the musical characteristics. The conclusion, however, that thus any aesthetic judgment is inadmissible would be misguided. For there are traces of functionality in autonomous music, too. Such traces are therefore not unique characteristics of a march that has been alienated for use as a concert piece, and they do not protect it from the verdict of triviality.

6.   Entertainment music serves either as a background for conversation or its replacement. "In Italy, the audience that gathered at the opera spent its evening with entertainment. Music sung on the stage was part of this entertainment, and one listened to it every once in a while during breaks in conversation. During conversation and while one paid visits to each other from box to box the music continued, and it did so with the same task that is assigned to *tafelmusik*[27] during large dinners, i.e., by means of its noise to encourage otherwise inhibited conversation to develop."[28] As filler of gaps in conversation or in the performance of an activity, entertainment music is neither *umgangsmäßig* and functional nor "objective" and autonomous. Too vague to be an object on the one hand, the state of absent-mindedness it presupposes and perpetuates appears as a caricature of "listening along" [*mithören*] on the other hand.

III

According to John H. Mueller, it is "wretchedly presumptuous" to judge trivial music on the basis of criteria abstracted from art works.[29] Those who believe in "absolute norms" are, says Mueller, metaphysically blinded (as if he were a Marxist, metaphysics assume the role of the supermundane justification of earthly privileges). In order to be science, he argues, aesthetics needs to become sociology; and as empirical social research, it is limited in its subject matter to irreducible "group norms."

Thus, the opinion that a work by Bach is "boring" and the judgment that a pop song is "primitive" are of equal value—as outcomes of two "group norms" of which neither may take precedence. The simple difference between judgments that are based on an understanding of the nature of an object, and those that are based on a lack of it, is suppressed and denied. This is the result of a peculiar crossing and interlocking of two basic premises: first, an aesthetic irrationalism that can solely understand music as release of emotions, not as intentional object, and second, a methodological empiricism that—out of fear of the uncertain—clings to "opinions" and "decisions" (the resolution to go listen to a concert or not) as its highest authority, and that suspects metaphysical excess as soon as the relationship of judgment and facts is addressed. What is most uncertain, vague "opinion," is regarded as most certain.

Mueller attributes universal validity to the empirical sociology of music. However, its aesthetic and methodological prerequisites or prejudices—the fact that it is caught up in a degenerated aesthetic of emotion, along with its origin out of market research—predestine it to a theory of trivial music.

1. Mueller links the method of the empirical sociology of music (i.e., the recording of opinions and decisions) with the claim to establish an aesthetic theory.[30] *Quaestio facti* and *quaestio iuris*[31] merge so that a judgment's degree of circulation turns out to be the only dependable legal source. However, this apparent impartiality is a deception. The descriptive sociologist highlights his lack of familiarity with art when dismissing musical works that cannot easily be fitted into the existing institutional system as "unsocial matter."[32]

2. The expression "quality" is equivocal; it means "make up" or "structure," yet also "value." Mueller exploits this ambiguity, first, in order to suppress the difference between judgments of taste that represent a "group norm" and cognitive judgments that refer to properties of a musical work, and second, in order to declare that both are mere projections. "We attribute to the art work qualities that in reality exist in our minds."[33] "Because of the human inclination to 'read into' the object what really spins around in our heads, it is often assumed that the value of a composition is inherent in it."[34] To Mueller, the thought that the relevance of a value judgment hinges on the adequacy of a judgment of fact—such as the ability of the judge to tell whether the parts of a work bear no relationship to one another, or are connected through developing variation—is alien. The concept of the qualified listener is printed in malicious quotation marks;[35] insight is denounced as hubris.

3. A qualitative analysis of musical opinions would impair the relevance of the statistical method, and in order to protect the claim of empirical sociology—to establish a scientific aesthetic—from doubt, Mueller is forced to deny the concept of the aesthetic object and reduce musical listening to the pattern of "stimulus and reaction." Thus, rather than an object that one can grasp or miss, music constitutes the design for an experiment. "Music history [is] a history of experiments that require the stamp of social approval."[36]

The dissolution of the aesthetic object into an ensemble of stimuli is one characteristic of trivial music; and a sociological theory that envisages musical works as experimental design, as provocations for "spontaneous enjoyment" and "aesthetic distraction,"[37] is nothing other than an apologia of the musically banal. It does not establish aesthetics as a rigorous science but disguises a "group norm." The accusation of empiricism against the metaphysical aesthetic—that of being an ideology—turns toward empiricism itself.

4. "The taste of small and financially weak minorities cannot last, except perhaps at the margins of society at large. Large musical systems of taste rest on material buttresses, embodied by enormous financial investments, whether it be concert halls, instrument making, pedagogical facilities, music printing or many other things."[38] This concession, that "systems of taste" are supported by interests, shows the weakness of the empirical method: It thwarts its own assumption (that opinions and decisions must represent the highest authority) and contradicts the claim that aesthetic pleasure is "spontaneous." Nevertheless, the unperturbed Mueller sticks to the claim that empirical social research—collecting reactions within the existing institutional system—represents the fundament of a scientific aesthetic. "Enormous financial investments" assume the function of its fundamental principle (after metaphysics have been expelled). That the *volonté de tous*—the prevailing musical opinion—is determined by extra-aesthetic interests does not prevent Mueller from pronouncing it *volonté générale* (i.e., aesthetic reason).

Under the assumptions of the empirical method, it is impossible to appeal against the musically banal and worn. In order for it to emerge as distortion and trivialization, opinions must be formed on the basis of the object, i.e., the facts and meanings inherent in aesthetic entities.

IV

Criticism of the trivial—the kind that goes further than contempt or disgust—is often based on the idea of a universal, undivided music. The separation of high and low art is blamed for the spread of the musically banal. An element of folk art sinking into triviality, it is argued, constitutes the reverse image—the contrasting complement—of an educational art that locks itself off in esotericism.

1. However, universality is a utopia rather than a past reality. An endangered balance of heterogeneous parts, it has been realized in a single work, the *Magic Flute* (whose text, however, has been alternately praised as brilliant and disdained as dreadful for one and a half centuries). And almost at the same time, in the *Critique of Judgment*, Kant proclaimed *sensus communis* as authority of aesthetic judgment.

The idea of a universal art was alien to the centuries before the philanthropic enlightenment, despite the fact that they were close to realizing it. Contempt of low music went without saying at a time when social thinking was penetrated by the concept of privilege.[39] The distance in the public consciousness that separated notated, artificial music and non-notated, common practices, is scarcely affected by the fact that folk songs were occasionally used as material for art works. Distance is emphasized rather than eliminated by contempt.

What is novel about the nineteenth century's musical history is not the separation itself, but the sense that it is bad fortune. The idea of the universal became a guiding principle of aesthetic conscience,[40] and ever since, a growing reserve against the banal—a sensitivity that leads towards esotericism—has been accompanied by the (opposite) feeling that the distance should be leveled out or eliminated. The *topos* that the future will correct any injustice that is done to a work in the present gives voice not only to the need to be understood and to survive one's own death, but it also expresses the longing for a state of affairs past and beyond the separation of high and low art.

2.   As diverse as efforts for an "elevation" of trivial music are in the nineteenth century, as vehement is the polemic against a *Juste-Milieu* where (philanthropically or commercially motivated) contempt coincides with parvenus of low music striving for ennoblement. The mediocre is the caricature of the universal.

Schumann expresses opposition against a musical "Juste-Milieu" that stretches from Henri Herz to Meyerbeer, and Wagner against the "mediocre" that "does not offer something unfamiliar and new, but the familiar in pleasing and flattering form."[41] Masked triviality produces a kind of rage that is rarely ever provoked when it is (cynically or naively) undisguised. "What remains is to aim not only at the deception of the audience, but of true artistic judgment—as if trying to sell light and flawed goods as being of proper weight and solid—thus producing the most repulsive appearance."[42] Undoubtedly, one of the motives for this polemic is the fact that the mediocre—constituting competition externally and menace internally—is closer to the important than is the bad. At the same time, though, it appears that the mediocre was experienced and thus despised as a distortion and as a decayed form of the universal—an idea to which one stuck, even though in reality it could hardly be achieved.

V

Dealing with trivial music, we need to get involved in the aesthetics of content. An abstract formal analysis would be inadequate: It would unearth the characteristic poverty of the trivial, yet this poverty remains incomprehensible if left unrelated to the "contents" that are represented.

1. It is no accident that attempts to justify the trivial against its despisers are all based, stereotypically, on the argument that the subject of criticism, its musical form, is secondary and its "content" decisive (i.e., for songs, the relationship between melodic character, text, and function). According to Philipp Spitta,[43] the men's choirs of the nineteenth century can only be understood as a unity of musical and patriotic factors. And the challenging comparison of a badly composed national anthem and a well composed cancan would justly have been experienced as a profession of faith in anarchy rather than in aesthetics.

Text, function, and melodic-rhythmic character form a complex whole whose elements are linked interactively and are interdependent. (Parody, a frequent means especially in trivial music, appears to thwart these relationships; yet fully rescinding a piece's original "content" would curtail or even eliminate the effect of many contrafacta: Both the profane parody of *couplets* and the sacred parody of salvation army songs draws on the ironic or emphatic contrast to what is being repressed.)

Social or institutional functions—and functions often stick in our consciousness more tenaciously than texts—shape musical character, and the nature of the latter is historical. It is not hard but unnecessary to demonstrate, on the basis of experimental psychology, that they are not a natural property of the melodic-rhythmic construction: If one lets listeners judge melodies without identifying their texts and functions, the "content" of the music vanishes as a result of the experimental design, while its historical existence remains undisputed.

Melodies that are closely associated with texts and functions are recognized as trivial only once their "contents"—emotional religion, revolutionary pathos or gymnastic patriotism—fade or become suspicious. The musical form that remains for an analysis of compositional technique and aesthetic criticism is a dead leftover.

2.   That form and content are inseparable is a commonplace idea that nobody denies, yet it falls short of dissolving the opposition between the aesthetic of form and content, or of reducing the latter to the status of a mock problem. The "pathological" enjoyment of music in Hanslick's polemics was not a phantom, but a quotidian reality[44]; and the fact that it has become suspicious must not conceal its historical existence and importance.

Due to intense discussions of the extent to which music is able to represent or suggest content (i.e., a variety of images or emotions), the question whether form is to be considered a function of content or vice versa has been neglected, even though it should hardly be of lesser importance than the question of music's aesthetic limits. Using the language of gestalt psychology, a content is either "ground" or "figure." As "figure," it constitutes the primary object of attention, and musical form, the epitome of harmonic relationships, functions merely as foil and support. The same content, however, can also be experienced as background without it being denied as a result. Rather than getting absorbed in a mood, musical listening is supported by it and focuses on form as a tonally moving object. Content becomes the function of form.

The aesthetics of content—the principle that considers form as "ground" and content as "figure"—is just as questionable as Hanslick claimed, yet it is so not because it can be proven wrong, but because it tends towards banality. The radius of contents that can be musically represented or described is narrowly limited. Contents, remaining vague per se, owe their apparent richness and differentiation to forms. Musical listening that clings to contents and reduces forms to their foil results in impoverishment: along with the forms, it shrinks contents into meager and abstract contours.

The weakness of the aesthetics of content thus lies with its misapprehension of the dialectic to which the contents of music are subject; it is its neglect of the paradoxical fact that just when they stand out, they turn to shadows. The consequence of its deficiency, however, is the affinity of the aesthetics of content to trivial music, where the reduction of listening—the disparagement of formal appearance to a mere material of which emotions and moods live—takes hold of the musical constructions themselves. Entertainment music executes, as it were, the verdict passed by the aesthetics of content. And it seems as if in order to pay justice to its historical meaning, we should consider Hanslick's rigorous formal aesthetics a polemic against the trivialization of music.

VI

Aesthetic judgment tends to be given prematurely; in contrast to judicial judgment, it anticipates analysis. Yet, in order for it not to appear arbitrary, it must be founded on the musical text.

The trivial resists attempts of analytical detection. Nobody would hesitate to reproach the potpourri's principle (i.e., formlessness that is declared form) of banality. However, when one attempts, on the basis of musical properties, to demonstrate the difference between a meaningful contrast and an empty lack of relation (i.e., the potpourri's flaw), the certainty with which judgment was previously passed quickly turns into embarrassment. It is harder to demonstrate heterogeneity than it is to discover relations.

In fact, it seems as if the banal cannot be analyzed. Hans Mersmann's *Attempt at a Musical Aesthetics of Value* is reared on the thesis that "the categories of analysis become more pronounced, or disappear, depending on the art work . . . Musical analysis and the aesthetics of value are neither mutually exclusive areas nor diametrically opposed extremes, but the determination of value seems to me to be the mature fruit of analysis."[45] Music that proceeds within "the natural orbit of the elements" constitutes the "nadir in the range of value." "Its melody moves along the rails provided by the scale and triad, its rhythm converges completely with the meter, its tensions are of a basic nature; its harmony is based on the respiration between tonic and dominant, touching rarely on the subdominant and avoiding both the color of the secondary chords[46] and the lightening of weight achieved by inversions and the stronger tensions of new leading notes." Since thus, "idling of the elements" is one characteristic of the banal, "then the creative process emerges as an image of engendering obstructions."[47] Musical quality can be grasped analytically as differentiation, originality, and abundance of relationships.

For simple songs, however, the criteria that have been abstracted from art works fail. Their "range of value" is, according to Mersmann—

Andante

Figure 1

who without doubt does not disdain folk songs—"arranged the other way round."[48] Thus, in order to mark the simple as banal, it does not suffice to demonstrate the "idling of the elements." What needs to simultaneously become clear is why it is legitimate to apply the criteria of an art work rather than those of folk music.

The octave descent with which Thekla Badarczewska's virgin is getting ready for prayer would be nothing else but "idling," were it not for the dragging appoggiaturas, the melting-away arpeggio, the suspenseful rest, and the abrupt sforzato that reverberates in the fermata— all of which give away its "striving for elevation" just as much as the title (see figure 1).[49]

However, the props that are meant to suggest a hint of "importance" bring out the music's destituteness all the more embarrassingly. By masking itself, and by striving both hard and vainly beyond its reach, the simple decays into triviality. The lofty accents highlight the wretchedness they are meant to disguise.

Trivial music is a mass product. In order not to disturb comfortable pleasure, it must not transcend the limits of the familiar. Yet at the same time, it needs to be conspicuous in order to stand out and stick in memory. Trivial music achieves its aesthetic ideal when it successfully makes the worn appear charming.

Banal accentuation (i.e., bragging with props) is distinct from artful differentiation because of its ornamental nature. Differentiation develops without deliberation out of simplicity. In contrast, the effect of the trivial—the parvenu of artistic means—can be distinguished because it is superficially grafted onto a simple creation, rather than penetrating it. The basic pattern and its pointed development remain distinct and, as a merger abounding with contradiction, they are responsible for the effect of the banal.

Figure 2

The vehement accent with which Meyerbeer furnishes a simple motif in *Robert le Diable* is a dynamic effect without melodic cause that attracts attention by force (see figure 2).

This contrast between light and dark is grounded neither in the character of the detail nor in the overarching formal trajectory (which motivates quite a few abrupt sforzati in Beethoven's symphonies). It is forced violently onto the harmless creation through the interference of a musical stage director. Theodor Billroth's judgment was that "Meyerbeer, like Weber, does not shy away from triviality, even roughness, and knows how to use it in order to intensify other, finer musical effects."[50]

In Meyerbeer's overture to *Romilda e Costanza* (1817), it is rhythm that comes across as a glued-on ornament (see figure 3).

Figure 3

The motif can be reduced to a simple pattern of two arpeggiated chords. And the repeated notes of the first and third measure shine through, despite the dotted rhythms that have been cast onto them as a disguise. Simplicity and pointed development do not join to produce a differentiated creation, but they act like different images that have been photographed on top of each other.

The method of potpourri—joining heterogeneous parts together—is a means of trivial accentuation that fulfills a function similar to unrelated dynamic and rhythmic effects. Constant switching to the unexpected is supposed to force attention out of the distracted listener. (The distracted listener is one of the fundamental assumptions for trivial music).[51]

The aria of Appio in Giovanni Pacini's *L'Ultimo Giorno di Pompei* (1825) starts simply *cantabile* (see figure 4). Yet Pacini cannot forego

Figure 4

to add a coquettish trill to the melody, unmasking simplicity as intentional gesture. After two measures Pacini breaks off; and rather than a closing phrase, what follows is a gesture that first expands determinately and then subsides resignedly, and whose pathos draws on the worn-out effect of the chromatically altered Phrygian cadence (f-a-d#/e-g#-e). And rather than justifying the abrupt turn by means of a development that negotiates between the extremes, Pacini is satisfied with yet another change of sets: Rossini-esque rhythms that do not complement what preceded them, but rather eliminate it ironically, constitute the conclusion of the "period."[51] The melody is a potpourri of minute effects that come so thick and fast that the listener cannot find a gap through which to escape from the music. Logic is replaced by assembly, persistence by the effort of constantly attempting to appear "interesting."

"Breaks in style"—the invasion of operatic tone into song, or of virtuosic display into chamber music—are, like potpourri technique (i.e., the lining up of unrelated parts), a calculated effect rather than an accidental deficiency. Ferdinand Hérold starts a romance in a mood of soulful homeliness (see figure 5).

In the middle section, however, he starts gesticulating: the accentuated octave leap, the chromatic upper neighbor note, and the pause on the fermata are props of operatic style. The bourgeois girl, for whom the romance is intended, is allowed to feel momentarily transported to the stage before being guided back into banal reality by means of a recapitulation of the initial melody.

Figure 5

When the artist . . . takes refuge in that touching device against reality, i.e., in longing and sentimentality, and applies tears all over the cheeks of meanness and puts an Oh God! into its mouth—whereby of course his characters are elevated far beyond reality towards heaven, but like bats, belonging neither to the species of birds nor animals, neither to earth nor heaven—and such beauty cannot be without ugliness, such morality not without weakness and vileness, such reason not without triteness; the fortune and misfortune that are involved not without fear, nor meanness, and both not without contempt . . .[53]

Hegel's judgment is mercilessly matter-of-fact.

NOTES

1. These two essays first appeared in a collection of essays edited by Carl Dahlhaus, entitled *Studien zur Trivialmusik des 19. Jahrhunderts*. [Regensburg, Germany: Bosse, 1967].

2. Carl Dahlhaus' style of writing creates a particular challenge for the translator. Given the need to strike a balance between faithfulness to the original and readability in the translated language, I chose as a basic premise to value the former over the latter where I had to, thus making some sacrifices in terms of the fluidity and idiomatic quality of the translated text. Neither native English speaker nor professional translator, I owe great debt to Chris Washburne for his help in editing. I would also like to express my gratitude to the two translation editors for their comments.

3. In the nineteenth and early twentieth centuries, *gassenhauer* means the popular song repertoire of the urban masses. Often exploiting the current "high" or "low" repertoires as a source, *gassenhauer* voiced the perspectives and concerns of the lower classes. [Trans.]

4. Hans Mersmann (1891–1971), German musicologist, studied with Riemann and Kretzschmar.

5. Dahlhaus bases his use of "gebrauchsmusik," "umgangsmusik" and "umgangsmäßig" on Heinrich Besseler. In his 1925 essay "Grundfragen des musikalischen Hörens" [Fundamental questions regarding musical listening], Besseler—informed by philosopher Martin Heidegger's concepts of the "present-at-hand" (vorhanden) and the "ready-to-hand" (zuhanden)—establishes "Gebrauchsmusik" and independent or autonomous music as distinct categories:

   The ordinariness from which high art wants to deliver us is *gebrauchsmusik*'s vital substance. . . . *gebrauchsmusik* constitutes something at level with our other activities, something we deal with [umgang] the same way we deal with items of everyday usage, where we do not need to first overcome a distance and assume a special aesthetic attitude. Thus, the fundamental nature of gebrauchsmusik shall be called *umgangsmäßig*. All other art . . . forms the opposite to this Dasein in that its reason lies, in some way or another, within itself, it is self-sufficient. (Besseler, 1925: 45–46)

Rather than using the original German term, I have chosen to translate "gebrauchsmusik" for better readability. I found "functional music" preferable to alternatives used by other translators or authors; including J. Bradford Robinson's "vernacular music" (in his translation of Dahlhaus' *Nineteenth-Century Music*); "utility music" or "music for use" chosen by Hindemith in a 1950 lecture; or "ambivalent music" as suggested by Hinton in his Grove entry for "Gebrauchsmusik". Although equivalent to "gebrauchsmusik", I have left *umgangsmäßig* untranslated for lack of an appropriate adjective in the English language. For a detailed cultural history of the concept of "gebrauchsmusik", see Stephen Hinton, *The Idea of Gebrauchsmusik* (New York, 1989). [Trans.]

6. The nineteenth century's couplet is a strophe of three, four, six, eight or more verses that form part of a chanson; it was prominent in the *comédie-vaudeville* and *comédie mêlée de couplets*. [Trans.]

7. The eighteenth century conceives of beer fiddler (*bierfiedler*) in contrast to artful violinists (*kunstgeiger*). They belong to the low arts, among the ranks of musicians in the streets, at inns and fairs. [Trans.]

8. The song "Schier dreißig Jahre bist du alt" [You're almost thirty years of age], referred to as "Mantellied" [Coat Song] and part of the nineteenth century's popular repertoire, originated from Karl von Holtei's 1828 patriotic play *Lenore*, where a soldier sings it to address his coat. The play was set to music by Carl Eberwein as *Lenore oder Die Vermählung im Grabe* and premiered in Berlin in 1828. [Trans.]

9. In his 1834 "Der Psychometer", Robert Schumann distinguishes three categories of composers: First, "Klassiker" (classical composers, backward-looking), second, "Juste-Milieuisten" (members of the "Juste Milieu," i.e., middle-of-the-road composers, philistines) and third, "Romantiker" (Romantic composers, looking towards the future). [Trans.]

10. Johann Wolfgang von Goethe's epic poem "Hermann und Dorothea" was published in 1798.

11. "U-Musik" and "e-Musik" distinguish "unterhaltungsmusik" (entertainment music) and "ernste Musik" (serious music). [Trans.]

12. H. G. Nägeli, *Vorlesungen über Musik mit Berücksichtigung der Dilettanten* (Stuttgart/Tübingen, 1826), 164 f.. cf. K. G. Fellerer, "Mozart in der Betrachtung H. G. Nägelis," *Mozart-Jahrbuch* (1957): 30 f.

13. E. Eggli, *Probleme der musikalischen Wertästhetik im 19. Jahrhundert. Ein Versuch zur schlechten Musik* (Winterthur, 1965), 88.

14. H. Broch, "Einige Bemerkungen zum Problem des Kitsches." *Dichten und Erkennen. Essays* (Zurich, 1955), 1:307. "Evil-mindedness and inner untruthfulness are also didactic, and aim to attract proselytes. That is why, full of vanity, they assume the given form, while always remaining inorganic and deliberate." F. Th. Vischer, *Ästhetik oder Wissenschaft des Schönen*, 2nd ed. (Munich, 1922), 2:459.

15. M. Greiner, Die Entstehung der modernen Unterhaltungsliteratur (Hamburg, 1964), 143.

16. See footnote 4 for (translations of) "Gebrauchsmusik," *umgangsmäßig* and associated terms. [Trans.]

17. The prefix "mit-" ["with-" or "along"] expresses simultaneity. Here, it means an activity performed by several individuals at the same time (someone doing something alongside others) or two or more activities performed by one individual (someone doing something alongside something else) . . . [Trans.]

18. H. Besseler, "Grundfragen des musikalischen Hörens," *Jahrbuch Peters* 32 (1925), 38; however, it remains to be considered whether the rhythmicization of the original impulse that provides the latter with duration isn't the first step of an "objectification"; emotion is at once carried forth by the order of dance and, as object, separated from the subject.

19. Ibid., 39; cf. also C. Vega, "Mesomusic. An Essay on the Music of the Masses," *Ethnomusicology* 10 (1966): 1 ff.

20. Besseler, 41.

21. Ibid., 42.

22. "Vollziehen" or "vollzug" in German can mean "understanding," "Fathoming" (as "nachvollziehen," literally "re-enacting in one's mind") and "executing," "carrying out" (as "vollziehen"). [Trans.]

23. "A dearth of original compositions is characteristic of entertainment music." (K. Lindemann, *Der Berufsstand der Unterhaltungsmusiker in Hamburg,* Diss. (1938), 34).

24. Besseler, 46.

25. Literally "song for a kommers." The kommers (various other spellings exist)— a ceremonious drinking bout—formed part of the nineteenth century's student fraternities' set of customs and traditions. The kommerslied, part of the kommers' ritual, was sung by the whole community of celebrants. [Trans.]

26. Besseler, 41.

27. Literally, "table music:" music accompanying feasts and banquets. [Trans.]

28. R. Wagner, *Gesammelte Schriften und Dichtungen,* ed. W. Golther (Berlin, n.d.), 7:124. "In Milan, where one is not used to be shy as in Germany and to hide one's nature, it has long become custom for intellectuals to devote themselves to playing cards at the theater, yet to applaud hard when something in the music reaches the heart, or a musical jump on the tightrope is made." A. F. J. Thibaut, *Über Reinheit der Tonkunst* (Freiburg / Leipzig, 1893), 49.

29. J. H. Mueller, *Fragen des musikalischen Geschmacks*, Kunst und Kommunikation 8 (Cologne/Opladen, 1963), 141.

30. Ibid., 106.

31. *Quaestio facti* means a question relating to facts, *quaestio iuris* means a question relating to the validity of legal claims, given the facts on which they are based. [Trans.]

32. Mueller, *Fragen des musikalischen Geschmacks,* 104.

33. Ibid., 113.

34. Ibid., 141.

35. Ibid., 141. Emerson and Thoreau "realized what characteristics were most needed by those parts of American society that were threatened not by the injustice of ossified traditions, but by the irresponsibility of the fluid opinion of the masses." W. H. Auden, *Des Färbers Hand und andere Essays* (Gütersloh, 1962), 431.

36. Ibid., 119. "Poetry and music have always created their mightiest effect—and maybe this applies to the present day—when they were at a very low and

imperfect stage of development." E. Burke, *Vom Erhabenen und Schönen* (Berlin, 1956), 60.

37. Mueller, *Fragen des musikalischen Geschmacks* 150. Goethe wrote to Schiller on August 9th, 1797: "The peculiar state of the audience of a large city has caught my attention. It lives in a continuous frenzy of acquiring and consuming, and what we call emotion can neither be produced nor imparted. All pleasure, even theater, is only supposed to distract. . . ."
38. Mueller, 147. "Indeed it is through the circle of manipulation and retroactive need that the system's unity becomes increasingly tight." M. Horkheimer and Th. W. Adorno, *Dialektik der Aufklärung* (Amsterdam, 1947), 147.
39. Cf. H.W. Schwab, *Sangbarkeit, Popularität und Kunstlied,* Studien zur Musikgeschichte des 19. Jahrhunderts 3 (Regensburg, 1965), 92f. Forkel reproached Burney for including beer fiddlers' tricks in his musical travel journals. (*Musikalisch-kritische Bibliothek* (Gotha, 1779), 3:119).
40. "We must at least keep the faith that—just as we have a uniform language—we can also acquire a uniform culture." H. Kretzschmar, "Volksmusik und höhere Tonkunst", *Gesammelte Aufsätze aus den Jahrbüchern der Musikbibliothek Peters* (Leipzig, 1911), 453. Cf. A. Halm, *Von zwei Kulturen der Musik* (Stuttgart, 1947), 3:199ff.
41. R. Wagner, 10:65.
42. Ibid., 10:77.
43. Ph. Spitta, *Musikgeschichtliche Aufsätze* (Berlin, 1894), 319f.; cf. also H. Heine, *Zeitungsberichte über Musik und Malerei* (Frankfurt, 1964), 23f. As early as 1814, a reviewer of Methfessel's *Sechs deutsche Kriegslieder* wrote in the *Allgemeine Musikalische Zeitung:* "What needs to penetrate the whole is that wonderful and spiritual something which cannot be couched in words, yet which, if the song is performed by a great mass of people, everybody notices immediately, feels immediately, and which used to be called unction, by which nothing more was meant than that it was a wonderful thing."
44. Eduard Hanslick (1825–1904) is maybe best known today for his book V*om Musikalisch-Schönen. Beiträge zur Revision der Ästhetik der Tonkunst* (first published in 1854).
45. H. Mersmann, "Versuch einer musikalischen Wertästhetik," *Zeitschrift für Musikwissenschaft* 17 (1935), 34. cf. W. Friedländer, "Das Problem der musikalischen Qualität," *Das Musikleben* 7 (1954), 301ff. E. Eggli, 5ff.
46. "Nebendreiklänge" (translated here as "secondary chords") means scale degrees other than the I, IV and V. [Trans.]
47. Mersmann, 37.
48. Ibid., 39. "Generally, however, the emptiness of a melody is not a necessary effect of the simplicity of its harmonic foundation." G. W. F. Hegel, Ästhetik (Frankfurt, n.d.), 2:300.
49. Thekla Badarczewska (1834–1861), Polish composer who published a piece called *Molitwa Dziewicy* [A Virgin's Prayer] in 1851. It became one of the most well-known pieces (and materials) of the nineteenth century's popular repertoire.
50. Th. Billroth, *Wer ist musikalisch?* (Berlin, 1898), 3:165.

51.   Ibid., 48. "First a mysterious beginning; then a warning shot; sudden silence; unexpectedly something waltz-like; but—just as that starts to ignite a certain fire—with the same brilliance a quick transition into the pensive and weepy; from there immediately into a wild tempest: right out of the middle of the storm, after a short exciting rest, on to something flirty, and at the end some kind of whoopee, at which point with screaming love all healthily embrace each other."

52.   "Periode" (musical period), like "satz" (musical phrase), relates to a component of musical syntax; it usually means an eight-bar unit. [Trans.]

53.   G. W. F. Hegel, quoted after H. Kuhn, *Die Vollendung der klassischen deutschen Ästhetik durch Hegel* (Berlin, 1931), 6.

Contributors

Eliot Bates is a PhD student in Ethnomusicology at the University of California Berkeley. His areas of research include electronic music cultures, music and technology, and Turkish popular music. He performs Turkish classical and popular music (oud, percussion, and vocals), and has engineered and mastered world music recordings at several studios.

Giorgio Biancorosso holds a PhD in Musicology from Princeton University. A former member of the Society of Fellows at Columbia University (2001–2003), he is currently a Visiting Assistant Professor in Musicology, also at Columbia. He is the author of "Beginning Credits and Beyond: Music and the Cinematic Imagination," *ECHO*, Vol. 3-1 (Spring 2001) [http://www.humnet.ucla.edu/echo.html]. He is currently working on a book entitled: *Where's the Music Coming From? Cinematic Reflections on the Listening Experience*.

Richard Carlin is Executive Editor at Routledge publishing. He is the author of *Country Music: A Biographical Dictionary* (2003); *Southern Exposure* (with Bob Carlin) (2000), and *Classical Music: An Informal Guide* (1992), among other books. He has contributed articles on traditional music to various journals, and has also produced ten albums of traditional music for Folkways Records.

Maiken Tandgaard Derno is a Research Fellow in the Department of Comparative Literature at the University of Copenhagen, Denmark. She is writing a book about Shakespeare's problem plays and the discursive transformation of literary genres in the English Renaissance. She is also currently a visiting scholar at Columbia University, and has worked as a freelance editor for Brøndums Forlag and Routledge Press.

Aaron A. Fox is Associate Professor of Music at Columbia University and the Director of Columbia's Center for Ethnomusicology. He is the author of *Real Country: Music, Language, and Feeling in Texas Working Class Culture* (2004), as well as numerous articles on country music and on the music/language relationship. He is the co-editor, with Christine Yano, of *Songs Out of Place: Country Musics of the World*, forthcoming on Duke University Press. He has also been a professional country guitarist for over a decade.

Walter Frisch is Professor of Music at Columbia University. He has written *Brahms and the Principle of Developing Variation* (1984); *The Early Works of Arnold Schoenberg, 1893-1908* (1993); and *Brahms: The Four Symphonies* (1996). He is currently completing a book on music and early German modernism in the years around 1900.

Simon Frith is Professor of Film and Media at the University of Stirling, Scotland. He is author of *Performing Rites: On the Value of Popular Music* (1996) and editor (with Will Straw and John Street) of the *Cambridge Companion to Pop and Rock* (2001). He chairs the judges of the Mercury Music Prize.

James Koehne is Artistic Adviser to the Adelaide Symphony Orchestra in South Australia. He has previously worked in various areas of music management and in policy development with the Australian Broadcasting Corporation and government arts agencies and performing arts organizations throughout Australia. As a writer, he has contributed articles and program essays for many Australian journals and for CD recordings and concert programs.

Jason Lee Oakes is a PhD Candidate at Columbia University. He is currently completing his dissertation on Elvis impersonators, Loser's Lounge, Stevie Nicks drag artists, and Punk Rock Heavy Metal Karaoke in New York City.

Angela Rodel is a PhD Candidate in ethnomusicology at the University of California, Los Angeles. In addition to popular music, her research interests include Balkan music and linguistics.

Torben Sangild is Lecturer at Copenhagen University in the Department of Culture and Fine Arts. He is also a freelance writer and author of *The Aesthetics of Noise* and several publications in Danish. He is currently writing a PhD dissertation entitled *Objective Sensibility: Adorno, emotions and contemporary art.*

Ulrike Sailer is a PhD candidate in Historical Musicology at New York University and works as a consultant for AEA Consulting. Her main interest concerns the effects of private philanthropyand board governance in U.S. arts organizations on cultural policy. She has translated and edited articles for the Andante record label.

Matthew Wheelock Stahl is a PhD Candidate and Lecturer in Communication at the University of California, San Diego and a member of the International Association for the Study of Popular Music (IASPM). He has recently published articles on micropolitics in indie rock sociality, boy bands, and on legitimacy and authorship struggles.

Timothy D. Taylor is an Associate Professor in the Music Department at Columbia University. His publications include *Global Pop: World Music, World Markets* (1997), *Strange Sounds: Music, Technology and Culture* (2001), and numerous articles on various popular and classical musics. He is currently writing a history of music used in advertising.

Elizabeth Tolbert is an ethnomusicologist and Professor at Johns Hopkins University, where she holds a joint appointment in the departments of Musicology and Anthropology. Her recent publications reflect her diverse interests in music and language, feminist theory, technoscience, ritual, and most recently, music and evolution. She is currently writing a book on music ideologies in evolutionary discourses, with the working title *Music, Meaning, and the Birth of Representation.*

Christopher Washburne is Assistant Professor of Music and Director of the Louis Armstrong Jazz Performance program at Columbia University. He has published numerous articles on jazz, Latin jazz, and salsa, and his book *New York Salsa* will be published in 2005 by Temple University Press. He is leader of the highly acclaimed Latin jazz group SYOTOS, one of the busiest and most in demand Latin jazz bands in New York, and has recently released the record *Paradise In Trouble* (Jazzheads Records). In addition to SYOTOS, he has performed and recorded extensively with Tito Puente, Eddie Palmieri, Celia Cruz,

Ray Barretto, Mark Anthony, Justin Timberlake, Celine Dion, Gloria Estefan, and the Duke Ellington Orchestra, and on occasion, takes pleasure in performing a wide array of "Bad" musics.

Deena Weinstein is a rock critic who works on both sides of the literary street with numerous publications and as Professor of Sociology at DePaul University in Chicago. She specializes in mass media and popular culture, and is the author of books and articles on social theory and rock music.

Elizabeth L. Wollman received her PhD in ethnomusicology from the Graduate Center, City University of New York, in September 2002. She is currently Assistant Professor of Music at Baruch College in Manhattan.

Index